Taste *of* Home®
healthy
cooking
COOKBOOK

Taste *of* Home® BOOKS

READER'S DIGEST —
REIMAN MEDIA GROUP, INC.

Taste of Home · Reader's Digest

A TASTE OF HOME/READER'S DIGEST BOOK

©2013 Reiman Media Group, Inc., 5400 S. 60th St., Greendale WI 53129. All rights reserved.
Taste of Home and Reader's Digest are registered trademarks of The Reader's Digest Association, Inc.

EDITORIAL

Editor-in-Chief: Catherine Cassidy
Creative Director: Howard Greenberg
Editorial Operations Director: Kerri Balliet

Managing Editor, Print and Digital Books: Mark Hagen
Associate Creative Director: Edwin Robles Jr.

Editors: Janet Briggs, Heather Ray, Amy Glander
Layout Designer: Catherine Fletcher
Editorial Production Manager: Dena Ahlers
Copy Chief: Deb Warlaumont Mulvey
Copy Editor: Alysse Gear
Content Operations Manager: Colleen King
Executive Assistant: Marie Brannon
Design Intern: Siya Motamedi
Editorial Intern: Devin Mulertt

Chief Food Editor: Karen Berner
Food Editors: James Schend; Peggy Woodward, RD
Associate Food Editor: Krista Lanphier
Associate Editor/Food Content: Annie Rundle
Recipe Editors: Mary King; Jenni Sharp, RD; Irene Yeh

Test Kitchen and Food Styling Manager: Sarah Thompson
Test Cooks: Matthew Hass, Lauren Knoelke
Food Stylists: Kathryn Conrad (senior), Shannon Roum, Leah Rekau
Prep Cooks: Megumi Garcia, Nicole Spohrleder, Beth VanOpdorp

Photography Director: Stephanie Marchese
Photographers: Dan Roberts, Jim Wieland
Photographer/Set Stylist: Grace Natoli Sheldon
Set Stylists: Stacey Genaw, Melissa Haberman, Dee Dee Jacq

Business Analyst: Kristy Martin
Billing Specialist: Mary Ann Koebernik

BUSINESS

General Manager, Taste of Home Cooking Schools: Erin Puariea

Vice President, Brand Marketing: Jennifer Smith
Vice President, Circulation and Continuity Marketing: Dave Fiegel

READER'S DIGEST NORTH AMERICA

Vice President, Business Development and Marketing: Alain Begun
President, Books and Home Entertainment: Harold Clarke
General Manager, Canada: Philippe Cloutier
Vice President, Operations: Mitch Cooper
Chief Operating Officer: Howard Halligan
Vice President, Chief Sales Officer: Mark Josephson
Vice President, General Manager, Milwaukee: Frank Quigley
Vice President, Digital Sales: Steve Sottile
Vice President, Chief Content Officer: Liz Vaccariello
Vice President, Global Financial Planning & Analysis: Devin White

THE READER'S DIGEST ASSOCIATION, INC.

President and Chief Executive Officer: Robert E. Guth

For other Taste of Home books and products, visit us at **tasteofhome.com.**

For more Reader's Digest products and information, visit
rd.com (in the United States) or see **rd.ca** (in Canada).

International Standard Book Number: 978-1-61765-235-6
Library of Congress Control Number: 2013940213

Cover Photography: Dan Roberts
Food Stylist: Kathryn Conrad
Set Stylist: Melissa Haberman

Pictured on front cover: Chicken Tacos with Avocado Salsa, page 97;
Taco Salad Tacos, page 116; and Black Bean and Corn Tacos, page 117
Pictured on spine: Chocolate-Raspberry Torte, page 287
Pictured on back cover: Creamy Macaroni and Cheese, page 258; Chocolate
Bliss Marble Cake, page 293; and Italian Beef Barley Stew, page 135

Printed in China.
1 3 5 7 9 10 8 6 4 2

PAGE 111

PAGE 278

PAGE 85

Contents

Delicious. Healthy. *Easy.*

Feel good about what your family's eating with 501 light and delicious recipes!

"I don't want to make different meals to accommodate picky eaters."

"I'm concerned about my family's eating habits."

"I need recipes that are quick and taste good."

"I don't want to give up the foods I love."

"We need recipes with practical ingredients."

"My family eats meatless several times a week."

HERE AT *TASTE OF HOME*, WE'RE ALWAYS LOOKING FOR WAYS TO MAKE LIFE EASIER, HEALTHIER AND MORE DELICIOUS! That's why *Healthy Cooking Cookbook* contains recipes that use what's already in your pantry, fridge and freezer to prepare **heart-smart meals and snacks fit for the whole family.**

Inside you'll find **kid-friendly suppers, complete menus and more than 90 easy entrees ready in 30 minutes or less.**

We've also dedicated **an entire chapter to gluten-free goodies** because even though you may not be on a gluten-restricted diet, you probably know someone who is—and we suspect they could use a cupcake now and then.

We think you'll appreciate that the recipes in this collection don't call for exotic ingredients or require intimidating cooking techniques. If you can turn on an oven or stove, you're set.

And here's the best part: **These recipes are submitted by health-minded home cooks from around the country.** They're reviewed by a Registered Dietitian and tested in the *Taste of Home* kitchens. You can feel good knowing these dishes not only work for other families, but they come with our **Test Kitchen-approved guarantee.**

Every recipe offers a complete set of **Nutrition Facts** as well as **Diabetic Exchanges** for applicable items. Simply **look for these handy icons** throughout each chapter to quickly identify which recipes are significantly **low in sodium** **S**, **fat** **F** and/or **carbohydrates** **C**, and which ones can be **table-ready in 30 minutes** **FAST FIX** or less!

Nutritional Guidelines

The recipes in the *Healthy Cooking Cookbook* represent a variety of foods that fit into any meal plan that is within the standards of the USDA's plan for moderately active adults (see chart below).

How We Calculated the Nutrition Facts

- Whenever a choice of ingredients is given in a recipe, the first ingredient listed is always the one calculated in the Nutrition Facts.

- When a range is given for an ingredient (such as 2 to 3 teaspoons), we calculate the first amount.

- Only the amount of marinade absorbed during preparation is calculated.

- Garnishes listed in recipes are generally included in calculations.

Diabetic Exchanges

All recipes in this book have been reviewed by a Registered Dietitian. Diabetic Exchanges are assigned to recipes in accordance with guidelines from the American Diabetic and American Dietetic associations. The majority of recipes in *Healthy Cooking Cookbook* are suitable for diabetics.

MAKE OVER MY DISH

We all have that **one food we refuse to give up.** Whether it's a creamy mac & cheese specialty or Grandma's coconut cream pie, **readers continually send us their favorite recipes** with the hopes that we can **re-create the same dish with fewer calories** and **less fat, sodium and cholesterol.** *Healthy Cooking Cookbook* includes **an entire chapter of our best makeovers** (see **page 252**), along with **tips and tricks for cutting fat and shaving calories** without sacrificing flavor.

When a **recipe arrives for a makeover,** it's first **reviewed by a Registered Dietitian,** who scans the ingredients and looks for potential substitutions. Then the full-fat version is **prepared in our test kitchen** so we know what we're up against. Next, our **test kitchen cooks get to work on a new lightened-up version,** which is compared to the original for taste, texture and appearance by a panel of food editors. When **everyone's happy** with the results, we send the **new and improved recipe** back to the reader to enjoy with her family.

DAILY NUTRITION GUIDE

	WOMEN 25-50	WOMEN OVER 50	MEN 50-65
Calories	2,000	1,800	2,400
Fat	67 g or less	60 g or less	80 g or less
Saturated Fat	22 g or less	20 g or less	27 g or less
Cholesterol	300 mg or less	300 mg or less	360 mg or less
Sodium	2,400 mg or less	2,400 mg or less	2,400 mg or less
Carbohydrates	300 g	270 g	360 g
Fiber	20-30 g	20-30 g	20-30 g
Protein	50 g	45 g or less	60 g

This chart is only a guide. Calorie requirements vary, depending on age, weight, height and amount of activity. Children's dietary needs vary as they grow.

CHICKEN WONTON CUPS
PAGE 21

**CATHY BARGER'S
CHEESE-STUFFED MUSHROOMS**
PAGE 10

**KAREN SULAK'S
SAUSAGE-STUFFED RED
POTATOES** *PAGE 14*

**KATRINA LOPES'
MEXICAN CHICKEN MEATBALLS**
PAGE 19

Starters & Snacks

Make lasting first impressions with light hors d'oeuvres so good there's no need for a main course. From **casual comforts to fancy finger foods,** you'll find yourself looking for **any excuse to have a party.**

C FAST FIX
Light and Delicious Guacamole

My husband told me this is the best guacamole he's ever tasted. Adding cream cheese and green chillies makes it unlike any other.

—**LISA SIEVERS** PHILIPSBURG, PA

START TO FINISH: 10 MIN.
MAKES: 2½ CUPS

- 2 medium ripe avocados, peeled and pitted
- 1 package (8 ounces) fat-free cream cheese
- 1 can (4 ounces) chopped green chilies, drained
- ¼ cup chopped onion
- 1 tablespoon lemon juice
- 1 garlic clove, peeled and halved
- ¼ teaspoon salt
- 2 plum tomatoes, seeded and finely chopped
  Baked tortilla chip scoops

In a food processor, combine the first seven ingredients. Cover and process until blended. Stir in tomatoes. Serve with chips.
PER SERVING ¼ cup equals 87 cal., 6 g fat (1 g sat. fat), 2 mg chol., 231 mg sodium, 6 g carb., 3 g fiber, 4 g pro.

F S C
Roasted Pepper Dip

I've brought this creamy dip to many events in our community, to family get-togethers and to the elementary school where I work as a school psychologist. It's easy to make ahead and store in the fridge overnight.

—**AMY BRASLEY** MERIDIAN, ID

PREP: 10 MIN. + CHILLING
MAKES: 2 CUPS

- 4 ounces fat-free cream cheese
- ½ cup reduced-fat sour cream
- ½ cup chopped roasted sweet red peppers
- ½ cup grated Parmesan cheese
- ⅓ cup shredded pepper Jack cheese
- ¼ cup finely chopped onion
- ⅛ teaspoon garlic powder
- ⅛ teaspoon pepper
  Assorted crackers

In a small bowl, beat cream cheese and sour cream until smooth. Stir in the peppers, cheeses, onion, garlic powder and pepper. Refrigerate for at least one hour. Serve with crackers.
PER SERVING 2 tablespoons equals 42 cal., 2 g fat (1 g sat. fat), 8 mg chol., 126 mg sodium, 2 g carb., trace fiber, 3 g pro.

F S C FAST FIX
Shrimp with Orange Pineapple Sauce

This is a very light appetizer that's easy to make; the sauce can be made ahead and chilled until ready to serve. My husband even likes it as a main dish.

—**RADELLE KNAPPENBERGER** OVIEDO, FL

START TO FINISH: 15 MIN.
MAKES: ABOUT 2½ DOZEN
(⅔ CUP SAUCE)

- ¼ cup pineapple preserves
- ¼ cup orange marmalade
- ¼ cup lemon juice
- 1 tablespoon water
- 1 teaspoon cornstarch
- 1 pound cooked medium shrimp, peeled and deveined

In a small saucepan, combine the first five ingredients. Bring to a boil; cook and stir for 2 minutes or until thickened. Chill until serving. Serve with shrimp.
PER SERVING 1 shrimp equals 29 cal., trace fat (trace sat. fat), 22 mg chol., 23 mg sodium, 4 g carb., trace fiber, 3 g pro.

S C FAST FIX ▶
Cranberry Popcorn Deluxe

I created this recipe when I needed a festive treat for the holidays. Now as a year-round snack, everyone finds the combination of popcorn, fruit and nuts irresistible.

—**CAROLYN SYKORA** BLOOMER, WI

PREP: 15 MIN. • **BAKE:** 15 MIN. + COOLING.
MAKES: 8 CUPS

- 8 **cups air-popped popcorn**
- ¾ **cup dried cranberries**
- ¼ **cup slivered almonds**
- ¼ **cup pecan halves**
- ¼ **cup honey**
- 3 **tablespoons butter**
- 2 **tablespoons maple syrup**
- ¼ **teaspoon almond extract**

1. In a shallow roasting pan, combine the popcorn, cranberries, almonds and pecans.

2. In a small saucepan, combine the honey, butter and syrup. Cook and stir over medium heat until butter is melted. Remove from the heat; stir in extract. Drizzle over popcorn mixture and toss to coat.

3. Bake at 325° for 15 minutes, stirring every 5 minutes. Cool on a wire rack, stirring occasionally. Store in an airtight container.

PER SERVING *½ cup equals 96 cal., 4 g fat (2 g sat. fat), 6 mg chol., 16 mg sodium, 14 g carb., 1 g fiber, 1 g pro. Diabetic Exchanges: 1 starch, 1 fat*

CRANBERRY POPCORN DELUXE

F FAST FIX ▶
Spinach & Black Bean Egg Rolls

Black beans and spinach provide lots of healthy nutrients in these delicious egg rolls. The flavors are perfect for dipping in ranch dressing or salsa.

—**MELANIE SCOTT** AMARILLO, TX

START TO FINISH: 30 MIN.
MAKES: 20 EGG ROLLS

- 2 **cups frozen corn, thawed**
- 1 **can (15 ounces) black beans, rinsed and drained**
- 1 **package (10 ounces) frozen chopped spinach, thawed and squeezed dry**
- 1 **cup (4 ounces) shredded reduced-fat Mexican cheese blend**
- 1 **can (4 ounces) chopped green chilies, drained**
- 4 **green onions, chopped**
- 1 **teaspoon ground cumin**
- ½ **teaspoon chili powder**
- ½ **teaspoon pepper**
- 20 **egg roll wrappers**
  Cooking spray
  Salsa and reduced-fat ranch salad dressing, optional

SPINACH & BLACK BEAN EGG ROLLS

1. In a large bowl, combine the first nine ingredients. Place ¼ cup mixture in the center of one egg roll wrapper. (Keep remaining wrappers covered with a damp paper towel until ready to use.) Fold bottom corner over filling. Fold sides toward center over filling. Moisten remaining corner with water; roll up tightly to seal. Repeat.

2. Place seam side down on baking sheets coated with cooking spray. Spray tops of egg rolls with cooking spray. Bake at 425° for 10-15 minutes or until lightly browned. Serve warm with salsa and dressing if desired. Refrigerate leftovers.

PER SERVING *147 cal., 2 g fat (1 g sat. fat), 7 mg chol., 298 mg sodium, 26 g carb., 2 g fiber, 7 g pro. Diabetic Exchanges: 1½ starch, 1 lean meat.*

F S C
Hoisin Cocktail Meatballs

Asian-inspired meatballs make a fun and flavorful appetizer for parties or get-togethers. Plus they can be made a day ahead and broiled just before serving.

—**DEIRDRE DEE COX** KANSAS CITY, KS

PREP: 20 MIN. • **BAKE:** 20 MIN.
MAKES: 32 APPETIZERS

- 2 tablespoons hoisin sauce
- 1 tablespoon reduced-sodium soy sauce
- 1 teaspoon sesame oil
- ¼ cup dry bread crumbs
- 3 tablespoons chopped green onions
- 3 tablespoons minced fresh parsley
- 2 garlic cloves, minced
- 1 teaspoon minced fresh gingerroot
- 1½ pounds lean ground beef

SAUCE
- ¼ cup rice vinegar
- ¼ cup hoisin sauce
- 2 tablespoons water
- 2 tablespoons sesame oil
- 2 tablespoons reduced-sodium soy sauce
- 1 tablespoon honey
- 2 garlic cloves, minced
- 1 teaspoon minced fresh gingerroot

1. In a large bowl, combine the first eight ingredients. Crumble beef over mixture and mix well.

2. Shape into 32 meatballs. Place in a 13-in. x 9-in. baking dish coated with cooking spray. Bake, uncovered, at 350° for 20-25 minutes or until meat is no longer pink.

3. Meanwhile, in a small saucepan, combine the sauce ingredients; heat through. Serve with meatballs.

PER SERVING *56 cal., 3 g fat (1 g sat. fat), 13 mg chol., 121 mg sodium, 3 g carb., trace fiber, 4 g pro.*

HOISIN COCKTAIL
MEATBALLS

CHEESE-STUFFED MUSHROOMS
AND MANDARIN
TURKEY PINWHEELS, PAGE 13

F S C

Cheese-Stuffed Mushrooms

Expect these to go fast when served at parties. This recipe is from a friend, but I modified it for a slimmer version that tastes as scrumptious as the original.

—**CATHY BARGER** CLARKSVILLE, MI

PREP: 25 MIN. • **BAKE:** 15 MIN.
MAKES: 2 DOZEN

- 24 **medium fresh mushrooms**
  Butter-flavored cooking spray
- 3 **tablespoons chopped shallot**
- 2 **teaspoons olive oil**
- ½ **cup white wine or reduced-sodium chicken broth**
- ¼ **cup plus 6 tablespoons shredded reduced-fat Swiss cheese, divided**
- ¼ **cup grated Parmesan cheese**
- 3 **tablespoons dry bread crumbs**
- 2 **to 3 tablespoons fat-free milk**
- 2 **tablespoons dried parsley flakes**
- ½ **teaspoon dried tarragon**
- ¼ **teaspoon salt**
- ¼ **teaspoon pepper**

1. Remove stems from mushrooms and finely chop. Place caps on a foil-lined baking sheet; spritz with cooking spray. Set aside.

2. In a small skillet, saute the shallots and chopped mushrooms in oil until tender. Stir in wine; bring to a boil. Reduce heat; simmer, uncovered, for 10-12 minutes or until liquid is absorbed. Remove from the heat.

3. Stir in ¼ cup Swiss cheese, Parmesan cheese, bread crumbs, milk, parsley, tarragon, salt and pepper. Spoon into reserved mushroom caps. Sprinkle with remaining cheese and spritz with cooking spray.

4. Bake at 375° for 15-20 minutes or until mushrooms are tender and cheese is melted.

PER SERVING *26 cal., 1 g fat (trace sat. fat), 2 mg chol., 54 mg sodium, 2 g carb., trace fiber, 2 g pro.*

Spiced Apple Tea

I love to try new recipes for my husband and our friends. This spiced tea is one of our favorites. I like to serve it warm, but it's also nice chilled over ice.

—SHARON DELANEY-CHRONIS
SOUTH MILWAUKEE, WI

START TO FINISH: 25 MIN.
MAKES: 5 SERVINGS

- 2 **cups unsweetened apple juice**
- 6 **whole cloves**
- 1 **cinnamon stick (3 inches)**
- 3 **cups water**
- 5 **individual tea bags**
  Additional cinnamon sticks (3 inches), optional

1. In a small saucepan, combine the apple juice, cloves and cinnamon stick. Bring to a boil. Reduce heat; simmer, uncovered, for 10-15 minutes.
2. Meanwhile, in a large saucepan, bring water to a boil. Remove from the heat; add tea bags. Cover and steep for 5 minutes. Discard tea bags. Strain juice mixture, discarding cloves and cinnamon. Stir into tea. Serve warm with additional cinnamon sticks if desired.
PER SERVING *47 cal., trace fat (trace sat. fat), 0 chol., 3 mg sodium, 12 g carb., trace fiber, trace pro.* **Diabetic Exchange:** *1 fruit.*

Crab Salad Tarts

These little bites are as easy as they are elegant. Guests will never know you made and froze them weeks ago.

—DONNA ROBERTS SHUMWAY, IL

START TO FINISH: 25 MIN.
MAKES: 15 APPETIZERS

- 1 **can (6 ounces) lump crabmeat, drained**
- ⅓ **cup shredded reduced-fat Swiss cheese**
- ¼ **cup Miracle Whip Light**
- 2 **tablespoons finely chopped celery**
- 2 **tablespoons finely chopped red onion**
- 1 **teaspoon dried parsley flakes**
- ¼ **teaspoon pepper**
- 1 **package (1.9 ounces) frozen miniature phyllo tart shells**

1. In a small bowl, combine the crabmeat, cheese, Miracle Whip Light, celery, onion, parsley and pepper.
2. Spoon filling into tart shells. Cover and freeze for up to 3 months. Or, place tart shells on an ungreased baking sheet. Bake at 350° for 10-12 minutes or until shells are lightly browned. Serve warm.
TO USE FROZEN TARTS *Place on an ungreased baking sheet. Bake at 350° for 13-15 minutes or until lightly browned.*
PER SERVING *47 cal., 2 g fat (trace sat. fat), 3 mg chol., 115 mg sodium, 5 g carb., trace fiber, 2 g pro.*

CRAB SALAD TARTS

F C FAST FIX
Prosciutto-Wrapped Asparagus with Raspberry Sauce

Grilling the prosciutto with the asparagus gives this appetizer a salty crunch that's perfect for dipping into the sweet glaze. When delicious dishes are this easy to prepare, it's hard not to try them at least once.

—NOELLE MYERS GRAND FORKS, ND

START TO FINISH: 30 MIN.
MAKES: 16 APPETIZERS

- ⅓ **pound thinly sliced prosciutto or deli ham**
- 16 **fresh asparagus spears, trimmed**
- ½ **cup seedless raspberry jam**
- 2 **tablespoons balsamic vinegar**

1. Cut prosciutto slices in half. Wrap a prosciutto piece around each asparagus spear; secure ends with toothpicks. Moisten a paper towel with cooking oil; using long-handled tongs, lightly coat the grill rack.
2. Grill asparagus, covered, over medium heat for 6-8 minutes or until prosciutto is crisp, turning once. Discard toothpicks.
3. In a small microwave-safe bowl, microwave jam and vinegar on high for 15-20 seconds or until jam is melted. Serve with asparagus.
PER SERVING *50 cal., 1 g fat (trace sat. fat), 8 mg chol., 184 mg sodium, 7 g carb., trace fiber, 3 g pro.* **Diabetic Exchange:** *½ starch.*

S C FAST FIX
Goat Cheese Crostini

My husband got this crostini recipe from a friend at work. At first, I thought the flavors wouldn't work well together, but it turned out to be delicious!

—REBECCA EBELING NEVADA CITY, CA

START TO FINISH: 10 MIN.
MAKES: 32 APPETIZERS

- 1 **cup crumbled goat cheese**
- 1 **teaspoon minced fresh rosemary**
- 1 **French bread baguette (10½ ounces), cut into ½-inch slices and toasted**
- 3 **tablespoons honey**
- ¼ **cup slivered almonds, toasted**

In a small bowl, combine cheese and rosemary; spoon over toast slices. Drizzle with honey; sprinkle with almonds.

BACON-ALMOND CROSTINI
Combine 2 cups shredded Monterey Jack cheese, ⅔ cup mayonnaise, ½ cup toasted sliced almonds, 6 slices crumbled cooked bacon, 1 chopped green onion and a dash of salt. Spread over toast. Bake for 5-7 minutes or until cheese is melted. Sprinkle with additional almonds if desired.
PER SERVING *76 cal., 4 g fat (2 g sat. fat), 6 mg chol., 92 mg sodium, 9 g carb., 1 g fiber, 3 g pro.* **Diabetic Exchanges:** *½ starch, ½ fat.*

GOAT CHEESE CROSTINI

Why We Love Goat Cheese

On average, goat cheese is lower in fat and calories than cream cheese and other cow's-milk cheeses. It's also higher in vitamins D, K, thiamine and niacin. And because it contains less lactose, some people find it easier to digest. Known for its distinct, rich flavor, a little goes a long way.

PROSCIUTTO-WRAPPED ASPARAGUS WITH RASPBERRY SAUCE

Spinach & Crab Dip

We love this recipe! I've lightened it considerably without sacrificing its richness, and no one can tell the difference. I also make this to serve as a potato topping.

—SANDIE HEINDEL LIBERTY, MO

START TO FINISH: 25 MIN.
MAKES: 4 CUPS

- 1 package (10 ounces) frozen chopped spinach, thawed and squeezed dry
- 1 package (8 ounces) reduced-fat cream cheese, cubed
- 1 cup (8 ounces) plain yogurt
- ½ cup grated Parmesan cheese
- ½ cup Miracle Whip Light
- 2 garlic cloves, minced
- 1 teaspoon crushed red pepper flakes
- ¼ teaspoon salt
- ¼ teaspoon pepper
- 1 can (6 ounces) lump crabmeat, drained
  Assorted crackers or baked tortilla chip scoops

1. In a large saucepan over low heat, combine the first nine ingredients. Cook and stir until cream cheese is melted. Stir in crab; heat through.
2. Transfer to a serving bowl; serve with crackers. Refrigerate leftovers.
PER SERVING *¼ cup equals 89 cal., 6 g fat (3 g sat. fat), 26 mg chol., 256 mg sodium, 3 g carb., 1 g fiber, 6 g pro.*

Mandarin Turkey Pinwheels

My cousin shared this recipe with me and we made dozens for our grandparents' 50th wedding anniversary open house. People kept coming back for seconds—and thirds!

—LORIE MINER KAMAS, UT

PREP: 15 MIN. + CHILLING
MAKES: 2½ DOZEN

- 1 package (8 ounces) reduced-fat cream cheese
- ½ teaspoon curry powder
- ½ cup mandarin oranges, drained and chopped
- 3 flour tortillas (12 inches), room temperature
- ½ pound sliced deli smoked turkey
- 3 cups fresh baby spinach
- 2 green onions, chopped

1. In a small bowl, beat cream cheese and curry powder until blended. Stir in oranges. Spread ½ cup mixture over each tortilla. Layer with turkey, spinach and green onions; roll up tightly. Wrap in plastic wrap and refrigerate for 2 hours or until firm enough to cut.
2. Unwrap and cut each roll into 10 slices.
PER SERVING *50 cal., 2 g fat (1 g sat. fat), 8 mg chol., 149 mg sodium, 4 g carb., 1 g fiber, 3 g pro.*

SPINACH & CRAB DIP

SAUSAGE-STUFFED
RED POTATOES

F C
Sausage-Stuffed Red Potatoes

My husband and I have a large garden with red potatoes so I'm always trying to come up with creative ways to use them in recipes. My son calls these tasty noshes potato poppers. They're delicious and low-calorie.

—**KAREN SULAK** LAMPASAS, TX

PREP: 25 MIN. • **COOK:** 10 MIN.
MAKES: 16 APPETIZERS

- 8 **small red potatoes**
- 1 **pound Italian turkey sausage links, casings removed**
- ½ **cup chopped sweet red pepper**
- 4 **green onions, chopped**
- 9 **teaspoons minced fresh parsley, divided**
- ⅓ **cup shredded reduced-fat cheddar cheese**

1. Scrub and pierce potatoes; place on a microwave-safe plate. Microwave, uncovered, on high for 8-9 minutes or until tender, turning once.

2. Meanwhile, in a large skillet, cook sausage and pepper over medium heat until sausage is no longer pink. Add onions and 4½ teaspoons parsley; cook 1-2 minutes longer. Remove from the heat; stir in cheese. Cut each potato in half lengthwise. Scoop out 1 tablespoon pulp (save for another use).

3. Spoon about 2 tablespoons sausage mixture into each half. Place on a microwave-safe plate. Microwave on high for 1-2 minutes or until cheese is melted. Sprinkle with remaining parsley.

NOTE *This recipe was tested in a 1,100-watt microwave.*

PER SERVING *63 cal., 3 g fat (1 g sat. fat), 19 mg chol., 186 mg sodium, 3 g carb., 1 g fiber, 5 g pro.* **Diabetic Exchanges:** *1 lean meat.*

Easy Buffalo Chicken Dip

With three simple ingredients, you can turn leftover chicken into the ultimate man food, perfect for a game-day snack. I often serve this fun dip with crackers or celery.

—**JANICE FOLTZ** HERSHEY, PA

START TO FINISH: 30 MIN.
MAKES: 4 CUPS

- 1 package (8 ounces) reduced-fat cream cheese
- 1 cup (8 ounces) reduced-fat sour cream
- ½ cup Louisiana-style hot sauce
- 3 cups shredded cooked chicken breast
  Assorted crackers

1. In a large bowl, beat the cream cheese, sour cream and hot sauce until smooth; stir in chicken.

2. Transfer to an 8-in. square baking dish coated with cooking spray. Cover and bake at 350° for 18-22 minutes or until heated through. Serve warm with crackers.

PER SERVING 3 tablespoons equals 77 cal., 4 g fat (2 g sat. fat), 28 mg chol., 71 mg sodium, 1 g carb., trace fiber, 8 g pro.

White Chocolate Popcorn Deluxe

I often take this to potlucks and the teachers' table at work. It's fun to try different types of chocolate and other mix-ins, too.

—**KAY SCOTT** HICO, TX

PREP: 15 MIN. + COOLING
MAKES: 2 QUARTS

- 8 cups air-popped popcorn
- 2 ounces white baking chocolate, chopped
- 1 teaspoon butter
- ⅓ cup dried cranberries
- ¼ cup chopped walnuts
- ¾ teaspoon salt

1. Place popcorn in a large bowl. In a microwave, melt white chocolate and butter; stir until smooth. Pour over popcorn mixture and toss to coat. Add the cranberries, nuts and salt.

2. Spread onto waxed paper. Cool until set. Store in an airtight container.

PER SERVING 1 cup equals 114 cal., 6 g fat (2 g sat. fat), 3 mg chol., 233 mg sodium, 15 g carb., 2 g fiber, 2 g pro.

EASY BUFFALO CHICKEN DIP

Party Pretzels

Turn ordinary pretzels into instant party food with a garlicky-dill seasoning. This could also be done with pretzel sticks and makes a popular after-school snack.

—CARRIE SHAUB MOUNT JOY, PA

START TO FINISH: 25 MIN.
MAKES: 12 CUPS

- 1 **package (16 ounces) fat-free miniature pretzels**
- ¼ **cup canola oil**
- 3 **teaspoons garlic powder**
- 1 **teaspoon dill weed**
- ½ **teaspoon lemon-pepper seasoning**

1. Place pretzels in an ungreased 15-in. x 10-in. x 1-in. baking pan. Combine the oil, garlic powder, dill and lemon-pepper; drizzle over pretzels and toss to coat.

2. Bake at 350° for 12 minutes, stirring twice. Cool on a wire rack. Store in an airtight container.

PER SERVING *½ cup equals 89 cal., 2 g fat (trace sat. fat), 0 chol., 290 mg sodium, 16 g carb., 1 g fiber, 2 g pro. Diabetic Exchanges: 1 starch, ½ fat.*

Ants on a Log

I make this snack as a protein pick-me-up. It reminds of "Ants on a Log" from my childhood, and it's great on an English muffin or apple slices.

—LISA HUMMITSCH TINLEY PARK, IL

PREP: 10 MIN.
MAKES: 4 SERVINGS

- 1 **celery rib, finely chopped**
- 2 **tablespoons raisins**
- 2 **tablespoons creamy peanut butter**
  Miniature whole wheat bagels or apple slices

In a small bowl, combine the celery, raisins and peanut butter. Serve with bagels or apples.

PER SERVING *2 tablespoons equals (calculated without bagels and apples) 63 cal., 4 g fat (1 g sat. fat), 46 mg sodium, 5 g carb., 1 g fiber, 2 g pro. Diabetic Exchange: ½ high-fat meat.*

CREAMY DILL DIP

Creamy Dill Dip

Beau Monde seasoning is the secret ingredient that adds a little special zing to this low-fat, classic dill dip. I usually double the recipe since I think it gets better after a few days in the fridge.

—CORKY HUFFSMITH INDIO, CA

PREP: 10 MIN. + CHILLING
MAKES: 1⅓ CUPS

- ⅔ **cup fat-free mayonnaise**
- ⅔ **cup reduced-fat sour cream**
- 1 **tablespoon chopped green onions**
- 1 **tablespoon dried parsley flakes**
- 2 **teaspoons Beau Monde seasoning**
- 2 **teaspoons dill weed**
  Assorted fresh vegetables

1. In a small bowl, combine the first six ingredients. Cover and refrigerate overnight. Serve with vegetables.

PER SERVING *49 cal., 3 g fat (1 g sat. fat), 10 mg chol., 371 mg sodium, 5 g carb., 1 g fiber, 2 g pro.*

PARTY PRETZELS

Curried Cran-Orange Snack Mix

A new salty-sweet twist on an old party favorite, this mix includes pistachios, craisins and a mild curry flavor that make it extraordinary. It's also a great gift from the kitchen to keep on hand during the holidays.

—MARY BETH HARRIS-MURPHREE
TYLER, TX

PREP: 15 MIN.
BAKE: 40 MIN. + COOLING
MAKES: 5½ CUPS

- **2 cups Wheat Chex**
- **1½ cups Corn Chex**
- **1 cup chow mein noodles**
- **⅓ cup shelled pistachios**
- **2 tablespoons butter, melted**
- **2 tablespoons orange juice**
- **2 teaspoons curry powder**
- **1 teaspoon salt**
- **1 teaspoon garlic powder**
- **1 teaspoon dried basil**
- **1 teaspoon grated orange peel**
- **¼ teaspoon pepper**
- **¾ cup dried cranberries**

1. In a large bowl, combine the cereals, noodles and pistachios; set aside. In a small bowl, combine the butter, orange juice, curry, salt, garlic powder, basil, orange peel and pepper. Drizzle over cereal mixture; toss to coat.

2. Transfer to a 15-in. x 10-in. x 1-in. baking pan coated with cooking spray. Bake at 275° for 40 minutes or until golden brown, stirring every 10 minutes. Stir in cranberries. Cool on wire racks. Store in an airtight container.

PER SERVING *½ cup equals 125 cal., 5 g fat (2 g sat. fat), 5 mg chol., 347 mg sodium, 19 g carb., 2 g fiber, 2 g pro.* ***Diabetic Exchanges:*** *1 starch, 1 fat.*

CURRIED
CRAN-ORANGE
SNACK MIX

F S C FAST FIX
Fresh Peach Salsa

When peaches are in season, I like to serve this with grilled chicken or fish. Since this fresh salsa comes together in a food processor, it really takes almost no time to make.

—SHAWNA LAUFER FT MYERS, FL

PREP: 15 MIN. + CHILLING
MAKES: 4 CUPS

- 4 medium peaches, peeled and pitted
- 2 large tomatoes, cut into wedges and seeded
- ½ sweet onion, cut into wedges
- ½ cup fresh cilantro leaves
- 2 garlic cloves, peeled and crushed
- 2 cans (4 ounces each) chopped green chilies
- 4 teaspoons cider vinegar
- 1 teaspoon lime juice
- ¼ teaspoon pepper
   Baked tortilla chip scoops

In a food processor, combine the first five ingredients; cover and pulse until coarsely chopped.

Add the chilies, vinegar, lime juice and pepper; cover and pulse just until blended. Transfer to a serving bowl; chill until serving. Serve with chips.

PER SERVING ¼ cup equals 20 cal., trace fat (trace sat. fat), 0 chol., 58 mg sodium, 5 g carb., 1 g fiber, 1 g pro. *Diabetic Exchange: Free food.*

F C
Cool and Creamy Spinach Dip

I always keep this easy dip on hand—it encourages me to eat more fresh veggies. The light cottage cheese adds protein and calcium without the fat.

—MELISSA HANSEN ROCHESTER, MN

PREP: 10 MIN. + CHILLING
MAKES: 2½ CUPS

- 1 cup (8 ounces) 2% cottage cheese
- 1 package (10 ounces) frozen chopped spinach, thawed and squeezed dry
- 1 cup (8 ounces) fat-free sour cream
- 2 tablespoons fat-free milk
- 1 tablespoon grated Parmesan-Romano or Parmesan cheese
- 1 tablespoon reduced-fat ranch salad dressing
- ¼ teaspoon dill weed
- ⅛ teaspoon garlic powder
   Assorted fresh vegetables

In a food processor, cover and process cottage cheese until smooth. Transfer to a small bowl; stir in the spinach, sour cream, milk, Parmesan-Romano cheese, ranch dressing, dill and garlic powder. Cover and refrigerate for 3-4 hours. Serve with vegetables.

PER SERVING ¼ cup equals 56 cal., 1 g fat (trace sat. fat), 8 mg chol., 145 mg sodium, 7 g carb., 1 g fiber, 5 g pro. *Diabetic Exchange: ½ starch.*

FRESH PEACH SALSA

F S C
Mexican Chicken Meatballs

As a fun alternative to meatballs, these cheesy chicken bites go great with salsa and tortilla chips. They brown up nicely in the oven, but remember to turn them every few minutes.

—KATRINA LOPES LYMAN, SC

PREP: 20 MIN. • **BAKE:** 15 MIN.
MAKES: ABOUT 5 DOZEN

- ½ cup egg substitute
- 1 can (4 ounces) chopped green chilies
- 1 cup crushed cornflakes
- 1 cup (4 ounces) shredded reduced-fat Mexican cheese blend
- ½ teaspoon seasoned salt
- ¼ teaspoon cayenne pepper
- 1 pound ground chicken
  Salsa, optional

1. In a large bowl, combine the first six ingredients. Crumble chicken over mixture and mix well. Shape into 1-in. balls. Place on baking sheets coated with cooking spray.
2. Bake at 375° for 12-15 minutes or until a thermometer reads 165° and juices run clear, turning occasionally. Serve with salsa if desired.
PER SERVING *21 cal., 1 g fat (trace sat. fat), 6 mg chol., 49 mg sodium, 1 g carb., trace fiber, 2 g pro.*

MEXICAN CHICKEN MEATBALLS

Crunchy Spiced Nuts

This is a recipe my mother gave to me for spiced nuts. The cinnamon-sugar coating gives them an extra-potent crunch, and hints of ginger and nutmeg make it difficult to stop reaching for more.

—SUZANNE WOOD HOUSTON, TX

PREP: 20 MIN. • **BAKE:** 45 MIN. + COOLING.
MAKES: 3 CUPS

- 2 egg whites
- 2 tablespoons water
- 2 cups confectioners' sugar
- 3 tablespoons ground cinnamon
- 2 tablespoons ground ginger
- 1 tablespoon ground cloves
- 2 teaspoons salt
- 1 teaspoon ground nutmeg
- 1 cup unblanched almonds
- ½ cup pecan halves
- ½ cup walnut halves

1. In a shallow bowl, whisk egg whites and water. Sift together the confectioners' sugar, cinnamon, ginger, cloves, salt and nutmeg; place in another shallow bowl. Coat nuts in egg mixture, then dip in sugar mixture.
2. Transfer to a baking sheet coated with cooking spray. Bake at 250° for 45 minutes, stirring occasionally. Cool completely. Store in an airtight container.
PER SERVING *¼ cup equals 182 cal., 12 g fat (1 g sat. fat), 0 chol., 243 mg sodium, 17 g carb., 3 g fiber, 4 g pro.*

Golden Pineapple Salsa

This delicious salsa adds lively flavor to pork or could be served with tortilla chips as an appetizer. Sweet pineapple and refreshing mint couple nicely with a splash of lime juice.

—**BRYNNE GARMAN** BELLEVUE, WA

PREP: 10 MIN. + CHILLING
MAKES: 2½ CUPS

- 2 **cups chopped fresh pineapple**
- ⅓ **cup finely chopped sweet onion**
- ¼ **cup finely chopped green pepper**
- 2 **tablespoons lime juice**
- 2 **garlic cloves, minced**
- 2 **tablespoons minced fresh mint**
- ¼ **teaspoon salt**
- ¼ **teaspoon ground cumin**
- ⅛ **teaspoon cayenne pepper**

1. In a small bowl, combine the pineapple, onion, green pepper, lime juice and garlic. Stir in the mint, salt, cumin and cayenne. Cover and refrigerate for at least 1 hour. Serve with your favorite pork, fish or poultry.

PER SERVING *20 cal., trace fat (trace sat. fat), 0 chol., 60 mg sodium, 5 g carb., 1 g fiber, trace pro.* **Diabetic Exchange:** *Free food.*

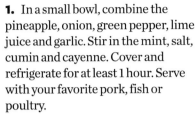

Zest Before Juicing

If you're using fresh citrus for lemon or lime juice, zest the fruit first. Then pop the zest into an airtight container or freezer-safe bag and store it in the freezer. Having it on hand is an easy way to add a little zip to baked goods, fruit salads, stir-fries and more .

GOLDEN PINEAPPLE SALSA

BLUE CHEESE-STUFFED STRAWBERRIES

Blue Cheese-Stuffed Strawberries

I was enjoying a salad with strawberries and blue cheese when the idea hit me to stuff the strawberries and serve them as an appetizer. It worked out great, and the flavors blend so nicely.

—**DIANE NEMITZ** LUDINGTON, MI

START TO FINISH: 25 MIN.
MAKES: 16 APPETIZERS

- ½ **cup balsamic vinegar**
- 3 **ounces fat-free cream cheese**
- 2 **ounces crumbled blue cheese**
- 16 **fresh strawberries**
- 3 **tablespoons finely chopped pecans, toasted**

1. Place vinegar in a small saucepan. Bring to a boil; cook until liquid is reduced by half. Cool to room temperature.
2. Meanwhile, in a small bowl, beat cream cheese until smooth. Beat in blue cheese. Remove stems and scoop out centers from strawberries; fill each with about 2 teaspoons cheese mixture. Sprinkle pecans over filling, pressing lightly. Chill until serving.

Drizzle with balsamic vinegar.
PER SERVING *36 cal., 2 g fat (1 g sat. fat), 3 mg chol., 80 mg sodium, 3 g carb., trace fiber, 2 g pro.* **Diabetic Exchange:** *½ fat.*

Chicken Wonton Cups

These little wonton cups are a great way for my family to enjoy the taste of jalapeno poppers without all the fat and calories. I simply use light mayonnaise and cream cheese to reduce the fat content.

—**NADINE MESCH** MOUNT HEALTHY, OH

START TO FINISH: 30 MIN.
MAKES: 3 DOZEN

- 36 **wonton wrappers**
  Cooking spray
- 1½ **cups shredded cooked chicken breasts**
- 1 **package (8 ounces) reduced-fat cream cheese**
- ½ **cup shredded Parmesan cheese**
- ⅓ **cup reduced-fat mayonnaise**
- 1 **can (4 ounces) chopped green chilies, undrained**
- 1 **jalapeno pepper, seeded and minced**

1. Press wonton wrappers into miniature muffin cups coated with cooking spray. Spritz wrappers with cooking spray. Bake at 350° for 5-6 minutes or until edges begin to brown.
2. Meanwhile, in a small bowl, combine the chicken, cream cheese, Parmesan cheese, mayonnaise, chilies and jalapeno. Spoon chicken mixture into cups. Bake 8-10 minutes longer or until filling is heated through. Serve warm. Refrigerate leftovers.
NOTE *Wear disposable gloves when cutting hot peppers; the oils can burn skin. Avoid touching your face.*
PER SERVING *62 cal., 3 g fat (1 g sat. fat), 12 mg chol., 126 mg sodium, 5 g carb., trace fiber, 4 g pro.*

CHICKEN WONTON CUPS

**BLUE CHEESE
WALDORF SALAD** *PAGE 32*

SALADS

**SARAH VASQUES'
GRILLED PORTOBELLOS WITH
MOZZARELLA SALAD**
PAGE 26

**GINGER SULLIVAN'S
CANTALOUPE CHICKEN SALAD**
PAGE 30

**CAROLE RESNICK'S
TURKEY BULGUR SALAD**
PAGE 33

Salads

There's coleslaw, and then there's macaroni coleslaw. Make your **next salad extraordinary** with **tangy flavors and fresh combinations** that will guarantee you an invite to the next potluck.

FAST FIX
Thai Pasta Side Salad

A tasty peanut dressing lightly coats pasta and cabbage in this easy-to-make side dish that's perfect for potlucks or outdoor events. Try sesame oil instead of olive oil if you have some on hand.

—**LAURIE DAVISON** CLEARWATER, FL

START TO FINISH: 25 MIN.
MAKES: 10 SERVINGS

- 2 cups uncooked bow tie pasta
- 4 cups chopped red cabbage
- 1 medium green pepper, chopped
- 1 medium sweet red pepper, chopped
- 4 green onions, thinly sliced
- ¼ cup rice vinegar
- ¼ cup reduced-fat creamy peanut butter
- 4½ teaspoons reduced-sodium soy sauce
- 1 tablespoon honey
- 1½ teaspoons olive oil
- ½ cup dry roasted peanuts

1. Cook the pasta according to package directions. Meanwhile, in a large bowl, combine the cabbage, peppers and onions. In a small bowl, whisk the vinegar, peanut butter, soy sauce, honey and oil.
2. Drain pasta and rinse in cold water; add to cabbage mixture. Pour dressing over salad; toss to coat. Just before serving, sprinkle with peanuts.

PER SERVING ¾ cup equals 161 cal., 7 g fat (1 g sat. fat), 0 chol., 194 mg sodium, 21 g carb., 3 g fiber, 6 g pro. *Diabetic Exchanges:* 1½ starch, 1 fat.

Refreshing Grilled Chicken Salad

I like to combine my favorite power foods—blueberries, walnuts, olive oil— into this light, zippy salad. It's my go-to for luncheons with friends.

—**DENISE RASMUSSEN** SALINA, KS

PREP: 20 MIN. + MARINATING
GRILL: 10 MIN. • **MAKES:** 4 SERVINGS

- ½ cup lime juice
- 2 tablespoons honey
- 4 teaspoons olive oil
- ½ teaspoon salt
- ½ teaspoon pepper
- 4 boneless skinless chicken breast halves (4 ounces each)
- 6 cups spring mix salad greens
- 2 cups cubed seedless watermelon
- 1 cup fresh blueberries
- 1 medium sweet yellow pepper, cut into 1-inch pieces
- ⅓ cup chopped walnuts, toasted

1. In a small bowl, combine the lime juice, honey, oil, salt and pepper. Pour ⅓ cup into a large resealable plastic bag; add chicken. Seal the bag and turn to coat; refrigerate for at least 1 hour.

Cover and refrigerate remaining lime juice mixture for dressing.
2. Drain and discard marinade. Using long-handled tongs, moisten a paper towel with cooking oil and lightly coat the grill rack. Grill chicken, covered, over medium heat or broil 4 in. from the heat for 4-7 minutes on each side or until a thermometer reads 165°.
3. In a large bowl, mix the salad greens, watermelon, blueberries and yellow pepper; add reserved dressing and toss to coat. Divide mixture among four serving plates. Slice the chicken; serve with the salads. Sprinkle each serving with 4 teaspoons walnuts.

PER SERVING 300 cal., 12 g fat (2 g sat. fat), 63 mg chol., 257 mg sodium, 25 g carb., 4 g fiber, 28 g pro. *Diabetic Exchanges:* 3 lean meat, 2 fat, 1 vegetable, 1 fruit, ½ starch.

Colorful Garbanzo Bean Salad

Here's a salad that's most flavorful after it chills in the refrigerator for a few hours. That makes it a nice make-ahead option for lunch.

—**DIANA TSEPERKAS** NORTH HAVEN, CT

PREP: 30 MIN. + STANDING
MAKES: 4 SERVINGS

- 1 medium sweet red pepper
- 1 can (15 ounces) garbanzo beans or chickpeas, rinsed and drained
- 6 cherry tomatoes, halved
- 2 tablespoons minced fresh basil or 2 teaspoons dried basil
- 2 tablespoons olive oil
- 1 tablespoon lemon juice
- 1 tablespoon red wine vinegar
- ½ teaspoon salt
- ½ teaspoon grated lemon peel
- ¼ teaspoon pepper

1. Broil pepper 4 in. from the heat until skin blisters, about 5 minutes. With tongs, rotate pepper a quarter turn. Broil and rotate until all sides are blistered and blackened. Immediately place pepper in a small bowl; cover and let stand for 20 minutes.

2. Peel off and discard charred skin. Remove stem and seeds; chop pepper. In a large bowl, combine pepper, garbanzo beans, tomatoes and basil. In a small bowl, whisk the oil, lemon juice, vinegar, salt, lemon peel and pepper. Pour over bean mixture; toss to coat. Chill until serving.

PER SERVING ⅔ *cup equals 174 cal., 9 g fat (1 g sat. fat), 0 chol., 436 mg sodium, 20 g carb., 5 g fiber, 5 g pro. Diabetic Exchanges: 1½ fat, 1 starch.*

Greek-Inspired Quinoa Salad

I like to serve this black bean and spinach salad with pita bread. You can also turn it into a main dish simply by tossing in cut-up chicken breast.

—**JULIE STOCKEL** FARMINGTON HILLS, MI

PREP: 30 MIN. + CHILLING
MAKES: 10 SERVINGS

- 2 cups water
- 1 cup quinoa, rinsed
- 1 package (10 ounces) frozen chopped spinach, thawed and squeezed dry
- 1½ cups (6 ounces) crumbled feta cheese
- 1 cup grape tomatoes
- ¾ cup canned black beans, rinsed and drained
- ½ cup chopped seeded peeled cucumber
- ½ cup sliced pepperoncini
- ½ cup Greek olives, pitted and halved
- ¾ cup reduced-fat Greek or Italian salad dressing, divided

1. In a small saucepan, bring water to a boil. Add quinoa. Reduce the heat; cover and simmer for 12-15 minutes or until water is absorbed. Remove from the heat.

2. In a large bowl, combine the quinoa, spinach, cheese, tomatoes, beans, cucumber, pepperoncini and olives. Pour ½ cup dressing over quinoa mixture and toss to coat. Cover and refrigerate for at least 1 hour.

3. Just before serving, drizzle the remaining dressing over salad; toss to coat.

NOTE *Look for quinoa in the cereal, rice or organic food aisle.*

PER SERVING ¾ *cup equals 184 cal., 8 g fat (2 g sat. fat), 9 mg chol., 472 mg sodium, 19 g carb., 4 g fiber, 7 g pro. Diabetic Exchanges: 1½ fat, 1 starch, 1 lean meat.*

GREEK-INSPIRED QUINOA SALAD

COLORFUL GARBANZO BEAN SALAD

Macaroni Coleslaw

My friend Peggy brought her coleslaw to one of our picnics, and everyone liked it so much, we all had to have the recipe. The water chestnuts are a fun touch and give the creamy salad a nice crunch.

—SANDRA MATTESON WESTHOPE, ND

PREP: 25 MIN. + CHILLING
MAKES: 16 SERVINGS

- 1 package (7 ounces) ring macaroni or ditalini
- 1 package (14 ounces) coleslaw mix
- 2 medium onions, finely chopped
- 2 celery ribs, finely chopped
- 1 medium cucumber, finely chopped
- 1 medium green pepper, finely chopped
- 1 can (8 ounces) whole water chestnuts, drained and chopped

DRESSING

- 1½ cups Miracle Whip Light
- ⅓ cup sugar
- ¼ cup cider vinegar
- ½ teaspoon salt
- ¼ teaspoon pepper

1. Cook the macaroni according to package directions; drain and rinse in cold water. Transfer to a large bowl; add the coleslaw mix, onions, celery, cucumber, green pepper and water chestnuts.
2. In a small bowl, whisk the dressing ingredients. Pour over salad; toss to coat. Cover and refrigerate for at least 1 hour.
PER SERVING ¾ cup equals 150 cal., 5 g fat (1 g sat. fat), 6 mg chol., 286 mg sodium, 24 g carb., 2 g fiber, 3 g pro. *Diabetic Exchanges: 1 starch, 1 vegetable, 1 fat.*

Buffalo Chicken Salad

We consider this a summer staple. Sometimes we grill the chicken outside, then sprinkle the hot sauce over it, because you've gotta have that kick!

—CORI COOPER BOISE, ID

START TO FINISH: 25 MIN.
MAKES: 4 SERVINGS

- 1 pound boneless skinless chicken breasts, cut into ½-inch cubes
- 1 tablespoon olive oil
- 2 tablespoons Louisiana-style hot sauce
- ¼ teaspoon salt
- ¼ teaspoon pepper
- 1 bunch romaine, chopped
- 2 celery ribs, chopped
- 1 cup shredded carrots
- ½ cup fat-free ranch salad dressing

1. In a large nonstick skillet, saute chicken in oil until no longer pink; drain. Stir in the hot sauce, salt and pepper.
2. In large bowl, combine romaine, celery and carrots. Divide among four plates. Top with chicken. Serve with ranch dressing.
PER SERVING 229 cal., 7 g fat (1 g sat. fat), 63 mg chol., 644 mg sodium, 16 g carb., 3 g fiber, 25 g pro. *Diabetic Exchanges: 3 lean meat, 1 starch, 1 vegetable, ½ fat.*

BUFFALO CHICKEN SALAD

GRILLED PORTOBELLOS
WITH MOZZARELLA SALAD

C **FAST FIX**

Grilled Portobellos with Mozzarella Salad

These colorful mushrooms are so filling, they're almost a meal in themselves. They can also be served with a small garden salad or as a hearty side dish.

—**SARAH VASQUES** MILFORD, NH

START TO FINISH: 30 MIN.
MAKES: 4 SERVINGS

- 2 **cups grape tomatoes, halved**
- 3 **ounces fresh mozzarella cheese, cubed**
- 3 **fresh basil leaves, thinly sliced**
- 2 **teaspoons olive oil**
- 2 **garlic cloves, minced**
- ¼ **teaspoon salt**
- ¼ **teaspoon pepper**
- 4 **large portobello mushrooms (4 to 4½ inches), stems removed**
  Cooking spray

1. In a small bowl, combine the first seven ingredients; cover and chill until serving.
2. Spritz mushrooms with cooking spray. Using long-handled tongs, moisten a paper towel with cooking oil and lightly coat the grill rack. Grill the mushrooms, covered, over medium heat or broil 4 in. from the heat for 6-8 minutes on each side or until tender. Spoon ½ cup of the tomato mixture into each mushroom cap.

PER SERVING *133 cal., 8 g fat (3 g sat. fat), 17 mg chol., 190 mg sodium, 9 g carb., 2 g fiber, 7 g pro.* **Diabetic Exchanges:** *2 vegetable, 1 lean meat, 1 fat.*

Sausage Potato Salad

I make this cool potato recipe on warm days. I modified the recipe by reducing the oil quite a bit and adding a little more honey mustard, which gives it a richer taste. Sausage, too, adds a savory touch to this salad.
—**GINETTE STARSHAK** DECATUR, IL

PREP: 20 MIN. • **COOK:** 15 MIN.
MAKES: 5 SERVINGS

- 1 **pound small red potatoes**
- 2 **tablespoons olive oil**
- 2 **tablespoons honey mustard**
- 1 **tablespoon white vinegar**
- 1 **tablespoon minced fresh parsley**
- 1 **teaspoon minced fresh tarragon or**
  ¼ teaspoon dried tarragon
- ¼ **teaspoon salt**
- ¼ **teaspoon pepper**
- ¼ **pound smoked turkey sausage,**
  halved and sliced
- 1 **small onion, chopped**

1. Scrub potatoes; place in a small saucepan and cover with water. Bring to a boil. Reduce heat; cover and cook for 15-20 minutes or until potatoes are tender.
2. For dressing, in a small bowl, combine the oil, honey mustard, vinegar and seasonings. Set aside. In a small nonstick skillet coated with cooking spray, cook and stir sausage until heated through.
3. Drain potatoes; cool slightly. Cut into ¼-in. slices and place in a bowl. Add the onion, sausage and dressing; toss to coat. Serve warm or chilled.
PER SERVING *⅔ cup equals 162 cal., 7 g fat (1 g sat. fat), 14 mg chol., 398 mg sodium, 19 g carb., 2 g fiber, 6 g pro. Diabetic Exchanges: 1½ fat, 1 starch.*

Thai-Style Black Bean Salad

Roasted or grilled fresh corn adds a deep undertone to this salad, but frozen corn works, too. The key is a splash of lime juice to really brighten the flavors.
—**JENNIFER WICKES** PINE BEACH, NJ

PREP: 15 MIN. + CHILLING
MAKES: 4 SERVINGS

- 1 **cup frozen corn**
- 1 **can (15 ounces) black beans,**
  rinsed and drained
- 1 **small onion, chopped**
- 1 **celery rib, thinly sliced**
- 1 **small sweet red pepper, chopped**
- ¼ **cup minced fresh cilantro**
- 1 **jalapeno pepper, seeded and finely**
  chopped
- 2 **tablespoons sesame oil**
- 1 **tablespoon rice vinegar**
- 1 **tablespoon lime juice**
- 2 **garlic cloves, minced**
- 1 **teaspoon minced fresh gingerroot**
- ½ **teaspoon salt**

1. Cook corn according to package directions. Transfer to a small bowl; add the beans, onion, celery, red pepper, cilantro and jalapeno.
2. In a small bowl, whisk the oil, vinegar, lime juice, garlic, ginger and salt. Pour over the bean mixture and toss to coat. Cover and refrigerate for at least 1 hour.
NOTE *Wear disposable gloves when cutting hot peppers; the oils can burn skin. Avoid touching your face.*
PER SERVING *¾ cup equals 198 cal., 7 g fat (1 g sat. fat), 0 chol., 517 mg sodium, 27 g carb., 6 g fiber, 7 g pro. Diabetic Exchanges: 1½ starch, 1 vegetable, 1 fat.*

THAI-STYLE
BLACK BEAN SALAD

Ⓒ Grecian Garden Salad

My mom likes to make this salad for guests. With a generous topping of cheese over fresh asparagus, tomato and basil, no wonder it's become her most-loved dish.

—**MELISSA SIPHERD** SALT LAKE CITY, UT

PREP: 20 MIN. + CHILLING
MAKES: 6 SERVINGS

- 1½ cups cut fresh asparagus (1-inch pieces)
- 3 medium tomatoes, seeded and chopped
- 2 tablespoons balsamic vinegar
- 4½ teaspoons minced fresh basil or 1½ teaspoons dried basil
- 1 tablespoon olive oil
- 1 teaspoon salt
- ½ teaspoon pepper
- 1 cup (4 ounces) crumbled feta cheese

1. In a large saucepan, bring 3 cups water to a boil. Add asparagus; cover and boil for 3 minutes. Drain and immediately place asparagus in ice water. Drain and pat dry. Transfer to a serving bowl. Stir in the tomatoes.

2. In a small bowl, whisk the vinegar, basil, oil, salt and pepper. Drizzle over vegetables; toss to coat. Cover and refrigerate for at least 1 hour. Just before serving, stir in cheese.

PER SERVING *⅔ cup equals 92 cal., 5 g fat (2 g sat. fat), 10 mg chol., 579 mg sodium, 6 g carb., 2 g fiber, 5 g pro.* **Diabetic Exchanges:** *1 vegetable, 1 fat.*

GRECIAN GARDEN SALAD

Ⓒ FAST FIX ▶ Southwest Crunch Chicken Salad

The blend of citrus, smoky cumin and bacon in this creamy chicken salad make it stand out from the rest. If you don't have cumin, chili powder is a spicy, flavorful substitution.

—**SALLY SIBTHORPE** SHELBY TOWNSHIP, MI

START TO FINISH: 30 MIN.
MAKES: 13 SERVINGS

- 1⅓ cups fat-free mayonnaise
- ½ cup minced fresh cilantro
- ¼ cup lime juice
- ¼ cup orange juice
- 2 garlic cloves, minced
- 1¾ teaspoons ground cumin
- ¾ teaspoon grated orange peel
- ½ teaspoon salt
- 9 cups cubed cooked chicken breast
- 1¾ cups julienned peeled jicama
- 1¾ cups chopped celery
- 1¾ cups chopped sweet red peppers
- 1 cup chopped cashews
- ½ pound turkey bacon strips, diced and cooked

In a small bowl, combine the first eight ingredients. In a large bowl, combine remaining ingredients. Add the mayonnaise mixture; toss to coat. Refrigerate until serving.

PER SERVING *1 cup equals 286 cal., 12 g fat (3 g sat. fat), 95 mg chol., 653 mg sodium, 11 g carb., 3 g fiber, 33 g pro.* **Diabetic Exchanges:** *4 lean meat, 1½ fat, 1 starch.*

Grilled Vegetable Orzo Salad

Vegetables that are in season make great additions to my orzo salad. It's the perfect side dish for a picnic, it can easily be doubled for a crowd, and you can add grilled chicken to make it a filling entree.

—**DANIELLE MILLER** WESTFIELD, IN

PREP: 35 MIN. • **GRILL:** 10 MIN.
MAKES: 8 SERVINGS

- 1¼ cups uncooked orzo pasta
- ½ pound fresh asparagus, trimmed
- 1 medium zucchini, cut lengthwise into ½-inch slices
- 1 medium sweet yellow or red pepper, halved
- 1 large portobello mushroom, stem removed
- ½ medium red onion, halved

DRESSING
- ⅓ cup olive oil
- ¼ cup balsamic vinegar
- 3 tablespoons lemon juice
- 4 garlic cloves, minced
- 1 teaspoon lemon-pepper seasoning

SALAD
- 1 cup grape tomatoes, halved
- 1 tablespoon minced fresh parsley
- 1 tablespoon minced fresh basil
- ½ teaspoon salt
- ¼ teaspoon pepper
- 1 cup (4 ounces) crumbled feta cheese

1. Cook orzo according to package directions. Place vegetables in a large bowl. In a small bowl, whisk dressing ingredients. Add to the vegetables and toss to coat.

2. Remove vegetables, reserving dressing. Grill mushroom, pepper and onion, covered, over medium heat 5-10 minutes or until tender, turning occasionally. Grill asparagus and zucchini, uncovered, 3-4 minutes or

CARROT RAISIN SALAD

until desired doneness, turning occasionally.

3. When cool enough to handle, cut vegetables into bite-size pieces. In a large bowl, combine cooked orzo, grilled vegetables, tomatoes, parsley, basil, salt, pepper and reserved dressing; toss to combine. Serve at room temperature or chill until cold. Just before serving, stir in cheese.

PER SERVING ¾ cup equals 260 cal., 12 g fat (3 g sat. fat), 8 mg chol., 352 mg sodium, 30 g carb., 2 g fiber, 8 g pro. *Diabetic Exchanges:* 2 fat, 1½ starch, 1 vegetable.

---

top tip **Freezer Carrots**

I shred carrots and freeze them in plastic bags in 1-cup portions. When a recipe calls for shredded carrots, I just pull a bag out of the freezer.

—**CANDANCE Z.** Eagar, AZ

F **S**

Carrot Raisin Salad

Vanilla yogurt gives this simple and traditional salad a subtle, sweet twist. It's wonderful with turkey, and it will go great with your favorite sandwich.

—**ELIZABETH BORGEMENKE** MASON, OH

PREP: 15 MIN. + CHILLING
MAKES: 4 SERVINGS

- 2½ cups shredded carrots
- 1 celery rib, chopped
- ½ cup raisins
- ¾ cup (6 ounces) vanilla yogurt

In a small bowl, combine all the ingredients. Cover and chill for at least 4 hours. Stir before serving.

PER SERVING ¾ cup equals 127 cal., 2 g fat (1 g sat. fat), 4 mg chol., 85 mg sodium, 27 g carb., 3 g fiber, 3 g pro. *Diabetic Exchanges:* 1 vegetable, 1 fruit, ½ starch.

CANTALOUPE CHICKEN SALAD

FAST FIX

Cantaloupe Chicken Salad

I found this recipe several years ago, and my son and I enjoy it often. It's just right for a cool-me-down lunch.

—**GINGER SULLIVAN** CUTLER BAY, FL

START TO FINISH: 20 MIN.
MAKES: 2 SERVINGS

- ¼ cup fat-free mayonnaise
- 2 tablespoons fat-free sour cream
- 1½ teaspoons sugar
- ½ teaspoon grated lemon peel
- ½ teaspoon lemon juice
- ¼ teaspoon ground ginger
  Dash salt and pepper
- 1 cup cubed cooked chicken breast
- ½ cup sliced celery
- ½ cup seedless red grapes, halved
- 2 green onions, chopped
- 1 small cantaloupe, halved and seeded
- ¼ cup slivered almonds, toasted

In a large bowl, combine the mayonnaise, sour cream, sugar, peel, lemon juice, ginger, salt and pepper. Add the chicken, celery, grapes and onions; toss to coat. Spoon 1 cup salad mixture into each cantaloupe half; sprinkle with the almonds.

PER SERVING 350 cal., 11 g fat (2 g sat. fat), 60 mg chol., 417 mg sodium, 40 g carb., 5 g fiber, 27 g pro. **Diabetic Exchanges:** 3 lean meat, 2 fruit, 1½ fat, ½ starch.

Artichoke Tomato Salad

For a little zip, crumble feta over the salad. Or add shredded rotisserie chicken for a hearty main dish.

—**DEB WILLIAMS** PEORIA, AZ

START TO FINISH: 20 MIN.
MAKES: 8 SERVINGS

- 5 **large tomatoes (about 2 pounds), cut into wedges**
- ¼ **teaspoon salt**
- ¼ **teaspoon pepper**
- 1 **jar (7½ ounces) marinated quartered artichoke hearts, drained**
- 1 **can (2¼ ounces) sliced ripe olives, drained**
- 2 **tablespoons minced fresh parsley**
- 2 **tablespoons white wine vinegar**
- 2 **garlic cloves, minced**

Arrange the tomato wedges on a large serving platter; sprinkle with salt and pepper. In a small bowl, combine the remaining ingredients. Spoon over the tomatoes. Refrigerate leftovers.

PER SERVING *¾ cup equals 74 cal., 5 g fat (1 g sat. fat), 0 chol., 241 mg sodium, 7 g carb., 2 g fiber, 1 g pro. Diabetic Exchanges: 1 vegetable, 1 fat.*

Fruited Mixed Greens Salad

Peppery arugula with citrus and berries is a fantastically fresh combination of bright flavors. This is a salad to remember!

—**ANN BAKER** TEXARKANA, TX

START TO FINISH: 15 MIN.
MAKES: 6 SERVINGS

- 1 **package (5 ounces) spring mix salad greens**
- 2 **cups fresh baby spinach**
- 1 **cup fresh arugula or additional fresh baby spinach**
- 1 **can (11 ounces) mandarin oranges, drained**
- ⅔ **cup chopped walnuts**
- ½ **cup fresh raspberries**
- ½ **cup canned diced beets**
- ½ **cup fresh blueberries**
- ¼ **cup sliced radishes**

DRESSING

- ⅔ **cup fat-free poppy seed salad dressing**
- 3 **tablespoons red raspberry preserves**
- 1 **teaspoon white wine vinegar**

In a large bowl, combine the first nine ingredients. In a small bowl, whisk dressing ingredients. Drizzle over salad; toss to coat.

PER SERVING *1⅔ cups equal 97 cal., 8 g fat (1 g sat. fat), 4 mg chol., 116 mg sodium, 28 g carb., 3 g fiber, 6 g pro. Diabetic Exchanges: 1 starch, 1 vegetable, 1 fat, ½ fruit.*

FRUITED MIXED GREENS SALAD

Fresh & Chunky Chicken Salad

I've served this twice to special guests at dinner parties, and both times, everyone loved it. People just kept coming back for more!

—CAROL DOGGETTE LOS ANGELES, CA

PREP: 20 MIN. + MARINATING
GRILL: 10 MIN. • **MAKES:** 4 SERVINGS

- 1 tablespoon lime juice
- 2 teaspoons olive oil
- ½ teaspoon salt
- ½ teaspoon garlic powder
- ½ teaspoon onion powder
- ¼ teaspoon pepper
- 3 boneless skinless chicken breast halves (4 ounces each)

SALAD

- ½ cup diced apple
- 2 tablespoons orange juice
- ¼ cup fat-free plain yogurt
- ¼ cup fat-free mayonnaise
- ⅛ teaspoon pepper
- 1 cup diced cantaloupe
- 1 medium peach, peeled and diced
- 1 celery rib, diced
- ¼ cup raisins
- ¼ cup chopped walnuts, toasted
- 1 green onion, chopped
- 4 lettuce leaves

1. In a large resealable plastic bag, combine the first six ingredients; add chicken. Seal bag and turn to coat. Refrigerate for 20 minutes.

2. In a small bowl, toss apple with orange juice; set aside. In a large bowl, whisk the yogurt, mayonnaise and pepper until blended. Stir in cantaloupe, peach, celery, raisins, walnuts, onion and apple mixture. Cover and chill.

3. Drain chicken if necessary, discarding any excess marinade. Using long-handled tongs, moisten a paper towel with cooking oil and lightly coat the grill rack. Grill chicken, covered, over medium heat or broil 4 in. from the heat for 4-7 minutes on each side or until a thermometer reads 165°.

4. Dice the chicken and stir into the yogurt mixture. Serve over lettuce leaves.

PER SERVING *1 cup equals 247 cal., 9 g fat (1 g sat. fat), 49 mg chol., 480 mg sodium, 22 g carb., 3 g fiber, 21 g pro. Diabetic Exchanges: 2 lean meat, 1½ fat, 1 fruit, ½ starch.*

FRESH & CHUNKY CHICKEN SALAD

Blue Cheese Waldorf Salad

Blue cheese perks up this version of a classic. It's lovely served over lettuce leaves for a light, bistro-style lunch.

—DEB WILLIAMS PEORIA, AZ

PREP: 20 MIN. + CHILLING
MAKES: 12 SERVINGS

- 4 large apples, chopped
- 2 cups green grapes, halved

BLUE CHEESE WALDORF SALAD

- 1⅓ cups chopped celery
- ½ cup raisins
- 1 tablespoon lemon juice
- ⅔ cup fat-free mayonnaise
- ⅔ cup buttermilk
- ⅓ cup crumbled blue cheese
- 1 tablespoon sugar
- ¼ cup chopped walnuts, toasted

1. In a large bowl, combine the apples, grapes, celery, raisins and lemon juice.

2. In a small bowl, combine the mayonnaise, buttermilk, blue cheese and sugar. Pour over apple mixture and toss to coat. Cover and refrigerate for at least 1 hour.

3. Just before serving, sprinkle with walnuts.

PER SERVING *¾ cup equals 126 cal., 4 g fat (1 g sat. fat), 5 mg chol., 192 mg sodium, 24 g carb., 3 g fiber, 3 g pro. Diabetic Exchanges: 1 fruit, ½ starch, ½ fat.*

Turkey & Bulgur Salad

Cranberry juice concentrate gives this wonderful luncheon salad a burst of flavor. I like to line a serving platter with bright, crunchy greens and mound the salad in the center for a pretty presentation.

—**CAROLE RESNICK** CLEVELAND, OH

PREP: 25 MIN. + STANDING
MAKES: 6 SERVINGS

- 1½ cups reduced-sodium chicken broth
- ½ cup water
- 1 cup bulgur
- 2 cups cubed cooked turkey breast
- 1 small cucumber, finely chopped
- 1 cup garbanzo beans or chickpeas, rinsed and drained
- 3 green onions, thinly sliced
- ¼ cup sliced ripe olives
- 3 tablespoons dried cranberries
- ¼ cup olive oil
- 3 tablespoons lime juice
- 2 tablespoons thawed cranberry juice concentrate
- 1 cup cherry tomatoes, halved
- 3 tablespoons minced fresh parsley

1. In a small saucepan, bring broth and water to a boil. Place bulgur in a large bowl. Stir in broth mixture. Cover and let stand for 30 minutes or until most of the liquid is absorbed. Drain. Stir in the turkey, cucumber, beans, onions, olives and cranberries.

2. In a small bowl, whisk the oil, lime juice and cranberry juice concentrate. Stir into bulgur mixture. Add the tomatoes and parsley; gently toss to coat. Serve at room temperature or chilled.

PER SERVING *1½ cups equal 302 cal., 11 g fat (2 g sat. fat), 40 mg chol., 283 mg sodium, 32 g carb., 7 g fiber, 20 g pro.* **Diabetic Exchanges:** *2 starch, 2 lean meat, 2 fat.*

top tip
The Bigger the Bulgur

Bulgur is a form of wheat that has been parboiled and ground into fine, medium, coarse or whole grains. It doubles in size when hydrated so be sure to use a big enough bowl or pan. Look for bulgur in the cereal, rice or organic food aisle of your grocery store.

TURKEY & BULGUR SALAD

C FAST FIX

Blackberry Spinach Salad

The combination of feta and blackberries in this salad will be a new summertime favorite. The tangy honey-mustard dressing is also a recipe you should keep handy for any green salad or pasta salad.

—MARY LOU TIMPSON COLORADO CITY, AZ

START TO FINISH: 20 MIN.
MAKES: 6 SERVINGS

- 6 **cups fresh baby spinach**
- 1 **cup fresh blackberries**
- 1 **cup cherry tomatoes, halved**
- 1 **green onion, sliced**
- 2 **tablespoons chopped walnuts, toasted**
- 2 **tablespoons olive oil**
- 1 **tablespoon balsamic vinegar**
- 2½ **teaspoons honey**
- 1 **garlic clove, minced**
- 1 **teaspoon Dijon mustard**
- ¼ **teaspoon salt**
- ¼ **teaspoon pepper**
- ⅔ **cup crumbled feta cheese**

1. In a large salad bowl, combine spinach, blackberries, tomatoes, onion and walnuts.

2. In a small bowl, whisk the oil, vinegar, honey, garlic, mustard, salt and pepper. Drizzle over salad and toss to coat. Sprinkle with cheese. Serve immediately.

PER SERVING *1 cup equals 116 cal., 8 g fat (2 g sat. fat), 7 mg chol., 266 mg sodium, 9 g carb., 3 g fiber, 4 g pro. Diabetic Exchanges: 1 vegetable, 1 fat, ½ lean meat.*

BLACKBERRY SPINACH SALAD

Summer-Fresh Quinoa Salad

This light and refreshing salad is easy to prepare and perfect for hot summer days. I often add zucchini or summer squash and use fresh tomatoes instead of sun-dried.

—LIZ GADBOIS WOODVILLE, WI

PREP: 25 MIN. + CHILLING
MAKES: 14 SERVINGS

- 2 **cups quinoa, rinsed**
- 1 **cup boiling water**
- ½ **cup sun-dried tomatoes (not packed in oil)**
- 1 **medium cucumber, peeled, seeded and chopped**
- 1 **each medium green, sweet red and yellow peppers, chopped**
- 6 **green onions, thinly sliced**
- 1 **package (4 ounces) crumbled garlic and herb feta cheese**
- ½ **cup reduced-fat sun-dried tomato salad dressing, divided**

1. Cook the quinoa according to package directions. Transfer to a large bowl; cool completely.

2. In a small bowl, combine the water and tomatoes; let stand for 5 minutes. Drain and chop the tomatoes; add to quinoa. Stir in the cucumber, peppers, onions, cheese and ¼ cup salad dressing.

3. Cover and refrigerate for 2 hours. Just before serving, stir in remaining salad dressing.

NOTE *Look for quinoa in the cereal, rice or organic food aisle.*

PER SERVING *¾ cup equals 148 cal., 4 g fat (1 g sat. fat), 6 mg chol., 248 mg sodium, 22 g carb., 2 g fiber, 5 g pro.* ***Diabetic Exchanges:*** *1½ starch, 1 fat.*

WILD RICE SALAD

Wild Rice Salad

Nutty, fruity and packed with flavor, this make-ahead dish is a wholesome side for all kinds of entrees.

—BARBARA SCHULTE PAYSON, AZ

PREP: 15 MIN. **COOK:** 55 MIN. + CHILLING
MAKES: 15 SERVINGS (⅔ CUP EACH)

- 3 **cups water**
- 2 **cups uncooked wild rice**
- 2 **cups finely chopped dried apricots**
- 2 **cups dried cherries**
- 1 **cup chopped walnuts**
- ½ **cup olive oil**
- ⅓ **cup lemon juice**
- 2 **tablespoons maple syrup**
- 1½ **teaspoons salt**

1. In a large saucepan, bring water and rice to a boil. Reduce heat; cover and simmer for 45-50 minutes or until rice is tender. Drain if necessary. Transfer to a large bowl; cool completely.

2. Meanwhile, place apricots in a small bowl; cover with boiling water. Let stand for 5 minutes; drain. Stir the apricots, cherries and walnuts into rice. In a small bowl, whisk the oil, lemon juice, maple syrup and salt. Pour over the rice mixture and mix well. Chill for at least 30 minutes.

PER SERVING *⅔ cup equals 293 cal., 12 g fat (1 g sat. fat), 0 chol., 234 mg sodium, 44 g carb., 3 g fiber, 5 g pro.*

SPINACH BEAN SALAD
WITH MAPLE DRESSING

F S FAST FIX
Crunchy Apple Salad

With fiber-rich fruit, light dressing and crunchy walnuts, this is a great snack. Try it with low-fat granola.
—**KATHY ARMSTRONG** POST FALLS, ID

START TO FINISH: 15 MIN.
MAKES: 5 SERVINGS

- 6 tablespoons fat-free sugar-free vanilla yogurt
- 6 tablespoons reduced-fat whipped topping
- ¼ teaspoon plus ⅛ teaspoon ground cinnamon, divided
- 2 medium red apples, chopped
- 1 large Granny Smith apple, chopped
- ¼ cup dried cranberries
- 2 tablespoons chopped walnuts

In a large bowl, combine the yogurt, whipped topping and ¼ teaspoon cinnamon. Add apples and cranberries; toss to coat. Refrigerate until serving. Sprinkle with walnuts and remaining cinnamon before serving.
PER SERVING *¾ cup equals 109 cal., 3 g fat (1 g sat. fat), trace chol., 12 mg sodium, 22 g carb., 3 g fiber, 2 g pro.* **Diabetic Exchanges:** *1 fruit, ½ starch, ½ fat.*

CRUNCHY APPLE
SALAD

F C FAST FIX
Spinach Bean Salad with Maple Dressing

In this clever recipe, warm maple dressing slightly wilts the spinach, giving it a delightful texture and flavor. If you want to be wowed by a salad, you've got to try this one.
—**SALLY MALONEY** DALLAS, GA

START TO FINISH: 15 MIN.
MAKES: 11 SERVINGS

- ¼ cup maple syrup
- 3 tablespoons cider vinegar
- 1 tablespoon olive oil
- 1 tablespoon Dijon mustard
- ¼ teaspoon salt
- ¼ teaspoon coarsely ground pepper
- 1 can (15½ ounces) great northern beans, rinsed and drained
- 2 packages (6 ounces each) fresh baby spinach
- 4 green onions, thinly sliced
- 1 small sweet red pepper, chopped
- 5 bacon strips, cooked and crumbled

1. For dressing, in a small microwave-safe bowl, combine first six ingredients; set aside. Place beans in another microwave-safe bowl; microwave, uncovered, for 1-2 minutes or until heated through.
2. In a large salad bowl, combine the spinach, onions, red pepper, bacon and beans. Microwave the dressing, uncovered, for 30-60 seconds or until heated through. Whisk until smooth; drizzle over salad and toss to coat.
PER SERVING *1 cup equals 90 cal., 3 g fat (1 g sat. fat), 3 mg chol., 272 mg sodium, 13 g carb., 3 g fiber, 4 g pro.* **Diabetic Exchanges:** *1 starch, 1 vegetable.*

C
Thai Shrimp Salad

Here's a deliciously different salad that blends grilled shrimp, a lean source of protein, with the low-calorie crunch of cucumber and onion. It's tossed and dressed with Thai flavors of sesame, cilantro, lime and refreshing mint.

—ANNETTE TRAVERSO SAN RAFAEL, CA

PREP: 25 MIN. • **GRILL:** 10 MIN.
MAKES: 4 SERVINGS

- ¼ cup lime juice
- 2 tablespoons sesame oil
- 2 tablespoons reduced-sodium soy sauce
- 1 tablespoon sesame seeds, toasted
- 1 tablespoon minced fresh mint
- 1 tablespoon minced fresh cilantro
- ⅛ teaspoon crushed red pepper flakes
- 1 pound uncooked large shrimp, peeled and deveined
- ¼ teaspoon salt
- ¼ teaspoon pepper
- 1 sweet onion, sliced
- 1 medium cucumber, peeled and sliced
- 4 cups torn leaf lettuce

1. In a large bowl, combine the first seven ingredients; set aside. Sprinkle shrimp with salt and pepper; thread onto four metal or soaked wooden skewers.

2. Using long-handled tongs, moisten a paper towel with cooking oil and lightly coat the grill rack. Grill, covered, over medium heat for 2-4 minutes on each side or until shrimp turn pink.

3. Stir the reserved dressing; add the shrimp, onion and cucumber. Toss to coat. Divide the lettuce among four salad plates; top with the shrimp mixture.

PER SERVING *202 cal., 9 g fat (1 g sat. fat), 168 mg chol., 661 mg sodium, 10 g carb., 3 g fiber, 21 g pro.* **Diabetic Exchanges:** *3 lean meat, 2 vegetable, 1½ fat.*

top tip
One Shrimp, Two Shrimp

When buying shrimp, the "count" represents the number of shrimp in a pound for a certain size category. For example, there are about 31 to 35 large shrimp in a pound as opposed to 21 to 25 jumbo shrimp per pound.

THAI SHRIMP SALAD

APRICOT TURKEY
SANDWICHES PAGE 53

**LORI TERRY'S
ITALIAN SAUSAGE KALE SOUP**
PAGE 42

**LILY JULOW'S
ROAST PORK SANDWICHES WITH
PEACH CHUTNEY** PAGE 46

**NATALIE HUGHES'
SPICY CHICKEN CHILI**
PAGE 57

Soups & Sandwiches

Few **culinary combinations** have stood the test of time like the pairing of soup and sandwich. Enjoy this comforting duo with ingredients **you can feel good about** serving your family.

Italian Beef Sandwiches

These sandwiches are fork-tender, mouthwatering good and so easy to fix. I love serving them during football season to our hungry friends.

—**CHER SCHWARTZ** ELLISVILLE, MO

PREP: 20 MIN. • **COOK:** 8 HOURS
MAKES: 12 SERVINGS

- 1 **beef rump roast or bottom round roast (3 pounds)**
- 3 **cups reduced-sodium beef broth**
- 1 **envelope Italian salad dressing mix**
- 1 **teaspoon garlic powder**
- 1 **teaspoon onion powder**
- 1 **teaspoon dried parsley flakes**
- 1 **teaspoon dried basil**
- 1 **teaspoon dried oregano**
- 1 **teaspoon pepper**
- 1 **large onion, julienned**
- 1 **large green pepper, julienned**
- 4½ **teaspoons olive oil**
- 12 **hamburger buns, split**
- 12 **slices reduced-fat provolone cheese**

1. Cut roast in half; place in a 4-qt. slow cooker. Combine the broth, dressing mix and seasonings; pour over meat. Cover and cook on low for 8 hours or until tender.
2. Remove roast; cool slightly. Skim fat from cooking juices; reserve 1 cup juices. Shred beef and return to slow cooker. Stir in reserved cooking juices; heat through.
3. Meanwhile, in a large skillet, saute onion and green pepper in oil until tender.
4. Using a slotted spoon, place beef on bun bottoms; layer with cheese and vegetables. Replace bun tops.
PER SERVING *346 cal., 12 g fat (5 g sat. fat), 79 mg chol., 707 mg sodium, 25 g carb., 2 g fiber, 32 g pro.* **Diabetic Exchanges:** *4 lean meat, 1½ starch, 1 fat.*

FAST FIX
Southwest Chicken Corn Chowder

My family really enjoys my lightened-up take on chowder. Even my little grandson likes it! The fat-free evaporated milk stands in beautifully for heavy cream.

—**EILEEN ROBITAILLE** RIVERSIDE, CA

START TO FINISH: 25 MIN.
MAKES: 9 SERVINGS (2¼ QUARTS)

- 1 **large onion, chopped**
- 1 **garlic clove, minced**
- ½ **teaspoon olive oil**
- 1 **can (14½ ounces) reduced-sodium chicken broth**
- 1 **can (10¾ ounces) reduced-fat reduced-sodium condensed cream of chicken soup, undiluted**
- 2 **cups cubed cooked chicken breast**
- 1 **can (4 ounces) chopped green chilies, drained**
- 2 **cans (14¾ ounces each) cream-style corn**
- 1 **can (12 ounces) fat-free evaporated milk**
- ½ **teaspoon chili powder**
- ½ **teaspoon ground cumin**
- 6 **tablespoons shredded reduced-fat cheddar cheese**
- 4½ **teaspoons chopped cilantro**

1. In a large nonstick saucepan, saute the onion and garlic in oil until tender.
2. Stir in the broth, soup, chicken and chilies until blended. Bring to a boil. Reduce the heat; stir in corn, milk, chili powder and cumin. Heat through (do not boil). Sprinkle each serving with the cheese and cilantro.
PER SERVING *206 cal., 5 g fat (2 g sat. fat), 35 mg chol., 669 mg sodium, 27 g carb., 2 g fiber, 16 g pro.* **Diabetic Exchanges:** *2 starch, 2 lean meat.*

Beef and Tortellini Soup

This recipe came from my mother many years ago. My family loves it and so do others who taste it. The tortellini makes such a fun and filling addition to savory beef soup.

—BARBARA KEMMER ROHNERT PARK, CA

PREP: 20 MIN. • **COOK:** 40 MIN.
MAKES: 6 SERVINGS (2¼ QUARTS)

- 5 **tablespoons all-purpose flour, divided**
- ½ **pound beef top sirloin steak, cut into ½-inch cubes**
- 3 **teaspoons butter, divided**
- 1 **medium onion, chopped**
- 1 **celery rib, chopped**
- 1 **medium carrot, chopped**
- 2 **garlic cloves, minced**
- 1 **can (28 ounces) diced tomatoes, undrained**
- 2 **cans (14½ ounces each) reduced-sodium beef broth**
- 1½ **cups water, divided**
- 1 **teaspoon dried thyme**
- ½ **teaspoon white pepper**
- ¼ **teaspoon salt**
- 2 **cups frozen beef tortellini**

1. Place 2 tablespoons flour in a large resealable plastic bag. Add beef, a few pieces at a time, and shake to coat. In a nonstick Dutch oven, brown beef in 2 teaspoons butter; remove and keep warm.

2. In the same pan, saute the onion, celery and carrot in the remaining butter until tender. Add garlic; cook 1 minute longer. Add the tomatoes, broth, 1 cup water, thyme, pepper, salt and reserved beef. Bring to a boil. Reduce heat; cover and simmer for 20 minutes. Add tortellini; cook 5-10 minutes longer or until tender.

3. Combine remaining flour and water until smooth. Stir into the pan. Bring to a boil; cook and stir for 2 minutes or until thickened.

NOTE *Top sirloin may be labeled as strip steak, Kansas City steak, New York strip steak, ambassador steak or boneless club steak in your area.*
PER SERVING *265 cal., 9 g fat (4 g sat. fat), 109 mg chol., 706 mg sodium, 27 g carb., 4 g fiber, 19 g pro.* **Diabetic Exchanges:** *2 lean meat, 2 vegetable, 1 starch, ½ fat.*

FAST FIX

Chicken Caesar Wraps

Here's a classic cold sandwich that's layered with tender chicken, Parmesan cheese and chopped Caesar croutons. It uses just the right amount of dressing, and makes a tasty summertime meal.

—NANCY PRATT LONGVIEW, TX

START TO FINISH: 15 MIN.
MAKES: 6 SERVINGS

- ¾ **cup fat-free creamy Caesar salad dressing**
- ¼ **cup grated Parmesan cheese**
- ½ **teaspoon garlic powder**
- ¼ **teaspoon pepper**
- 3 **cups cubed cooked chicken breast**
- 2 **cups torn romaine**
- ¾ **cup Caesar salad croutons, coarsely chopped**
- 6 **whole wheat tortillas (8 inches), room temperature**

In a large bowl, combine dressing, cheese, garlic powder and pepper. Add the chicken, romaine and croutons. Spoon ⅔ cup chicken mixture down the center of each tortilla; roll up.

PER SERVING *332 cal., 7 g fat (1 g sat. fat), 57 mg chol., 689 mg sodium, 37 g carb., 4 g fiber, 27 g pro.* **Diabetic Exchanges:** *3 lean meat, 2½ starch, ½ fat.*

BEEF AND TORTELLINI SOUP

Pork Tenderloin Panini with Fig Port Jam

I serve these rather sophisticated yet simple sandwiches for dinner or cut them into smaller servings for appetizers. They're great hot or cold, but if serving cold, I like to add some watercress for a bit more color.

—CASEY GALLOWAY COLUMBIA, MO

PREP: 1 HOUR • **COOK:** 5 MIN.
MAKES: 4 SERVINGS

- ⅓ **cup port wine or grape juice**
- 2 **tablespoons water**
- 2 **dried figs, chopped**
- 1 **fresh rosemary sprig**
- 1 **tablespoon honey**
- ⅛ **teaspoon salt**
  Dash pepper

SANDWICHES

- 1 **pork tenderloin (¾ pound)**
- ¼ **teaspoon salt**
- ¼ **teaspoon pepper**
- 8 **slices sourdough bread**
- ¼ **cup crumbled goat cheese**
- 1 **cup watercress, optional**
  Cooking spray

1. For jam, in small saucepan, combine first seven ingredients. Bring to a boil. Reduce the heat; simmer, uncovered, until liquid is reduced to about ¼ cup, about 15 minutes.
2. Remove from the heat. Cool slightly; discard the rosemary. Transfer mixture to blender; cover and process until blended. Cover and chill until serving.
3. Meanwhile, sprinkle the tenderloin with salt and pepper; place on a rack in a shallow roasting pan. Bake, uncovered, at 350° for 40-50 minutes or until a thermometer reads 160°. Let stand for 10 minutes before slicing. Cut

PORK TENDERLOIN PANINI WITH FIG PORT JAM

pork into ⅛-in. slices.
4. On four bread slices, layer the pork, jam, cheese and watercress if desired; top with remaining bread. Coat outsides of sandwiches with cooking spray.
5. Cook on a panini maker or indoor grill for 3-4 minutes or until bread is lightly browned.
PER SERVING *381 cal., 8 g fat (4 g sat. fat), 59 mg chol., 746 mg sodium, 48 g carb., 3 g fiber, 28 g pro.*

FAST FIX
Super-Duper Tuna Sandwiches

If packing this fantastic sandwich for a brown-bag lunch, keep the bread separate from the salad so it doesn't get soggy. You can also try serving the tuna salad with crackers, as a wrap or on lettuce.

—RENEE BARTOLOMEO INDIANOLA, IA

START TO FINISH: 15 MIN.
MAKES: 4 SERVINGS

- 2 **cans (5 ounces each) light water-packed tuna, drained and flaked**
- ⅓ **cup shredded peeled apple**
- ⅓ **cup finely shredded cabbage**
- ⅓ **cup finely shredded carrot**
- 3 **tablespoons finely chopped celery**
- 3 **tablespoons finely chopped onion**
- 3 **tablespoons sweet pickle relish**
- 2 **tablespoons reduced-fat mayonnaise**
- 8 **slices whole wheat bread**

In a large bowl, combine the first eight ingredients. Spread ½ cup tuna mixture over four slices of bread; top with the remaining bread slices.
PER SERVING *291 cal., 5 g fat (1 g sat. fat), 28 mg chol., 717 mg sodium, 31 g carb., 5 g fiber, 29 g pro.* **Diabetic Exchanges:** *3 lean meat, 2 starch, ½ fat.*

Italian Sausage Kale Soup

My mom dehydrates the last pick of tomatoes from her garden each fall—perfect for quick soups like this one. Mom used dried beans, but I find canned beans are a real time saver and work just as well.

—**LORI TERRY** CHICAGO, IL

PREP: 15 MIN. • **COOK:** 20 MIN.
MAKES: 8 SERVINGS (2 QUARTS)

- 1½ pounds Italian turkey sausage links, casings removed
- 1 medium onion, chopped
- 8 cups chopped fresh kale
- 2 garlic cloves, minced
- ¼ teaspoon crushed red pepper flakes, optional
- ½ cup white wine or chicken stock
- 1 carton (26 ounces) chicken stock
- 1 can (15 ounces) white kidney or cannellini beans, rinsed and drained
- 1 can (14½ ounces) no-salt-added diced tomatoes
- ½ cup sun-dried tomatoes (not packed in oil), chopped
- ¼ teaspoon pepper

1. Crumble sausage into a Dutch oven; add onion. Cook and stir over medium heat until the meat is no longer pink. Drain, reserving ¼ cup drippings; set sausage aside. Saute kale in reserved drippings until wilted. Add the garlic and, if desired, pepper flakes; cook for 1 minute. Add the wine; cook 2 minutes longer.

2. Stir in the stock, beans, diced tomatoes, dried tomatoes, pepper and sausage mixture. Bring to a boil. Reduce heat; cover and simmer for 15-20 minutes or until kale is tender.

PER SERVING *217 cal., 8 g fat (2 g sat. fat), 51 mg chol., 868 mg sodium, 15 g carb., 4 g fiber, 18 g pro.*

Artichoke Chicken Pockets

You'll have a hard time believing these hefty, pizza-crust pockets are light. Packed full of cheese, artichokes, chicken, spinach and fabulous flavor, they're great even without the sauce and sure to become a family favorite.

—**BEVERLY OFERRALL** LINKWOOD, MD

PREP: 20 MIN. • **BAKE:** 15 MIN.
MAKES: 6 SERVINGS

- 2 cups shredded cooked chicken breast
- 2 cups thinly sliced fresh spinach
- 1¼ cups shredded provolone cheese
- ¾ cup water-packed artichoke hearts, rinsed, drained and chopped

ARTICHOKE CHICKEN POCKETS

- 1 garlic clove, minced
- ¼ teaspoon pepper
- 1 tube (13.8 ounces) refrigerated pizza crust
- 2 teaspoons cornmeal
  Marinara sauce, optional

1. In a large bowl, combine the first six ingredients. Unroll pizza dough; cut into six 4½-in. squares. Spoon 1 cup chicken mixture onto the center of each square; brush edges of dough with water. Fold one corner of each square over filling to the opposite corner, forming a triangle. Using a fork, crimp edges to seal.

2. Sprinkle cornmeal over a 15-in. x 10-in. x 1-in. baking pan coated with cooking spray. Place pockets in pan; prick tops with a fork. Bake at 425° for 12-15 minutes or until golden brown. Serve with marinara sauce if desired.

PER SERVING *355 cal., 11 g fat (5 g sat. fat), 55 mg chol., 776 mg sodium, 34 g carb., 1 g fiber, 27 g pro.* **Diabetic Exchanges:** *3 lean meat, 2 starch, 1 fat.*

ITALIAN SAUSAGE KALE SOUP

Pretty Autumn Soup

Carrots, squash and sweet potato combine to make a healthy and colorful soup, which I enjoy in the fall or spring.

—**MARGARET ALLEN** ABINGDON, VA

PREP: 15 MIN. • **COOK:** 20 MIN.
MAKES: 6 SERVINGS

- 2½ cups cubed peeled butternut squash
- 1 large sweet potato, peeled and cubed
- 3 medium carrots, sliced
- ¼ cup thawed orange juice concentrate
- 3 cups fat-free milk
- ¼ teaspoon salt
- ¼ teaspoon pepper
- 3 tablespoons reduced-fat sour cream
- 2 tablespoons minced chives
- 1 tablespoon sesame seeds, toasted

1. Place the squash, sweet potato and carrots in a steamer basket; place in a large saucepan over 1 in. of water. Bring to a boil; cover and steam for 12-16 minutes or until tender. Cool slightly. Transfer to a food processor; add the orange juice concentrate. Cover and process until smooth.

2. Transfer to a large saucepan; stir in the milk, salt and pepper. Cook and stir over low heat until heated through (do not boil). Top each serving with 1½ teaspoons sour cream, 1 teaspoon chives and ½ teaspoon sesame seeds.

PER SERVING *166 cal., 1 g fat (1 g sat. fat), 5 mg chol., 190 mg sodium, 33 g carb., 6 g fiber, 7 g pro.* ***Diabetic Exchanges:*** *1½ starch, 1 vegetable, ½ fat-free milk.*

FAST FIX
Smoked Turkey & Slaw Wraps

Crunchy, colorful coleslaw adds a tangy twist to these wholesome, quick and easy wraps. They're equally great for lunch or dinner.

—**DEB WILLIAMS** PEORIA, AZ

START TO FINISH: 15 MIN.
MAKES: 4 SERVINGS

- 1 cup shredded green cabbage
- ½ cup shredded red cabbage
- 1 small carrot, grated
- 1 green onion, thinly sliced
- 3 tablespoons reduced-fat mayonnaise
- 1 tablespoon lemon juice
- 2 teaspoons Dijon mustard
- ¼ teaspoon sugar
- 4 whole wheat tortillas (8 inches), room temperature
- ½ pound sliced deli smoked turkey
- 1 small tomato, sliced

1. In a small bowl, combine the first four ingredients. Combine the mayonnaise, lemon juice, mustard and sugar; pour over the cabbage mixture and toss to coat.

2. Spoon cabbage mixture down the center of each tortilla. Top with turkey and tomato; roll up.

PER SERVING *260 cal., 8 g fat (1 g sat. fat), 24 mg chol., 761 mg sodium, 28 g carb., 3 g fiber, 17 g pro.* ***Diabetic Exchanges:*** *2 lean meat, 1½ starch, 1 vegetable, 1 fat.*

PRETTY AUTUMN SOUP

SPICED-UP HEALTHY SOUP

Spiced-Up Healthy Soup

My spiced-up soup has been a hit since the first time I tried it. It's low in fat and filled with good-for-you ingredients.

—DIANE TAYMAN

DIXON/GRAND DETOUR, IL

PREP: 15 MIN. • **COOK:** 40 MIN.
MAKES: 14 SERVINGS (3½ QUARTS)

- 1 **medium onion, chopped**
- ⅓ **cup medium pearl barley**
- 2 **tablespoons canola oil**
- 4 **garlic cloves, minced**
- 5 **cans (14½ ounces each) reduced-sodium chicken broth**
- 2 **boneless skinless chicken breast halves (4 ounces each)**
- 1 **cup dried lentils, rinsed**
- 1 **jar (16 ounces) picante sauce**
- 1 **can (15 ounces) garbanzo beans or chickpeas, rinsed and drained**
- ½ **cup minced fresh cilantro**
- 8 **cups chopped fresh spinach**

1. In a Dutch oven, saute onion and barley in oil until onion is tender. Add garlic; cook 1 minute longer. Add the broth, chicken and lentils; bring to a boil. Reduce heat; cover and simmer for 15 minutes or until chicken is no longer pink. Remove chicken and set aside.

2. Add the picante sauce, garbanzo beans and cilantro to soup; cover and simmer 10 minutes longer or until barley and lentils are tender.

3. Shred chicken with two forks. Add spinach and chicken to soup. Simmer, uncovered, for 5 minutes or until spinach is wilted.

PER SERVING *156 cal., 3 g fat (trace sat. fat), 9 mg chol., 601 mg sodium, 21 g carb., 7 g fiber, 11 g pro.*
Diabetic Exchanges: *1 starch, 1 lean meat, 1 vegetable, ½ fat.*

OPEN-FACED
TUNA MELTS

FSC
Herbed Turkey Stock

Sometimes spending a little extra time in the kitchen comes with big and flavorful rewards. After trying this delicious homemade stock, you may never want to buy canned broth or stock again!

—TASTE OF HOME TEST KITCHEN

PREP: 1¼ HOURS • **COOK:** 2 HOURS
MAKES: 14 SERVINGS (3½ QUARTS)

- 1 leftover turkey carcass (from a 12- to 14-pound turkey)
- 2 medium onions, cut into wedges
- 2 celery ribs, cut into 1-inch pieces
- 2 medium carrots, cut into 1-inch pieces
- 6 garlic cloves, peeled
- 4 quarts plus 1 cup water, divided
- ½ cup packed fresh parsley sprigs
- ⅓ cup fresh sage leaves
- ¼ cup fresh thyme sprigs
- 4 bay leaves
- 1 tablespoon whole peppercorns

1. Place the turkey carcass, onions, celery, carrots and garlic in a shallow roasting pan coated with cooking spray. Bake, uncovered, at 400° for 1 hour, turning once.

2. Transfer the turkey carcass and vegetables to a stockpot; add 4 quarts water. Pour remaining the water into roasting pan, stirring to loosen browned bits; add to the stockpot. Place the parsley, sage, thyme, bay leaves and peppercorns on a double thickness of cheesecloth; bring up corners of cloth and tie with string to form a bag; add to stockpot. Slowly bring to a boil over low heat; cover and simmer for 1½ hours.

3. Discard the carcass and herb bag. Strain broth through a cheesecloth-lined colander. If using immediately, skim fat. Or cool, then refrigerate for 8 hours or overnight; remove fat from surface before using. The broth may be refrigerated for up to 3 days or frozen for 4-6 months.

PER SERVING *33 cal., 1 g fat (trace sat. fat), 1 mg chol., 89 mg sodium, 6 g carb., 1 g fiber, 2 g pro.*

FAST FIX
Open-Faced Tuna Melts

I've enjoyed these melts for 20 years and usually serve them for Sunday lunch. It's a simple yet comforting recipe that never gets old.

—ALICE STRAPP-MEISTER
NEW ROSS, NS

START TO FINISH: 25 MIN.
MAKES: 2 SERVINGS

- ¼ cup fat-free mayonnaise
- 2 tablespoons chopped green pepper
- 1½ teaspoons chopped onion
- 1½ teaspoons chopped celery
- 1½ teaspoons prepared mustard
- ¼ teaspoon Worcestershire sauce
- 1 can (6 ounces) tuna, drained and flaked
- 2 hamburger buns, split and toasted
- 4 slices tomato
- 2 tablespoons shredded reduced-fat cheddar cheese

1. In a small bowl, combine the first six ingredients; stir in tuna. Spread over each bun half; top with a tomato slice. Sprinkle with the cheese.

2. Place sandwiches on a baking sheet. Broil 3-4 in. from the heat for 3-5 minutes or until lightly browned and cheese is melted.

PER SERVING *276 cal., 5 g fat (2 g sat. fat), 34 mg chol., 833 mg sodium, 28 g carb., 2 g fiber, 28 g pro.*

Roast Pork Sandwiches with Peach Chutney

This combination of roast pork with peach chutney used to be a favorite Sunday dinner. Since most of my family's on their own now, I cut the recipe down to four unforgettable sandwiches.

—LILY JULOW GAINESVILLE, FL

PREP: 15 MIN. • **BAKE:** 30 MIN.
MAKES: 4 SERVINGS

- 1 pork tenderloin (1 pound)
- 2 tablespoons spicy brown mustard

PEACH CHUTNEY
- ¼ cup peach preserves
- 3 tablespoons finely chopped onion
- 2 tablespoons red wine vinegar
- 1 small garlic clove, minced
- ¼ teaspoon mustard seed
- ⅛ teaspoon salt
- ⅛ teaspoon ground ginger
- ⅛ teaspoon ground cinnamon
   Dash cayenne pepper
   Dash ground cloves
- ¼ cup fat-free mayonnaise
- 4 onion rolls, split and toasted
- 4 lettuce leaves

1. Brush pork with mustard; place on a rack in a shallow roasting pan. Bake at 425° for 30-40 minutes or until a thermometer reads 145°. Let stand for 5 minutes before slicing.
2. Meanwhile, for chutney, in a small saucepan, combine the preserves, onion, vinegar, garlic and seasonings. Bring to a boil. Reduce heat; simmer, uncovered, for 7-8 minutes or until thickened. Set aside to cool. Spread mayonnaise over roll bottoms. Layer with lettuce, pork slices and chutney. Replace tops.

PER SERVING *357 cal., 7 g fat (2 g sat. fat), 65 mg chol., 589 mg sodium, 42 g carb., 2 g fiber, 29 g pro.* **Diabetic Exchanges:** *3 lean meat, 2½ starch.*

Sausage Bean Soup

Cozy up to this rich and rustic soup to take the chill off any evening. Multigrain pasta increases fiber, but whole wheat pasta works well, too.

—TASTE OF HOME TEST KITCHEN

PREP: 20 MIN. • **COOK:** 20 MIN.
MAKES: 6 SERVINGS

- ½ pound Italian turkey sausage links, casings removed
- 1 medium green pepper, chopped
- 1 medium onion, chopped
- 2 garlic cloves, minced
- 2 cans (14½ ounces each) reduced-sodium chicken broth
- 1 can (15 ounces) pinto beans, rinsed and drained
- 1 can (14½ ounces) no-salt-added diced tomatoes
- 4 ounces uncooked multigrain spaghetti, broken into 2-inch pieces
- 1 teaspoon Italian seasoning
- ¼ teaspoon pepper

In a Dutch oven, saute the sausage, green pepper and onion until meat is no longer pink; drain. Add garlic; cook 1 minute longer. Stir in the remaining ingredients. Bring to a boil. Reduce the heat; cover and simmer for 10-15 minutes or until spaghetti is tender.

PER SERVING *225 cal., 4 g fat (1 g sat. fat), 23 mg chol., 752 mg sodium, 32 g carb., 6 g fiber, 16 g pro.* **Diabetic Exchanges:** *2 starch, 2 lean meat, 1 vegetable.*

ROAST PORK SANDWICHES
WITH PEACH CHUTNEY

TURKEY MEATBALL GYROS

FAST FIX
Turkey Meatball Gyros

My whole family loves these, and I appreciate how quick and easy they are. The meatballs can be made the night before or prepped in a big batch to freeze and use as needed.

—**JENNIFER CODUTO** KENT, OH

START TO FINISH: 30 MIN.
MAKES: 4 SERVINGS

- ½ **cup seasoned bread crumbs**
- 1 **egg**
- 1 **teaspoon garlic powder**
- ½ **teaspoon salt**
- ¼ **teaspoon pepper**
- 1 **pound lean ground turkey**

- ¾ **cup (6 ounces) reduced-fat plain yogurt**
- ½ **cup finely chopped peeled cucumber**
- 2 **tablespoons finely chopped onion**
- 1½ **teaspoons lemon juice**
- 8 **whole wheat pita pocket halves**
- 2 **cups shredded lettuce**
- 1 **cup chopped tomatoes**

1. In a large bowl, combine the bread crumbs, egg and seasonings. Crumble turkey over mixture and mix well. Shape into 16 balls.
2. Place meatballs on a rack coated with cooking spray in a shallow baking pan. Bake, uncovered, at 400° for 15-20 minutes or until no longer pink.
3. Meanwhile, in a small bowl, combine the yogurt, cucumber, onion and lemon juice. Line pitas with lettuce and tomatoes; add the meatballs and drizzle with the yogurt sauce.

PER SERVING *439 cal., 14 g fat (4 g sat. fat), 145 mg chol., 975 mg sodium, 48 g carb., 6 g fiber, 32 g pro.*

Vegetable Pork Soup

Tender pork, potatoes and carrots fill this aromatic stew that's lightly flavored with honey, thyme and a hint of beer.

—**DEB HALL** HUNTINGTON, IN

PREP: 20 MIN. • **COOK:** 7 HOURS
MAKES: 6 SERVINGS (2 QUARTS)

- 1 pork tenderloin (1 pound), cut into 1-inch pieces
- 1 teaspoon garlic powder
- 2 teaspoons canola oil
- 1 can (28 ounces) diced tomatoes
- 4 medium carrots, cut into ½-inch pieces
- 2 medium potatoes, cubed
- 1 can (12 ounces) light or nonalcoholic beer
- ¼ cup quick-cooking tapioca
- 2 bay leaves
- 1 tablespoon Worcestershire sauce
- 1 tablespoon honey
- 1 teaspoon dried thyme
- ¼ teaspoon salt
- ¼ teaspoon pepper
- ⅛ teaspoon ground nutmeg

1. Sprinkle the pork with garlic powder. In a large skillet, brown pork in oil; drain.
2. Transfer to a 4-qt. slow cooker. Add the remaining ingredients. Cover and cook on low for 7-8 hours or until meat is tender. Discard bay leaves.
PER SERVING *258 cal., 4 g fat (1 g sat. fat), 42 mg chol., 357 mg sodium, 34 g carb., 5 g fiber, 18 g pro.* **Diabetic Exchanges: 2 lean meat, 2 vegetable, 1½ starch.**

VEGETABLE PORK SOUP

Cranberry Chicken Focaccia

This recipe takes chicken to new heights. Combining some of our favorite ingredients, goat cheese, cranberries and pecans, it's a real hit with everyone I serve it to.

—**CHARLENE CHAMBERS**
ORMOND BEACH, FL

PREP: 25 MIN.
BAKE: 40 MIN. + COOLING
MAKES: 6 SERVINGS

- 1¾ pounds bone-in chicken breast halves
- 6 fresh thyme sprigs
- ½ teaspoon salt
- ¼ teaspoon pepper
- 1 cup fresh or frozen cranberries, thawed
- ½ cup orange segments
- 2 tablespoons sugar
- 1 loaf (12 ounces) focaccia bread

CRANBERRY CHICKEN FOCACCIA

- ⅓ cup crumbled goat cheese
- 3 large lettuce leaves
- ¼ cup chopped pecans, toasted

1. With fingers, carefully loosen skin from the chicken breast to form a pocket. Place thyme sprigs under the skin and sprinkle with salt and pepper. Place in an 11-in. x 7-in. baking dish coated with cooking spray. Bake, uncovered, at 350° for 40-45 minutes or until a thermometer reads 170°.
2. Set chicken aside until cool enough to handle. Remove meat from bones; discard bones and slice chicken. Place the cranberries, orange segments and sugar in a small food processor; cover and process until blended.
3. Cut focaccia in half horizontally. Layer with the cheese, lettuce, cranberry mixture, chicken and pecans; replace top. Cut focaccia into six wedges.
PER SERVING *363 cal., 11 g fat (4 g sat. fat), 63 mg chol., 628 mg sodium, 40 g carb., 3 g fiber, 27 g pro.*

Breaded Eggplant Sandwiches

Eggplant Parmesan is one of my family's favorite comfort foods. We love this spin on it, and often serve the sandwiches open-faced with a salad.

—HOLLY GOMEZ SEABROOK, NH

PREP: 30 MIN. • **BAKE:** 25 MIN.
MAKES: 6 SERVINGS

- ¼ cup minced fresh basil
- 2 teaspoons olive oil
- ¼ teaspoon dried oregano
- ¼ teaspoon pepper
- ⅛ teaspoon salt
- 2 egg whites, lightly beaten
- 1 cup seasoned bread crumbs
- 1 medium eggplant
- 2 large tomatoes
- 1½ cups (6 ounces) shredded part-skim mozzarella cheese
- 2 tablespoons grated Parmesan cheese
- 1 garlic clove, peeled
- 12 slices Italian bread (½ inch thick), toasted

1. Combine the basil, oil, oregano, pepper and salt; set aside. Place egg whites and bread crumbs in separate shallow bowls. Cut eggplant lengthwise into six slices. Dip slices in egg whites, then coat in crumbs.
2. Place on a baking sheet coated with cooking spray. Bake at 375° for 20-25 minutes or until tender and golden brown, turning once.
3. Cut each tomato into six slices; place two slices on each eggplant slice. Spoon reserved basil mixture over tomatoes and sprinkle with cheeses. Bake for 3-5 minutes or until cheese is melted.
4. Meanwhile, rub garlic over one side of each slice of bread; discard garlic. Place each eggplant stack on a slice of bread, garlic side up. Top with the remaining bread, garlic side down.
PER SERVING *288 cal., 9 g fat (4 g sat. fat), 18 mg chol., 628 mg sodium, 38 g carb., 5 g fiber, 15 g pro.* **Diabetic Exchanges:** *2 starch, 1 lean meat, 1 vegetable, 1 fat.*

FAST FIX
Apple-Beef Panini

Horseradish sauce and apple slices make for an interesting and surprisingly addictive beef sandwich. I don't have a panini press, so I use my countertop grill instead.

—DONNA MARIE RYAN TOPSFIELD, MA

START TO FINISH: 10 MIN.
MAKES: 2 SERVINGS

- 4 slices multigrain bread
- 2 slices reduced-fat cheddar cheese
- 2 teaspoons horseradish sauce
- ½ medium apple, thinly sliced
- 4 ounces sliced deli roast beef
  Cooking spray

1. Layer two bread slices with cheese, horseradish sauce, apple and beef. Top with remaining bread. Spritz outsides of the sandwiches with cooking spray.
2. Cook on a panini maker or indoor grill for 3-4 minutes or until the bread is browned and cheese is melted.
PER SERVING *317 cal., 12 g fat (3 g sat. fat), 49 mg chol., 742 mg sodium, 31 g carb., 4 g fiber, 23 g pro.* **Diabetic Exchanges:** *3 lean meat, 2 starch, ½ fat.*

APPLE-BEEF PANINI

My Favorite Burger

After having a burger similar to this one at a diner years ago, I tried to lighten it up without losing the great flavors. Now I can enjoy one more often without feeling guilty!

—**KRIS SWIHART** PERRYSBURG, OH

PREP: 25 MIN. **GRILL:** 15 MIN.
MAKES: 4 SERVINGS

- ¼ **cup grated onion**
- ½ **teaspoon garlic powder**
- ¼ **teaspoon salt**
- ¼ **teaspoon pepper**
- 1 **pound lean ground beef (90% lean)**
- 1 **cup sliced fresh mushrooms**
- ½ **cup sliced sweet onion**
- 4 **kaiser rolls, split**
- 4 **ounces fat-free cream cheese**
- 2 **bacon strips, cooked and crumbled**

1. In a large bowl, combine onion, garlic powder, salt and pepper. Crumble beef over mixture and mix well. Shape into four patties.

2. Using long-handled tongs, moisten a paper towel with cooking oil; lightly coat the grill rack. Grill, covered, over medium heat or broil 4 in. from heat for 4-6 minutes on each side or until a thermometer reads 160° and juices run clear.

3. Meanwhile, in a small skillet coated with cooking spray, cook and stir mushrooms and onion over medium heat until onion is golden brown. Grill rolls for 1-2 minutes or until lightly toasted.

4. Spread rolls with cream cheese; top with burgers and mushroom mixture. Sprinkle with bacon.

PER SERVING *410 cal., 13 g fat (5 g sat. fat), 75 mg chol., 737 mg sodium, 37 g carb., 2 g fiber, 33 g pro.*

MY FAVORITE BURGER

Cranberry BBQ Turkey Sandwiches

Perfect for a post-Thanksgiving pitch-in or neighborhood potluck, these sweet and tangy sandwiches are a great way to use up leftover turkey and feed a crowd.

—**SUSAN MATTHEWS** ROCKFORD, IL

PREP: 10 MIN. • **COOK:** 30 MIN.
MAKES: 12 SERVINGS

- 1 can (14 ounces) jellied cranberry sauce
- 1 cup reduced-sodium beef broth
- ¼ cup sugar
- ¼ cup ketchup
- 2 tablespoons cider vinegar
- 1 tablespoon Worcestershire sauce
- 1 teaspoon yellow mustard
- ¼ teaspoon garlic powder
- ⅛ teaspoon seasoned salt
- ⅛ teaspoon paprika
- 6 cups shredded cooked turkey breast
- 12 sandwich buns, split

1. In a large saucepan, combine the first 10 ingredients. Bring to a boil. Reduce the heat; simmer, uncovered, for 20 minutes or until sauce is thickened.

2. Stir in the turkey; simmer 4-5 minutes or until heated through. Spoon ½ cup onto each bun.

PER SERVING *296 cal., 3 g fat (1 g sat. fat), 61 mg chol., 388 mg sodium, 41 g carb., 1 g fiber, 25 g pro.* **Diabetic Exchanges:** *3 lean meat, 2½ starch.*

PESTO EGG SALAD SANDWICHES

FAST FIX

Pesto Egg Salad Sandwiches

For a casual springtime meal with a twist, boil up some eggs and dinner will be done pronto. I call this an Italian picnic delight!

—**TENLEY HARALDSON**
FORT ATKINSON, WI

START TO FINISH: 10 MIN.
MAKES: 4 SERVINGS

- ½ cup fat-free mayonnaise
- ¼ cup finely chopped red onion
- 4 teaspoons prepared pesto
- ¼ teaspoon salt
- ⅛ teaspoon pepper
- 4 hard-cooked eggs, chopped
- 3 hard-cooked egg whites, chopped
- 8 slices whole wheat bread, toasted
- 8 spinach leaves

In a small bowl, combine the first five ingredients. Gently stir in eggs and egg whites. Spread over four toast slices; top with spinach and remaining toast.

PER SERVING *285 cal., 11 g fat (3 g sat. fat), 217 mg chol., 811 mg sodium, 30 g carb., 5 g fiber, 18 g pro.* **Diabetic Exchanges:** *2 medium-fat meat, 1½ starch.*

HEARTY TURKEY CHILI

Hearty Turkey Chili

My mother-in-law introduced our family to this chili a few years ago, and we can't seem to get enough of it! It makes a lot, so why not freeze extra portions for warming lunches or dinners on hectic nights ahead?

—JUDY NIEMEYER BRENHAM, TX

PREP: 15 MIN. • **COOK:** 25 MIN.
MAKES: 8 SERVINGS (2½ QUARTS)

- 2 **pounds lean ground turkey**
- 1 **large onion, chopped**
- 2 **celery ribs, chopped**
- 4 **garlic cloves, minced**
- 2 **cans (16 ounces each) kidney beans, rinsed and drained**
- 6 **cans (5½ ounces each) reduced-sodium V8 juice**
- 1 **cup reduced-sodium beef broth**
- 1 **can (6 ounces) tomato paste**
- 3 **teaspoons ground cumin**
- 1 **teaspoon salt**
- ½ **teaspoon crushed red pepper flakes**
- 2 **bay leaves**

1. In a Dutch oven, cook the turkey, onion and celery over medium heat or until the meat is no longer pink. Add garlic; cook 1 minute longer. Drain. Stir in the remaining ingredients. Bring to a boil.

2. Reduce heat; simmer, uncovered, for 15 minutes to allow flavors to blend. Discard bay leaves.

PER SERVING *329 cal., 10 g fat (3 g sat. fat), 90 mg chol., 738 mg sodium, 31 g carb., 8 g fiber, 29 g pro.* ***Diabetic Exchanges:*** *4 lean meat, 2 vegetable, 1 starch.*

Chipotle BBQ Pork Sandwiches

I first made these for a summer barbecue with guests who love traditional BBQ pork sandwiches but wanted something lighter. They loved my creation and didn't miss the extra calories one bit. Crunchy coleslaw tames the heat!

—**PRISCILLA YEE** CONCORD, CA

PREP: 20 MIN. • **GRILL:** 20 MIN.
MAKES: 4 SERVINGS

- ½ **cup barbecue sauce**
- 1 **tablespoon honey**
- 2 **chipotle peppers in adobo sauce, chopped**
- 1 **pork tenderloin (1 pound)**
- 1½ **cups coleslaw mix**
- 2 **tablespoons reduced-fat sour cream**
- 2 **tablespoons Miracle Whip Light**
- 1 **tablespoon Dijon mustard**
- 4 **hamburger buns, split**

1. In a bowl, combine the barbecue sauce, honey and peppers. Set aside ¼ cup sauce.
2. Moisten a paper towel with cooking oil; using long-handled tongs, lightly coat the grill rack. Prepare grill for indirect heat, using a drip pan.
3. Place pork over drip pan and grill, covered, over indirect medium-hot heat for 20-25 minutes or until a thermometer reads 145°, basting occasionally with the remaining barbecue sauce. Let stand for 5 minutes before slicing.
4. Meanwhile, combine the coleslaw mix, sour cream, Miracle Whip Light and mustard. Brush cut sides of the buns with reserved barbecue sauce. Cut pork into ¼-in. slices; place on bun bottoms. Top with coleslaw and bun tops.
PER SERVING *337 cal., 9 g fat (2 g sat. fat), 68 mg chol., 753 mg sodium, 35 g carb., 2 g fiber, 28 g pro.* **Diabetic Exchanges:** *3 lean meat, 2 starch, 1 fat.*

FAST FIX
Apricot Turkey Sandwiches

Apricot jam and Dijon mustard come together for a wonderful spread on this sandwich stacked with Swiss cheese, turkey bacon and peppered turkey slices.

—**CHARLOTTE GEHLE**
BROWNSTOWN, MI

START TO FINISH: 15 MIN.
MAKES: 2 SERVINGS

- 2 **turkey bacon strips**
- 4 **pieces multigrain bread, toasted**
- 2 **tablespoons apricot jam**
- 3 **ounces thinly sliced deli peppered turkey**
- 2 **slices tomato**
- 2 **slices red onion**
- 2 **pieces leaf lettuce**
- 2 **slices reduced-fat Swiss cheese**
- 4 **teaspoons Dijon mustard**

1. In a small skillet, cook bacon over medium heat until crisp. Remove to paper towels to drain.
2. Spread two toast slices with jam. Layer with turkey, bacon, tomato, onion, lettuce and cheese. Spread remaining toast with mustard; place on top.
PER SERVING *338 cal., 10 g fat (3 g sat. fat), 40 mg chol., 1,109 mg sodium, 43 g carb., 4 g fiber, 23 g pro.*

APRICOT TURKEY SANDWICHES

F Stacy's Black Bean Soup

We love this low-fat black bean soup, and it's packed with good-for-you vegetables and beans. To make it completely vegetarian, substitute vegetable broth for the chicken broth.

—STACY MARTI JENKS, OK

PREP: 35 MIN. + SOAKING
COOK: 1½ HOURS
MAKES: 8 SERVINGS (2 QUARTS)

- 1½ cups dried black beans
- 3 celery ribs, chopped
- 3 medium carrots, chopped
- 1 large onion, chopped
- 2 teaspoons olive oil
- 2 garlic cloves, minced
- 6½ cups reduced-sodium chicken broth
- 1 teaspoon dried oregano
- ½ teaspoon dried thyme
- ½ teaspoon salt
- ¼ teaspoon cayenne pepper
- 1 bay leaf
- 3 tablespoons lime juice
- ½ cup reduced-fat sour cream
- ¼ cup minced fresh cilantro

1. Place beans in a large saucepan; add water to cover by 2 in. Bring to a boil; boil for 2 minutes. Remove from the heat; cover and let stand for 1 to 4 hours or until beans are softened. Drain and rinse beans, discarding liquid.
2. In a Dutch oven coated with cooking spray, saute the celery, carrots and onion in oil until vegetables are tender. Add garlic; cook 1 minute longer. Add the beans, broth, oregano, thyme, salt, cayenne and bay leaf. Bring to a boil. Reduce heat; cover and simmer for 1 to 1¼ hours or until beans are tender. Discard bay leaf. Cool slightly.
3. In a blender, cover and process soup in batches until smooth. Return to pan; heat though. Stir in lime juice. Garnish each serving with sour cream and cilantro.
PER SERVING *210 cal., 3 g fat (1 g sat. fat), 5 mg chol., 686 mg sodium, 34 g carb., 8 g fiber, 13 g pro.* **Diabetic Exchanges:** *2 starch, 1 lean meat, 1 vegetable.*

STACY'S BLACK BEAN SOUP

FAST FIX

Italian BLTs

Toasting BLTs in a coating of crispy bread crumbs takes these sandwiches from satisfying to spectacular. What a brilliant method.

—JOYCE MOUL YORK HAVEN, PA

START TO FINISH: 20 MIN.
MAKES: 2 SERVINGS

ITALIAN BLTS

- 2 turkey bacon strips, diced
- 4 slices Italian bread (½ inch thick)
- 2 slices reduced-fat provolone cheese
- 2 lettuce leaves
- 1 small tomato, sliced
- 4 teaspoons fat-free Italian salad dressing
- ⅓ cup panko (Japanese) bread crumbs
- Butter-flavored cooking spray
- ½ teaspoon olive oil

1. In a small skillet, cook bacon over medium heat until crisp. Layer two bread slices with cheese, bacon, lettuce and tomato; top with remaining bread.
2. Brush outsides of sandwiches with salad dressing. Place the bread crumbs in a shallow bowl. Coat the sandwiches with bread crumbs; spray with the butter-flavored cooking spray.
3. In a large skillet over medium heat, toast sandwiches in oil for 2-3 minutes on each side or until bread is lightly browned.
PER SERVING *272 cal., 11 g fat (4 g sat. fat), 25 mg chol., 761 mg sodium, 30 g carb., 2 g fiber, 13 g pro.* **Diabetic Exchanges:** *2 starch, 2 lean meat.*

Butternut Soup with Parmesan Croutons

Roasting creates a rich, caramelized flavor, but you can cook the squash cubes directly in the broth if you're short on time. They should pierce easily with a fork when they're done.

—**JEN LEHNER** SEATTLE, WA

PREP: 50 MIN. • **COOK:** 25 MIN.
MAKES: 8 SERVINGS (2 QUARTS)

- 1 **medium butternut squash (about 3 pounds), peeled, seeded and cut into 1-inch cubes**
- 2 **tablespoons olive oil, divided**
- ¼ **teaspoon pepper**
- 1 **large onion, chopped**
- 3 **celery ribs, chopped**
- 2 **tablespoons minced fresh sage or 2 teaspoons rubbed sage**
- 3 **cans (14½ ounces each) reduced-sodium chicken broth**

CROUTONS
- 2 **tablespoons grated Parmesan cheese**
- 2 **tablespoons olive oil**
- 1 **tablespoon minced fresh sage or 1 teaspoon rubbed sage**
- 2 **garlic cloves, minced**
- 2 **cups cubed French bread (½-inch cubes)**
  Cooking spray
  Additional grated Parmesan cheese, optional

1. Place the squash in a 15-in. x 10-in. x 1-in. baking pan lightly coated with cooking spray. Drizzle with 1 tablespoon oil; sprinkle with the pepper. Toss to coat. Bake, uncovered, at 425° for 30-35 minutes or until tender, stirring every 15 minutes. Set aside.

2. In a Dutch oven, saute onion, celery and sage in remaining oil until tender. Stir in the broth and squash. Bring to a boil. Reduce heat; cover and simmer for 15-20 minutes to allow flavors to blend. Cool slightly.

3. In a blender, puree soup in batches until smooth. Return to the pan; heat through.

4. For croutons, in a small bowl, combine the cheese, oil, sage and garlic. Add bread cubes and spritz with cooking spray; toss to coat. Place on a baking sheet coated with cooking spray.

5. Bake at 425° for 5-8 minutes or until golden brown, stirring occasionally. Sprinkle each serving of soup with the croutons and additional cheese if desired.

PER SERVING *179 cal., 8 g fat (1 g sat. fat), 1 mg chol., 541 mg sodium, 25 g carb., 6 g fiber, 5 g pro.* ***Diabetic Exchanges:*** *1½ starch, 1 fat.*

BUTTERNUT SOUP
WITH PARMESAN CROUTONS

Portobello Crab Open-Faced Sandwiches

I used yogurt instead of mayo to lighten up an extraordinary crab and portobello sandwich. This is the food to try when you're in the mood for something new.

—ROSALIND POPE GREENSBORO, NC

PREP: 45 MIN. + STANDING
BAKE: 15 MIN.
MAKES: 4 SERVINGS

- 1 large sweet red pepper
- ½ cup fat-free plain yogurt
- 1 teaspoon sherry or reduced-sodium chicken broth
- 1 garlic clove, crushed
- ½ teaspoon hot pepper sauce
- ¼ teaspoon salt

STUFFED MUSHROOMS

- 1 small onion, finely chopped
- 1 small sweet red pepper, finely chopped
- 1 teaspoon canola oil
- 1 egg, lightly beaten
- 3 tablespoons fat-free plain yogurt
- ½ teaspoon Worcestershire sauce
- 1 cup crushed saltines (about 30 crackers)
- 1 tablespoon minced fresh parsley
- 2 teaspoons Dijon mustard
- ½ teaspoon seafood seasoning
- ½ teaspoon paprika
  Dash pepper
- 1 can (6 ounces) lump crabmeat, drained
- 4 large portobello mushrooms (4 to 4½ inches), stems removed

FOR SERVING

- 2 hamburger buns, split and toasted
- 1 cup watercress

1. Broil the large red pepper 4 in. from the heat until skin blisters, about 5 minutes. With tongs, rotate pepper a quarter turn. Broil and rotate until all sides are blistered and blackened. Immediately place pepper in a small bowl; cover and let stand for 15-20 minutes.

2. Peel off and discard charred skin. Remove stems and seeds. Place in a food processor; add the yogurt, sherry, garlic, pepper sauce, and salt. Cover and process until blended. Set aside.

3. For stuffing, in a small nonstick skillet, saute onion and chopped red pepper in oil until tender. In a small bowl, combine egg, yogurt, Worcestershire sauce, saltines, parsley, mustard and seasonings. Stir in onion mixture; fold in crab. Spoon into mushroom caps. Place in a 15-in. x 10-in. x 1-in. baking pan coated with cooking spray.

4. Bake at 400° for 15-20 minutes or until stuffing is golden brown and mushrooms are tender. Serve on bun halves with watercress and reserved red pepper sauce.

PER SERVING *268 cal., 6 g fat (1 g sat. fat), 92 mg chol., 794 mg sodium, 36 g carb., 4 g fiber, 19 g pro.* **Diabetic Exchanges:** *2 lean meat, 2 vegetable, 1½ starch, ½ fat.*

PORTOBELLO CRAB
OPEN-FACED SANDWICHES

Hearty Breaded Fish Sandwiches

Fishing for a burger alternative? Consider it caught. A hint of cayenne is cooled by a creamy yogurt and mayo sauce that will put your local drive-thru to shame.

—TASTE OF HOME TEST KITCHEN

START TO FINISH: 30 MIN.
MAKES: 4 SERVINGS

- ½ cup dry bread crumbs
- ½ teaspoon garlic powder
- ½ teaspoon cayenne pepper
- ½ teaspoon dried parsley flakes
- 4 cod fillets (6 ounces each)
- 4 whole wheat hamburger buns, split
- ¼ cup plain yogurt
- ¼ cup fat-free mayonnaise
- 2 teaspoons lemon juice
- 2 teaspoons sweet pickle relish
- ¼ teaspoon dried minced onion
- 4 lettuce leaves
- 4 slices tomato
- 4 slices sweet onion

1. In a shallow bowl, combine the bread crumbs, garlic powder, cayenne and parsley. Coat fillets with bread crumb mixture.

2. Moisten a paper towel with cooking oil; using long-handled tongs, lightly coat the grill rack. Grill cod, covered, over medium heat or broil 4 in. from the heat for 4-5 minutes on each side or until fish flakes easily with a fork. Grill buns over medium heat for 30-60 seconds or until toasted.

3. Meanwhile, in a small bowl, combine the yogurt, mayonnaise, lemon juice, relish and minced onion; spread over bun bottoms. Top with cod, lettuce, tomato and onion; replace bun tops.

SALSA FISH SANDWICHES *Follow method as directed but replace plain yogurt with salsa and omit lemon juice, relish and dried minced onion. Top sandwiches with sliced tomato and fresh cilantro.*
PER SERVING *292 cal., 4 g fat (1 g sat. fat), 68 mg chol., 483 mg sodium, 32 g carb., 4 g fiber, 32 g pro. Diabetic Exchanges: 5 lean meat, 2 starch.*

Spicy Chicken Chili

My recipe was inspired when I was on a low-calorie, low-fat, high fiber diet. I entered it in a chili cook-off and had several people say that it was the best chili they'd ever had!

—NATALIE HUGHES JOPLIN, MO

PREP: 30 MIN. • **COOK:** 30 MIN.
MAKES: 12 SERVINGS (4 QUARTS)

- 1 small onion, chopped
- 1 small green pepper, chopped
- 1 small sweet red pepper, chopped
- 2 jalapeno peppers, seeded and chopped
- 1 serrano pepper, seeded and chopped
- 1 tablespoon olive oil
- 3 garlic cloves, minced
- 1 can (28 ounces) crushed tomatoes
- 1 can (14½ ounces) stewed tomatoes, cut up
- 1 can (14½ ounces) diced tomatoes with mild green chilies
- 1 can (16 ounces) kidney beans, rinsed and drained
- 1 can (15 ounces) black beans, rinsed and drained
- 1 carton (32 ounces) reduced-sodium chicken broth
- 3 tablespoons chili powder
- 1 tablespoon ground cumin

SPICY CHICKEN CHILI

- 1 to 2 teaspoons crushed red pepper flakes
- 2 to 4 tablespoons Louisiana-style hot sauce
- 2½ cups cubed cooked chicken breast
- 2 cups frozen corn
- ¾ cup reduced-fat sour cream
- ¾ cup shredded reduced-fat cheddar cheese

1. In a Dutch oven, saute the first five ingredients in oil until tender. Add garlic, cook 1 minute longer. Add the tomatoes, beans, broth, seasonings and hot sauce. Bring to a boil. Reduce heat; simmer, uncovered, for 15 minutes.

2. Stir in chicken and corn; heat through. Garnish each serving with 1 tablespoon each of sour cream and cheese.

NOTE *Wear disposable gloves when cutting hot peppers; the oils can burn skin. Avoid touching your face.*
PER SERVING *242 cal., 6 g fat (2 g sat. fat), 32 mg chol., 694 mg sodium, 31 g carb., 7 g fiber, 19 g pro. Diabetic Exchanges: 2 lean meat, 2 vegetable, 1 starch, 1 fat.*

VEGGIE-TOPPED
POLENTA SLICES *PAGE 62*

**TASTE OF HOME TEST KITCHEN'S
ROASTED ROOT VEGETABLES**

PAGE 63

**SENJA MERRILL'S
FAVORITE MASHED SWEET
POTATOES** *PAGE 67*

**ELLEN GOVERTSEN'S
SPICED RICE**

PAGE 73

Side Dishes & Breads

Take pride in your sides—**spice up those veggies,** add pizazz to pilaf and **pass a basket of homemade bread.** All the fixings for a healthy meal are here.

F Potluck Baked Beans

I acquired this recipe from a dear friend many years ago, and it has remained a favorite for family get-togethers.

—**VIRGINIA SANDER**
NORTH HOLLYWOOD, CA

PREP: 10 MIN. • **BAKE:** 30 MIN.
MAKES: 12 SERVINGS

- 4 **bacon strips, chopped**
- 1 **medium onion, chopped**
- 1 **can (28 ounces) baked beans**
- 1 **can (16 ounces) kidney beans, rinsed and drained**
- 1 **can (15 ounces) pinto beans, rinsed and drained**
- ½ **cup packed brown sugar**
- ⅓ **cup ketchup**
- 2 **teaspoons Worcestershire sauce**

1. In a large skillet, saute bacon and onion over medium heat until bacon is crisp; drain. In a large bowl, combine the beans, brown sugar, ketchup, Worcestershire sauce and bacon mixture.
2. Pour into a shallow 2-qt. baking dish coated with cooking spray. Bake at 350° for 30-35 minutes or until heated through.
PER SERVING *192 cal., 2 g fat (1 g sat. fat), 7 mg chol., 528 mg sodium, 37 g carb., 7 g fiber, 8 g pro.*

C Cauliflower au Gratin

A lighter version of a classic white sauce coats this cauliflower dish that's perfect for a potluck buffet. Thick and creamy with a golden brown topping, it's a comforting side dish that tastes as homey as it looks.

—**TASTE OF HOME TEST KITCHEN**

PREP: 30 MIN. • **BAKE:** 30 MIN.
MAKES: 12 SERVINGS

- 3 **packages (16 ounces each) frozen cauliflower, thawed**
- 1 **large onion, chopped**
- ⅓ **cup butter, cubed**
- ⅓ **cup all-purpose flour**
- ½ **teaspoon salt**
- ¼ **teaspoon ground mustard**
- ¼ **teaspoon pepper**
- 2 **cups fat-free milk**
- ½ **cup grated Parmesan cheese**

TOPPING
- ½ **cup soft whole wheat bread crumbs**
- 2 **tablespoons butter, melted**
- ¼ **teaspoon paprika**

1. Place 1 in. of water in a Dutch oven; add cauliflower. Bring to a boil. Reduce heat; cover and cook for 4-6 minutes or until crisp-tender. Drain and pat dry.
2. Meanwhile, in a large saucepan, saute onion in butter until tender. Stir in the flour, salt, mustard and pepper until blended; gradually add milk.

Bring to a boil; cook and stir for 1-2 minutes or until thickened. Remove from the heat. Add cheese; stir until melted.
3. Place the cauliflower in a 13-in. x 9-in. baking dish coated with cooking spray. Pour the sauce over the top.
4. For topping, combine the bread crumbs, butter and paprika. Sprinkle over the sauce. Bake, uncovered, at 350° for 30-35 minutes or until bubbly.
PER SERVING *142 cal., 8 g fat (5 g sat. fat), 22 mg chol., 257 mg sodium, 13 g carb., 3 g fiber, 6 g pro.* **Diabetic Exchanges:** *1½ fat, 1 vegetable, ½ starch.*

top tip

Have Food, Will Travel

It's not easy to keep warm sides hot while traveling. Instead, consider cooking the dish the night before, cool to room temperature and store in the refrigerator overnight. Then pack the dish in a cooler for traveling and reheat at your destination.

Crab-Stuffed Potatoes

If you love crab, you definitely need to try my recipe. It takes twice-baked potatoes to a new level. It pairs perfectly with seafood or chicken.

—JOHN KENNEY MARCO ISLAND, FL

PREP: 35 MIN. • **BAKE:** 20 MIN.
MAKES: 8 SERVINGS

- 4 large potatoes (about 3 pounds)
- 1 small onion, finely chopped
- ¼ cup finely chopped celery
- 1 tablespoon butter
- 2 garlic cloves, minced
- ½ cup reduced-fat sour cream
- 2 cans (6 ounces each) lump crabmeat, drained
- ½ cup fat-free milk
- 1 tablespoon minced fresh parsley
- ½ teaspoon salt
- ¼ teaspoon pepper

1. Scrub and pierce the potatoes; place on a microwave-safe plate. Microwave, uncovered, on high for 18-22 minutes or until potatoes are tender, turning once. Let stand for 5 minutes or until cool enough to handle.

2. Meanwhile, in a small skillet, saute onion and celery in butter until tender. Add the garlic; cook 1 minute longer. Set aside. Cut each potato in half lengthwise. Scoop out pulp, leaving thin shells.

3. In a small bowl, mash the pulp with the sour cream. Stir in the crabmeat, milk, parsley, salt, pepper and reserved vegetable mixture. Spoon the mixture into potato shells. Place on a baking sheet. Bake, uncovered, at 375° for 20-25 minutes or until potatoes are heated through.

PER SERVING *231 cal., 3 g fat (2 g sat. fat), 47 mg chol., 330 mg sodium, 36 g carb., 3 g fiber, 14 g pro*

CRAB-STUFFED POTATOES

HONEY WHEAT ROLLS

Honey Wheat Rolls

The recipe for these light wheat rolls is one that I save in my exclusive book of most-liked dishes. They're not at all difficult to make and they have the most wonderful honey flavor.

—SANDY KLOCINSKI SUMMERVILLE, SC

PREP: 40 MIN. + RISING • **BAKE:** 10 MIN.
MAKES: 2 DOZEN

- 2 packages (¼ ounce each) active dry yeast
- 1¾ cups warm fat-free milk (110°-115°)
- 2 eggs
- ½ cup honey
- ¼ cup mashed potatoes (without added milk and butter)
- ¼ cup butter, melted
- 1 teaspoon salt
- 3 cups whole wheat flour
- 2¼ to 2¾ cups all-purpose flour

1. In a small bowl, dissolve yeast in warm milk. In a large bowl, combine 1 egg, honey, mashed potatoes, butter, salt, whole wheat flour, yeast mixture and 1½ cups all-purpose flour; beat on medium speed for 3 minutes. Stir in enough remaining flour to form a soft dough (dough will be sticky).

2. Turn onto a floured surface; knead until smooth and elastic, about 6-8 minutes. Place in a bowl coated with cooking spray, turning once to coat the top. Cover with plastic wrap and let rise in a warm place until doubled, about 1 hour.

3. Turn onto a floured surface; divide into 24 balls. Roll each into a 7-in. rope. Holding one end of rope, loosely wrap dough around, forming a coil. Tuck end under; pinch to seal. Place in muffin cups coated with cooking spray. Cover and let rise until doubled, about 30 minutes.

4. Beat remaining egg; brush over rolls. Bake at 400° for 9-11 minutes or until golden brown. Remove from pans to wire racks to cool.

PER SERVING *146 cal., 3 g fat (1 g sat. fat), 19 mg chol., 126 mg sodium, 27 g carb., 2 g fiber, 5 g pro.* **Diabetic Exchange:** *2 starch.*

Orange & Mint Snap Peas

A classic steaming method produces vibrant, crisp-tender vegetables. Tossed with a syrupy orange sauce and accented with fresh mint, this curious combination is worth a taste.

—TASTE OF HOME TEST KITCHEN

START TO FINISH: 25 MIN.
MAKES: 4 SERVINGS

- ½ cup orange juice
- 2 tablespoons brown sugar
- 1 tablespoon butter
- 2 teaspoons grated orange peel
- ½ teaspoon salt
- 3 cups fresh sugar snap peas, trimmed
- 2 tablespoons minced fresh mint

1. In a small saucepan, combine the first five ingredients; bring to a boil. Reduce the heat; simmer, uncovered, until the mixture is reduced by half, about 15 minutes.

2. Meanwhile, place peas in a steamer basket in a large saucepan over 1 in. of water; bring to a boil. Cover and steam for 3-5 minutes or until crisp-tender; drain. Transfer to a serving bowl. Add orange juice mixture and mint; toss to coat.

PER SERVING *117 cal., 3 g fat (2 g sat. fat), 8 mg chol., 323 mg sodium, 19 g carb., 4 g fiber, 4 g pro.* **Diabetic Exchanges:** *1 starch, 1 vegetable, ½ fat.*

Roasted Garlic and Cheese Corn on the Cob

My corn on the cob is so garlicky and cheesy that even veggie-haters love it! I make it for every cookout because it's the only way my family will eat corn.

—MARY BETH HARRIS-MURPHREE
TYLER, TX

PREP: 1 HOUR • **GRILL:** 20 MIN.
MAKES: 8 SERVINGS

- 1 whole garlic bulb
- ⅛ teaspoon olive oil
  Dash salt
  Dash plus ½ teaspoon pepper, divided
- 8 medium ears sweet corn in husks
- ½ cup fat-free mayonnaise
- 1 teaspoon paprika
- ¾ cup grated Romano cheese

1. Remove papery outer skin from garlic (do not peel or separate cloves). Cut top off of garlic bulb. Brush with oil; sprinkle with salt and dash pepper.

Wrap bulb in heavy-duty foil. Bake at 425° for 30-35 minutes or until softened. Cool for 10 minutes. Remove cloves from bulb.

2. Carefully peel back corn husks to within 1 in. of bottoms; remove silk. In a food processor, combine the garlic, mayonnaise, paprika and remaining pepper until blended; spread over corn. Sprinkle with cheese. Rewrap corn in husks and secure with kitchen string.

3. Grill corn, covered, over medium heat for 18-22 minutes or until tender, turning often.

PER SERVING *142 cal., 5 g fat (3 g sat. fat), 13 mg chol., 344 mg sodium, 21 g carb., 3 g fiber, 8 g pro.*

ROASTED GARLIC AND CHEESE CORN ON THE COB

SWEET POTATO DIPPERS

Veggie-Topped Polenta Slices

This recipe was created at a time when our pantry was looking bare; however, this amazing appetizer was still able to be made. My boyfriend calls dishes like these "cabinet vibrations."

—JENN TIDWELL FAIR OAKS, CA

PREP: 20 MIN. • **COOK:** 20 MIN.
MAKES: 4 SERVINGS

- 1 tube (1 pound) polenta, cut into 12 slices
- 2 tablespoons olive oil, divided
- 1 medium zucchini, chopped
- 2 shallots, minced
- 2 garlic cloves, minced
- 3 tablespoons reduced-sodium chicken broth
- ½ teaspoon pepper
- ⅛ teaspoon salt
- 4 plum tomatoes, seeded and chopped
- 2 tablespoons minced fresh basil or 2 teaspoons dried basil
- 1 tablespoon minced fresh parsley
- ½ cup shredded part-skim mozzarella cheese

1. In a large nonstick skillet, cook polenta in 1 tablespoon oil over medium heat for 9-11 minutes on each side or until golden brown.
2. Meanwhile, in another large skillet, saute zucchini in remaining oil until tender. Add shallots and garlic; cook 1 minute longer. Add the broth, pepper and salt. Bring to a boil; cook until liquid is almost evaporated.
3. Stir in the tomatoes, basil and parsley; heat through. Serve with polenta; sprinkle with cheese.
PER SERVING *222 cal., 9 g fat (2 g sat. fat), 8 mg chol., 558 mg sodium, 28 g carb., 2 g fiber, 7 g pro. Diabetic Exchanges: 1½ starch, 1½ fat, 1 vegetable.*

Sweet Potato Dippers

A spicy and creamy dip accompanies these tender sweet potato slices. Any leftover sauce can be served with crackers or on a baked potato the next night.

—CHERYL WILT EGLON, WV

PREP: 10 MIN. • **BAKE:** 25 MIN.
MAKES: 4 SERVINGS

- 1¼ pounds sweet potatoes (about 2 medium), peeled
- 1 tablespoon olive oil
- ¼ teaspoon salt
- ¼ teaspoon pepper
- **DIP**
- 3 ounces fat-free cream cheese
- 3 tablespoons reduced-fat sour cream
- 2 teaspoons finely chopped green onion
- 2 teaspoons finely chopped seeded jalapeno pepper

GARNISH
- Additional finely chopped green onion, optional

1. Cut potatoes into ⅛-in. slices. Place in a large bowl. Drizzle with oil. Sprinkle with salt and pepper; toss to coat.
2. Arrange in a single layer in two ungreased 15-in. x 10-in. x 1-in. baking pans. Bake at 375° for 25-30 minutes or until golden brown, turning once.
3. In a small bowl, beat the dip ingredients. Serve with the sweet potatoes. Garnish with additional onion if desired.
NOTE *Wear disposable gloves when cutting hot peppers; the oils can burn skin. Avoid touching your face.*
PER SERVING *155 cal., 5 g fat (1 g sat. fat), 5 mg chol., 280 mg sodium, 23 g carb., 3 g fiber, 5 g pro. Diabetic Exchanges: 1½ starch, 1 fat.*

Steamed Hawaiian Bread

S

Steaming bread is unusual, but the method produces a soft and flavorful loaf of bread without overheating your kitchen. You'll love the mild sweetness of banana and coconut.

—**ROXANNE CHAN** ALBANY, CA

PREP: 20 MIN. • **COOK:** 45 MIN. + STANDING
MAKES: 1 LOAF (6 WEDGES)

- ¾ cup all-purpose flour
- ½ cup ground almonds, toasted
- ¼ cup flaked coconut
- 1 teaspoon baking powder
- ¼ teaspoon baking soda
- ⅓ cup coconut milk
- ¼ cup honey
- 3 tablespoons mashed ripe banana
- ¼ teaspoon coconut extract

1. In a large bowl, combine the first five ingredients. Combine the coconut milk, honey, banana and extract; stir into dry ingredients just until moistened. Pour into a 2-cup stoneware dish or bowl coated with cooking spray; cover with foil.

2. Place on a rack in a deep stockpot; add 1 in. of hot water to pot. Bring to a gentle boil; cover and steam for 45-50 minutes or until a toothpick inserted near the center comes out clean, adding more water as needed.

3. Remove dish from pan; let stand for 15 minutes before removing bread from dish.

PER SERVING *197 cal., 8 g fat (4 g sat. fat), 0 chol., 132 mg sodium, 29 g carb., 2 g fiber, 4 g pro.*

Roasted Root Vegetables

F S C

After experimenting with several combinations of fresh, aromatic herbs and a touch of olive oil, we came up with a sensational blend to coat a batch of naturally sweet root vegetables.

—**TASTE OF HOME TEST KITCHEN**

PREP: 20 MIN. • **BAKE:** 25 MIN.
MAKES: 4 SERVINGS

- 2 cups cubed peeled rutabaga
- ¾ cup chopped peeled turnip
- 1 small onion, cut into wedges
- 1 small carrot, chopped
- ½ cup chopped peeled parsnip
- 1½ teaspoons olive oil
- ½ teaspoon minced fresh thyme or ¼ teaspoon dried thyme
- ½ teaspoon minced fresh oregano or ¼ teaspoon dried oregano
- ½ teaspoon minced fresh rosemary or ¼ teaspoon dried rosemary, crushed
- ¼ teaspoon pepper
- ⅛ teaspoon salt

1. In a large bowl, combine all the ingredients; toss to coat. Transfer to a 15-in. x 10-in. x 1-in. baking pan coated with cooking spray.

2. Bake, uncovered, at 425° for 25-30 minutes or until vegetables are tender, stirring occasionally.

PER SERVING *72 cal., 2 g fat (trace sat. fat), 0 chol., 115 mg sodium, 13 g carb., 4 g fiber, 2 g pro. **Diabetic Exchange:** 2 vegetable.*

ROASTED ROOT VEGETABLES

Simple Spanish Rice

I prefer this side dish to traditional recipes because it's vegetarian and lower in fat. While you're preparing the rest of your meal, it simmers on the stove, allowing the flavors to blend beautifully.

—EMILY HOCKETT FEDERAL WAY, WA

PREP: 5 MIN. • **COOK:** 45 MIN.
MAKES: 6 SERVINGS

- 1   cup uncooked brown rice
- 1   large onion, chopped
- 1   medium green pepper, chopped
- 2   tablespoons butter
- 1   can (14½ ounces) diced tomatoes with mild green chilies, undrained
- ¼   teaspoon salt

SIMPLE SPANISH RICE

1. Cook the brown rice according to package directions.
2. Meanwhile, in a large nonstick skillet, saute the onion and pepper in butter until tender. Stir in the tomatoes and salt. Bring to a boil. Reduce heat; simmer, uncovered, for 5-10 minutes or until slightly thickened. Stir in the cooked rice; heat through.

SPICY SPANISH RICE *Along with the tomatoes, add 1 teaspoon chili powder and ¼ teaspoon each dried oregano and garlic powder.*
PER SERVING *183 cal., 5 g fat (3 g sat. fat), 10 mg chol., 390 mg sodium, 32 g carb., 3 g fiber, 3 g pro.*

F S C FAST FIX

Green Beans Provence

Dressed with fresh basil and just enough vinegar to add a bit of tang, these green beans complement most any entree.

—TASTE OF HOME TEST KITCHEN

START TO FINISH: 20 MIN.
MAKES: 4 SERVINGS

- 1   pound fresh green beans, trimmed
- 1   cup cherry tomatoes, halved
- 2   tablespoons minced fresh basil or 2 teaspoons dried basil
- 1   tablespoon tarragon vinegar
- 2   teaspoons olive oil
- 1   garlic clove, minced
- ¼   teaspoon pepper
     Dash salt

1. Place beans in a large saucepan and cover with water. Bring to a boil. Cover and cook for 4 to 7 minutes or until crisp-tender. Drain and immediately place beans in ice water. Drain and pat dry.
2. In a large bowl, combine beans and tomatoes. Combine the basil, vinegar, oil, garlic, pepper and salt; drizzle over beans and toss to coat.

GREEN BEANS PROVENCE

PER SERVING *60 cal., 3 g fat (trace sat. fat), 0 chol., 46 mg sodium, 9 g carb., 4 g fiber, 2 g pro.* **Diabetic Exchanges:** *1 vegetable, ½ fat.*

top tip

Bean There, Done That

For a change of pace from green beans, try using wax beans instead. Wax beans are a variety of string bean with yellow pods, a mild flavor and a waxy texture. They can be used interchangeably in recipes. Keep in mind that 1 pound of either bean, cut, equals about 4 cups.

Potato Smashers

My potato smashers are meant as a side dish, but I think they make a quick and delicious lunch. The potatoes hold together like a patty, and they turn out crisp, cheesy and full of flavor. Kids would love them.

—JANET STEIGER BUCYRUS, OH

START TO FINISH: 20 MIN.
MAKES: 2 SERVINGS

- **6 small red potatoes (about ¾ pound)**
- **½ cup water**
- **2 center-cut bacon strips**
- **2 tablespoons reduced-fat Italian salad dressing**
- **¼ cup shredded sharp cheddar cheese**
  Reduced-fat sour cream, optional

1. Place the potatoes in a small microwave-safe dish; add water. Microwave, uncovered, on high for 8-9 minutes or until tender, stirring once.
2. Meanwhile, in a large nonstick skillet, cook bacon over medium heat until crisp. Remove to paper towels to drain. Crumble bacon and set aside.
3. With the bottom of a glass, flatten potatoes to 1/2-in. thickness. In the same skillet coated with cooking spray, cook potatoes in Italian dressing over medium heat for 2-3 minutes or until bottoms are golden brown.
4. Turn potatoes; sprinkle with cheese and reserved bacon. Cover and cook 2-3 minutes longer or until cheese is melted. Serve with sour cream if desired.
PER SERVING *224 cal., 8 g fat (4 g sat. fat), 23 mg chol., 314 mg sodium, 29 g carb., 3 g fiber, 9 g pro.* **Diabetic Exchanges:** *2 starch, 1 medium-fat meat, 1/2 fat.*

C
Cheese Flatbread

The convenience of frozen dough and dried herbs makes this treat about as easy as it gets. To boost fiber, you can also use frozen whole wheat bread dough.

—SHARON DELANEY-CHRONIS
SOUTH MILWAUKEE, WI

PREP: 5 MIN. + RISING • **BAKE:** 20 MIN.
MAKES: 16 SERVINGS

- **1 loaf (1 pound) frozen bread dough, thawed**
- **2 tablespoons butter, softened**
- **2 teaspoons paprika**
- **½ teaspoon garlic powder**
- **½ teaspoon dried oregano**
- **½ teaspoon dried basil**
- **1 cup (4 ounces) shredded part-skim mozzarella cheese**

1. On a lightly floured surface, roll dough into a 16-in. x 11-in. rectangle. Transfer to a 15-in. x 10-in. x 1-in. baking pan coated with cooking spray; build up edges slightly. Spread with butter. Sprinkle with paprika, garlic powder, oregano and basil. Prick the dough several times with a fork; sprinkle with cheese. Cover and let rise for 30 minutes.
2. Bake at 375° for 20-25 minutes or until crust is golden brown and cheese is melted. Serve warm.
PER SERVING *111 cal., 4 g fat (2 g sat. fat), 8 mg chol., 202 mg sodium, 14 g carb., 1 g fiber, 5 g pro.* **Diabetic Exchanges:** *1 starch, 1/2 fat.*

CHEESE FLATBREAD

BRUSSELS SPROUTS
WITH BACON

C **FAST FIX**

Brussels Sprouts with Bacon

Bacon lends a wonderful salty flavor while balsamic vinegar adds a hint of spicy tang. Try serving this to someone who has never tried Brussels sprouts so they get a good first impression of the yummy vegetable.

—**PAULA YOUNG** TIFFIN, OH

START TO FINISH: 30 MIN.
MAKES: 12 SERVINGS

- **3** **bacon strips**
- **1¼** **pounds fresh or frozen Brussels sprouts, thawed, quartered**
- **1** **large onion, chopped**
- **2** **tablespoons water**
- **¼** **teaspoon salt**
- **⅛** **teaspoon pepper**
- **2** **tablespoons balsamic vinegar**

1. In a large skillet, cook bacon over medium heat until crisp. Remove to paper towels; drain, reserving 1 tablespoon drippings. Crumble bacon and set aside.

2. In the same pan, saute Brussels sprouts and onion in reserved drippings until crisp-tender. Add the water, salt and pepper. Bring to a boil. Reduce heat; cover and simmer for 4-5 minutes or until Brussels sprouts are tender. Stir in bacon and vinegar.

PER SERVING *90 cal., 4 g fat (1 g sat. fat), 6 mg chol., 200 mg sodium, 11 g carb., 4 g fiber, 5 g pro.* **Diabetic Exchanges:** *2 vegetable, 1 fat.*

Cheesy Canadian Bacon & Potato Casserole

When I first came across this dish, I noticed it used full-fat ingredients—cottage cheese, sour cream, soup, cheddar cheese—so I gave it a makeover by using lower-fat versions. It turns out so rich and creamy, you'd never guess it was lighter.

—**CHRISTINA PRICE** WHEELING, WV

PREP: 15 MIN. • **BAKE:** 50 MIN. + STANDING
MAKES: 12 SERVINGS

- 1 can (10¾ ounces) reduced-fat condensed broccoli cheese soup, undiluted
- 1 cup (8 ounces) 1% cottage cheese
- 1 cup (8 ounces) reduced-fat sour cream
- 1 package (28 ounces) frozen O'Brien potatoes, thawed
- 1 teaspoon garlic powder
- ½ teaspoon pepper
- ½ pound Canadian bacon, chopped
- ¼ cup shredded reduced-fat cheddar cheese

1. In a food processor, combine the soup, cottage cheese and sour cream; cover and process until mixture is smooth.
2. In a large bowl, combine the potatoes, garlic powder and pepper; stir in Canadian bacon and soup mixture. Transfer to a 13-in. x 9-in. baking dish coated with cooking spray; sprinkle with cheddar cheese.
3. Bake, uncovered, at 350° for 50-55 minutes or until bubbly. Let stand for 15 minutes before serving.
PER SERVING *133 cal., 4 g fat (2 g sat. fat), 17 mg chol., 478 mg sodium, 15 g carb., 2 g fiber, 9 g pro. **Diabetic Exchanges:** 1 starch, 1 lean meat.*

Favorite Mashed Sweet Potatoes

My family begs me to make this recipe during the holidays. They like it because pumpkin pie spice enhances the flavor of the sweet potatoes. I like the fact that it can be made a day ahead and warmed before serving.

—**SENJA MERRILL** SANDY, UTAH

START TO FINISH: 20 MIN.
MAKES: 8 SERVINGS

- 6 medium sweet potatoes, peeled and cubed
- 3 tablespoons orange juice
- 2 tablespoons brown sugar
- 2 tablespoons maple syrup
- ¼ teaspoon pumpkin pie spice

Place potatoes in a Dutch oven and cover with water. Bring to a boil. Reduce heat; cover and cook for 10-15 minutes or until tender. Drain. Mash potatoes with remaining ingredients.
PER SERVING *117 cal., trace fat (trace sat. fat), 0 chol., 10 mg sodium, 28 g carb., 3 g fiber, 1 g pro. **Diabetic Exchange:** 2 starch.*

FAVORITE MASHED SWEET POTATOES

C FAST FIX

Cajun Spiced Broccoli

I usually make this minus the Creole seasoning, but a few weeks ago, I decided to try adding a different spice just to see what would happen. I loved it! It's garlicy, spicy and crunchy.

—KRISTA FRANK RHODODENDRON, OR

START TO FINISH: 15 MIN.
MAKES: 4 SERVINGS

- 1 bunch broccoli, cut into florets
- 2 tablespoons canola oil
- 2 large garlic cloves, minced
- ¾ teaspoon Creole seasoning

In a large nonstick skillet coated with cooking spray, saute broccoli in oil until crisp-tender, adding the garlic and Creole seasoning during the last 2 minutes of cooking.

NOTE *The following spices may be substituted for 1 teaspoon Creole seasoning ¼ teaspoon each salt, garlic powder and paprika; and a pinch each of dried thyme, ground cumin and cayenne pepper.*

PER SERVING *107 cal., 8 g fat (1 g sat. fat), 0 chol., 166 mg sodium, 8 g carb., 5 g fiber, 5 g pro.* **Diabetic Exchanges:** *2 vegetable, 1 fat.*

F S

Brown Rice Pilaf

Brown rice, a whole grain, contains all the nutrients and essential parts of the entire grain seed. It adds almost three times as much heart-healthy fiber to this side dish as white would.

—TASTE OF HOME TEST KITCHEN

PREP: 10 MIN. • **COOK:** 45 MIN.
MAKES: 6 SERVINGS

- 1 medium onion, chopped
- 1 medium green pepper, chopped
- 1 tablespoon olive oil
- 1¼ cups uncooked brown rice
- 2 garlic cloves, minced
- 1½ cups water
- 1 cup reduced-sodium chicken broth
- ½ teaspoon dried thyme
- ¼ teaspoon pepper

1. In a large saucepan, saute onion and green pepper in oil until tender. Add rice and garlic; cook and stir for 3-4 minutes or until rice is lightly browned.
2. Add the water, broth, thyme and pepper. Bring to a boil. Reduce heat; cover and simmer for 35-40 minutes or until rice is tender. Fluff with a fork.
PER SERVING *181 cal., 3 g fat (1 g sat. fat), 0 chol., 99 mg sodium, 34 g carb., 2 g fiber, 4 g pro.* **Diabetic Exchanges:** *2 starch, ½ fat.*

CAJUN SPICED BROCCOLI

F C FAST FIX
Dilled Carrots & Green Beans

I never ate carrots until I tasted this recipe. I just love the dill flavor. Besides being good for an everyday family dish, it's also great for entertaining!

—HARRIETT LEE GLASGOW, MT

START TO FINISH: 25 MIN.
MAKES: 4 SERVINGS

- ¾ cup water
- 1 teaspoon sugar
- ½ teaspoon salt
- ½ teaspoon dill weed
- 4 medium carrots, julienned
- ½ pound fresh green beans
- ¼ cup reduced-fat Italian salad dressing

1. In small saucepan, bring the water, sugar, salt and dill to a boil. Add carrots and beans. Cook, uncovered, for 5-8 minutes or until vegetables are crisp-tender; drain.

2. Drizzle with the Italian dressing; toss to coat.

PER SERVING *69 cal., 2 g fat (trace sat. fat), trace chol., 298 mg sodium, 11 g carb., 4 g fiber, 2 g pro.* **Diabetic Exchanges:** *2 vegetable, ½ fat.*

top tip
Quinoa Care

Quinoa is coated with a bitter-tasting chemical called saponin and needs to be rinsed thoroughly before cooking. When cooked, it has a mild flavor with a light, fluffy texture. Store uncooked quinoa in an airtight container in the refrigerator.

QUINOA WITH PEAS AND ONION

Quinoa with Peas and Onion

Even picky eaters will love this dish. I like to make this with fresh peas but frozen are good, too.

—LORI PANARELLA PHOENIXVILLE, PA

PREP: 30 MIN. • **COOK:** 10 MIN.
MAKES: 6 SERVINGS

- 2 cups water
- 1 cup quinoa, rinsed
- 1 small onion, chopped
- 1 tablespoon olive oil
- 1½ cups frozen peas
- ½ teaspoon salt
- ¼ teaspoon pepper
- 2 tablespoons chopped walnuts

1. In a large saucepan, bring water to a boil. Add the quinoa. Reduce the heat; cover and simmer for 12-15 minutes or until water is absorbed. Remove from the heat; fluff with a fork.

2. Meanwhile, in a small skillet, saute onion in oil until tender. Stir into cooked quinoa. Add the peas, salt and pepper; heat through. Sprinkle with walnuts.

NOTE *Look for quinoa in the cereal, rice or organic food aisle.*

PER SERVING *174 cal., 6 g fat (1 g sat. fat), 0 chol., 244 mg sodium, 26 g carb., 4 g fiber, 6 g pro.* **Diabetic Exchanges:** *1½ starch, 1 fat.*

Walnut Apple Bread

Whenever I make this bread, it's like being in my Grandma's kitchen. Swirled with apples, walnuts and cinnamon, it's one of the best breads I've ever tasted.

—**NANCY DAUGHERTY** CORTLAND, OH

PREP: 40 MIN. + RISING
BAKE: 30 MIN. + COOLING
MAKES: 2 LOAVES (16 SLICES EACH)

- 2 **packages (¼ ounce each) active dry yeast**
- ½ **cup warm water (110° to 115°)**
- ¾ **cup sugar**
- ½ **cup warm 2% milk (110° to 115°)**
- ¼ **cup reduced-fat butter, softened**
- 2 **eggs**
- 1 **teaspoon salt**
- 4 **to 4½ cups all-purpose flour**

FILLING

- 2 **cups chopped peeled apples**
- ½ **cup chopped walnuts**
- ⅔ **cup sugar**
- 1 **tablespoon all-purpose flour**
- 2 **teaspoons ground cinnamon**
- 2 **tablespoons reduced-fat butter, softened**

GLAZE

- 1 **cup confectioners' sugar**
- 2 **tablespoons apple cider or juice**

1. In a large bowl, dissolve yeast in warm water. Add the sugar, milk, butter, eggs, salt and 2 cups flour. Beat until smooth. Stir in enough remaining flour to form a soft dough (dough will be sticky).

2. Turn onto a lightly floured surface; knead until smooth and elastic, about 6-8 minutes. Place in a bowl coated with cooking spray, turning once to coat the top. Cover and let rise in a warm place until doubled, about 1 hour.

3. For filling, in a small bowl, combine apples and walnuts. Combine the sugar, flour and cinnamon; stir into apple mixture. Punch dough down. Roll into a 14x12-in. rectangle. Spread butter to within ½ in. of edges; sprinkle with apple mixture. Roll up jelly-roll style, starting with a long side. Cut in half. Pinch seams to seal and tuck ends under.

4. Place loaves seam side down in two 9x5-in. loaf pans coated with cooking spray. Cover and let rise until doubled, about 30 minutes.

5. Preheat oven to 350°. With a sharp knife, make eight shallow slashes across top of each loaf. Bake 30-35 minutes or until golden brown. Remove from pans to wire racks to cool.

6. In a small bowl, combine glaze ingredients; drizzle over bread.

NOTE *This recipe was tested with Land O'Lakes light stick butter.*
PER SERVING *140 cal., 3 g fat (1 g sat. fat), 16 mg chol., 99 mg sodium, 27 g carb., 1 g fiber, 3 g pro.* ***Diabetic Exchanges:*** *1½ starch, ½ fat.*

WALNUT APPLE BREAD

ALMOND COLESLAW

Almond Coleslaw

As a twist to my mother's original recipe, I added toasted almonds to this slaw for extra crunch, flavor and nutrition.
—**SARAH NEVIN** GILA, NM

START TO FINISH: 25 MIN.
MAKES: 14 SERVINGS

- 2 packages (16 ounces each) coleslaw mix
- 1 cup reduced-fat mayonnaise
- 2 tablespoons cider vinegar
- 1 tablespoon sugar
- ¾ teaspoon seasoned salt
- ½ teaspoon pepper
- ½ cup slivered almonds, toasted

Place coleslaw mix in a serving bowl. In a small bowl, combine the mayonnaise, vinegar, sugar, seasoned salt and pepper. Pour over coleslaw mix; toss to coat. Chill until serving. Just before serving, sprinkle with almonds.

PER SERVING *103 cal., 8 g fat (1 g sat. fat), 6 mg chol., 237 mg sodium, 7 g carb., 2 g fiber, 2 g pro.* **Diabetic Exchanges:** *1½ fat, ½ starch.*

FAST FIX
Sweet Peas Parma

If you're looking for new ways to prepare vegetables, give this simple pea recipe a try. I think the Italian flavors are delicious.
—**JILL ANDERSON** SLEEPY EYE, MN

START TO FINISH: 20 MIN.
MAKES: 4 SERVINGS

- 1 package (16 ounces) frozen peas
- 4 thin slices prosciutto or deli ham, coarsely chopped
- 1 tablespoon olive oil
- 1 tablespoon butter
- 1 garlic clove, minced
- 1 medium tomato, seeded and chopped
- ¼ teaspoon salt
- ⅛ teaspoon pepper

1. Place peas in a steamer basket; place in a saucepan over 1 in. of water. Bring to a boil; cover and steam for 4 minutes.
2. Meanwhile, in a large skillet, cook prosciutto in oil and butter over medium heat until prosciutto is crisp. Add garlic; cook 1 minute longer. Add the tomato, salt and pepper; heat through. Stir in peas.

SWEET PEAS AND MUSHROOMS
Cook peas as directed. Omit remaining ingredients. Saute 2 cups sliced fresh mushrooms and ½ cup chopped onion in ¼ cup butter. Add peas, 2 teaspoons sugar, ¾ teaspoon salt and a dash of pepper; heat through. Makes: 5 servings.

PEAS AMANDINE *Cook peas as directed. Omit remaining ingredients. Saute ¼ cup slivered almonds in 3 tablespoons butter until lightly browned. Remove with a slotted spoon; add to cooked peas. Saute 1 jar (4½ oz.) sliced mushrooms (drained) and ¼ cup chopped onion until tender; add to peas. Season with salt and pepper. Makes: 4 servings.*

HERBED PEAS *Cook peas as directed. Omit remaining ingredients. Saute ½ cup thinly sliced green onions in 2 tablespoons butter until tender. Add the peas, 2 tablespoons each minced fresh parsley and basil, ¾ teaspoon sugar, ½ teaspoon salt and ¼ teaspoon pepper; heat through. Makes: 4 servings.*

PER SERVING *181 cal., 8 g fat (3 g sat. fat), 20 mg chol., 569 mg sodium, 17 g carb., 6 g fiber, 10 g pro.* **Diabetic Exchanges:** *1 starch, 1 lean meat, 1 fat.*

SWEET PEAS PARMA

CRANBERRY-PECAN
CORN MUFFINS

Hominy with Peppers

My mother-in-law hated to eat light, but she would devour this casserole when I served it. It's my family's favorite side dish.
—**ANNA BREEDING** MARION, OH

START TO FINISH: 25 MIN.
MAKES: 6 SERVINGS

- 1 each large green pepper, sweet red and yellow peppers
- 2 cans (15½ ounces each) hominy, rinsed and drained
- 2 tablespoons canola oil
- 1½ teaspoons garlic pepper blend

In a large bowl, combine the peppers, hominy, oil and garlic pepper; toss to coat. Spread into an ungreased 15-in. x 10-in. x 1-in. baking pan. Bake at 450° for 14-16 minutes or until peppers are tender, stirring once.
PER SERVING *130 cal., 5 g fat (trace sat. fat), 0 chol., 692 mg sodium, 20 g carb., 5 g fiber, 2 g pro.* **Diabetic Exchanges:** *1 starch, 1 vegetable, 1 fat.*

Cranberry-Pecan Corn Muffins

I added cranberries and pecans to a low-fat corn muffins recipe. I think they're best served warm with a touch of honey butter.
—**LISA VARNER** EL PASO, TX

PREP: 15 MIN. • **BAKE:** 20 MIN.
MAKES: ABOUT 1 DOZEN

- 1¾ cups yellow cornmeal
- ¾ cup all-purpose flour
- 1¼ teaspoons baking soda
- ½ teaspoon salt
- 1½ cups (12 ounces) fat-free plain yogurt
- 1 egg
- ¼ cup canola oil
- ¼ cup honey
- ½ cup dried cranberries
- ¼ cup chopped pecans

1. In a large bowl, combine the cornmeal, flour, baking soda and salt. In another bowl, combine the yogurt, egg, oil and honey. Stir into the dry ingredients just until moistened. Fold in cranberries and pecans. Coat muffin cups with cooking spray; fill three-fourths full with batter.
2. Bake at 375° for 18-20 minutes or until a toothpick inserted near the center comes out clean. Cool for 5 minutes before removing from pans. Serve warm.
PER SERVING *185 cal., 6 g fat (1 g sat. fat), 16 mg chol., 217 mg sodium, 29 g carb., 2 g fiber, 4 g pro.* **Diabetic Exchanges:** *2 starch, 1 fat.*

top tip

Try Hominy

Never had it? What are you waiting for? Hominy is made from kernels of corn that are soaked in lime or lye to remove the hull and germ. The process causes the corn to soften and puff up to double its size. The tender, chewy bits are a tasty way to round out a meal.

F C FAST FIX
Roasted Parmesan Green Beans

I'm not a big fan of the classic green bean casserole, so I came up with this easy, no-fuss version using Greek seasoning, which is a combination of mint, thyme, basil, marjoram, dried onion and dried garlic.

—**CHRISTIE LADD** MECHANICSBURG, PA

START TO FINISH: 30 MIN.
MAKES: 4 SERVINGS

- 1 **pound fresh green beans, trimmed**
- 2 **teaspoons olive oil**
- 1½ **teaspoons Greek seasoning**
- 2 **tablespoons shredded Parmesan cheese**

1. Place the beans in a 15-in. x 10-in. x 1-in. baking pan coated with cooking spray. Drizzle with oil. Sprinkle with seasoning; stir to coat.
2. Bake, uncovered, at 425° for 12-15 minutes or until beans are tender, stirring once. Sprinkle with the cheese.
PER SERVING *61 cal., 3 g fat (1 g sat. fat), 2 mg chol., 410 mg sodium, 7 g carb., 3 g fiber, 3 g pro.* ***Diabetic Exchanges:*** *1 vegetable, ½ fat.*

F FAST FIX
Spiced Rice

Honey, raisins and cinnamon lend a slightly sweet flavor to this Mediterranean-inspired side dish. I think it makes a tasty dish for women's luncheons or brunches.

—**ELLEN GOVERTSEN** WHEATON, IL

START TO FINISH: 25 MIN.
MAKES: 4 SERVINGS

- ⅔ **cup uncooked long grain rice**
- 1¼ **cups water**
- ¾ **cup chopped sweet onion**

SPICED RICE

- 1½ **teaspoons olive oil**
- 1½ **teaspoons honey**
- ¾ **cup reduced-sodium chicken broth**
- ¼ **cup golden raisins**
- 1 **teaspoon curry powder**
- ¼ **teaspoon salt**
- ¼ **teaspoon ground cumin**
- ¼ **teaspoon ground cinnamon**
- ¼ **cup chopped sweet red pepper**

1. In a large saucepan, bring rice and water to a boil. Reduce heat; cover and simmer for 14-16 minutes or until tender.

2. Meanwhile, in a small nonstick skillet, saute the onion in oil for 1 minute. Stir in honey and cook 2 minutes longer. Stir in the broth, raisins, curry, salt, cumin and cinnamon. Bring to a boil. Reduce the heat; simmer, uncovered, for 5 minutes. Stir in the red pepper and rice until well blended. Cook 2 minutes longer or until the rice is heated through.
PER SERVING *183 cal., 2 g fat (trace sat. fat), 0 chol., 259 mg sodium, 38 g carb., 2 g fiber, 4 g pro.*

HASH BROWN BAKE

4 medium green peppers

4 ounces reduced-fat Monterey Jack cheese or part-skim mozzarella cheese, cut into 8 pieces

2 teaspoons minced fresh marjoram or ¾ teaspoon dried marjoram

1 can (8 ounces) tomato sauce

TOPPING

3 tablespoons panko (Japanese) bread crumbs

2 tablespoons grated Parmesan cheese

1 tablespoon olive oil

⅛ teaspoon cayenne pepper

1. Place the eggplant and zucchini in a large bowl; sprinkle with ½ teaspoon salt and toss to coat. Cover and let stand for 30 minutes. Rinse with cold water; drain and pat dry.

2. In a large skillet, saute onion and garlic in oil until tender. Add eggplant mixture, tomatoes, pepper and remaining salt. Bring to boil. Reduce heat; cover and simmer for 20 minutes. Remove from the heat.

3. Meanwhile, cut green peppers in half lengthwise; discard seeds. Place in a 13-in. x 9-in. baking dish coated with cooking spray. Place about 3 tablespoons eggplant mixture in each pepper half; top with a piece of cheese and sprinkle with marjoram. Top with tomato sauce and remaining eggplant mixture.

4. Cover and bake at 350° for 40-45 minutes or until peppers are tender. Combine the topping ingredients; sprinkle over peppers. Bake, uncovered, 3-5 minutes longer or until the topping is golden brown.

PER SERVING *128 cal., 8 g fat (3 g sat. fat), 11 mg chol., 430 mg sodium, 11 g carb., 3 g fiber, 6 g pro.* ***Diabetic Exchanges:** 2 vegetable, 1 lean meat, ½ fat.*

Hash Brown Bake

My family has no idea they're eating a low-fat recipe with this hearty side dish. It's cheesy and simply delicious.

—**DARLA KAHLER** BISON, SD

PREP: 20 MIN. • **BAKE:** 45 MIN.
MAKES: 6 SERVINGS

1¼ cups fat-free milk

3 ounces reduced-fat cream cheese

1 envelope ranch salad dressing mix

6 cups frozen shredded hash brown potatoes, thawed

½ cup shredded reduced-fat cheddar cheese

1 bacon strip, cooked and crumbled

1. In a blender, combine the milk, cream cheese and salad dressing mix. Cover and process until smooth. Place potatoes in an 8-in. square baking dish coated with cooking spray; top with the milk mixture. Cover and bake at 350° for 35 minutes.

2. Sprinkle with cheddar cheese and bacon. Bake, uncovered, 8-10 minutes longer or until cheese is melted and potatoes are tender.

PER SERVING *155 cal., 5 g fat (4 g sat. fat), 19 mg chol., 552 mg sodium, 19 g carb., 1 g fiber, 8 g pro.* ***Diabetic Exchanges:** 1 starch, 1 lean meat, 1 fat.*

C
Baked Ratatouille Boats

To cut down on starch, I use only vegetables in the filling for these peppers instead of rice. You could also omit the panko topping, but I like the crispiness it adds.

—**ROSALIND POPE** GREENSBORO, NC

PREP: 30 MIN. + STANDING • **BAKE:** 45 MIN.
MAKES: 8 SERVINGS

2 cups cubed eggplant

1 medium zucchini, chopped

¾ teaspoon salt, divided

1 small onion, chopped

3 garlic cloves, minced

4 teaspoons olive oil

2 large tomatoes, chopped

¼ teaspoon pepper

TANGY MASHED POTATOES

F
Veggie Mushroom Rice

There's plenty of herb and mushroom flavor for friends and family to savor in this filling, healthful side dish. It goes well with a variety of meats and main dishes.

—**TAMMY CONDIT** LEAGUE CITY, TX

PREP: 15 MIN. • **BAKE:** 45 MIN.
MAKES: 7 SERVINGS

- 1 **small onion, chopped**
- 1 **small green pepper, chopped**
- 1 **small sweet red pepper, chopped**
- ¼ **cup chopped celery**
- 1 **tablespoon canola oil**
- 1½ **cups sliced fresh mushrooms**
- 1 **garlic clove, minced**
- 1¼ **cups uncooked long grain rice**
- 2½ **cups water**
- 1½ **teaspoons rubbed sage**
- 1 **teaspoon dried parsley flakes**
- 1 **teaspoon dried thyme**
- ¾ **teaspoon salt**
- ⅛ **teaspoon pepper**

1. In a large nonstick saucepan, saute the onion, peppers and celery in oil for 2 minutes. Add mushrooms and garlic; saute 3 minutes longer or until the vegetables are crisp-tender. Stir in the rice, water and seasonings; bring to a boil.

2. Carefully transfer to a 2-qt. baking dish coated with cooking spray. Cover and bake at 350° for 45-50 minutes or until the rice is tender.

PER SERVING *154 cal., 2 g fat (trace sat. fat), 0 chol., 260 mg sodium, 30 g carb., 1 g fiber, 3 g pro.* **Diabetic Exchanges:** *2 starch, ½ fat.*

F
Tangy Mashed Potatoes

Here is one of my favorite items to serve alongside oven-fried chicken. Using plain yogurt in the mashed potatoes gives them a tangy flavor and a creamy body.

—**DONNA NOEL** GRAY, ME

PREP: 20 MIN. • **COOK:** 20 MIN.
MAKES: 13 SERVINGS

- 4 **pounds potatoes, peeled and cubed (about 12 medium)**
- 1½ **cups (12 ounces) reduced-fat plain yogurt**
- 4 **green onions, minced**
- 2 **tablespoons butter**
- 1 **teaspoon salt**
- ½ **teaspoon pepper**

Place potatoes in a Dutch oven and cover with water. Bring to a boil. Reduce heat; cover and cook for 10-15 minutes or until tender. Drain potatoes; mash with yogurt, onions, butter, salt and pepper.

PER SERVING *114 cal., 2 g fat (1 g sat. fat), 6 mg chol., 216 mg sodium, 21 g carb., 1 g fiber, 3 g pro.* **Diabetic Exchange:** *1½ starch.*

VEGGIE MUSHROOM RICE

GREEN CHILI
BREAKFAST BURRITOS
PAGE 88

**SHARMAN SHUBERT'S
SAGE TURKEY SAUSAGE PATTIES**

PAGE 80

**BEV LEHRMAN'S
VEGGIE BREAKFAST PIZZA**

PAGE 86

**NICKI LAZORIK'S
BAKED LONG JOHNS**

PAGE 90

Good Mornings

This chapter proves **there's more than cereal for breakfast.** Treat the family to a special Sunday morning brunch, or whip up a satisfying smoothie for those **early hours on the go**.

Energizing Granola

Adding flaxseed to my granola is an easy way for me to add omega-3s to my diet, and the combination of nuts, grains and fruit packs a healthy and great-tasting punch!

—**NINA WISEMAN** BATAVIA, OH

PREP: 25 MIN. • **BAKE:** 25 MIN. + COOLING
MAKES: 6 CUPS

- 2½ cups old-fashioned oats
- ¾ cup chopped walnuts
- ½ cup unsalted sunflower kernels
- ⅓ cup packed brown sugar
- ¼ cup flaked coconut
- ¼ cup toasted wheat germ
- 2 tablespoons sesame seeds
- 2 tablespoons ground flaxseed
- ⅓ cup water
- 2 tablespoons honey
- 2 tablespoons molasses
- 1 tablespoon canola oil
- ¾ teaspoon vanilla extract
- ½ teaspoon salt
- ½ teaspoon ground cinnamon
- ⅓ cup dried cranberries
- ⅓ cup golden raisins
- ¼ cup dried banana chips

1. In a large bowl, combine the first eight ingredients. In a small saucepan, combine the water, honey, molasses and oil. Heat for 3-4 minutes over medium until heated through. Remove from the heat; stir in the vanilla, salt and cinnamon. Pour over the oat mixture; stir to coat.

2. Transfer to a 15-in. x 10-in. x 1-in. baking pan coated with cooking spray. Bake at 350° for 25-30 minutes or until lightly browned, stirring every 10 minutes. Cool completely on a wire rack. Stir in dried fruits. Store in an airtight container.

PER SERVING *260 cal., 12 g fat (2 g sat. fat), 0 chol., 110 mg sodium, 35 g carb., 4 g fiber, 7 g pro.* **Diabetic Exchanges:** *2½ starch, 1½ fat.*

Smoked Salmon Quiche

My son fishes for salmon on the Kenai River in Alaska and smokes much of what he catches. My mother passed this recipe on to me to help me find new ways to cook with salmon. Regular salmon also works in this quiche, but the smoked flavor can't be beat!

—**ROSE MARIE CHERVEN** ANCHORAGE, AK

PREP: 30 MIN. • **BAKE:** 35 MIN. + STANDING
MAKES: 8 SERVINGS

- 1 sheet refrigerated pie pastry
- 1 cup (4 ounces) shredded reduced-fat Swiss cheese
- 1 tablespoon all-purpose flour
- 3 plum tomatoes, seeded and chopped
- 2 tablespoons finely chopped onion
- 2 teaspoons canola oil
- 3 ounces smoked salmon fillet, flaked (about ½ cup)
- 4 eggs
- 1 cup whole milk
- ¼ teaspoon salt

1. On a lightly floured surface, unroll pastry. Transfer to a 9-in. pie plate. Trim pastry to ½ in. beyond edge of plate; flute edges.

2. In a small bowl, combine cheese and flour. Transfer to pastry.

3. In a large skillet, saute tomatoes and onion in oil just until tender. Remove from the heat; stir in salmon. Spoon over cheese mixture.

4. In a small bowl, whisk the eggs, milk and salt. Pour into pastry. Bake at 350° for 35-40 minutes or until a knife inserted near the center comes out clean. Let stand for 15 minutes before cutting.

PER SERVING *235 cal., 13 g fat (5 g sat. fat), 122 mg chol., 348 mg sodium, 17 g carb., trace fiber, 12 g pro.* **Diabetic Exchanges:** *2 medium-fat meat, 1 starch.*

FAST FIX ▶

Green Eggs and Ham Sandwiches

This is my kid-friendly version of green eggs and ham. For my adult version, I use prosciutto instead of ham and fontina cheese for the provolone. It's a fun sandwich for breakfast, lunch or dinner.

—**BETH DAUENHAUER** PUEBLO, CO

START TO FINISH: 20 MIN.
MAKES: 4 SERVINGS

- 4 **eggs**
- ¼ **cup fat-free milk**
- 3 **tablespoons prepared pesto**
- 4 **whole wheat English muffins, split and toasted**
- 2 **slices deli ham, halved**
- 4 **slices reduced-fat provolone cheese**

1. Heat a 10-in. nonstick skillet coated with cooking spray over medium heat. Whisk the eggs, milk and pesto. Add to skillet (mixture should set immediately at edges).

GREEN EGGS AND
HAM SANDWICHES

2. As eggs set, push cooked edges toward the center, letting uncooked portion flow underneath. When the eggs are set and top appears glossy, remove from skillet and cut into quarters.

3. On each English muffin bottom, layer ham, eggs and cheese. Replace tops.

PER SERVING *329 cal., 15 g fat (5 g sat. fat), 230 mg chol., 716 mg sodium, 29 g carb., 5 g fiber, 22 g pro.*

Southwest Spinach Strata

I've made this strata with pinto beans and cannellini beans instead of black beans, and it's just as delicious. It's a fun dish to serve for breakfast, or even dinner, if you're in the mood for something different.

—**DEBORAH BIGGS** OMAHA, NE

PREP: 20 MIN. • **BAKE:** 45 MIN. + STANDING
MAKES: 6 SERVINGS

- 2½ **cups cubed day-old white bread**
- 2½ **cups cubed day-old whole wheat bread**
- ⅔ **cup black beans, rinsed and drained**
- 1 **package (10 ounces) frozen chopped spinach, thawed and squeezed dry**
- 1½ **cups (6 ounces) shredded reduced-fat cheddar cheese, divided**
- 1 **cup Southwestern-style egg substitute**
- 2 **cups fat-free milk**
- ¼ **cup minced fresh cilantro**
- ¼ **teaspoon salt**
- 6 **tablespoons reduced-fat sour cream**
- 6 **tablespoons salsa**

1. Place half of the bread cubes in an 8-in. square baking dish coated with cooking spray. Layer with beans, spinach and half of the cheese. Top with remaining bread cubes.

2. In a large bowl, whisk the egg substitute, milk, cilantro and salt. Pour over top. Let stand for 5 minutes.

3. Bake, uncovered, at 350° for 40 minutes. Sprinkle with remaining cheese. Bake 5 minutes longer or until cheese is melted and a knife inserted near the center comes out clean. Let stand for 10 minutes before cutting. Serve with sour cream and salsa.

PER SERVING *264 cal., 9 g fat (5 g sat. fat), 27 mg chol., 736 mg sodium, 28 g carb., 4 g fiber, 20 g pro.*
Diabetic Exchanges: *2 starch, 2 lean meat, ½ fat.*

French Toast with Apple Topping

Topped with warm cinnamon apples, this indulgent French toast is a simple way to make your family feel extra special.

—JANIS SCHARNOTT FONTANA, WI

START TO FINISH: 20 MIN.
MAKES: 2 SERVINGS

- 1 **medium apple, peeled and thinly sliced**
- 1 **tablespoon brown sugar**
- ¼ **teaspoon ground cinnamon**
- 2 **tablespoons reduced-fat butter, divided**
- 1 **egg**
- ¼ **cup 2% milk**
- 1 **teaspoon vanilla extract**
- 4 **slices French bread (½ inch thick)**
  Maple syrup, optional

1. In a large skillet, saute the apple, brown sugar and cinnamon in 1 tablespoon butter until apple is tender.

2. In a shallow bowl, whisk the egg, milk and vanilla. Dip both sides of bread in egg mixture.

3. In a large skillet, melt remaining butter over medium heat. Cook bread on both sides until golden brown. Serve with apple mixture and maple syrup if desired.

NOTE *This recipe was tested with Land O'Lakes light stick butter.*
PER SERVING *219 cal., 10 g fat (5 g sat. fat), 113 mg chol., 279 mg sodium, 29 g carb., 2 g fiber, 6 g pro.* **Diabetic Exchanges:** *1½ starch, 1½ fat, ½ fruit.*

Buttermilk Pumpkin Waffles

My girlfriend loves pumpkin, so I enjoy making this for her on cool Sunday mornings. I like to freeze homemade pumpkin puree in 1-cup batches because I find the flavor infinitely more satisfying.

—CHARLES INSLER SILVER SPRING, MD

PREP: 20 MIN. • **COOK:** 5 MIN./BATCH
MAKES: 6 SERVINGS

- ¾ **cup all-purpose flour**
- ½ **cup whole wheat flour**
- 2 **tablespoons brown sugar**
- 1 **teaspoon baking powder**
- 1 **teaspoon ground cinnamon**
- ½ **teaspoon ground ginger**
- ¼ **teaspoon baking soda**
- ¼ **teaspoon salt**
- ¼ **teaspoon ground cloves**
- 2 **eggs**
- 1¼ **cups buttermilk**
- ½ **cup fresh or canned pumpkin**
- 2 **tablespoons butter, melted**
  Butter and maple syrup, optional

1. In a large bowl, combine the first nine ingredients. In a small bowl, whisk the eggs, buttermilk, pumpkin and butter. Stir into dry ingredients just until moistened.

2. Bake in a preheated waffle iron according to manufacturer's directions until golden brown. Serve with butter and syrup if desired.
PER SERVING *194 cal., 6 g fat (3 g sat. fat), 83 mg chol., 325 mg sodium, 28 g carb., 3 g fiber, 7 g pro.* **Diabetic Exchanges:** *2 starch, 1 fat.*

BUTTERMILK PUMPKIN WAFFLES

SAGE TURKEY
SAUSAGE PATTIES

TO USE FROZEN PATTIES *Unwrap patties and place on a baking sheet coated with cooking spray. Bake at 350° for 15 minutes on each side or until heated through.*
PER SERVING *104 cal., 6 g fat (2 g sat. fat), 46 mg chol., 227 mg sodium, trace carb., trace fiber, 11 g pro.* **Diabetic Exchanges:** *1 lean meat, 1 fat.*

S Chia Orange Yogurt

I love this chia yogurt parfait because it tastes like you're eating dessert for breakfast. Plus, chia seeds deliver a big dose of omega-3 fatty acids, and they're rich in fiber, calcium, phosphorus, magnesium, manganese, copper, iron and zinc.
—**MARION MCNEILL** MAYFIELD HEIGHTS, OH

PREP: 10 MIN. + CHILLING
MAKES: 1 SERVING.

- ⅓ **cup fat-free milk or almond milk**
- ¼ **cup old-fashioned oats**
- ¼ **cup reduced-fat plain Greek yogurt**
- 1 **tablespoon orange marmalade spreadable fruit**
- 1½ **teaspoons chia seeds**
- ¼ **teaspoon vanilla extract**
- ⅓ **cup orange segments, chopped**

In a jar with a tight-fitting lid, combine the milk, oats, yogurt, marmalade, chia seeds and vanilla. Cover and shake to combine. Stir in the orange segments. Cover and refrigerate for 8 hours or overnight.
PER SERVING *245 cal., 5 g fat (1 g sat. fat), 5 mg chol., 59 mg sodium, 39 g carb., 6 g fiber, 13 g pro.* **Diabetic Exchanges:** *2½ starch, 1 lean meat.*

C FAST FIX
Sage Turkey Sausage Patties

As an alternative to pork, my homemade turkey sausage is full of flavor but cuts down on fat. Most people are surprised how easy these are to make.
—**SHARMAN SCHUBERT** SEATTLE, WA

START TO FINISH: 30 MIN.
MAKES: 12 SERVINGS

- ¼ **cup grated Parmesan cheese**
- 3 **tablespoons minced fresh parsley or 1 tablespoon dried parsley flakes**
- 2 **tablespoons fresh sage or 2 teaspoons dried sage leaves**
- 2 **garlic cloves, minced**
- 1 **teaspoon fennel seed, crushed**
- ¾ **teaspoon salt**
- ½ **teaspoon pepper**
- 1½ **pounds lean ground turkey**
- 1 **tablespoon olive oil**

1. In a large bowl, combine the first seven ingredients. Crumble turkey over mixture and mix well. Shape into twelve 3-in. patties.
2. In a large skillet coated with cooking spray, cook patties in oil in batches over medium heat for 3-5 minutes on each side or until meat is no longer pink. Drain on paper towels if necessary.
3. To freeze, wrap each patty in plastic wrap; transfer to a resealable plastic freezer bag. May be frozen for up to 3 months.

Peachy Pecan Bread

With a cup of hot tea, this tasty sweet bread hits the spot in the morning. Not only does it bring a little fruit to your diet, it also packs 7 grams of fiber per serving.
—**KATHY FLEMING** LISLE, IL

PREP: 15 MIN. • **BAKE:** 45 MIN. + COOLING
MAKES: 1 LOAF (12 SLICES)

- 1½ cups all-purpose flour
- ½ cup uncooked oat bran cereal
- ⅔ cup packed brown sugar
- 1½ teaspoons baking powder
- ½ teaspoon baking soda
- ¼ teaspoon salt
- ¼ cup water
- ½ cup orange juice
- ½ cup egg substitute
- ¼ cup canola oil
- 1 teaspoon vanilla extract
- ½ cup dried peaches or apricots, finely chopped
- ¼ cup chopped pecans

1. In a large bowl, combine the first six ingredients. In a small bowl, combine the water, orange juice, egg substitute, oil and vanilla. Stir into dry ingredients just until moistened. Fold in peaches and pecans.

2. Transfer to an 8-in. x 4-in. loaf pan coated with cooking spray. Bake at 350° for 45-55 minutes or until a toothpick inserted near the center comes out clean. Cool for 10 minutes before removing from pan to a wire rack.

NOTE *Look for oat bran cereal near the hot cereals or in the natural foods section.*

PER SERVING *200 cal., 7 g fat (1 g sat. fat), 0 chol., 178 mg sodium, 32 g carb., 2 g fiber, 4 g pro.*

S | **FAST FIX**

Creamy Orange Smoothies

Smoothies make a great morning pick-me-up or afternoon snack. I love the citrus-showcasing combo of orange juice and mandarin oranges blended with cream cheese and yogurt.
—**ROXANNE CHAN** ALBANY, CA

START TO FINISH: 15 MIN.
MAKES: 12 SERVINGS (¾ CUP EACH)

- 4 cups orange juice
- 3 containers (6 ounces each) orange creme yogurt
- 3 medium bananas, peeled and cut into chunks
- 2 cans (11 ounces each) mandarin oranges, drained
- 6 ounces reduced-fat cream cheese, cubed

Place half of each ingredient in a blender; cover and process until blended. Transfer to a large pitcher. Repeat, adding second batch to the same pitcher; stir to combine. Serve immediately or chill until serving.

PER SERVING *159 cal., 4 g fat (2 g sat. fat), 12 mg chol., 85 mg sodium, 29 g carb., 1 g fiber, 4 g pro.*

CREAMY ORANGE SMOOTHIES

Spinach Swiss Quiche

As comforting as it is colorful, a warm slice of my quiche is never a bad idea when you want to start the day right. To save time, I sometimes saute the bacon-veggie mixture the night before.
—**APRIL MILNER** DEARBORN HEIGHTS, MI

PREP: 25 MIN. • **BAKE:** 35 MIN. + STANDING
MAKES: 6 SERVINGS

- 1 refrigerated pie pastry
- 4 turkey bacon strips, diced
- ¼ cup chopped onion
- ¼ cup chopped sweet red pepper
- 1 package (10 ounces) frozen chopped spinach, thawed and squeezed dry
- 2 cups egg substitute
- ½ cup fat-free cottage cheese
- ¼ cup shredded reduced-fat Swiss cheese
- ½ teaspoon dried oregano
- ¼ teaspoon dried parsley flakes
- ¼ teaspoon each salt, pepper and paprika
- 6 tablespoons fat-free sour cream

1. On a lightly floured surface, unroll pastry. Transfer to a 9-in. pie plate. Trim pastry to ½ in. beyond edge of plate; flute edges. Line unpricked pastry with a double thickness of heavy-duty foil.

2. Bake at 450° for 8 minutes. Remove foil; bake 5 minutes longer. Cool on a wire rack. Reduce heat to 350°.

3. In a small skillet, cook the bacon, onion and red pepper until vegetables are tender; drain. Stir in spinach. Spoon spinach mixture into pastry.

4. In a small bowl, combine the egg substitute, cottage cheese, Swiss cheese and seasonings; pour over spinach mixture.

5. Bake for 35-40 minutes or until a knife inserted near the center comes out clean. Let stand for 10 minutes before cutting. Serve with sour cream.
PER SERVING *278 cal., 12 g fat (5 g sat. fat), 22 mg chol., 659 mg sodium, 26 g carb., 2 g fiber, 17 g pro.* **Diabetic Exchanges:** *2 lean meat, 2 fat, 1½ starch.*

F S FAST FIX

A.M. Rush Espresso Smoothie

Want an early-morning pick-me-up that's good for you, too? Fruit and flaxseed give this sweet espresso a nutritious twist.
—**AIMEE WILSON** CLOVIS, CA

START TO FINISH: 10 MIN.
MAKES: 1 SERVING.

- ½ cup cold fat-free milk
- 1 tablespoon vanilla flavoring syrup
- 1 cup ice cubes
- ½ medium banana, cut up
- 1 to 2 teaspoons instant espresso powder
- 1 teaspoon ground flaxseed
- 1 teaspoon baking cocoa

In a blender, combine all the ingredients; cover and process for 1-2 minutes or until blended. Pour into a chilled glass; serve immediately.
NOTE *This recipe was tested with Torani brand flavoring syrup. Look for it in the coffee section.*
PER SERVING *148 cal., 2 g fat (trace sat. fat), 2 mg chol., 54 mg sodium, 31 g carb., 3 g fiber, 6 g pro.*

SPINACH SWISS QUICHE

HEARTY CONFETTI BREAKFAST

FAST FIX

Blueberry Orange Scones

Tender, flaky and bursting with blueberries, these buttery scones are great for breakfast, brunch or as a midday snack with coffee or tea.

—KATY RADTKE APPLETON, WI

START TO FINISH: 30 MIN.
MAKES: 8 SCONES

- 2 **cups all-purpose flour**
- 3 **tablespoons sugar**
- 2 **teaspoons baking powder**
- 2 **teaspoons grated orange peel**
- 1 **teaspoon salt**
- ¼ **teaspoon baking soda**
- ¼ **teaspoon ground cloves**
- ¼ **cup cold butter**
- ½ **cup buttermilk**
- ¼ **cup orange juice**
- ½ **cup fresh or frozen unsweetened blueberries**

1. In a large bowl, combine the first seven ingredients. Cut in butter until mixture resembles coarse crumbs. Stir in buttermilk and orange juice just until moistened. Gently fold in blueberries.
2. Turn onto a floured surface; gently knead 10 times. Pat into an 8-in. circle. Cut into eight wedges. Separate wedges and place on a baking sheet coated with cooking spray. Bake at 425° for 10-12 minutes or until golden brown. Serve warm.
NOTE *If using frozen blueberries, use without thawing to avoid discoloring the batter.*
PER SERVING *198 cal., 6 g fat (4 g sat. fat), 16 mg chol., 509 mg sodium, 32 g carb., 1 g fiber, 4 g pro.*
Diabetic Exchanges: 2 starch, 1 fat.

Hearty Confetti Breakfast

You know it's going to be a good day when it starts with an all-in-one potato-and-egg skillet. But that doesn't mean you should rule out this hearty dish as a dinner option, too.

—LORI MERRICK DANVERS, IL

PREP: 35 MIN. • **BROIL:** 5 MIN.
MAKES: 4 SERVINGS

- 1 **large sweet potato, peeled and cut into ½-inch cubes**
- 1 **large Yukon Gold potato, cut into ½-inch cubes**
- 1 **medium red potato, cut into ½-inch cubes**
- 1 **small onion, finely chopped**
- ¾ **teaspoon minced fresh rosemary or ¼ teaspoon dried rosemary, crushed**
- ¾ **teaspoon minced fresh thyme or ¼ teaspoon dried thyme**
- ¼ **teaspoon salt**
- ¼ **teaspoon pepper**
- 2 **teaspoons butter**
- 2 **teaspoons olive oil**
- 4 **eggs**
- ¼ **cup shredded Asiago cheese**

1. In a 10-in. ovenproof skillet, saute the potatoes, onion and seasonings in butter and oil until vegetables are golden brown and tender. With the back of a spoon, make four wells in the potato mixture; add an egg to each well. Remove from the heat; sprinkle with cheese.
2. Broil 3-4 in. from the heat for 3-4 minutes or until eggs are completely set.
PER SERVING *297 cal., 11 g fat (4 g sat. fat), 223 mg chol., 262 mg sodium, 37 g carb., 4 g fiber, 12 g pro. Diabetic Exchanges: 2 starch, 1½ fat, 1 medium-fat meat.*

HASH BROWN
BREAKFAST CASSEROLE

FAST FIX ›

Strawberry Puff Pancake

I've cut this recipe to 2 eggs and ½ cup milk for my husband and me, and it works just fine. It's yummy with strawberry or blueberry topping. You could even garnish it with whipped topping for a light dessert.

—**BRENDA MORTON** HALE CENTER, TX

START TO FINISH: 30 MIN.
MAKES: 4 SERVINGS

- 2 **tablespoons butter**
- 3 **eggs**
- ¾ **cup fat-free milk**
- 1 **teaspoon vanilla extract**
- ¾ **cup all-purpose flour**
- ⅛ **teaspoon salt**
- ⅛ **teaspoon ground cinnamon**
- ¼ **cup sugar**
- 1 **tablespoon cornstarch**
- ½ **cup water**
- 1 **cup sliced fresh strawberries**
  Confectioners' sugar

1. Place butter in a 9-in. pie plate; place in a 400° oven for 4-5 minutes or until melted. Meanwhile, in a small bowl, whisk the eggs, milk and vanilla. In another small bowl, combine the flour, salt and cinnamon; whisk into egg mixture until blended.

2. Pour into prepared pie plate. Bake for 15-20 minutes or until sides are crisp and golden brown.

3. In a small saucepan, combine sugar and cornstarch. Stir in water until smooth; add strawberries. Cook and stir over medium heat until thickened. Coarsely mash strawberries. Serve with pancake. Dust with confectioners' sugar.

PER SERVING *277 cal., 10 g fat (5 g sat. fat), 175 mg chol., 187 mg sodium, 38 g carb., 2 g fiber, 9 g pro.* **Diabetic Exchanges:** *2½ starch, 1 medium-fat meat, 1 fat.*

Hash Brown Breakfast Casserole

This is my quick and easy recipe for a savory brunch bake. To keep fat and cholesterol in check, I use egg substitute and chicken breast instead of high-calorie bacon.

—**CINDY SCHNEIDER** SARASOTA, FL

PREP: 10 MIN. • **BAKE:** 40 MIN.
MAKES: 4 SERVINGS

- 4 **cups frozen shredded hash brown potatoes, thawed**
- 1½ **cups egg substitute**
- 1 **cup finely chopped cooked chicken breast**
- ½ **teaspoon garlic powder**
- ½ **teaspoon pepper**
- ¾ **cup shredded reduced-fat cheddar cheese**

1. In a large bowl, combine the hash browns, egg substitute, chicken, garlic powder and pepper. Transfer to an 8-in. square baking dish coated with cooking spray; sprinkle with cheese.

2. Bake, uncovered, at 350° for 40-45 minutes or until a knife inserted near the center comes out clean. Let stand for 5 minutes before serving.

PER SERVING *220 cal., 6 g fat (3 g sat. fat), 42 mg chol., 355 mg sodium, 16 g carb., 1 g fiber, 26 g pro.* **Diabetic Exchanges:** *3 lean meat, 1 starch.*

STRAWBERRY
PUFF PANCAKE

top tip

The Egg-Quation

When substituting whole eggs with egg whites or egg substitute, remember that one large egg equals two large egg whites or ¼ cup egg substitute.

Spring Brunch Bake

My husband grows a great vegetable garden, and asparagus is always the first crop. We like to make this casserole when we have leftover ham.

—NANCY ZIMMERMAN

CAPE MAY COURT HOUSE, NJ

PREP: 15 MIN. • **BAKE:** 35 MIN. + STANDING
MAKES: 6 SERVINGS

- 8 **cups cubed French bread**
- 2 **cups cut fresh asparagus (1-inch pieces)**
- 1 **cup cubed fully cooked lean ham**
- ¾ **cup shredded part-skim mozzarella cheese**
- 6 **egg whites**
- 3 **eggs**
- 1½ **cups fat-free milk**
- 2 **tablespoons lemon juice**
- ¼ **teaspoon garlic powder**

1. In a large bowl, combine the bread, asparagus, ham and cheese. Whisk the egg whites, eggs, milk, lemon juice and garlic powder; pour over bread mixture and stir until blended. Transfer to a 13-in. x 9-in. baking dish coated with cooking spray.

2. Cover and bake at 350° for 25 minutes. Uncover and bake 8-10 minutes longer or until a knife inserted near the center comes out clean. Let stand for 10 minutes before serving.

PER SERVING *224 cal., 6 g fat (3 g sat. fat), 124 mg chol., 640 mg sodium, 20 g carb., 2 g fiber, 21 g pro.*

Apple Walnut Pancakes

If you like your pancakes fluffy and full of sweet, crunchy apples and nuts, this batter is a must-try. I really enjoy the subtle taste of whole wheat in this hearty breakfast.

—KERRY BLONDHEIM DENMARK, WI

PREP: 15 MIN. • **COOK:** 5 MIN./BATCH
MAKES: 18 PANCAKES

- 1 **cup all-purpose flour**
- 1 **cup whole wheat flour**
- 1 **tablespoon brown sugar**
- 2 **teaspoons baking powder**
- 1 **teaspoon salt**
- 2 **egg whites**
- 1 **egg, lightly beaten**
- 2 **cups fat-free milk**
- 2 **tablespoons canola oil**
- 1 **medium apple, peeled and chopped**
- ½ **cup chopped walnuts**
  Maple syrup

1. In a large bowl, combine the flours, brown sugar, baking powder and salt. Combine the egg whites, egg, milk and oil; add to dry ingredients just until moistened. Fold in apple and walnuts.

2. Pour batter by ¼ cupfuls onto a hot griddle coated with cooking spray; turn when bubbles form on top. Cook until the second side is golden brown. Serve with syrup.

PER SERVING *208 cal., 8 g fat (1 g sat. fat), 25 mg chol., 396 mg sodium, 27 g carb., 3 g fiber, 8 g pro.* **Diabetic Exchanges:** *2 starch, 1 fat.*

APPLE WALNUT PANCAKES

VEGGIE BREAKFAST PIZZA

4. Meanwhile, drain salsa, discarding the liquid. In a large skillet over medium heat, cook and stir the tomatoes, onion and green pepper in oil until crisp-tender. Combine eggs and seasonings; add to the pan. Cook and stir until eggs are set.

5. Spoon salsa and egg mixture over crust; sprinkle with cheese. Bake for 3-5 minutes or until cheese is melted.

PER SERVING *285 cal., 10 g fat (3 g sat. fat), 168 mg chol., 731 mg sodium, 34 g carb., 2 g fiber, 13 g pro.* ***Diabetic Exchanges:*** *2 starch, 1 lean meat, 1 vegetable, 1 fat.*

F **S** **FAST FIX**

Creamy Berry Smoothies

No one can tell there's tofu in these silky smoothies. For me, the blend of berries and pomegranate juice is a welcome delight.

—**SONYA LABBE** WEST HOLLYWOOD, CA

START TO FINISH: 10 MIN.
MAKES: 2 SERVINGS

- ½ cup pomegranate juice
- 1 tablespoon agave syrup or honey
- 3 ounces silken firm tofu (about ½ cup)
- 1 cup frozen unsweetened mixed berries
- 1 cup frozen unsweetened strawberries

Place all ingredients in a blender; cover and process until blended. Serve immediately.

PER SERVING *157 cal., 1 g fat (trace sat. fat), 0 chol., 24 mg sodium, 35 g carb., 3 g fiber, 4 g pro.*

Veggie Breakfast Pizza

We love Mexican food, so we combined several recipes to come up with this pizza. It's often our breakfast on Saturdays, when we can enjoy time around the table. Our kids look forward to getting up just for this!

—**BEV LEHRMAN** GIJOCA, BRAZIL,

PREP: 50 MIN. • **BAKE:** 15 MIN.
MAKES: 8 SLICES

- 1¼ teaspoons active dry yeast
- ¾ cup warm water (110° to 115°)
- 1 tablespoon sugar
- 1 tablespoon olive oil
- 1 teaspoon salt
- 2¼ cups all-purpose flour

TOPPINGS
- 1 cup salsa
- 2 medium tomatoes, seeded and chopped
- 1 large onion, chopped
- 1 small green pepper, chopped
- 1 tablespoon olive oil
- 6 eggs, beaten
- ½ teaspoon seasoned salt
- ¼ teaspoon salt
- ¼ teaspoon garlic pepper blend
- 1 cup (4 ounces) shredded part-skim mozzarella cheese

1. In a large bowl, dissolve yeast in warm water. Add the sugar, oil, salt and 1¼ cups flour. Beat until dough is smooth. Stir in enough remaining flour to form a soft dough (dough will be sticky). Turn onto a lightly floured surface, knead until smooth and elastic, about 6-8 minutes.

2. Place in a bowl coated with cooking spray, turning once to coat the top. Cover and let rise in a warm place for 30 minutes.

3. Punch dough down; roll into a 13-in. circle. Transfer to a 12-in. pizza pan coated with cooking spray. Build up edges slightly. Prick dough thoroughly with a fork. Bake at 425° for 8-10 minutes or until golden brown.

Cranberry Coffee Cake Wedges

A friend gave me this recipe, but it was with raisins and regular sugar, butter and sour cream, which I changed to dried cranberries and Splenda, light butter and fat-free yogurt. My husband can't tell I've changed anything but the raisins.

—CAROL BARBEE JASPER, MO

PREP: 20 MIN. • **BAKE:** 15 MIN.
MAKES: 8 SERVINGS

- ⅓ **cup dried cranberries**
- 1 **cup boiling water**
- 2 **cups all-purpose flour**
- 3 **tablespoons plus 1 teaspoon sugar blend, divided**
- 2 **teaspoons baking powder**
- ½ **teaspoon baking soda**
- ½ **teaspoon salt**
- 5 **tablespoons cold reduced-fat butter**
- 1 **cup (8 ounces) fat-free plain yogurt**
- 1 **egg, separated**
- ½ **teaspoon ground cinnamon**

1. Place cranberries in a small bowl; add boiling water. Cover and let stand for 5 minutes. Drain and set aside.

2. In a large bowl, combine the flour, 3 tablespoons sugar blend, baking powder, baking soda and salt. Cut in butter until mixture resembles coarse crumbs; stir in reserved cranberries. Combine yogurt and egg yolk; add to crumb mixture and stir until a soft dough forms (dough will be sticky).

3. Turn onto a floured surface; gently dough knead 6-8 times. Transfer to a baking sheet coated with cooking spray. Pat into a 9-in. circle; cut into eight wedges, but do not separate. Beat the egg white; brush over dough. Combine cinnamon and remaining sugar blend; sprinkle over the top. Bake at 425° for 15-18 minutes or until golden brown. Remove to wire rack. Serve warm.

NOTE *This recipe was tested with Splenda sugar blend and Land O'Lakes light stick butter.*

PER SERVING *202 cal., 5 g fat (2 g sat. fat), 36 mg chol., 412 mg sodium, 36 g carb., 1 g fiber, 5 g pro.* **Diabetic Exchanges:** *2½ starch, 1 fat.*

CRANBERRY COFFEE CAKE WEDGES

Banana Date-Nut Mini Muffins

F S C

These little muffins don't need butter or jam or anything else to make them complete. I like them warm right out of the oven or after a few seconds in the microwave.

—**LILY JULOW** GAINESVILLE, FL

PREP: 15 MIN. • **BAKE:** 15 MIN./BATCH
MAKES: 4 DOZEN

- 1 **cup mashed ripe bananas (about 2 medium)**
- ¾ **cup sugar**
- ⅓ **cup unsweetened applesauce**
- 3 **tablespoons canola oil**
- 1 **egg**
- ¾ **cup all-purpose flour**
- ¾ **cup whole wheat flour**
- ½ **cup quick-cooking oats**
- 1½ **teaspoons baking powder**
- ½ **teaspoon baking soda**
- ⅓ **cup chopped dates**
- ¼ **cup finely chopped walnuts**
- 1 **teaspoon grated lemon peel**

1. In a large bowl, beat bananas, sugar, applesauce, oil and egg until well blended. Combine the flours, oats, baking powder and baking soda; gradually beat into banana mixture until blended. Stir in the dates, walnuts and lemon peel.

2. Coat miniature muffin cups with cooking spray or use paper liners; fill half full with batter. Bake at 350° for 12-14 minutes or until a toothpick comes out clean. Cool for 5 minutes before removing from pans to wire racks.

PER SERVING *49 cal., 1 g fat (trace sat. fat), 4 mg chol., 27 mg sodium, 9 g carb., 1 g fiber, 1 g pro.* **Diabetic** **Exchange:** *½ starch.*

BANANA DATE-NUT
MINI MUFFINS

GREEN CHILI
BREAKFAST BURRITOS

FAST FIX

Green Chili Breakfast Burritos

In the Southwest, we wrap everything in a tortilla. Breakfast burritos in every possible combination are very popular, especially those with green chilies.

—**ANGELA SPENGLER** CLOVIS, NM

START TO FINISH: 25 MIN.
MAKES: 6 SERVINGS

- 6 **eggs**
- 3 **egg whites**
- 1 **jalapeno pepper, seeded and minced**
  Dash cayenne pepper
- 4 **breakfast turkey sausage links, casings removed**
- ¾ **cup shredded reduced-fat Mexican cheese blend**
- 1 **can (4 ounces) chopped green chilies, drained**
- 6 **whole wheat tortillas (8 inches), warmed**
- 6 **tablespoons salsa**

1. In a small bowl, whisk the eggs, egg whites, jalapeno and cayenne; set aside.

2. Crumble sausage into a large skillet; cook over medium heat until no longer pink. Drain. Push sausage to the sides of pan. Pour egg mixture into center of pan. Cook and stir until set. Sprinkle with cheese and chilies. Remove from the heat; cover and let stand until cheese is melted.

3. Place ⅓ cup mixture off center on each tortilla. Fold sides and end over filling; roll up. Top with salsa.

NOTE *Wear disposable gloves when cutting hot peppers; the oils can burn skin. Avoid touching your face.*

PER SERVING *290 cal., 12 g fat (3 g sat. fat), 232 mg chol., 586 mg sodium, 25 g carb., 2 g fiber, 19 g pro.* **Diabetic Exchanges:** *2 medium-fat meat, 1½ starch.*

Ham & Egg Pita Pockets

I made these egg pockets when my kids were running late for school one morning and I needed a quick and healthy handheld breakfast. They come together in the microwave and are ready to eat in 10 minutes.

—SUE OLSEN FREMONT, CA

START TO FINISH: 10 MIN.
MAKES: 1 SERVING.

- 2 **egg whites**
- 1 **egg**
- ⅛ **teaspoon smoked or plain paprika**
- ⅛ **teaspoon freshly ground pepper**
- 1 **slice deli ham, chopped**
- 1 **green onion, sliced**
- 2 **tablespoons shredded reduced-fat cheddar cheese**
- 2 **whole wheat pita pocket halves**

In a microwave-safe bowl, whisk egg whites, egg, paprika and pepper until blended; stir in ham, green onion and cheese. Microwave, covered, on high for 1 minute. Stir; cook on high 30-60 seconds longer or until almost set. Serve in pitas.

NOTE *This recipe was tested in a 1,100-watt microwave.*

PER SERVING *323 cal., 10 g fat (4 g sat. fat), 231 mg chol., 769 mg sodium, 34 g carb., 5 g fiber, 27 g pro.*
Diabetic Exchanges: 3 lean meat, 2 starch.

C Spinach Pantry Souffle

We have always loved souffles, but I got tired of slaving over the white sauce. One day I substituted condensed soup for the white sauce, and we all thought it was great. When we started watching our fat intake, I switched to the reduced-fat, reduced-sodium soup, reduced-fat cheese and just two egg yolks, and it turned out amazing!

—DIANE CONRAD NORTH BEND, OR

PREP: 35 MIN. • **BAKE:** 30 MIN.
MAKES: 6 SERVINGS

- 6 **egg whites**
- 2 **tablespoons grated Parmesan cheese**
- 1 **can (10¾ ounces) reduced-fat reduced-sodium condensed cream of mushroom soup, undiluted**
- 1 **cup (4 ounces) shredded reduced-fat Mexican cheese blend**
- 1 **teaspoon ground mustard**
- 1 **package (10 ounces) frozen chopped spinach, thawed and squeezed dry**
- 2 **egg yolks, beaten**

1. Let egg whites stand at room temperature for 30 minutes. Coat a 2-qt. souffle dish with cooking spray and lightly sprinkle with Parmesan cheese; set aside.

2. In a small saucepan, combine the soup, cheese blend and mustard; cook and stir over medium heat for 5 minutes or until cheese is melted. Transfer to a large bowl; stir in spinach. Stir a small amount of soup mixture into egg yolks; return all to the bowl, stirring constantly.

3. In a small bowl with clean beaters, beat egg whites until stiff peaks form. With a spatula, stir a fourth of the egg whites into spinach mixture until no white streaks remain. Fold in remaining egg whites until combined. Transfer to prepared dish.

4. Bake at 375° for 30-35 minutes or until the top is puffed and center appears set. Serve immediately.

PER SERVING *140 cal., 8 g fat (3 g sat. fat), 90 mg chol., 453 mg sodium, 7 g carb., 1 g fiber, 12 g pro.*
Diabetic Exchanges: 2 medium-fat meat, ½ starch.

SPINACH PANTRY SOUFFLE

BAKED LONG JOHNS

2 eggs
¼ cup unsweetened applesauce
½ cup buttermilk
½ cup strong brewed coffee
1 tablespoon instant coffee granules
½ teaspoon vanilla extract
1 cup all-purpose flour
¾ cup whole wheat flour
1½ teaspoons baking powder
½ teaspoon baking soda
½ teaspoon ground cinnamon
¼ teaspoon salt
½ cup finely chopped pecans,
    divided *Choc. Chips*

1. Preheat oven to 375°. In a large bowl, beat butter and brown sugar until crumbly, about 2 minutes. Add the eggs; mix well. Beat in the applesauce. In a small bowl, whisk buttermilk, coffee, coffee granules and vanilla until granules are dissolved; gradually add to butter mixture.
2. In another bowl, whisk the flours, baking powder, baking soda, cinnamon and salt. Add to butter mixture; stir just until moistened. Fold in ¼ cup pecans.
3. Coat muffin cups with cooking spray or use paper liners; fill three-fourths full. Sprinkle with remaining pecans. Bake 15-20 minutes or until a toothpick inserted in center comes out clean. Cool 5 minutes before removing from pan to a wire rack. Serve warm.
PER SERVING *220 cal., 9 g fat (3 g sat. fat), 46 mg chol., 209 mg sodium, 33 g carb., 2 g fiber, 4 g pro.*
Diabetic Exchanges: *2 starch, 1½ fat.*

400° for loaf 45 min.

Baked Long Johns

Long Johns are a Saturday morning favorite for us. The tradition started with the doughnut pans I ordered from the *Taste of Home* Country Store years ago, and the recipe has evolved into this fantastic chocolate-glazed baked treat using mini loaf pans.
—**NICKI LAZORIK** MELLEN, WI

PREP: 15 MIN. • **BAKE:** 20 MIN. + COOLING
MAKES: 8 SERVINGS

2 cups all-purpose flour
½ cup sugar
2 teaspoons baking powder
½ teaspoon salt
¼ teaspoon ground cinnamon
2 eggs
¾ cup fat-free milk
1 tablespoon butter, melted
1 teaspoon vanilla extract
GLAZE
¾ cup semisweet chocolate chips
1 tablespoon butter
4½ teaspoons fat-free milk

1. In a small bowl, combine the flour, sugar, baking powder, salt and cinnamon. In another bowl, whisk the eggs, milk, butter and vanilla. Stir into dry ingredients just until moistened.
2. Transfer to eight 4½-in. x 2½-in. x 1½-in. loaf pans coated with cooking spray. Bake at 325° for 18-22 minutes or until golden brown. Immediately remove from the pans to a wire rack to cool completely.
3. In a microwave, melt chocolate chips and butter. Add milk; stir until smooth. Dip tops of Long Johns in glaze. Return to wire rack; let stand until set.
PER SERVING *291 cal., 9 g fat (5 g sat. fat), 61 mg chol., 298 mg sodium, 48 g carb., 2 g fiber, 6 g pro.*

FAST FIX

Good

Java Muffins

These muffins sure do get me going in the morning, and they're especially delicious with a good cup of coffee.
—**ZAINAB AHMED** MOUNTLAKE TERRACE, WA

START TO FINISH: 30 MIN.
MAKES: 1 DOZEN

¼ cup butter, softened
1 cup packed brown sugar

Banana Pancakes

My daughter Karen created these pancakes to add to our usual Sunday brunch spread. They have a rich banana flavor and have become a favorite in our house.

—KAREN GWILLIM STRASBOURG, , SK

START TO FINISH: 25 MIN.
MAKES: 10 PANCAKES

- 2 **cups all-purpose flour**
- 2 **tablespoons brown sugar**
- 1 **teaspoon baking soda**
- ½ **teaspoon salt**
- ½ **teaspoon ground cardamom**
- 2 **eggs, lightly beaten**
- 2 **cups buttermilk**
- 2 **tablespoons canola oil**
- 1 **teaspoon vanilla extract**
- 1 **small firm banana, finely chopped**

1. In a small bowl, combine the flour, brown sugar, baking soda, salt and cardamom. Combine the eggs, buttermilk, oil and vanilla; stir into dry ingredients just until moistened. Fold in banana.

BANANA PANCAKES

2. Pour batter by ¼ cupfuls onto a hot griddle coated with cooking spray. Turn when bubbles form on top; cook until second side is golden brown.
PER SERVING *342 cal., 9 g fat (2 g sat. fat), 89 mg chol., 619 mg sodium, 53 g carb., 2 g fiber, 11 g pro.*

Potato Egg Bake

I came up with this egg bake while vacationing with my family at our Michigan cabin. We had lots of leftover potatoes and veggies so this was my way of using them up. My husband commented that I'm always using friends as guinea pigs for my recipes, but everyone loved it!

—RENA CHARBONEAU GANSEVOORT, NY

PREP: 20 MIN. • **BAKE:** 35 MIN.
MAKES: 8 SERVINGS

- 2 **pounds Yukon Gold potatoes (about 6 medium), peeled and diced**
- ½ **cup water**
- 1 **cup frozen chopped broccoli, thawed**
- 6 **green onions, thinly sliced**
- 1 **small sweet red pepper, chopped**
- 6 **eggs**
- 8 **egg whites**
- 1 **cup (8 ounces) 1% cottage cheese**
- 1 **cup (4 ounces) shredded reduced-fat cheddar cheese**
- ½ **cup grated Parmesan cheese**
- ½ **cup fat-free milk**
- 2 **tablespoons dried parsley flakes**
- ½ **teaspoon salt**
- ¼ **teaspoon pepper**

1. Place potatoes and water in a microwave-safe dish. Cover and microwave on high for 7 minutes or until tender; drain.
2. Spread potatoes in a 13-in. x 9-in. baking dish coated with cooking spray.

POTATO EGG BAKE

Top with the broccoli, onions and red pepper.
3. In a large bowl, whisk the remaining ingredients until blended. Pour over vegetables. Bake, uncovered, at 350° for 35-40 minutes or until center is set.
PER SERVING *235 cal., 9 g fat (4 g sat. fat), 174 mg chol., 555 mg sodium, 20 g carb., 2 g fiber, 20 g pro.* **Diabetic Exchanges:** *2 medium-fat meat, 1 starch.*

top tip

Cardamom

Cardamom has a strong, spicy-sweet taste which is slightly aromatic. It tends to be more expensive than average spices, so a good substitution is a combination of equal parts cinnamon and nutmeg or cinnamon and ginger.

SAUSAGE PASTA WITH
VEGETABLES *PAGE 107*

**LORI ANN PANCHISIN'S
ZEUS BURGERS**

PAGE 100

**KENDRA KATT'S
CHICKEN VEGGIE WRAPS**
PAGE 113

**ELLEN FINGER'S
BARBECUED CHICKEN-STUFFED
POTATOES** *PAGE 120*

DINNER IN 30

DINNER IN 30

SAUSAGE PASTA WITH VEGETABLES *PAGE 107*

LORI ANN PANCHISIN'S ZEUS BURGERS
PAGE 100

KENDRA KATT'S CHICKEN VEGGIE WRAPS
PAGE 113

ELLEN FINGER'S BARBECUED CHICKEN-STUFFED POTATOES *PAGE 120*

Dinner in 30

You want **something quick.** You want **something healthy.** And you don't want a sandwich again. Here you'll find an exciting variety of dishes that **fit your needs**—fast!

FAST FIX▶

Chili Mac

Family and friends love this recipe. I use three power foods: tomatoes, black beans and olive oil, plus whole wheat pasta...it's comfort food to feel good about!

—**KRISSY BLACK** MT. VERNON, OH

START TO FINISH: 30 MIN.
MAKES: 6 SERVINGS

- 2 cups uncooked whole wheat elbow macaroni
- 1 pound lean ground turkey
- 1 small onion, chopped
- 2 to 3 jalapeno peppers, seeded and chopped
- 2 teaspoons olive oil
- 2 garlic cloves, minced
- 1 can (15 ounces) black beans, rinsed and drained
- 1 can (14½ ounces) diced tomatoes, undrained
- 1 can (8 ounces) tomato sauce
- 1 to 2 tablespoons hot pepper sauce
- 2 to 3 teaspoons chili powder
- 1 teaspoon ground cumin
- ¼ teaspoon cayenne pepper
- ¼ teaspoon pepper
- ¾ cup shredded reduced-fat cheddar cheese

1. Cook macaroni according to package directions. Meanwhile, in a large nonstick skillet coated with cooking spray, cook the turkey, onion and jalapenos in oil over medium heat until meat is no longer pink. Add garlic; cook 1 minute longer. Drain.
2. Add the beans, tomatoes, tomato sauce, pepper sauce and seasonings. Drain macaroni; stir into turkey mixture. Cook over medium-low heat for 5 minutes or until heated through.
3. Sprinkle with cheese. Remove from the heat; cover and let stand until cheese is melted.
NOTE *Wear disposable gloves when cutting hot peppers; the oils can burn skin. Avoid touching your face.*
PER SERVING *396 cal., 12 g fat (4 g sat. fat), 70 mg chol., 581 mg sodium, 45 g carb., 9 g fiber, 28 g pro.*
***Diabetic Exchanges:** 3 lean meat, 2½ starch, 1 vegetable, 1 fat.*

FAST FIX▶

Mexican Beans and Rice

This skillet supper is terrific for a cold or rainy day. It's easy, comforting and really fills the tummy. Sometimes I switch white rice for brown.

—**LORRAINE CALAND** SHUNIAH, ON

START TO FINISH: 30 MIN.
MAKES: 4 SERVINGS

- 1 tablespoon canola oil
- 2 celery ribs, chopped
- 1 medium green pepper, chopped
- 1 medium onion, chopped
- 1 can (28 ounces) diced tomatoes, undrained
- 1 can (16 ounces) kidney beans, rinsed and drained
- 2 cups cooked brown rice
- 2 teaspoons Worcestershire sauce
- 1½ teaspoons chili powder
- ¼ teaspoon pepper
- ¼ cup shredded cheddar cheese
- ¼ cup reduced-fat sour cream
- 2 green onions, chopped

1. In a large nonstick skillet, heat oil over medium-high heat. Add celery, green pepper and onion; cook and stir until tender.
2. Stir in the tomatoes, beans, rice, Worcestershire sauce, chili powder and pepper; bring to a boil. Reduce the heat; simmer, covered, 7-9 minutes or until heated through. Top with cheese, sour cream and green onions.
PER SERVING *354 cal., 8 g fat (3 g sat. fat), 13 mg chol., 549 mg sodium, 58 g carb., 12 g fiber, 15 g pro.*

Snappy Chicken Stir-Fry

Don't just reheat leftover chicken, stir-fry it up with some frozen vegetables (the ones you have hiding in your freezer) for a super-fast weeknight meal. We don't call this recipe snappy for nothing.

—TASTE OF HOME TEST KITCHEN

START TO FINISH: 30 MIN.
MAKES: 4 SERVINGS

- 3 tablespoons cornstarch
- 1½ cups reduced-sodium chicken broth
- 3 tablespoons reduced-sodium soy sauce
- ¾ teaspoon garlic powder
- ¾ teaspoon ground ginger
- ¼ teaspoon crushed red pepper flakes
- 1 package (16 ounces) frozen sugar snap stir-fry vegetable blend
- 1 tablespoon sesame or canola oil
- 2 cups cubed cooked chicken breast
- 2 cups hot cooked brown rice
- ¼ cup sliced almonds, toasted

1. In a small bowl, combine the cornstarch, broth, soy sauce, garlic powder, ginger and pepper flakes; set aside.

2. In a large skillet or wok, stir-fry vegetable blend in oil for 5-7 minutes or until the vegetables are tender.

3. Stir the cornstarch mixture and add to the pan. Bring to a boil; cook and stir for 2 minutes or until thickened. Add the chicken; heat through. Serve with rice; sprinkle with almonds.

PER SERVING *365 cal., 9 g fat (1 g sat. fat), 54 mg chol., 753 mg sodium, 39 g carb., 5 g fiber, 27 g pro.* **Diabetic Exchanges:** *3 lean meat, 2½ starch, 1 fat.*

SNAPPY CHICKEN STIR-FRY

Turkey Burgers with Mango Salsa

This is the cookout recipe that will have everyone talking. The secret is mixing a creamy, spreadable cheese into the turkey patties for a rich but not overpowering taste.

—NANCEE MELIN TUCSON, AZ

START TO FINISH: 30 MIN.
MAKES: 6 SERVINGS

- ½ cup dry bread crumbs
- ⅓ cup reduced-fat garlic-herb spreadable cheese
- 2 green onions, chopped
- 4½ teaspoons lemon juice
- 1½ teaspoons grated lemon peel
- 1 teaspoon minced fresh thyme or ¼ teaspoon dried thyme
- ½ teaspoon salt
- ½ teaspoon pepper
- 1½ pounds lean ground turkey
- 6 whole wheat hamburger buns, split
- ¾ cup mango salsa

1. In a large bowl, combine the first eight ingredients. Crumble turkey over mixture and mix well. Shape into six patties.

2. Moisten a paper towel with cooking oil; using long-handled tongs, lightly coat the grill rack. Grill burgers, covered, over medium heat or broil 4 in. from the heat for 4-6 minutes on each side or until a thermometer reads 165° and juices run clear.

3. Grill buns, uncovered, for 1-2 minutes or until toasted. Place burgers on bun bottoms. Top with salsa. Replace bun tops.

PER SERVING *359 cal., 14 g fat (4 g sat. fat), 98 mg chol., 825 mg sodium, 31 g carb., 4 g fiber, 26 g pro.* **Diabetic Exchanges:** *3 lean meat, 2 starch.*

TURKEY BURGERS WITH MANGO SALSA

Simple Sausage Pasta Toss

Italian turkey sausage is one of our favorite ingredients for adding bold flavor to a simple pasta dish. Try it on your next spaghetti night.

—TASTE OF HOME TEST KITCHEN

START TO FINISH: 30 MIN.
MAKES: 5 SERVINGS

- 8 **ounces uncooked multigrain spaghetti**
- ¼ **cup seasoned bread crumbs**
- 1 **teaspoon olive oil**
- ¾ **pound Italian turkey sausage links, cut into ½-inch slices**
- 1 **garlic clove, minced**
- 2 **cans (14½ ounces each) no-salt-added diced tomatoes, drained**
- 1 **can (2¼ ounces) sliced ripe olives, drained**

1. Cook spaghetti according to package directions. Meanwhile, in a small skillet, toast bread crumbs in oil over medium heat; remove from the heat and set aside.

2. In a large nonstick skillet, cook sausage over medium heat until no longer pink. Add the garlic; cook 1 minute longer. Stir in tomatoes and olives. Cook and stir until heated through. Drain the pasta; add to skillet. Sprinkle with the bread crumbs.

PER SERVING *340 cal., 10 g fat (2 g sat. fat), 41 mg chol., 689 mg sodium, 44 g carb., 6 g fiber, 21 g pro.* ***Diabetic Exchanges:*** *3 lean meat, 2 starch, 1 vegetable, ½ fat.*

Beef and Blue Cheese Penne with Pesto

Steak and cheese over pasta is a dinnertime dream for hearty eaters, and this healthy option packs in 9 grams of fiber per serving.

—FRANCES PIETSCH FLOWER MOUND, TX

START TO FINISH: 30 MIN.
MAKES: 4 SERVINGS

- 2 **cups uncooked whole wheat penne pasta**
- 2 **beef tenderloin steaks (6 ounces each)**
- ¼ **teaspoon salt**
- ¼ **teaspoon pepper**
- 6 **cups fresh baby spinach, chopped**
- 2 **cups grape tomatoes, halved**
- 5 **tablespoons prepared pesto**
- ¼ **cup chopped walnuts**
- ¼ **cup crumbled Gorgonzola cheese**

1. Cook the pasta according to package directions.

2. Meanwhile, sprinkle the steaks with salt and pepper. Grill steaks, covered, over medium heat or broil 4 in. from the heat for 5-7 minutes on each side or until the meat reaches desired doneness (for medium-rare, a thermometer should read 145°; medium, 160°; well-done, 170°).

3. Drain pasta and transfer to a large bowl. Add the spinach, tomatoes, pesto and walnuts; toss to coat. Thinly slice steaks. Divide pasta mixture among four serving plates. Top with beef; sprinkle with the cheese.

PER SERVING *532 cal., 22 g fat (6 g sat. fat), 50 mg chol., 434 mg sodium, 49 g carb., 9 g fiber, 35 g pro.*

BEEF AND BLUE CHEESE PENNE WITH PESTO

SASSY CHICKEN & PEPPERS

Hearty Turkey & Rice

We just love this dish, especially when we want a fast, yummy dinner. The sauce is also excellent on tortilla chips, which we serve on the side.

—JOAN HALLFORD

NORTH RICHLAND HILLS, TX

START TO FINISH: 25 MIN.
MAKES: 4 SERVINGS

- 1½ cups instant brown rice
- 1 pound extra-lean ground turkey
- 1 medium onion, chopped
- 1½ cups salsa
- 1 can (8 ounces) no-salt-added tomato sauce
- 1 teaspoon reduced-sodium chicken bouillon granules
- ¼ teaspoon salt
- ¼ cup shredded reduced-fat cheddar cheese
- ¼ cup reduced-fat sour cream
  Chopped tomatoes, baked tortilla chip scoops and sliced ripe olives, optional

1. Cook the rice according to package directions.

2. Meanwhile, in a large nonstick skillet coated with cooking spray, cook the turkey and onion over medium heat until meat is no longer pink. Add the salsa, tomato sauce, bouillon and salt; heat through.

3. Serve with rice; top with the cheese and sour cream. Garnish with tomatoes, chips and olives if desired.

PER SERVING *354 cal., 5 g fat (2 g sat. fat), 55 mg chol., 732 mg sodium, 40 g carb., 3 g fiber, 34 g pro.* **Diabetic Exchanges:** *4 lean meat, 2 starch, 2 vegetable, ½ fat.*

C **FAST FIX**

Sassy Chicken & Peppers

This quick chicken supper tastes like a naked taco and is bursting with fresh flavors. And it can all be prepared in the same pan for easy cleanup.

—DORIS HEATH FRANKLIN, NC

START TO FINISH: 25 MIN.
MAKES: 2 SERVINGS

- 2 boneless skinless chicken breast halves (4 ounces each)
- 2 teaspoons taco seasoning
- 4 teaspoons canola oil, divided
- 1 small onion, halved and sliced
- ½ small green bell pepper, julienned
- ½ small sweet red pepper, julienned
- ¼ cup salsa
- 1 tablespoon lime juice

1. Sprinkle the chicken with seasoning. In a small nonstick skillet, cook chicken in 2 teaspoons oil over medium heat for 4-5 minutes on each side or until juices run clear. Remove and keep warm.

2. Saute onion and peppers in remaining oil until crisp-tender; stir in salsa and lime juice. Spoon mixture over chicken.

PER SERVING *239 cal., 12 g fat (1 g sat. fat), 63 mg chol., 377 mg sodium, 8 g carb., 1 g fiber, 24 g pro.* **Diabetic Exchanges:** *3 lean meat, 2 fat, 1 vegetable.*

Easy Greek Pizza

I created this recipe when trying to use leftovers from a dinner party. If you prefer to go meatless, it's great without the chicken, too.

—JENNIFER BECK MERIDIAN, ID

START TO FINISH: 30 MIN.
MAKES: 6 SERVINGS

- 1 prebaked 12-inch pizza crust
- ½ cup pizza sauce
- 1 teaspoon lemon-pepper seasoning, divided
- 2 cups shredded cooked chicken breast
- 1½ cups chopped fresh spinach
- 1 small red onion, thinly sliced and separated into rings
- ¼ cup sliced ripe olives
- ¾ cup shredded part-skim mozzarella cheese
- ½ cup crumbled feta cheese

1. Place crust on an ungreased baking sheet; spread with the pizza sauce and sprinkle with ½ teaspoon lemon-pepper. Top with the chicken, spinach, onion, olives, cheeses and remaining lemon-pepper.
2. Bake at 450° for 12-15 minutes or until edges are lightly browned and cheese is melted.
PER SERVING *321 cal., 9 g fat (4 g sat. fat), 49 mg chol., 719 mg sodium, 32 g carb., 2 g fiber, 26 g pro.* **Diabetic Exchanges:** *3 lean meat, 2 starch, ½ fat.*

Chicken Tacos with Avocado Salsa

My family members have various food allergies. It's a blessing when I find a dish we can all enjoy. This one fits that requirement so it's a keeper for me.

—CHRISTINE SCHENHER EXETER, CA

START TO FINISH: 30 MIN.
MAKES: 4 SERVINGS

- 1 pound boneless skinless chicken breasts, cut into ½-inch strips
- ⅓ cup water
- 1 tablespoon chili powder
- 1 teaspoon sugar
- 1 teaspoon onion powder
- 1 teaspoon paprika
- 1 teaspoon ground cumin
- 1 teaspoon dried oregano
- ½ teaspoon salt
- ½ teaspoon garlic powder
- 1 medium ripe avocado, peeled and cubed
- 1 cup fresh or frozen corn
- 1 cup cherry tomatoes, quartered
- 2 teaspoons lime juice
- 8 taco shells, warmed

1. In a large nonstick skillet coated with cooking spray, brown chicken. Add the water, chili powder, sugar, onion powder, paprika, cumin, oregano, salt and garlic powder. Cook over medium heat for 5-6 minutes or until chicken is no longer pink, stirring occasionally.
2. Meanwhile, in small bowl, combine avocado, corn, tomatoes and lime juice. Spoon chicken mixture into taco shells; top with avocado salsa.
PER SERVING *354 cal., 15 g fat (3 g sat. fat), 63 mg chol., 474 mg sodium, 30 g carb., 6 g fiber, 27 g pro.* **Diabetic Exchanges:** *3 lean meat, 2 starch, 1 fat.*

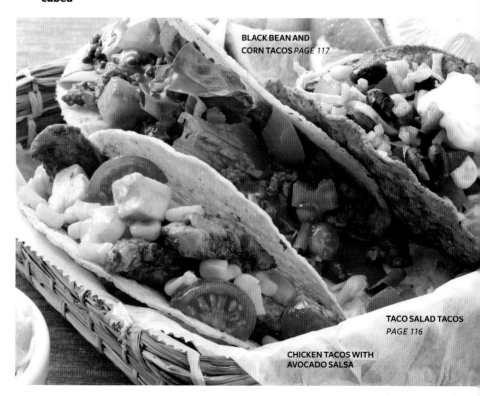

BLACK BEAN AND CORN TACOS *PAGE 117*

TACO SALAD TACOS *PAGE 116*

CHICKEN TACOS WITH AVOCADO SALSA

FAST FIX

Asian Pork Linguine

Peanut butter, ginger and honey make the sauce for this noodle toss. If I have fresh ginger, I grate a quarter of a teaspoon to use in place of ground.

—**LISA VARNER** EL PASO, TX

START TO FINISH: 30 MIN.
MAKES: 5 SERVINGS

- 6 ounces uncooked linguine
- 2 teaspoons cornstarch
- ½ cup water
- ¼ cup reduced-fat creamy peanut butter
- 2 tablespoons reduced-sodium soy sauce
- 1 tablespoon honey
- ½ teaspoon garlic powder
- ⅛ teaspoon ground ginger
- 1 pound boneless pork loin chops, cubed
- 3 teaspoons sesame oil, divided
- 2 medium carrots, sliced
- 1 medium onion, halved and sliced

1. Cook linguine according to package directions. For sauce, in a small bowl, combine cornstarch and water until smooth. Whisk in the peanut butter, soy sauce, honey, garlic powder and ginger until blended; set aside.
2. In a large nonstick skillet or wok coated with cooking spray, stir-fry pork in 2 teaspoons oil until no longer pink. Remove and keep warm. Stir-fry carrots and onion in remaining oil until crisp-tender. Stir the sauce and add to the pan. Bring to a boil; cook and stir for 2 minutes or until thickened.
3. Return pork to the pan. Drain linguine; add to the pan and stir to coat.
PER SERVING *376 cal., 13 g fat (3 g sat. fat), 44 mg chol., 358 mg sodium, 39 g carb., 3 g fiber, 27 g pro.*

FAST FIX

Scallops & Shrimp with Yellow Rice

I tasted a dish similar to this while vacationing in Bermuda years ago and wanted to duplicate it at home. I'm guessing my version is healthier than the one I had, but my husband and I just love it.

—**LILLIAN CHARVES** NEW BERN, NC

START TO FINISH: 30 MIN.
MAKES: 4 SERVINGS

- 1 large onion, chopped
- 1 tablespoon olive oil
- 1 garlic clove, minced
- 1 cup uncooked long grain rice
- ½ teaspoon ground turmeric
- 1 can (14½ ounces) reduced-sodium chicken broth
- ¾ cup water
- ½ pound uncooked medium shrimp, peeled and deveined
- ½ pound bay scallops
- 1 cup frozen peas
- ¼ teaspoon salt
- ⅛ teaspoon pepper

1. In a large nonstick skillet, saute onion in oil until tender. Add garlic; cook 1 minute longer. Add rice and turmeric; stir to coat. Stir in the broth and water. Bring to a boil. Reduce heat; cover and simmer for 15 minutes or until rice is tender.
2. Stir in remaining ingredients; return to a boil. Reduce heat; cover and simmer for 5 minutes or until shrimp turn pink.
PER SERVING *349 cal., 5 g fat (1 g sat. fat), 88 mg chol., 646 mg sodium, 48 g carb., 3 g fiber, 26 g pro.* **Diabetic Exchanges:** *3 starch, 3 lean meat, ½ fat.*

ASIAN PORK LINGUINE

FAST FIX ▶

Thai Chicken Pasta

Next time you're in the mood for something a little different, you'll know just what to make. Simply re-create your favorite Thai dish with what's in the pantry.

—JENI PITTARD COMMERCE, GA

START TO FINISH: 25 MIN.
MAKES: 2 SERVINGS

- 3 ounces uncooked multigrain linguine
- ½ cup salsa
- 2 tablespoons reduced-fat creamy peanut butter
- 1 tablespoon orange juice
- 1½ teaspoons honey
- 1 teaspoon reduced-sodium soy sauce
- 1 cup cubed cooked chicken breast
- 1 tablespoon chopped unsalted peanuts
- 1 tablespoon minced fresh cilantro

1. Cook linguine according to package directions.
2. Meanwhile, in a microwave-safe dish, combine the salsa, peanut butter, orange juice, honey and soy sauce. Cover and microwave on high for 1 minute; stir. Add the chicken; heat through.

3. Drain linguine. Serve with chicken mixture. Garnish with peanuts and cilantro.
NOTE *This recipe was tested in a 1,100-watt microwave.*
PER SERVING *409 cal., 10 g fat (2 g sat. fat), 54 mg chol., 474 mg sodium, 46 g carb., 6 g fiber, 33 g pro.*

top tip
Chicken at the Ready

I try to buy fresh chicken when it's on sale. I cook a big batch in the slow cooker, then shred it and package it in amounts suitable for recipes.
—JENI PITTARD COMMERCE, GA

DIJON PORK MEDALLIONS

C FAST FIX ▶

Dijon Pork Medallions

My husband likes anything with Dijon, so these quick-fix pork medallions are one of his favorites.

—JOYCE MOYNIHAN LAKEVILLE, MN

START TO FINISH: 20 MIN.
MAKES: 4 SERVINGS

- 1 pork tenderloin (1 pound)
- 1½ teaspoons lemon-pepper seasoning
- 2 tablespoons butter
- 2 tablespoons lemon juice
- 1 tablespoon Worcestershire sauce
- 1 teaspoon Dijon mustard
- 1 tablespoon minced fresh parsley

1. Cut the pork into eight slices; flatten to 1-in. thickness. Sprinkle with lemon-pepper. In a large nonstick skillet, cook pork in butter over medium heat for 3-4 minutes on each side or until tender. Remove and keep warm.
2. Stir lemon juice, Worcestershire sauce and mustard into skillet; heat through. Serve with pork; sprinkle with parsley.
PER SERVING *189 cal., 10 g fat (5 g sat. fat), 78 mg chol., 330 mg sodium, 2 g carb., trace fiber, 23 g pro.* **Diabetic Exchanges:** *3 lean meat, 1 fat.*

Salmon with Honey Pecan Sauce

You'll get an explosion of sweet and buttery flavors in every bite of this dish. In summer, sauteed zucchini makes the perfect side dish.

—**ALICE STANKO** WARREN, MI

START TO FINISH: 30 MIN.
MAKES: 4 SERVINGS

- 4 **salmon fillets (4 ounces each)**
- ½ **teaspoon seasoned salt**
- ¼ **teaspoon pepper**
- ¼ **cup finely chopped pecans, toasted**
- ¼ **cup honey**
- 3 **tablespoons reduced-fat butter**

1. Place salmon skin side down on a broiler pan; sprinkle with the seasoned salt and pepper. Broil 3-4 in. from the heat for 7-9 minutes or until fish flakes easily with a fork.
2. Meanwhile, in a small saucepan, cook the pecans, honey and butter

SALMON WITH HONEY PECAN SAUCE

over medium heat for 8-10 minutes or until bubbly. Serve with salmon.
NOTE *This recipe was tested with Land O'Lakes light stick butter.*
PER SERVING *330 cal., 20 g fat (5 g sat. fat), 68 mg chol., 319 mg sodium, 19 g carb., 1 g fiber, 20 g pro.* **Diabetic Exchanges:** *3 lean meat, 2½ fat, 1 starch.*

Zeus Burgers

I like to experiment with food, so I put together some common Greek ingredients and came up with this fantastic combination. These burgers are especially delicious with roasted-garlic ciabatta rolls!

—**LORI ANN PANCHISIN** HOLLY HILL, FL

START TO FINISH: 30 MIN.
MAKES: 4 SERVINGS

- 3 **tablespoons fat-free mayonnaise**
- 2 **teaspoons lemon juice**
- 1 **garlic clove, minced**
- ¼ **teaspoon dried oregano**
- ⅛ **teaspoon salt**

BURGERS

- ¼ **cup frozen chopped spinach, thawed and squeezed dry**
- ¼ **cup crumbled reduced-fat feta cheese**
- 2 **tablespoons lemon juice**
- 1 **tablespoon pine nuts, finely chopped**
- 1 **garlic clove, minced**
- 1 **teaspoon dried oregano**
- ¼ **teaspoon salt**
- ¼ **teaspoon pepper**
- 1 **pound lean ground beef (90% lean)**
- 4 **hamburger buns, split**

ZEUS BURGERS

1. In a small bowl, combine the mayonnaise, lemon juice, garlic, oregano and salt. Cover and refrigerate until serving.
2. In a large bowl, combine the spinach, cheese, lemon juice, pine nuts, garlic, oregano, salt and pepper. Crumble the beef over mixture and mix well. Shape into four patties.
3. Using long-handled tongs, moisten a paper towel with cooking oil and lightly coat the grill rack. Grill burgers, covered, over medium heat or broil 4 in. from the heat for 5-7 minutes on each side or until a thermometer reads 160° and juices run clear.
4. Toast the buns on for 1 minute or until lightly browned. Serve the burgers on the buns with the reserved sauce.
PER SERVING *335 cal., 13 g fat (5 g sat. fat), 73 mg chol., 669 mg sodium, 26 g carb., 2 g fiber, 28 g pro.*

Bow Ties with Walnut-Herb Pesto

I can't resist pasta, so I eat it once a week. I developed a recipe that isn't loaded with fat and extra calories...and it's done in just 20 minutes!

—DIANE NEMITZ LUDINGTON, MI

START TO FINISH: 20 MIN.
MAKES: 6 SERVINGS

- 4 **cups uncooked whole wheat bow tie pasta**
- 1 **cup fresh arugula**
- ½ **cup packed fresh parsley sprigs**
- ½ **cup loosely packed basil leaves**
- ¼ **cup grated Parmesan cheese**
- ½ **teaspoon salt**
- ⅛ **teaspoon crushed red pepper flakes**
- ¼ **cup chopped walnuts**
- ⅓ **cup olive oil**
- 1 **plum tomato, seeded and chopped**

1. Cook the pasta according to package directions.
2. Meanwhile, place the arugula, parsley, basil, cheese, salt and pepper flakes in a food processor; cover and pulse until chopped. Add the walnuts; cover and process until blended. While processing, gradually add oil in a steady stream.
3. Drain the pasta, reserving 3 tablespoons cooking water. In a large bowl, toss pasta with pesto, tomato and reserved water.
PER SERVING *323 cal., 17 g fat (3 g sat. fat), 3 mg chol., 252 mg sodium, 34 g carb., 6 g fiber, 10 g pro.* **Diabetic Exchanges:** *2½ fat, 2 starch.*

Cantaloupe Chicken Salad with Yogurt Chive Dressing

It's hard to find a dish that my four children and husband will all enjoy. That's why this refreshing combination of melon and chicken is so special to us.

—BETSY KING DULUTH, MN

START TO FINISH: 30 MIN.
MAKES: 5 SERVINGS

- ½ **cup plain yogurt**
- ½ **cup reduced-fat mayonnaise**
- 1 **tablespoon minced chives**
- 1 **tablespoon lime juice**
- ¼ **teaspoon salt**

- 5 **cups cubed cantaloupe**
- 2½ **cups cubed cooked chicken breast**
- 1 **medium cucumber, seeded and chopped**
- 1 **cup green grapes, halved**

In a large bowl, combine the first five ingredients. Add cantaloupe, chicken, cucumber and grapes; toss gently to combine. Cover and refrigerate until serving.
PER SERVING *290 cal., 11 g fat (2 g sat. fat), 65 mg chol., 380 mg sodium, 24 g carb., 2 g fiber, 24 g pro.* **Diabetic Exchanges:** *3 lean meat, 1½ fruit, 1 fat.*

CANTALOUPE CHICKEN SALAD WITH YOGURT CHIVE DRESSING

FAST FIX

Pork Chops with Cherry Sauce

Port wine and cherries make a rich-tasting sauce for these chops. This flavorful dinner certainly doesn't taste like it was prepared in under 30 minutes.

—KENDRA DOSS COLORADO SPRINGS, CO

START TO FINISH: 25 MIN.
MAKES: 2 SERVINGS

- 1 tablespoon finely chopped shallot
- 1 teaspoon olive oil
- 1 cup fresh or frozen pitted dark sweet cherries, halved
- ⅓ cup ruby port wine
- 1 teaspoon balsamic vinegar
- ⅛ teaspoon salt

PORK CHOPS

- 1 teaspoon coriander seeds, crushed
- ¾ teaspoon ground mustard
- ¼ teaspoon salt
- ¼ teaspoon pepper
- 2 bone-in pork loin chops (7 ounces each)
- 2 teaspoons olive oil

1. In a small saucepan, saute the shallot in oil until tender. Stir in the cherries, wine, vinegar and salt. Bring to a boil; cook until liquid is reduced by half, about 10 minutes.

2. Meanwhile, in a small bowl, combine coriander, mustard, salt and pepper; rub over chops. In a large skillet, cook chops in oil over medium heat for 4-5 minutes on each side or until a thermometer reads 145°. Let stand for 5 minutes. Serve with sauce.

PER SERVING *356 cal., 16 g fat (4 g sat. fat), 86 mg chol., 509 mg sodium, 16 g carb., 2 g fiber, 32 g pro.* **Diabetic Exchanges:** *4 lean meat, 1½ fat, 1 fruit.*

FAST FIX

Easy Chicken Broccoli Pasta

In a pinch, this is the recipe I turn to for a quick, throw-together Alfredo that's high in protein and full of veggies. You could also use whole-wheat penne for more fiber.

—RENEE PAJESTKA BRUNSWICK, OH

START TO FINISH: 25 MIN.
MAKES: 4 SERVINGS

- 2 cups uncooked penne pasta
- 2 cups frozen broccoli florets
- 1 pound boneless skinless chicken breasts, cut into 1-inch cubes
- ¼ teaspoon salt
- ¼ teaspoon pepper
- 1 tablespoon canola oil
- 1 small sweet red pepper, chopped
- ½ cup white wine or reduced-sodium chicken broth
- 1 cup reduced-fat Alfredo sauce

1. Cook the pasta according to package directions, adding the broccoli during the last 5 minutes of cooking.

2. Meanwhile, sprinkle chicken with salt and pepper. In a large nonstick skillet, saute chicken in oil until lightly browned. Add pepper; saute 3-5 minutes longer or until chicken is no longer pink and pepper is tender.

3. Drain pasta mixture; add to the pan. Reduce heat to low. Stir in the wine, then Alfredo sauce; cook and stir until heated through.

PER SERVING *400 cal., 13 g fat (5 g sat. fat), 88 mg chol., 654 mg sodium, 33 g carb., 2 g fiber, 31 g pro.*

PORK CHOPS WITH CHERRY SAUCE

Taco Pita Pizzas

Friday nights are pizza night at our house. This lighter alternative of the taco pizza at a place in town is our favorite!

—**JOANNE WILTZ** SANTEE, CA

START TO FINISH: 25 MIN.
MAKES: 4 SERVINGS

- 1 **pound lean ground turkey**
- ⅓ **cup finely chopped onion**
- 1 **can (4 ounces) chopped green chilies, drained**
- 4 **whole wheat pita breads (6 inches)**
- 1 **cup salsa**
- 1 **cup (4 ounces) shredded reduced-fat Mexican cheese blend**
- 1 **cup shredded lettuce**
- 1 **medium tomato, seeded and chopped**

1. In a large skillet, cook turkey and onion over medium heat until the meat is no longer pink; drain. Stir in the chilies. Place pitas on an ungreased baking sheet.

2. Spread 2 tablespoons salsa over each pita. Top with turkey mixture; sprinkle with cheese. Bake at 400° for 5-10 minutes or until cheese is melted. Serve with lettuce, tomato and remaining salsa.

PER SERVING *459 cal., 17 g fat (6 g sat. fat), 110 mg chol., 1,006 mg sodium, 45 g carb., 6 g fiber, 35 g pro.* **Diabetic Exchanges:** *4 lean meat, 2 starch, 2 vegetable, 1 fat.*

Orange Salmon with Sauteed Spinach

I love orange marmalade and wanted a lighter version of orange salmon without a heavy spice rub or brown sugar. What a rewarding outcome this was.

—**JANET CAICO** HILLSBOROUGH, NC

START TO FINISH: 30 MIN.
MAKES: 4 SERVINGS

- 4 **salmon fillets (4 ounces each)**
- ¼ **teaspoon plus ⅛ teaspoon pepper, divided**
- ¼ **teaspoon salt, divided**
- ½ **cup orange marmalade spreadable fruit**
- 2 **tablespoons half-and-half cream**
- 2 **tablespoons reduced-sodium soy sauce**
- 1 **tablespoon minced fresh gingerroot**
- 4½ **teaspoons plus 1 tablespoon reduced-fat butter, divided**
- 2 **garlic cloves, minced**
- 1 **tablespoon olive oil**
- 1 **package (6 ounces) fresh baby spinach**

1. Sprinkle the salmon with ¼ teaspoon pepper and ⅛ teaspoon salt; set aside.

2. In a saucepan, mix marmalade, cream, soy sauce, ginger and 4½ teaspoons butter. Bring to a boil. Reduce the heat; simmer, uncovered, until slightly thickened, about 5 minutes; set aside.

3. Moisten a paper towel with cooking oil; using long-handled tongs, lightly coat the grill rack. Place salmon skin side down on grill rack. Grill, covered, over medium heat or broil 4 in. from the heat for 10-12 minutes or until fish flakes easily with a fork.

4. In a large skillet, saute the garlic in oil and remaining butter for 1 minute. Add the spinach and

ORANGE SALMON WITH SAUTEED SPINACH

remaining salt and pepper; cook for 4-5 minutes or until spinach is wilted. Divide spinach among four plates; top each with salmon. Drizzle with marmalade sauce.

PER SERVING *346 cal., 19 g fat (5 g sat. fat), 70 mg chol., 604 mg sodium, 24 g carb., 1 g fiber, 21 g pro.* **Diabetic Exchanges:** *3 lean meat, 2 fat, 1½ starch, 1 vegetable.*

The Perfect Pair for Iron

Iron plays a role in immunity, energy and body temperature, and it comes in two forms: heme and non-heme. Pairing foods with heme iron (salmon, red meat, chicken) with foods rich in non-heme iron (spinach) helps boost iron absorption.

SOUTHWESTERN
CHICKEN SALAD

FAST FIX

Southwestern Chicken Salad

Creative and colorful ingredients make this fresh-tasting dish really stand out. Mix up your salad with tropical fruits seasoned with Southwestern spices.

—JEANNE HOLT MENDOTA HEIGHTS, MN

START TO FINISH: 30 MIN.
MAKES: 6 SERVINGS

- ½ cup orange juice
- 2 tablespoons olive oil
- 1 tablespoon minced fresh cilantro
- 1 tablespoon lime juice
- 1 tablespoon jalapeno pepper jelly
- 1 tablespoon honey
- ¼ teaspoon ground cumin
- 2½ cups cubed cooked chicken breast
- 1 can (15 ounces) black beans, rinsed and drained
- 1 cup cubed peeled mango
- ⅔ cup julienned sweet red pepper
- ⅔ cup julienned peeled jicama
- 4 green onions, chopped
- 3 cups fresh baby spinach
- 3 cups torn mixed salad greens
- ⅓ cup pepitas or salted pumpkin seeds

1. For dressing, in a small bowl, whisk the first seven ingredients. In a large bowl, combine the chicken, beans, mango, red pepper, jicama and onions. Drizzle with dressing and toss to coat. Chill for at least 10 minutes.

2. Just before serving, toss chicken mixture with spinach and salad greens. Sprinkle with pepitas.

PER SERVING *314 cal., 12 g fat (2 g sat. fat), 45 mg chol., 266 mg sodium, 28 g carb., 6 g fiber, 26 g pro.* **Diabetic Exchanges:** *3 lean meat, 2 fat, 1 starch, 1 vegetable, ½ fruit.*

C FAST FIX

Jerk Turkey Tenderloins

The salsa for the tenderloins is best with fresh pineapple; however, on particularly busy days, I have used canned pineapple tidbits in an effort to speed up the preparation.

—HOLLY BAUER WEST BEND, WI

START TO FINISH: 30 MIN.
MAKES: 5 SERVINGS (2 CUPS SALSA)

- 1 package (20 ounces) turkey breast tenderloins
- ½ teaspoon seasoned salt
- 2 tablespoons olive oil
- 1 tablespoon dried rosemary, crushed
- 1 tablespoon Caribbean jerk seasoning
- 1 tablespoon brown sugar

SALSA

- 1½ cups cubed fresh pineapple
- 1 medium sweet red pepper, chopped
- ¼ cup chopped red onion
- ¼ cup minced fresh cilantro
- 1 jalapeno pepper, seeded and minced
- 2 tablespoons lime juice
- 2 garlic cloves, minced
- ¼ teaspoon salt
- ⅛ teaspoon pepper

1. Sprinkle tenderloins with seasoned salt. Combine the oil, rosemary, jerk seasoning and brown sugar. Rub over tenderloins. Broil 3-4 in. from the heat for 7-9 minutes on each side or until a meat thermometer reads 165°.

2. Meanwhile, in a large bowl, combine the salsa ingredients. Serve with turkey.

NOTE *Substitute a fruity salsa from the deli for the homemade salsa. Wear disposable gloves when cutting hot peppers; the oils can burn skin. Avoid touching your face.*

PER SERVING *216 cal., 7 g fat (1 g sat. fat), 56 mg chol., 503 mg sodium, 12 g carb., 2 g fiber, 27 g pro.* **Diabetic Exchanges:** *3 lean meat, 1 vegetable, 1 fat, ½ fruit.*

JERK TURKEY
TENDERLOINS

Honey Mustard Pork

Dijon mustard and honey create a sweet and subtly tangy sauce that perfectly complements lean pork tenderloin.

—JANET LES CHILLIWACK, BC

START TO FINISH: 30 MIN.
MAKES: 4 SERVINGS

- 1 **pound pork tenderloin, cut into thin strips**
- 1 **tablespoon canola oil**
- 1 **cup reduced-sodium beef broth, divided**
- ¼ **cup honey**
- 1 **tablespoon Dijon mustard**
- 1 **tablespoon cornstarch**
- 2 **tablespoons cold water**
  Hot cooked long grain and wild rice, optional

1. In a large nonstick skillet, brown the pork in oil on all sides. Add ½ cup broth. Bring to a boil. Reduce heat; cover and simmer for 10 minutes or until meat is tender. Remove pork with a slotted spoon and keep warm.
2. Stir in the honey, mustard and remaining broth. Combine the cornstarch and water until smooth. Gradually stir into the pan. Bring to a boil; cook and stir for 2 minutes or until thickened. Return pork to the pan; heat through. Serve with rice if desired.

PER SERVING *242 cal., 7 g fat (2 g sat. fat), 64 mg chol., 246 mg sodium, 20 g carb., trace fiber, 23 g pro.* **Diabetic Exchanges:** *3 lean meat, 1 starch, 1 fat.*

CHICKEN SOBA NOODLE TOSS

Chicken Soba Noodle Toss

This is one of my favorite meals for busy weeknights. You can prep all the ingredients the day before and then put the dish together in minutes.

—ELIZABETH BROWN LOWELL, MA

START TO FINISH: 30 MIN.
MAKES: 4 SERVINGS

- 2 **teaspoons cornstarch**
- ½ **cup reduced-sodium chicken broth**
- 2 **tablespoons brown sugar**
- 3 **garlic cloves, minced**
- 1 **tablespoon butter, melted**
- 1 **tablespoon reduced-sodium soy sauce**
- 1 **tablespoon hoisin sauce**
- 2 **teaspoons minced fresh gingerroot**
- 2 **teaspoons rice vinegar**
- ¼ **teaspoon pepper**
- 6 **ounces uncooked Japanese soba noodles**
- ¾ **pound chicken tenderloins, cubed**
- 4 **teaspoons canola oil, divided**
- 3 **cups fresh broccoli stir-fry blend**
- ¼ **cup chopped unsalted cashews**

1. In a small bowl, combine the first 10 ingredients until blended; set aside.
2. Cook the noodles according to package directions. Meanwhile, in a large skillet or wok, stir-fry the chicken in 2 teaspoons oil until no longer pink. Remove; keep warm.
3. Stir-fry the broccoli blend in remaining oil for 4-6 minutes or until vegetables are crisp-tender.
4. Stir cornstarch mixture and add to the pan. Bring to a boil; cook and stir for 2 minutes or until thickened. Drain noodles; add to pan. Add chicken; heat through. Sprinkle with cashews.

PER SERVING *417 cal., 12 g fat (3 g sat. fat), 58 mg chol., 715 mg sodium, 52 g carb., 2 g fiber, 30 g pro.*

C FAST FIX
Baked Cod Piccata with Asparagus

It takes longer for the oven to preheat than it does to prepare this delicious, good-for-you dish. While it's baking, I throw together a quick salad.

—BARBARA LENTO HOUSTON, PA

START TO FINISH: 30 MIN.
MAKES: 4 SERVINGS

- 1 **pound fresh asparagus, trimmed**
- ¼ **cup water**
- 1 **pound cod fillet, cut into four pieces**
- 2 **tablespoons lemon juice**
- 1 **teaspoon salt-free lemon-pepper seasoning**
- ½ **teaspoon garlic powder**
- 2 **tablespoons butter, cubed**
- 2 **teaspoons capers**
  Minced fresh parsley, optional

1. Place asparagus in an ungreased 11-in. x 7-in. baking dish; add water. Arrange cod over asparagus. Sprinkle with lemon juice, lemon-pepper and garlic powder. Dot with butter; sprinkle with capers.
2. Bake, uncovered, at 400° for 12-15 minutes or until the fish flakes easily with a fork and asparagus is tender. If desired, sprinkle with parsley.
PER SERVING *150 cal., 7 g fat (4 g sat. fat), 58 mg chol., 265 mg sodium, 3 g carb., 1 g fiber, 20 g pro. Diabetic Exchanges: 3 lean meat, 1 fat.*

BAKED COD PICCATA WITH ASPARAGUS

FAST FIX
Chicken Chow Mein

When we go out for Chinese food, my husband always orders chicken chow mein. I created this recipe to make at home, only I use richer-flavored tamari sauce rather than soy.

—BETH DAUENHAUER PUEBLO, CO

START TO FINISH: 30 MIN.
MAKES: 2 SERVINGS

- 1 **tablespoon cornstarch**
- ⅔ **cup reduced-sodium chicken broth**
- 1 **teaspoon reduced-sodium soy sauce**
- ½ **teaspoon salt**
- ¼ **teaspoon ground ginger**
- ¼ **pound sliced fresh mushrooms**
- ⅔ **cup thinly sliced celery**
- ¼ **cup sliced onion**
- ¼ **cup thinly sliced green pepper**
- 2 **tablespoons julienned carrot**
- 1 **teaspoon canola oil**
- 1 **garlic clove, minced**
- 1 **cup cubed cooked chicken breast**
- 1 **cup cooked brown rice**
- 2 **tablespoons chow mein noodles**

CHICKEN CHOW MEIN

1. In a small bowl, combine the cornstarch, broth, soy sauce, salt and ginger until smooth; set aside.
2. In a large skillet or wok, stir-fry mushrooms, celery, onion, pepper and carrot in oil for 5 minutes. Add garlic; stir-fry 1-2 minutes longer or until vegetables are crisp-tender.
3. Stir cornstarch mixture and add to the pan. Bring to a boil; cook and stir for 2 minutes or until thickened. Add the chicken; heat through. Serve with rice; sprinkle with chow mein noodles.
PER SERVING *307 cal., 7 g fat (1 g sat. fat), 54 mg chol., 984 mg sodium, 35 g carb., 4 g fiber, 27 g pro. Diabetic Exchanges: 3 lean meat, 2 starch, 1 vegetable, ½ fat.*

FAST FIX ▶

Sausage Pasta with Vegetables

I made this tempting pasta for my pastor and his family. They loved it so much we nicknamed it Jason's Pasta. It's a sneaky way to get kids and adults alike to eat more veggies.

—**SUZIE FOUTTY** MANSFIELD, OH

START TO FINISH: 25 MIN.
MAKES: 4 SERVINGS

- 2 **cups uncooked whole wheat penne pasta**
- 1 **pound Italian turkey sausage links, casings removed**
- 1¾ **cups sliced fresh mushrooms**
- 1 **can (14½ ounces) fire-roasted diced tomatoes with garlic, undrained**
- 1 **package (6 ounces) fresh baby spinach**
- ¼ **cup shredded part-skim mozzarella cheese**

1. Cook the penne according to package directions.
2. Meanwhile, in a Dutch oven, cook sausage and mushrooms over medium heat until meat is no longer pink; drain. Stir in tomatoes; bring to a boil. Add spinach; cook and stir until spinach is wilted.
3. Drain pasta; stir into turkey mixture. Sprinkle with cheese; remove from the heat. Cover and let stand until cheese is melted.
PER SERVING *445 cal., 13 g fat (3 g sat. fat), 72 mg chol., 1,020 mg sodium, 51 g carb., 8 g fiber, 32 g pro.*

FAST FIX ▶

Curried Chicken Paninis

If there's leftover chutney from the paninis, I serve it with chicken or pork tenderloin, or with fat-free cream cheese as a cracker spread.

—**MICHAELA ROSENTHAL**

WOODLAND HILLS, CA

START TO FINISH: 20 MIN.
MAKES: 4 SERVINGS

- 2 **cups cubed cooked chicken breast**
- ¼ **cup chopped celery**
- ¼ **cup fat-free mayonnaise**
- ¾ **teaspoon curry powder**
- ¼ **teaspoon grated lemon peel**
- 8 **slices whole wheat bread**
- ⅓ **cup mango chutney**
- 1 **cup watercress or fresh arugula**
- 2 **tablespoons butter, softened**

1. In a small bowl, combine the first five ingredients.
2. Spread four bread slices with chutney. Layer each with ½ cup chicken salad and ¼ cup watercress; top with remaining bread. Spread outsides of sandwiches with butter.
3. Cook on a panini maker or indoor grill for 3-4 minutes or until bread is browned.
PER SERVING *389 cal., 10 g fat (5 g sat. fat), 71 mg chol., 705 mg sodium, 44 g carb., 4 g fiber, 28 g pro. Diabetic Exchanges: 3 starch, 3 lean meat, 1½ fat.*

CURRIED CHICKEN PANINIS

CHICKEN SAUSAGES
WITH PEPPER

¼ teaspoon salt
¼ teaspoon pepper
½ cup minced fresh cilantro
Lime wedges, optional

1. Soak the noodles according to package directions. Meanwhile, in a large dry skillet over medium heat, toast curry powder until aromatic, about 1-2 minutes. Stir in the coconut milk, shrimp, salt and pepper. Bring to a boil. Reduce heat; simmer, uncovered, for 5-6 minutes or until shrimp turn pink.
2. Drain noodles; add to pan. Stir in cilantro; heat through. Serve with lime wedges if desired.
PER SERVING *361 cal., 9 g fat (5 g sat. fat), 138 mg chol., 284 mg sodium, 44 g carb., 2 g fiber, 22 g pro.* **Diabetic Exchanges:** *3 lean meat, 2½ starch, 1 fat.*

C ❘ **FAST FIX** ▶

Chicken Sausages with Peppers

Apple-chicken sausage is our favorite flavor. This low-calorie dish doesn't skimp on the bold, savory flavors you expect from a entree that includes sausage.
—**DEBORAH SCHAEFER** DURAND, MI

START TO FINISH: 30 MIN.
MAKES: 4 SERVINGS

1 small onion, halved and sliced
1 small sweet orange pepper, julienned
1 small sweet red pepper, julienned
1 tablespoon olive oil
1 garlic clove, minced
1 package (12 ounces) fully cooked apple chicken sausage links or flavor of your choice, cut into 1-inch pieces

In a large nonstick skillet, saute onion and peppers in oil until crisp-tender. Add garlic; cook 1 minute longer. Stir in sausages; heat through.

PER SERVING *208 cal., 11 g fat (2 g sat. fat), 60 mg chol., 483 mg sodium, 14 g carb., 1 g fiber, 15 g pro.* **Diabetic Exchanges:** *2 lean meat, 1 vegetable, ½ starch, ½ fat.*

FAST FIX ▶

Thai Shrimp Pasta

I came up with this recipe when my son was home from the Navy. He loves Thai food and I wanted to make something special but simple. There wasn't a noodle left in the bowl!
—**JANA RIPPEE** CASA GRANDE, AZ

START TO FINISH: 30 MIN.
MAKES: 4 SERVINGS

8 ounces thin flat rice noodles
3 teaspoons curry powder
1 can (13.66 ounces) light coconut milk
1 pound uncooked medium shrimp, peeled and deveined

Use Your Noodle

Rice noodles come in a variety of thicknesses, similar to Italian pastas like fettuccini, linguine and vermicelli. The linguine-style thin, flat noodles used in the Thai Shrimp Pasta recipe are usually soaked in hot water for 8-10 minutes, then the noodles are drained and used in stir-fries, salads and soups.

Spanish Rice Supper

My mom made Spanish Rice when I was growing up, and now it's in the rotation for my family meals. It's one of the few that both of my kids love!

—**CATHY FLIKKEMA** SALT LAKE CITY, UT

START TO FINISH: 30 MIN.
MAKES: 6 SERVINGS

- 1 **pound lean ground beef (90% lean)**
- 3 **cups instant brown rice**
- 1 **can (29 ounces) tomato puree**
- 1½ **cups water**
- 1 **can (4 ounces) chopped green chilies**
- 1 **can (2¼ ounces) sliced ripe olives, drained**
- 1 **envelope chili seasoning**
- ½ **cup shredded reduced-fat cheddar cheese**

1. In a large skillet, cook beef over medium heat until no longer pink; drain. Stir in rice, tomato puree, water, chilies, olives and chili seasoning. Bring to a boil. Reduce heat; cover and simmer for 10-12 minutes or until rice is tender.

2. Remove from the heat. Sprinkle with cheese; cover and let stand until cheese is melted.

PER SERVING *380 cal., 10 g fat (4 g sat. fat), 44 mg chol., 741 mg sodium, 47 g carb., 4 g fiber, 24 g pro.*

Gourmet Deli Turkey Wraps

These wraps are a staple for my family. They're easy, incredibly delicious and can be served for dinner or lunch or sliced to make appetizers.

—**TAMARA HANSON** BIG LAKE, MN

START TO FINISH: 15 MIN.
MAKES: 6 SERVINGS

- 2 **tablespoons water**
- 2 **tablespoons red wine vinegar**
- 1 **tablespoon olive oil**
- ⅛ **teaspoon pepper**
- ¾ **pound sliced deli turkey**
- 6 **flour tortillas (8 inches), room temperature**
- 4 **cups spring mix salad greens**
- 2 **medium pears, peeled and sliced**
- 6 **tablespoons crumbled blue cheese**
- 6 **tablespoons dried cranberries**
- ¼ **cup chopped walnuts**

In a small bowl, whisk the water, vinegar, oil and pepper. Divide the turkey among tortillas; top with the salad greens, pears, cheese, cranberries and walnuts. Drizzle with dressing. Roll up tightly. Secure with toothpicks.

PER SERVING *330 cal., 11 g fat (2 g sat. fat), 25 mg chol., 819 mg sodium, 44 g carb., 3 g fiber, 17 g pro.*

GOURMET DELI
TURKEY WRAPS

F FAST FIX
Mustard Turkey Cutlets

Loaded with protein, turkey cutlets are low in fat and fast to the table. Fragrant rosemary perks up the apple juice, and the Dijon cuts the sweetness in the glaze, offering a delightful blend of flavors.

—DEB WILLIAMS PEORIA, AZ

START TO FINISH: 25 MIN.
MAKES: 4 SERVINGS

- 2 teaspoons cornstarch
- ½ teaspoon salt, divided
- ⅛ teaspoon plus ¼ teaspoon pepper, divided
- ½ cup thawed apple juice concentrate
- ¼ cup Dijon mustard
- 1½ tablespoons minced fresh rosemary or 1½ teaspoons dried rosemary, crushed
- 1 package (17.6 ounces) turkey breast cutlets
- 1 teaspoon olive oil

1. In a small saucepan, combine the cornstarch, ¼ teaspoon salt and ⅛ teaspoon pepper. Gradually whisk in the concentrate, mustard and rosemary until blended. Cook and stir over medium-high heat until thickened and bubbly. Reduce heat; cook and stir 2 minutes longer. Set aside ¼ cup sauce.
2. Brush turkey with oil; sprinkle with remaining salt and pepper. Using long-handled tongs, moisten a paper towel with cooking oil and lightly coat the grill rack.
3. Grill, covered, over medium heat or broil 4 in. from the heat for 2-3 minutes on each side or until no longer pink, basting occasionally with remaining sauce. Brush with reserved sauce before serving.
PER SERVING *230 cal., 2 g fat (trace sat. fat), 77 mg chol., 725 mg sodium, 19 g carb., trace fiber, 31 g pro.* **Diabetic Exchanges:** *4 lean meat, 1 starch.*

SOUTHWEST FLANK STEAK

MUSTARD TURKEY CUTLETS

S C FAST FIX
Southwest Flank Steak

A perfectly balanced rub imparts the flavor of an hours-long marinade without the waiting time. Leftovers are great for topping Caesar salads.

—KENNY FISHER LANCASTER, OH

START TO FINISH: 25 MIN.
MAKES: 6 SERVINGS

- 3 tablespoons brown sugar
- 3 tablespoons chili powder
- 4½ teaspoons ground cumin
- 1 tablespoon garlic powder
- 1 tablespoon cider vinegar
- 1½ teaspoons Worcestershire sauce
- ½ teaspoon cayenne pepper
- 1 beef flank steak (1½ pounds)

1. In a small bowl, combine the first seven ingredients; rub over the steak.
2. Moisten a paper towel with cooking oil; using long-handled tongs, lightly coat the grill rack. Grill steak, covered, over medium heat or broil 4 in. from the heat for 6-8 minutes on each side or until meat reaches desired doneness (for medium-rare, a thermometer should read 145°; medium, 160°; well-done, 170°).
3. Let stand for 5 minutes. To serve, thinly slice across the grain.
PER SERVING *219 cal., 9 g fat (4 g sat. fat), 54 mg chol., 127 mg sodium, 11 g carb., 2 g fiber, 23 g pro.* **Diabetic Exchanges:** *3 lean meat, 1 starch.*

Turkey & Swiss Quesadillas

My favorite sandwich is turkey with avocado, so I created this healthy quesadilla with the ingredients I have in the fridge and pantry.

—**KAREN O'SHEA** SPARKS, NV

START TO FINISH: 20 MIN.
MAKES: 2 SERVINGS

- 2 tablespoons reduced-fat Parmesan peppercorn ranch salad dressing
- 1 tablespoon Dijon mustard
- 2 whole wheat tortillas (8 inches)
- 2 slices reduced-fat Swiss cheese, halved
- ½ medium ripe avocado, peeled and thinly sliced
- 6 ounces sliced cooked turkey breast
  Diced sweet red pepper, optional

1. In a small bowl, combine salad dressing and mustard; spread over one side of each tortilla. Place the tortillas, spread side up, on a griddle coated with cooking spray.

2. Layer cheese, avocado and turkey over half of each tortilla. Fold over and cook over low heat for 1-2 minutes on each side or until cheese is melted. Garnish with red pepper if desired.

PER SERVING *421 cal., 16 g fat (3 g sat. fat), 86 mg chol., 566 mg sodium, 32 g carb., 5 g fiber, 38 g pro.* **Diabetic Exchanges:** *4 lean meat, 2 starch, 2 fat.*

Chicken Cutlets with Citrus Cherry Sauce

You'll love the sweet-tart tanginess of this restaurant-quality chicken dish. I also make this with pork cutlets and dried cranberries instead of chicken and dried cherries.

—**CHARLENE CHAMBERS**

ORMOND BEACH, FL

START TO FINISH: 30 MIN.
MAKES: 4 SERVINGS

- 4 boneless skinless chicken breast halves (6 ounces each)
- ½ teaspoon salt
- ¼ teaspoon pepper
- ¼ cup all-purpose flour
- ½ cup ruby red grapefruit juice
- ½ cup orange juice
- ⅓ cup dried cherries
- 2 teaspoons Dijon mustard
- 1 tablespoon butter
- 1 tablespoon canola oil

1. Flatten chicken breasts to ½-in. thickness; sprinkle with salt and pepper. Place the flour in a large resealable plastic bag. Add chicken, a few pieces at a time, and shake to coat; set aside.

2. In a small saucepan, combine the juices, cherries and mustard. Bring to a boil; cook until liquid is reduced to ½ cup.

3. In a large skillet over medium heat, cook chicken in butter and oil for 5-7 minutes on each side or until juices run clear. Serve with the sauce.

PER SERVING *316 cal., 10 g fat (3 g sat. fat), 102 mg chol., 458 mg sodium, 18 g carb., trace fiber, 35 g pro.* **Diabetic Exchanges:** *5 lean meat, 1 starch, 1 fat.*

CHICKEN CUTLETS WITH CITRUS CHERRY SAUCE

C FAST FIX

Sausage Spinach Salad

A fast way to turn a tangy summer salad into a hearty meal is to add sausage. I use chicken sausage but you can use different varieties and flavors. The mustard dressing is also nice with smoked salmon or chicken.

—**DEB WILLIAMS** PEORIA, AZ

START TO FINISH: 20 MIN.
MAKES: 2 SERVINGS

- 2 **fully cooked Italian chicken sausage links (3 ounces each), cut into ¼-inch slices**
- ½ **medium onion, halved and sliced**
- 4 **teaspoons olive oil, divided**
- 4 **cups fresh baby spinach**
- 1½ **teaspoons balsamic vinegar**
- 1 **teaspoon stone-ground mustard**

1. In a large nonstick skillet coated with cooking spray, cook sausage and onion in 1 teaspoon oil until sausage is browned.

2. Meanwhile, place spinach in a large bowl. In a small bowl, whisk the vinegar, mustard and remaining oil. Drizzle over spinach; toss to coat. Stir in sausage mixture; serve immediately.

PER SERVING *244 cal., 16 g fat (3 g sat. fat), 65 mg chol., 581 mg sodium, 8 g carb., 2 g fiber, 17 g pro.* **Diabetic Exchanges:** *2 lean meat, 2 vegetable, 2 fat.*

SAUSAGE SPINACH SALAD

C FAST FIX
Mediterranean Tilapia

I recently became a fan of tilapia because of its mild taste; it's also low in calories and fat. Plus, it's easy to top with my favorite ingredients.

—**ROBIN BRENNEMAN** HILLIARD, OH

START TO FINISH: 25 MIN.
MAKES: 6 SERVINGS

- 6 tilapia fillets (6 ounces each)
- 1 cup canned Italian diced tomatoes
- ½ cup water-packed artichoke hearts, chopped
- ½ cup sliced ripe olives
- ½ cup crumbled feta cheese

Preheat oven to 400°. Place fillets in a 15-in. x 10-in. x 1-in. baking pan coated with cooking spray. Top with tomatoes, artichoke, olives and cheese. Bake 15-20 minutes or until fish flakes easily with a fork.

ITALIAN TILAPIA *Follow method as directed but top fillets with 1 cup diced tomatoes with roasted garlic, ½ cup each julienned roasted sweet red pepper, sliced fresh mushrooms, diced fresh mozzarella cheese and ½ tsp. dried basil.*

PER SERVING *197 cal., 4 g fat (2 g sat. fat), 88 mg chol., 446 mg sodium, 5 g carb., 1 g fiber, 34 g pro.* **Diabetic Exchanges:** *5 lean meat, ½ fat.*

top tip
Tilapia Sub

When substituting tilapia in a recipe, choose fish with a mild flavor and similar texture. Cod, haddock and halibut are all good choices.

CHICKEN VEGGIE WRAPS

FAST FIX
Chicken Veggie Wraps

I gathered bits and pieces of things I like about Southwest cooking to come up with this economical recipe. Serve with a green salad and vinaigrette dressing for a refreshing meal.

—**KENDRA KATT** ALBUQUERQUE, NM

START TO FINISH: 30 MIN.
MAKES: 6 SERVINGS

- 1½ cups uncooked instant rice
- 1 medium tomato, chopped
- 2 cans (4 ounces each) chopped green chilies
- 7 tablespoons lime juice, divided
- 1½ teaspoons chili powder
- 1½ teaspoons ground cumin
- ½ teaspoon salt
- 1 pound boneless skinless chicken breasts, cubed
- 3 teaspoons canola oil, divided
- 1 large onion, halved and sliced
- 1 large green pepper, julienned
- 1 large sweet red pepper, julienned
- 3 garlic cloves, minced
- 1 tablespoon brown sugar
- 6 flour tortillas (8 inches), warmed

1. Cook rice according to package directions. Stir in the tomato, chilies and 3 tablespoons lime juice.
2. Meanwhile, combine the chili powder, cumin and salt; sprinkle over chicken. In a large nonstick skillet coated with cooking spray, saute chicken in 2 teaspoons oil until no longer pink. Remove and keep warm.
3. In the same skillet, cook onion and peppers in remaining oil until crisp-tender. Add garlic; cook 1 minute longer. Stir in the brown sugar, chicken and remaining lime juice; heat through.
4. Spoon ⅔ cup each of rice mixture and chicken mixture down the center of each tortilla; roll up.
PER SERVING *395 cal., 8 g fat (1 g sat. fat), 42 mg chol., 646 mg sodium, 59 g carb., 3 g fiber, 23 g pro.*

EASY CURRIED SHRIMP

Easy Curried Shrimp

I like to serve this dish with grapes or green veggies for added color. It's also nice with dried coconut or pineapple instead of apricots.

—DONA STONE CLEARWATER, FL

START TO FINISH: 20 MIN.
MAKES: 4 SERVINGS

- 1 tablespoon butter
- 2 teaspoons curry powder
- ¾ teaspoon ground cumin
- ¼ teaspoon salt
- ¼ teaspoon garlic powder
- ¼ teaspoon ground coriander
- ¼ teaspoon ground cinnamon
- 1 cup light coconut milk
- 1 pound uncooked large shrimp, peeled and deveined
- ⅓ cup chopped dried apricots
- 2 cups hot cooked brown rice

1. In a large skillet, melt butter. Add the curry, cumin, salt, garlic powder, coriander and cinnamon; cook over medium heat until the spices are lightly browned. Stir in the coconut milk. Bring to a boil. Reduce heat; simmer, uncovered, for 3-4 minutes or until thickened.

2. Add shrimp; cook and stir for 2-4 minutes or until shrimp turn pink. Stir in apricots; heat through. Serve with rice.

PER SERVING *309 cal., 10 g fat (5 g sat. fat), 145 mg chol., 316 mg sodium, 33 g carb., 3 g fiber, 21 g pro.* **Diabetic Exchanges:** *3 lean meat, 2 starch, 1 fat.*

Skillet Chicken Burritos

This is a go-to dish when I'm in a rush at dinnertime. Preparing the burritos in the skillet not only saves time, it gives them a crispy outside and ooey, gooey inside.

—SCARLETT ELROD NEWNAN, GA

START TO FINISH: 30 MIN.
MAKES: 8 SERVINGS

- 1 cup (8 ounces) reduced-fat sour cream
- ¼ cup chopped fresh cilantro
- 2 tablespoons chopped pickled jalapeno slices
- 2 teaspoons chopped onion
- 2 teaspoons Dijon mustard
- 1 teaspoon grated lime peel

BURRITOS
- 2 cups cubed cooked chicken breast
- 1 can (15 ounces) black beans, rinsed and drained
- 1 can (11 ounces) Mexicorn, drained
- 1 cup (4 ounces) shredded reduced-fat cheddar cheese
- ¼ teaspoon salt
- 8 whole wheat tortillas (8 inches), warmed
  Cooking spray
  Salsa, optional

1. In a small bowl, combine first six ingredients. In a large bowl, mix chicken, beans, corn, cheese, salt and ½ cup sour cream mixture. Spoon ½ cup chicken mixture on each tortilla. Fold sides and ends over filling and roll up. Spritz both sides with cooking spray.

2. In a large nonstick skillet or griddle coated with cooking spray, cook burritos in batches over medium heat for 3-4 minutes on each side or until golden brown. Serve with remaining sour cream mixture and salsa if desired.

PER SERVING *349 cal., 10 g fat (4 g sat. fat), 46 mg chol., 770 mg sodium, 40 g carb., 5 g fiber, 23 g pro.* **Diabetic Exchanges:** *3 lean meat, 2½ starch.*

SKILLET CHICKEN BURRITOS

CHIPOTLE-RASPBERRY
PORK CHOPS

Chipotle-Raspberry Pork Chops

My husband and I love this dinner. With only four ingredients, it's easy to throw together after a hectic day. Plus, if there's sauce left over, I freeze it for the next time.

—**JENNIFER RAY** PONCHA SPRINGS, CO

START TO FINISH: 20 MIN.
MAKES: 4 SERVINGS (¼ CUP SAUCE)

- ½ cup seedless raspberry preserves
- 1 chipotle pepper in adobo sauce, finely chopped
- ½ teaspoon salt
- 4 bone-in pork loin chops (7 ounces each)

1. In a small saucepan, combine preserves and chipotle peppers over medium heat until heated through. Reserve ¼ cup for serving. Sprinkle the pork with salt; brush with the remaining raspberry sauce.

2. Moisten a paper towel with cooking oil; using long-handled tongs, rub on grill rack to coat lightly. Place chops on grill rack and grill, covered, over medium heat 4-5 minutes on each side or until a thermometer reads 145°. Let stand 5 minutes. Serve with reserved sauce.

PER SERVING *308 cal., 9 g fat (3 g sat. fat), 86 mg chol., 395 mg sodium, 27 g carb., trace fiber, 30 g pro.*

F | FAST FIX

Simple Chicken Soup

I revised a recipe that my family loved so it would be lighter and easier to make. It's a hearty and healthy meal served with a green salad and fresh bread.

—**SUE WEST** ALVORD, TX

START TO FINISH: 20 MIN.
MAKES: 6 SERVINGS

- 2 cans (14½ ounces each) reduced-sodium chicken broth
- 1 tablespoon dried minced onion
- 1 package (16 ounces) frozen mixed vegetables
- 2 cups cubed cooked chicken breast
- 2 cans (10¾ ounces each) reduced-fat reduced-sodium condensed cream of chicken soup, undiluted

1. In a large saucepan, bring broth and onion to a boil. Reduce heat. Add the vegetables; cover and cook for 6-8 minutes or until crisp-tender. Stir in chicken and soup; heat through.
PER SERVING *195 cal., 3 g fat (1 g sat. fat), 44 mg chol., 820 mg sodium, 21 g carb., 3 g fiber, 19 g pro.*

SIMPLE CHICKEN SOUP

C | FAST FIX

Broiled Apricot Chicken

A little sweet blends perfectly with the bold taste of horseradish. What a nice treatment for lean, tender chicken breasts. This works great on the grill, too.

—**SUSAN WARREN** NORTH MANCHESTER, IN

START TO FINISH: 30 MIN.
MAKES: 6 SERVINGS

- 1 cup apricot nectar
- 3 tablespoons brown sugar
- 2 tablespoons ketchup
- 2 teaspoons cornstarch
- 1 teaspoon grated orange peel
- 1 teaspoon horseradish mustard
- 6 boneless skinless chicken breast halves (6 ounces each)

1. In a small saucepan, combine the first six ingredients. Bring to a boil. Cook and stir for 1 minute or until thickened.
2. Place chicken on a broiler pan coated with cooking spray. Broil 4 in. from the heat for 6-8 minutes on each side or until chicken juices run clear, basting frequently with apricot mixture.
PER SERVING *241 cal., 4 g fat (1 g sat. fat), 94 mg chol., 158 mg sodium, 15 g carb., trace fiber, 34 g pro.* **Diabetic Exchanges:** *5 lean meat, 1 starch.*

FAST FIX

Taco Salad Tacos

I was making tacos one night and noticed I was out of spicy taco sauce. Using a combination of spices and fat-free Catalina salad dressing rescued our family taco night.

—**CHERYL PLAINTE** PRUDENVILLE, MI

START TO FINISH: 30 MIN.
MAKES: 4 SERVINGS

- 1 pound extra-lean ground beef (95% lean)
- 1 medium onion, chopped
- 1 tablespoon chili powder
- 1 teaspoon garlic powder
- 1 teaspoon reduced-sodium beef bouillon granules
- 1 teaspoon ground cumin
- ¼ teaspoon salt

SALAD

- 3 cups torn romaine
- 1 large tomato, seeded and chopped
- 1 medium sweet orange pepper, chopped
- 3 green onions, chopped
- 8 taco shells, warmed
- ½ cup fat-free Catalina salad dressing
  Shredded reduced-fat Colby-Monterey Jack cheese and reduced-fat sour cream, optional

1. In a large skillet, cook beef and onion over medium heat until meat is no longer pink. Stir in the chili powder, garlic powder, bouillon, cumin and salt; remove from the heat.
2. In a large bowl, combine the romaine, tomato, orange pepper and green onions. Spoon beef mixture into taco shells; top with salad mixture. Drizzle with dressing. Serve with cheese and sour cream if desired.
PER SERVING *334 cal., 11 g fat (4 g sat. fat), 65 mg chol., 722 mg sodium, 33 g carb., 6 g fiber, 26 g pro.* **Diabetic Exchanges:** *3 lean meat, 2 vegetable, 1½ starch.*

Black Bean and Corn Tacos

We eat meatless meals a few times a week, so I replaced the beef with nutty brown rice to bulk up these tacos. I also like to swap quinoa for the rice.

—KRISTIN RIMKUS SNOHOMISH, WA

START TO FINISH: 30 MIN.
MAKES: 4 SERVINGS

- 1 medium onion, finely chopped
- 1 medium green pepper, finely chopped
- 1 small sweet red pepper, finely chopped
- 1 can (15 ounces) black beans, rinsed and drained
- 2 large tomatoes, seeded and chopped
- 2 cups shredded cabbage
- 1 cup fresh or frozen corn
- 2 tablespoons reduced-sodium taco seasoning
- 2 tablespoons lime juice
- 2 garlic cloves, minced
- 1 cup ready-to-serve brown rice
- 8 taco shells, warmed
- ½ cup shredded reduced-fat Mexican cheese blend
- ½ cup reduced-fat sour cream

1. In a large nonstick skillet coated with cooking spray, saute onion and peppers until crisp-tender. Add the beans, tomatoes, cabbage, corn, taco seasoning, lime juice and garlic. Cook and stir over medium heat for 8-10 minutes or until vegetables are tender. Stir in rice; heat through.
2. Spoon bean mixture into taco shells. Top with the cheese and sour cream.

PER SERVING *423 cal., 12 g fat (4 g sat. fat), 20 mg chol., 682 mg sodium, 64 g carb., 10 g fiber, 17 g pro.*

TURKEY SCALLOPINI

Turkey Scallopini

ok, bland

Great for family gatherings, this dish is easy to double. I typically serve it with rice or pasta for a quick dinner.

—SUSAN WARREN NORTH MANCHESTER, IN

START TO FINISH: 25 MIN.
MAKES: 4 SERVINGS

- ⅓ cup all-purpose flour
- ¼ teaspoon dried rosemary, crushed
- ¼ teaspoon dried thyme
- ⅛ teaspoon white pepper
- 1 package (17.6 ounces) turkey breast cutlets
- 4 teaspoons canola oil
- ¼ cup white wine or reduced-sodium chicken broth
- ½ teaspoon cornstarch
- ⅓ cup reduced-sodium chicken broth
- ½ cup reduced-fat sour cream
- 1 teaspoon spicy brown mustard
  Paprika, optional

1. In a large resealable plastic bag, combine the flour, rosemary, thyme and pepper. Add turkey; seal bag and shake to coat. In a large nonstick skillet coated with cooking spray, cook turkey in oil over medium heat for 2-4 minutes on each side or until no longer pink. Remove; keep warm.
2. Add wine to skillet; cook and stir for 30 seconds, stirring to loosen browned bits from pan. Combine cornstarch and broth until smooth; stir into the skillet. Bring to a boil; cook and stir for 2 minutes or until slightly thickened. Add the sour cream and mustard; heat through. Pour over the turkey; sprinkle with paprika if desired.

PER SERVING *263 cal., 8 g fat (2 g sat. fat), 88 mg chol., 194 mg sodium, 11 g carb., trace fiber, 34 g pro.* **Diabetic Exchanges:** *4 lean meat, 1 starch, 1 fat.*

FAST FIX
Asian Pork Stir-Fry

Working two jobs leaves little time for grocery shopping and cooking. This recipe can be made with almost anything you have at hand, including different vegetables and meats.
—DEBORAH SHEAHEN HICKORY, NC

START TO FINISH: 30 MIN.
MAKES: 4 SERVINGS

- 2 tablespoons cornstarch
- ½ cup water
- ½ cup reduced-sodium chicken broth
- 2 garlic cloves, minced
- 2 teaspoons minced fresh gingerroot
- 1 pound pork tenderloin, cut into ½-inch pieces
- 2 tablespoons sesame or canola oil, divided
- 1½ cups sliced fresh mushrooms
- 1 cup bean sprouts
- 1 cup sliced bok choy
- 1 cup fresh snow peas
- 1 small sweet red pepper, cut into ¾-inch pieces
- 2 tablespoons reduced-sodium soy sauce
- 2 cups hot cooked brown rice

1. In a small bowl, combine the cornstarch and water until smooth. Stir in the broth, garlic and ginger; set aside.

2. In a large skillet or wok, stir-fry pork in 1 tablespoon oil until no longer pink. Remove; keep warm.

3. Stir-fry the mushrooms, bean sprouts, bok choy, peas, pepper and soy sauce in remaining oil for 4-5 minutes or until vegetables are crisp-tender.

4. Stir cornstarch mixture and add to the pan. Bring to a boil; cook and stir for 1 minute or until thickened. Add the pork; heat through. Serve with rice.

PER SERVING *386 cal., 12 g fat (3 g sat. fat), 63 mg chol., 565 mg sodium, 38 g carb., 6 g fiber, 32 g pro.* **Diabetic Exchanges:** *3 lean meat, 2 vegetable, 1½ starch, 1½ fat.*

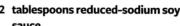
F FAST FIX
Tuscan Chicken and Beans

Who doesn't enjoy flavorful meals that are quick and easy to make? I really like the combination of rosemary and beans in this rustic Italian dish.
—MARIE RIZZIO INTERLOCHEN, MI

START TO FINISH: 30 MIN.
MAKES: 4 SERVINGS

- 1 pound boneless skinless chicken breasts, cut into ¾-inch pieces
- 2 teaspoons minced fresh rosemary or ½ teaspoon dried rosemary
- ¼ teaspoon salt
- ¼ teaspoon coarsely ground pepper
- 1 cup reduced-sodium chicken broth
- 2 tablespoons sun-dried tomatoes (not packed in oil), chopped
- 1 can (15½ ounces) white kidney or cannellini beans, rinsed and drained

1. In a small bowl, combine the chicken, rosemary, salt and pepper. In a large nonstick skillet coated with cooking spray, cook chicken over medium heat until browned.

2. Stir in broth and tomatoes. Bring to a boil. Reduce heat; simmer, uncovered, for 3-5 minutes or until chicken juices run clear. Add beans; heat through.

PER SERVING *216 cal., 3 g fat (1 g sat. fat), 63 mg chol., 517 mg sodium, 17 g carb., 4 g fiber, 28 g pro.* **Diabetic Exchanges:** *3 lean meat, 1 starch.*

ASIAN PORK STIR-FRY

GRILLED SESAME
ORANGE TUNA STEAKS

2. Brush tuna with 2 tablespoons marinade. Moisten a paper towel with cooking oil; using long-handled tongs, lightly coat the grill rack. Grill tuna, covered, over high heat or broil 3-4 in. from the heat for 3-4 minutes on each side for medium-rare or until slightly pink in center.

3. Brush tuna with remaining marinade; serve with rice and snap pea mixture.

PER SERVING *506 cal., 10 g fat (3 g sat. fat), 84 mg chol., 822 mg sodium, 56 g carb., 4 g fiber, 47 g pro.*

Grilled Sesame Orange Tuna Steaks

My son and I collaborated on these tuna steaks. We entered them in a contest because he aspires to be a chef someday, and our recipe placed in the top four.

—**LORNA MCFADDEN** PORT ORCHARD, WA

START TO FINISH: 25 MIN.
MAKES: 4 SERVINGS

- 1½ cups instant brown rice
- 2 cups fresh sugar snap peas
- 2 tablespoons honey
- 1 tablespoon butter
- 1 snack-size cup (4 ounces) mandarin oranges, drained
- ¼ cup unsalted cashews, coarsely chopped
- 4 tuna steaks (6 ounces each)
- 5 tablespoons sesame ginger marinade, divided

1. Cook rice according to package directions. In a large skillet, saute peas and honey in butter until crisp-tender. Add oranges and cashews; cook and stir 1 minute longer.

Turkey Enchilada Stack

As a child, my husband was one of the pickiest kids around, but my mother-in-law could always get him to dig in to this enchilada dish. So I knew the enchilada stack would be a winner!

—**ASHLEY WOLF** ALABASTER, AL

START TO FINISH: 20 MIN.
MAKES: 4 SERVINGS

- 1 pound lean ground turkey
- 2 cans (8 ounces each) no-salt-added tomato sauce
- 3 teaspoons dried minced onion
- ½ teaspoon garlic powder
- ½ teaspoon pepper
- ¼ teaspoon salt
- 4 whole wheat tortillas (8 inches)
- ⅔ cup shredded reduced-fat cheddar cheese
  Optional toppings: shredded lettuce, chopped tomatoes and reduced-fat sour cream

1. In a large skillet, cook turkey over medium heat until meat is no longer pink; drain. Stir in tomato sauce, minced onion, garlic powder, pepper and salt; heat through.

2. In a 2½-qt. round microwave-safe dish coated with cooking spray, layer one tortilla, about ¾ cup meat mixture and a scant 3 tablespoons cheese. Repeat layers three times. Cover and cook on high for 4-5 minutes or until cheese is melted. Let stand for 5 minutes before cutting. Serve with toppings if desired.

NOTE *This recipe was tested in a 1,100-watt microwave.*

PER SERVING *404 cal., 16 g fat (5 g sat. fat), 103 mg chol., 582 mg sodium, 31 g carb., 3 g fiber, 29 g pro.*
Diabetic Exchanges: 4 lean meat, 2 starch, 1 fat.

TURKEY
ENCHILADA STACK

BARBECUED CHICKEN-
STUFFED POTATOES

Barbecued Chicken-Stuffed Potatoes

This tasty dish combines some of my favorite things—the toppings for supreme nachos, tender chicken and the warm comfort of a baked potato.

—**ELLEN FINGER** LANCASTER, PA

START TO FINISH: 30 MIN.
MAKES: 8 SERVINGS

- 4 **large potatoes**
  Cooking spray
- 1 **teaspoon garlic salt with parsley**
- 1½ **cups cubed cooked chicken breast**
- ⅔ **cup barbecue sauce**
- 1 **can (16 ounces) chili beans, undrained**
- 1 **can (2¼ ounces) sliced ripe olives, drained**
- 2 **green onions, sliced**
- 1½ **cups (6 ounces) shredded reduced-fat Colby-Monterey Jack cheese**
- 2 **plum tomatoes, chopped**
- ½ **cup reduced-fat sour cream**

1. Scrub and pierce potatoes. Coat with cooking spray and rub with garlic salt with parsley. Place on a microwave-safe plate. Microwave, uncovered, on high for 18-22 minutes or until tender, turning once. Meanwhile, in a bowl, mix the chicken and barbecue sauce.

2. Cut each potato in half lengthwise. Scoop out the pulp, leaving ½-in. shells. Discard pulp or save for another use. Spoon chicken mixture into potato shells. Top with beans, olives and green onions; sprinkle with cheese. Place potatoes on a baking sheet.

3. Bake, uncovered, at 375° for 10-12 minutes or until heated through. Serve with tomatoes and sour cream.

NOTE *This recipe was tested in a 1,100-watt microwave.*

PER SERVING *237 cal., 8 g fat (4 g sat. fat), 36 mg chol., 737 mg sodium, 25 g carb., 5 g fiber, 19 g pro.* **Diabetic Exchanges:** *2 lean meat, 1½ starch, ½ fat.*

Cheese Ravioli with Pumpkin Alfredo Sauce

When I first made this recipe everyone thought: Pumpkin on pasta? Eww! But once they tasted it, they couldn't believe how much they liked it!

—**CHERI NEUSTIFTER** STURTEVANT, WI

START TO FINISH: 30 MIN.
MAKES: 6 SERVINGS

- 1 **package (25 ounces) frozen cheese ravioli**
- 3 **tablespoons all-purpose flour**
- 2 **cups fat-free milk**
- 1 **can (14½ ounces) reduced-sodium chicken broth**
- 3 **garlic cloves, minced**
- 2 **tablespoons butter**
- ½ **cup shredded Parmesan cheese**
- ½ **cup canned pumpkin**
- ¼ **cup minced fresh parsley**
- 1½ **teaspoons minced fresh sage**
  Dash ground nutmeg
- ¼ **cup pine nuts, toasted**
- ¼ **cup chopped walnuts, toasted**

1. Cook the ravioli according to package directions. Meanwhile, in a large bowl, whisk the flour, milk and broth.

2. In a large skillet, saute the garlic in butter until tender. Stir in the milk mixture, cheese, pumpkin, parsley, sage and nutmeg. Cook, uncovered, over medium heat for 10-15 minutes or until thickened, stirring occasionally.

3. Drain ravioli and stir into sauce. Sprinkle with nuts.

PER SERVING *420 cal., 16 g fat (6 g sat. fat), 29 mg chol., 662 mg sodium, 50 g carb., 4 g fiber, 19 g pro.*

CHEESE RAVIOLI WITH
PUMPKIN ALFREDO SAUCE

Easy Chicken Chasseur

I clipped a variation of this recipe from a magazine many years ago and have made changes to reduce the amount of fat and sodium. When I serve it, there are never any leftovers.

—**LILLIAN CHARVES** NEW BERN, NC

START TO FINISH: 30 MIN.
MAKES: 4 SERVINGS

- ½ **cup cornstarch**
- 1 **pound boneless skinless chicken breasts, cut into 1-inch strips**
- 4 **teaspoons olive oil, divided**
- 1 **cup sliced fresh mushrooms**
- 3 **green onions, thinly sliced**
- ½ **cup reduced-sodium chicken broth**
- ½ **cup sherry or reduced-sodium chicken broth**
- ½ **teaspoon dried tarragon**
- ½ **teaspoon dried thyme**
- ¼ **teaspoon salt**
- ¼ **teaspoon pepper**
- 2 **medium tomatoes, cut into wedges and seeded**
  Hot cooked rice, optional

1. Place cornstarch in a large resealable plastic bag. Add the chicken, a few pieces at a time, and shake to coat. In a large nonstick skillet coated with cooking spray, brown chicken in 2 teaspoons oil. Remove and set aside.
2. In the same skillet, saute the mushrooms and onions in the remaining oil until tender. Add the broth, sherry and seasonings; bring to a boil. Carefully return chicken to the pan; simmer, uncovered, for 4-6 minutes or until chicken is no longer pink. Stir in tomatoes; heat through. Serve with rice if desired.

PER SERVING *260 cal., 7 g fat (1 g sat. fat), 63 mg chol., 283 mg sodium, 18 g carb., 2 g fiber, 25 g pro.* ***Diabetic Exchanges:*** *3 lean meat, 1 starch, 1 vegetable, 1 fat.*

Tomato-Walnut Pesto on Linguine

We used sun-dried tomatoes to make this tangy alternative to traditional pesto. Walnuts lend an appealing nutty flavor to the stand-out dish.

—**TASTE OF HOME TEST KITCHEN**

START TO FINISH: 30 MIN.
MAKES: 8 SERVINGS

- ½ **cup sun-dried tomatoes (not packed in oil)**
- ½ **cup boiling water**
- 12 **ounces uncooked linguine**
- 2 **cups loosely packed basil leaves**
- ¼ **cup grated Parmesan cheese**
- 1 **garlic clove, peeled**
- ⅓ **cup reduced-sodium chicken broth**
- ¼ **cup chopped walnuts, toasted**
- ¼ **teaspoon salt**
- ⅛ **teaspoon pepper**
- 3 **tablespoons olive oil**

1. Place the tomatoes in a small bowl; add boiling water. Cover and let stand for 5 minutes. Meanwhile, cook linguine according to package directions.
2. Place the basil, Parmesan cheese and garlic in a food processor; cover and pulse until chopped. Add the tomatoes with liquid, broth, walnuts, salt and pepper; cover and process until blended. While processing, gradually add oil in a steady stream.
3. Drain linguine; toss with pesto. Serve immediately.

PER SERVING *244 cal., 9 g fat (2 g sat. fat), 2 mg chol., 212 mg sodium, 33 g carb., 3 g fiber, 7 g pro.*

TOMATO-WALNUT PESTO ON LINGUINE

top tip

Just Add Pesto

Freeze leftover pesto in ice-cube trays for those moments when you need a flavor boost. Once frozen, store the pesto cubes in a freezer bag in the freezer. Add frozen cubes to sauces or thaw and spread on sandwiches or crostini for a quick and tasty bite.

F **C** **FAST FIX**

Stuffed-Olive Cod

Take advantage of the olive bar in your supermarket and put a new twist on cod. This simple high-protein, low-fat entree is a weeknight lifesaver.

—**TRIA OLSEN** QUEEN CREEK, AZ

START TO FINISH: 25 MIN.
MAKES: 4 SERVINGS

- 4 **cod fillets (6 ounces each)**
- 1 **teaspoon dried oregano**
- ¼ **teaspoon salt**
- 1 **medium lemon, thinly sliced**
- ⅓ **cup garlic-stuffed olives, halved**
- 1 **shallot, thinly sliced**
- 2 **tablespoons water**
- 2 **tablespoons olive juice**

1. Sprinkle fillets with oregano and salt. Place in a large nonstick skillet coated with cooking spray; top fillets with lemon.
2. Arrange olives and shallot around fillets; add water and olive juice. Bring to a boil. Reduce heat; cover and steam for 8-10 minutes or until fish flakes easily with a fork.
PER SERVING *163 cal., 3 g fat (trace sat. fat), 65 mg chol., 598 mg sodium, 4 g carb., trace fiber, 27 g pro.* **Diabetic Exchange:** *4 lean meat.*

FAST FIX

Hoisin Shrimp & Broccoli

Get out the chopsticks—this Asian-inspired dinner is our healthier alternative to takeout and is so easy to prepare. Sesame, ginger and soy sauce add a rich flavor that enhances the taste of fresh broccoli.

—**MARY KISINGER** CALGARY, AB

START TO FINISH: 30 MIN.
MAKES: 4 SERVINGS

- 1 **tablespoon cornstarch**
- ⅓ **cup reduced-sodium chicken broth**
- 4½ **teaspoons reduced-sodium soy sauce**
- 4½ **teaspoons hoisin sauce**
- 1 **teaspoon sesame oil**
- 3 **cups fresh broccoli florets**
- 1 **tablespoon canola oil**
- 4 **green onions, chopped**
- 3 **garlic cloves, minced**
- 1 **teaspoon minced fresh gingerroot**
- 1 **pound uncooked medium shrimp, peeled and deveined**
- 2 **cups hot cooked rice**

HOISIN SHRIMP & BROCCOLI

1. In a small bowl, combine the cornstarch and broth until smooth. Stir in the soy sauce, hoisin sauce and sesame oil; set aside.
2. In a large nonstick skillet or wok, stir-fry broccoli in canola oil until crisp-tender. Add the onions, garlic and ginger; stir-fry for 3-4 minutes or until vegetables are tender. Add shrimp; stir-fry 4-5 minutes longer or until shrimp turn pink.
3. Stir cornstarch mixture and add to the pan. Bring to a boil; cook and stir for 2 minutes or until sauce is thickened. Serve with rice.
PER SERVING *289 cal., 7 g fat (1 g sat. fat), 138 mg chol., 524 mg sodium, 33 g carb., 2 g fiber, 23 g pro.* **Diabetic Exchanges:** *3 lean meat, 1½ starch, 1 vegetable, 1 fat.*

STUFFED-OLIVE COD

Crispy Asian Chicken Salad

Asian flavor, crunchy almonds and crispy breaded chicken make this hearty salad something special.

—BETH DAUENHAUER PUEBLO, CO

START TO FINISH: 30 MIN.
MAKES: 2 SERVINGS

- 2 **boneless skinless chicken breast halves (4 ounces each)**
- 2 **teaspoons hoisin sauce**
- 1 **teaspoon sesame oil**
- ½ **cup panko (Japanese) bread crumbs**
- 4 **teaspoons sesame seeds**
- 2 **teaspoons canola oil**

- 4 **cups spring mix salad greens**
- 1 **small green pepper, julienned**
- 1 **small sweet red pepper, julienned**
- 1 **medium carrot, julienned**
- ½ **cup sliced fresh mushrooms**
- 2 **tablespoons thinly sliced onion**
- 2 **tablespoons sliced almonds, toasted**
- ¼ **cup reduced-fat sesame ginger salad dressing**

1. Flatten chicken breasts to ½-in. thickness. Combine hoisin sauce and sesame oil; brush over chicken. In a shallow bowl, combine panko and sesame seeds; dip chicken in the mixture.

2. In a large nonstick skillet coated with cooking spray, cook chicken in oil for 5-6 minutes on each side or until no longer pink.

3. Meanwhile, divide salad greens between two plates. Top with peppers, carrot, mushrooms and onion. Slice chicken; place on top. Sprinkle with almonds and drizzle with dressing.

PER SERVING *386 cal., 17 g fat (2 g sat. fat), 63 mg chol., 620 mg sodium, 29 g carb., 6 g fiber, 30 g pro.* **Diabetic Exchanges:** *3 lean meat, 2 vegetable, 2 fat, 1 starch.*

CRISPY ASIAN CHICKEN SALAD

BEEF

TENDER SALSA BEEF
PAGE 141

CHRISTINE RICHARDSON'S MEXICAN BEEF & PASTA
PAGE 128

BLAIR LONERGAN'S MAKEOVER EASY BEEF-STUFFED SHELLS *PAGE 134*

CHARLENE CHAMBERS' SESAME BEEF STIR-FRY
PAGE 138

Beef

Following a heart-healthy diet **doesn't mean the meat has to go missing.** Next time someone in your bunch asks, "Where's the beef?" reach for one of these lean, **fit-for-the-family recipes.**

FAST FIX
Curried Beef Pitas with Cucumber Sauce

A friend gave this recipe to me when I got married, and the ingredients looked so strange. I was scared to try it for a while, but now it has become one of our favorite fast dinners.

—SHANNON KOENE BLACKSBURG, VA

START TO FINISH: 25 MIN.
MAKES: 4 SERVINGS (1½ CUPS SAUCE)

- 1 cup fat-free plain Greek yogurt
- 1 cup finely chopped peeled cucumber
- 1 tablespoon minced fresh mint
- 2 garlic cloves, minced
- 2 teaspoons snipped fresh dill
- 2 teaspoons lemon juice
- ¼ teaspoon salt

PITAS
- 1 pound lean ground beef (90% lean)
- 1 small onion, chopped
- 1 medium Golden Delicious apple, finely chopped
- ¼ cup raisins
- 2 teaspoons curry powder
- ¼ teaspoon salt
- 8 whole wheat pita pocket halves

1. In a small bowl, mix the first seven ingredients. Refrigerate until serving.
2. In a large skillet, cook beef and onion over medium heat 6-8 minutes or until beef is no longer pink, breaking up the beef into crumbles; drain. Add apple, raisins, curry powder and salt; cook until the apples are tender, stirring occasionally. Serve in pita halves with sauce.
PER SERVING *429 cal., 11 g fat (4 g sat. fat), 71 mg chol., 686 mg sodium, 50 g carb., 6 g fiber, 36 g pro*

FAST FIX
Hamburger Chop Suey

Fast, hearty and colorful, my chop suey uses up those summer garden peppers and spinach. If you happen to have a bag of pea pods, they'd be delicious thrown into the mix.

—BETH PISULA FREEPORT, IL

START TO FINISH: 30 MIN.
MAKES: 6 SERVINGS

- 1 tablespoon cornstarch
- 2 teaspoons minced fresh gingerroot
- 1 teaspoon reduced-sodium beef bouillon granules
- ¾ cup water
- ⅓ cup reduced-sodium soy sauce

CHOP SUEY
- 1 pound lean ground beef (90% lean)
- 2 celery ribs, sliced
- 1 cup sliced fresh mushrooms
- 1 medium green pepper, sliced
- 1 medium sweet red pepper, sliced
- 1 medium onion, halved and thinly sliced
- 1 can (14 ounces) bean sprouts, drained
- 1 can (8 ounces) sliced water chestnuts, drained
- 1 cup fresh spinach, torn
- 3 cups hot cooked rice

1. In a small bowl, combine the cornstarch, ginger and bouillon; stir in water and soy sauce until blended. Set aside.
2. In a large nonstick skillet or wok, stir-fry beef, celery, mushrooms, peppers and onion until the meat is no longer pink and vegetables are tender. Drain. Stir in bean sprouts, water chestnuts and spinach.
3. Stir reserved sauce mixture; add to pan. Bring to a boil; cook and stir for 1-2 minutes or until thickened. Serve with rice.
PER SERVING *287 cal., 6 g fat (2 g sat. fat), 37 mg chol., 679 mg sodium, 37 g carb., 4 g fiber, 20 g pro.* **Diabetic Exchanges:** *2 lean meat, 2 vegetable, 1½ starch.*

Grilled Beef Tenderloins

The aroma from these tenderloins sizzling on the grill often attracts the neighbors. It's one of our favorite dinners to make year-round.

—**PATRICIA SWART** GALLOWAY, NJ

PREP: 10 MIN. + MARINATING
GRILL: 10 MIN.
MAKES: 2 SERVINGS

- ¼ cup dry red wine
- ¼ cup reduced-sodium soy sauce
- ½ teaspoon garlic powder
- ½ teaspoon dried oregano
- ¼ teaspoon ground cumin
- ¼ teaspoon ground ancho chili pepper
- ¼ teaspoon pepper
- 2 beef tenderloin steaks (6 ounces each)

GRILLED BEEF TENDERLOINS

1. In a large resealable plastic bag, combine first seven ingredients. Add the steaks; seal bag and turn to coat. Refrigerate for up to 4 hours.
2. Drain and discard marinade. Using long-handled tongs, moisten a paper towel with cooking oil and lightly coat the grill rack. Grill steaks, covered, over medium heat or broil 4 in. from the heat for 4-6 minutes on each side or until meat reaches desired doneness (for medium-rare, a thermometer should read 145°; medium, 160°; well-done, 170°).

PER SERVING *263 cal., 10 g fat (4 g sat. fat), 75 mg chol., 402 mg sodium, 1 g carb., trace fiber, 37 g pro. Diabetic Exchange: 5 lean meat.*

Beef & Blue Cheese Tart

The scent of onions, garlic and beef along with the tantalizing aroma of baking bread will have everyone excited to slice into this rustic tart.

—**JUDY BATSON** TAMPA, FL

PREP: 20 MIN. • **BAKE:** 15 MIN.
MAKES: 6 SERVINGS

- ½ pound lean ground beef (90% lean)
- 1¾ cups sliced fresh mushrooms
- ½ medium red onion, thinly sliced
- ¼ teaspoon salt
- ¼ teaspoon pepper
- 1 tube (13.8 ounces) refrigerated pizza crust
- ½ cup reduced-fat sour cream
- 2 teaspoons Italian seasoning
- ½ teaspoon garlic powder
- ¾ cup crumbled blue cheese

1. In a large skillet, cook the beef, mushrooms and onion over medium heat until the meat is no longer pink; drain. Stir in salt and pepper; set aside.
2. On a lightly floured surface, roll

BEEF & BLUE CHEESE TART

crust into a 15-in. x 12-in. rectangle. Transfer to a parchment paper-lined baking sheet.
3. In a small bowl, combine the sour cream, Italian seasoning and garlic powder; spread over crust to within 2 in. of edges. Spoon the beef mixture over top. Fold up edges of crust over filling, leaving center uncovered.
4. Bake at 425° for 15-18 minutes or until crust is golden. Using the parchment paper, slide tart onto a wire rack. Sprinkle with the blue cheese; let stand for 5 minutes before slicing.

PER SERVING *328 cal., 12 g fat (5 g sat. fat), 43 mg chol., 803 mg sodium, 35 g carb., 1 g fiber, 19 g pro. Diabetic Exchanges: 2 starch, 2 lean meat, 2 fat.*

Mom's Sloppy Tacos

My mom used to make this recipe for me when I was a little girl, and now I make it for my daughter. She loves it! I have found it's a great starter for chili, or it can be made into a burrito filling by adding a can of drained beans.

—KAMI JONES AVONDALE, AZ

START TO FINISH: 30 MIN.
MAKES: 6 SERVINGS

- 1½ pounds extra-lean ground beef (95% lean)
- 1 can (15 ounces) tomato sauce
- ¾ teaspoon garlic powder
- ½ teaspoon salt
- ¼ teaspoon pepper
- ¼ teaspoon cayenne pepper
- 12 taco shells, warmed
  Optional toppings: shredded lettuce and cheese, chopped tomatoes, avocado and olives

1. In a large skillet, cook beef over medium heat until no longer pink. Stir in the tomato sauce, garlic powder, salt, pepper and cayenne. Bring to a boil. Reduce heat; simmer, uncovered, for 10 minutes.

2. Fill each taco shell with ¼ cup of the beef mixture and toppings of your choice.

PER SERVING *264 cal., 10 g fat (4 g sat. fat), 65 mg chol., 669 mg sodium, 17 g carb., 1 g fiber, 25 g pro.* **Diabetic Exchanges:** *3 lean meat, 1 starch, 1 fat.*

ⓒ Italian Mushroom Meat Loaf

Healthful oats and flaxseed amp up the nutrition in this tasty Italian meat loaf.

—KYLIE(PETRULIA) WERNING CANDLER, NC

PREP: 30 MIN. • **BAKE:** 1 HOUR
MAKES: 8 SERVINGS

- 1 egg, lightly beaten
- ¼ pound medium fresh mushrooms, chopped
- ½ cup old-fashioned oats
- ½ cup chopped red onion
- ¼ cup ground flaxseed
- ½ teaspoon pepper
- 1 package (19½ ounces) Italian turkey sausage links, casings removed and crumbled
- 1 pound lean ground beef (90% lean)
- 1 cup marinara or meatless spaghetti sauce

1. In a large bowl, combine the egg, mushrooms, oats, onion, flax and pepper. Crumble turkey and beef over mixture and mix well.

2. Shape into a 10-in. x 4-in. loaf. Place in a 13-in. x 9-in. baking dish coated with cooking spray. Bake, uncovered, at 350° for 50 minutes; drain. Top with the marinara sauce. Bake for 10-15 minutes or until no pink remains and a thermometer reads 165°.

PER SERVING *261 cal., 14 g fat (3 g sat. fat), 103 mg chol., 509 mg sodium, 10 g carb., 2 g fiber, 25 g pro.* **Diabetic Exchanges:** *3 lean meat, ½ starch.*

ITALIAN MUSHROOM MEAT LOAF

BEEF

FAST FIX

Mexican Beef & Pasta

Good don't make anymore

Fast home cooking done light and chock-full of southwestern flavor—what's not to love? (Especially when it's topped off with crunchy tortilla chips!)

—CHRISTINE RICHARDSON

MAPLE GROVE, MN

START TO FINISH: 30 MIN.
MAKES: 8 SERVINGS

- 3 cups uncooked whole wheat spiral pasta
- 1 pound lean ground beef (90% lean)
- 1 small onion, chopped
- 2 cans (14½ ounces each) no-salt-added diced tomatoes, undrained
- 1 can (15 ounces) black beans, rinsed and drained
- 1 cup frozen corn, thawed
- 1 cup chunky salsa
- 1 can (4 ounces) chopped green chilies
- 1 can (2¼ ounces) sliced ripe olives, drained
- 3 tablespoons taco seasoning
- ½ cup reduced-fat sour cream
  Crushed tortilla chips, optional

1. Cook the pasta according to package directions; drain. Meanwhile, in a large skillet, cook beef and onion over medium heat until meat is no longer pink; drain.

2. Stir in pasta, tomatoes, beans, corn, salsa, green chilies, olives and taco seasoning. Bring to a boil. Reduce heat; simmer, uncovered, for 8-10 minutes or until heated through. Serve with sour cream and chips if desired.

PER SERVING *305 cal., 7 g fat (3 g sat. fat), 40 mg chol., 737 mg sodium, 40 g carb., 7 g fiber, 20 g pro.* **Diabetic Exchanges:** *2 starch, 2 lean meat, 2 vegetable.*

Good

Soup-Bowl Cabbage Rolls

With this generous portion, you get all the flavors and nutrition of stuffed cabbage without all the work. Cayenne pepper gives it a nice kick, but it's not too hot for kids.

—TERRI PEARCE HOUSTON, TX

PREP: 15 MIN. • **COOK:** 35 MIN.
MAKES: 4 SERVINGS

- 1 **pound lean ground beef (90% lean)**
- 1 **garlic clove, minced**
- 1 **small head cabbage, chopped**
- 2½ **cups water** *beef broth 1 box*
- ⅔ **cup uncooked long grain rice**
- 1 **tablespoon Worcestershire sauce**
- 1 **teaspoon onion powder**
- 1 **teaspoon dried basil**
- ¼ **teaspoon cayenne pepper**
- ¼ **teaspoon pepper**
- 1 **can (28 ounces) crushed tomatoes**
- ½ **teaspoon salt**
  Grated Parmesan cheese, optional
  — perm rind

1. In a nonstick Dutch oven, cook beef and garlic over medium heat until meat is no longer pink; drain. Stir in the cabbage, water, rice, Worcestershire sauce, onion powder, basil, cayenne and pepper; bring to a boil. Reduce heat; cover and simmer for 25-30 minutes or until rice is tender.

2. Stir in the tomatoes and salt; heat through. Sprinkle with the cheese if desired.

PER SERVING *397 cal., 9 g fat (4 g sat. fat), 56 mg chol., 707 mg sodium, 51 g carb., 9 g fiber, 30 g pro.*

— onion
— seasonings xtra

FAST FIX

Black Bean and Beef Tostadas

Just a handful of ingredients add up to one of our family's favorites. It's also easy to double for company!

—SUSAN BROWN KANSAS CITY, KS

START TO FINISH: 30 MIN.
MAKES: 4 SERVINGS

- 8 **ounces lean ground beef (90% lean)**
- 1 **can (10 ounces) diced tomatoes and green chilies, undrained**
- 1 **can (15 ounces) black beans, rinsed and drained**
- 1 **can (16 ounces) refried beans**
- 8 **tostada shells**
  Optional toppings: shredded lettuce, shredded reduced-fat Mexican cheese blend, sour cream and/or salsa

1. In a large skillet, cook the beef over medium heat until no longer pink; drain. Stir in the tomatoes. Bring to a boil. Reduce heat; simmer, uncovered, for 6-8 minutes or until liquid is reduced to 2 tablespoons. Stir in the black beans; heat through.

2. Spread refried beans over tostada shells. Top with beef mixture. Serve with toppings of your choice.

PER SERVING *390 cal., 11 g fat (3 g sat. fat), 44 mg chol., 944 mg sodium, 49 g carb., 12 g fiber, 24 g pro. **Diabetic Exchanges:** 3 starch, 3 lean meat.*

SOUP-BOWL CABBAGE ROLLS

C
Grilled Sirloin Teriyaki

The marinade for this super-tender Asian-style beef also works well with fish, chicken and pork. It can only be described as fast and fabulous!

—AGNES WARD STRATFORD, ON

PREP: 10 MIN. + MARINATING
GRILL: 10 MIN.
MAKES: 2 SERVINGS

- 3 tablespoons reduced-sodium soy sauce
- 4½ teaspoons brown sugar
- 1 tablespoon rice vinegar
- 1½ teaspoons minced fresh gingerroot
- 1 garlic clove, minced
- ⅛ teaspoon crushed red pepper flakes
- 1 beef top sirloin steak (1 inch thick and ½ pound)

1. In a large resealable plastic bag, combine the first six ingredients. Add the steak; seal bag and turn to coat. Refrigerate for 8 hours or overnight.
2. Drain and discard marinade. Using long-handled tongs, moisten a paper towel with cooking oil and lightly coat the grill rack. Grill beef, covered, over medium heat or broil 4 in. from the heat for 4-5 minutes on each side or until the meat reaches desired doneness (for medium-rare, a thermometer should read 145°; medium, 160°; well-done, 170°).

PER SERVING *163 cal., 5 g fat (2 g sat. fat), 46 mg chol., 279 mg sodium, 4 g carb., trace fiber, 25 g pro.* **Diabetic Exchange:** *3 lean meat.*

GRILLED SIRLOIN TERIYAKI

FAST FIX ▶
Hearty Vegetable Beef Ragout

With this recipe, I can have a healthy, satisfying meal on the table in under 30 minutes, and my children all join the "Clean Plate Club," too!

—KIM VAN DUNK CALDWELL, NJ

START TO FINISH: 30 MIN.
MAKES: 8 SERVINGS

- 4 cups uncooked whole wheat spiral pasta
- 1 pound lean ground beef (90% lean)
- 1 large onion, chopped
- 3 garlic cloves, minced
- 2 cans (14½ ounces each) Italian diced tomatoes, undrained
- 1 jar (24 ounces) meatless spaghetti sauce
- 2 cups finely chopped fresh kale
- 1 package (9 ounces) frozen peas, thawed
- ¾ teaspoon garlic powder
- ¼ teaspoon pepper
  Grated Parmesan cheese, optional

1. Cook the pasta according to package directions. Meanwhile, in a Dutch oven, cook the beef, onion and garlic over medium heat until meat is no longer pink; drain.
2. Stir in the tomatoes, spaghetti sauce, kale, peas, garlic powder and pepper. Bring to a boil. Reduce heat; simmer, uncovered, for 8-10 minutes or until kale is tender. Drain pasta; stir into sauce. Serve with cheese if desired.

PER SERVING *302 cal., 5 g fat (2 g sat. fat), 35 mg chol., 837 mg sodium, 43 g carb., 7 g fiber, 20 g pro.* **Diabetic Exchanges:** *2 starch, 2 lean meat, 2 vegetable.*

Top-Rated Italian Pot Roast

I'm always collecting recipes from newspapers and magazines, and this one just sounded too good not to try! You'll love the the blend of wholesome ingredients and aromatic spices.

—**KAREN BURDELL** LAFAYETTE, CO

PREP: 30 MIN. • **COOK:** 6 HOURS
MAKES: 8 SERVINGS

- 6 **whole peppercorns**
- 4 **whole cloves**
- 3 **whole allspice**
- 1 **cinnamon stick (3 inches)**
- 1 **boneless beef chuck roast (2 pounds)**
- 2 **teaspoons olive oil**
- 2 **celery ribs, sliced**
- 2 **medium carrots, sliced**
- 1 **large onion, chopped**
- 4 **garlic cloves, minced**
- 1 **cup sherry or reduced-sodium beef broth**
- 1 **can (28 ounces) crushed tomatoes**
- ¼ **teaspoon salt**
  Hot cooked egg noodles, optional

1. Place the peppercorns, cloves, allspice and cinnamon stick on a double thickness of cheesecloth; bring up corners of cloth and tie with string to form a bag. Set aside.
2. In a large skillet, brown meat in oil on all sides; transfer to a 4-qt. slow cooker. Top with celery, carrots and spice bag.
3. In the same pan, saute onion in drippings until tender. Add garlic; cook 1 minute longer. Add sherry, stirring to loosen browned bits from pan. Bring to a boil; cook and stir until liquid is reduced to ⅔ cup. Stir in tomatoes and salt; pour over vegetables.
4. Cover and cook on low for 6-7 hours or until meat and vegetables are tender. Remove meat to a serving platter; keep warm. Discard spice bag. Skim fat from vegetable mixture; serve with beef and noodles if desired.
PER SERVING *251 cal., 12 g fat (4 g sat. fat), 74 mg chol., 271 mg sodium, 11 g carb., 3 g fiber, 24 g pro.* **Diabetic Exchanges:** *3 lean meat, 2 vegetable, ½ fat.*

CHOCOLATE-CHIPOTLE SIRLOIN STEAK

Chocolate-Chipotle Sirloin Steak

Looking to do something a little different with grilled sirloin? Add a smoky heat and chocolaty rich color with this easy five-ingredient rub.

—**TASTE OF HOME TEST KITCHEN**

PREP: 10 MIN.+ CHILLING
GRILL: 20 MIN.
MAKES: 4 SERVINGS

- 3 **tablespoons baking cocoa**
- 2 **tablespoons chopped chipotle peppers in adobo sauce**
- 4 **teaspoons Worcestershire sauce**
- 2 **teaspoons brown sugar**
- ½ **teaspoon salt**
- 1½ **pounds beef top sirloin steak**

1. Place the first five ingredients in a blender; cover and process until blended. Rub over beef. Cover and refrigerate for at least 2 hours.
2. Grill the beef, covered, over medium heat or broil 4 in. from the heat for 8-10 minutes on each side or until meat reaches desired doneness (for medium-rare, a thermometer should read 145°; medium, 160°; well-done, 170°).
PER SERVING *246 cal., 7 g fat (3 g sat. fat), 69 mg chol., 477 mg sodium, 6 g carb., 1 g fiber, 37 g pro.* **Diabetic Exchange:** *5 lean meat.*

SUCCULENT
BEEF SKEWERS

C
Succulent Beef Skewers

These are no ordinary beef kabobs! They're herb-infused and need to marinate at least an hour or overnight for the finest flavor. If you feel like splurging, this recipe's also fantastic with beef tenderloin.

—AGNES WARD STRATFORD, ON

PREP: 15 MIN. + MARINATING
GRILL: 10 MIN.
MAKES: 6 SKEWERS

- 2 tablespoons Dijon mustard
- 2 tablespoons balsamic vinegar
- 1 tablespoon brown sugar
- 1 tablespoon olive oil
- 1 tablespoon minced fresh rosemary or 1 teaspoon dried rosemary, crushed
- 1½ teaspoons minced fresh thyme or ½ teaspoon dried thyme
- 2 garlic cloves, minced
- ½ teaspoon salt
- ½ teaspoon pepper
- 1½ pounds boneless beef sirloin steak, cut into 1½-inch cubes

1. In a large resealable plastic bag, combine the first nine ingredients; add beef; seal bag and turn to coat. Refrigerate for at least 2 hours or overnight, turning occasionally.
2. Drain and discard marinade. Thread beef onto six metal or soaked wooden skewers. Using long-handled tongs, moisten a paper towel with cooking oil and lightly coat the grill rack.
3. Grill steak, covered, over medium-hot heat or broil 4 in. from the heat for 8-10 minutes or until the beef reaches desired doneness (for medium-rare, a thermometer should read 145°; medium, 160°; well-done, 170°), turning occasionally.
PER SERVING *170 cal., 7 g fat (2 g sat. fat), 64 mg chol., 297 mg sodium, 4 g carb., trace fiber, 22 g pro.* **Diabetic Exchanges:** *3 lean meat, 1 fat.*

C FAST FIX
Mexican Fiesta Steak Stir-Fry

The best part of throwing a weeknight party is being able to enjoy time with family. With this flavorful stir-fry on the menu, you'll be out of the kitchen with time to spare!

—PATRICIA SWART GALLOWAY, NJ

START TO FINISH: 30 MIN.
MAKES: 4 SERVINGS

- 1 pound boneless beef top loin steak, trimmed and cut into thin strips
- 3 garlic cloves, minced
- 1 to 2 tablespoons canola oil
- 1 package (14 ounces) frozen pepper strips, thawed
- 1⅓ cups chopped sweet onion
- 2 plum tomatoes, chopped
- 1 can (4 ounces) chopped green chilies
- ½ teaspoon salt
- ½ teaspoon dried oregano
- ¼ teaspoon pepper
  Hot cooked rice

1. In a large skillet or wok, stir-fry the beef and garlic in oil until the meat is no longer pink. Remove and keep warm.
2. Add peppers and onion to pan; stir-fry until tender. Stir in the tomatoes, chilies, salt, oregano, pepper and beef; heat through. Serve with rice.
PER SERVING *247 cal., 9 g fat (2 g sat. fat), 50 mg chol., 473 mg sodium, 13 g carb., 3 g fiber, 26 g pro.* **Diabetic Exchanges:** *3 lean meat, 2 vegetable, 1 fat.*

MEXICAN FIESTA
STEAK STIR-FRY

Bean Beef Burgers

When it comes to health, I know how important it is to boost fiber with something as simple as whole grains. So if you want to enjoy a burger without the fat and, as a bonus, sneak in more fiber, give these a try.

—JENNIFER KUNZ AUSTIN, TX

START TO FINISH: 30 MIN.
MAKES: 6 SERVINGS

- 1 cup water
- ½ cup bulgur
- 1 can (15 ounces) black beans, rinsed and drained
- 3 green onions, sliced
- 1 tablespoon stone-ground mustard
- 1 garlic clove, halved
- ¼ teaspoon salt
- ¼ teaspoon pepper
- 1 egg, lightly beaten
- ½ pound lean ground beef (90% lean)
- 1 tablespoon canola oil
- 6 whole wheat hamburger buns, split
  Spinach leaves, sliced red onion and tomato

1. In a small saucepan, bring water to a boil. Stir in the bulgur. Reduce heat; cover and simmer for 15-20 minutes or until tender. In a food processor, combine the beans, onions, mustard and garlic. Cover and pulse until blended. Stir in salt and pepper.

2. In a large bowl, combine the egg, bulgur and bean mixture. Crumble beef over mixture and mix well. Shape into six patties.

3. In a large nonstick skillet, cook patties in oil in batches for 4-5 minutes on each side or until a thermometer reads 160° and juices run clear. Serve on buns with spinach, onion and tomato.

PER SERVING *307 cal., 8 g fat (2 g sat. fat), 54 mg chol., 517 mg sodium, 42 g carb., 9 g fiber, 17 g pro. Diabetic Exchanges: 2 starch, 2 lean meat, 1 fat.*

Fired Up for Leftovers

When firing up the grill or broiler for tonight's steak dinner, think about tomorrow's supper, too. Prepare twice as much and use leftovers in fajitas, on salad or in scrambled eggs the next day.

C | FAST FIX ▶

Chili Steak & Peppers

In the mood for steak tonight? Chili sauce, lime juice and brown sugar is a simple combination for kicking up flavor, and the entire entree is under 275 calories.

—TASTE OF HOME TEST KITCHEN

START TO FINISH: 30 MIN.
MAKES: 4 SERVINGS

- 2 tablespoons chili sauce
- 1 tablespoon lime juice
- 1 teaspoon brown sugar
- ½ teaspoon crushed red pepper flakes
- ½ teaspoon salt, divided
- 1 beef top sirloin steak (1¼ pounds), cut into four steaks
- 1 medium onion, halved and sliced
- 1 medium green pepper, cut into strips
- 1 medium sweet yellow pepper, cut into strips

CHILI STEAK & PEPPERS

- 2 teaspoons olive oil
- 1 small garlic clove, minced
- ⅛ teaspoon pepper
- ¼ cup reduced-fat sour cream
- 1 teaspoon prepared horseradish

1. Combine the chili sauce, lime juice, brown sugar, pepper flakes and ¼ teaspoon salt; brush over steaks. Broil steaks 4-6 in. from the heat for 5-7 minutes on each side or until the meat reaches desired doneness (for medium-rare, a thermometer should read 145°; medium, 160°; well-done, 170°).

2. Meanwhile, in a large skillet, saute onion and green and yellow peppers in oil until tender. Add the garlic, pepper and remaining salt; cook 1 minute longer. In a small bowl, combine sour cream and horseradish. Serve steaks with pepper mixture and sauce.

PER SERVING *265 cal., 9 g fat (3 g sat. fat), 62 mg chol., 491 mg sodium, 12 g carb., 2 g fiber, 32 g pro. Diabetic Exchanges: 4 lean meat, 1 vegetable, 1 fat.*

FAST FIX ▶
Greek Sloppy Joes

Amazing how a little feta cheese adds a depth of flavor like no other to a simple sloppy-joe recipe. Leftovers make a tasty pita filling the next day.

—**SONYA LABBE** WEST HOLLYWOOD, CA

START TO FINISH: 25 MIN.
MAKES: 6 SERVINGS

- 1 **pound lean ground beef (90% lean)**
- 1 **small red onion, chopped**
- 1 **can (15 ounces) tomato sauce**
- 1 **teaspoon dried oregano**
- 2 **cups chopped romaine**
- 6 **kaiser rolls, split and toasted**
- ½ **cup crumbled feta cheese**

1. In a large skillet, cook the beef and onion over medium heat until the meat is no longer pink; drain. Stir in the tomato sauce and oregano. Bring to a boil. Reduce heat; simmer, uncovered, for 8-10 minutes or until sauce thickens slightly, stirring occasionally.

GREEK SLOPPY JOES

2. Place romaine on roll bottoms. Top each with ½ cup meat mixture and sprinkle with the feta. Replace roll tops.

PER SERVING *335 cal., 10 g fat (4 g sat. fat), 52 mg chol., 767 mg sodium, 36 g carb., 3 g fiber, 23 g pro.* **Diabetic Exchanges:** *3 lean meat, 2 starch, 1 vegetable.*

Easy Beef-Stuffed Shells

I like to make this ahead of time and bake it the next day for a simple, comforting meal. The pesto is the best part; it makes a surprising filling for the cheesy shells.

—**BLAIR LONERGAN** ROCHELLE, VA

PREP: 45 MIN. + CHILLING
BAKE: 45 MIN.
MAKES: 10 SERVINGS

- 20 **uncooked jumbo pasta shells**
- 1 **pound lean ground beef (90% lean)**
- 1 **large onion, chopped**
- 1 **medium green pepper, chopped**
- 1¼ **cups reduced-fat ricotta cheese**
- 1½ **cups (6 ounces) shredded reduced-fat Italian cheese blend, divided**
- ¼ **cup grated Parmesan cheese**
- ¼ **cup prepared pesto**
- 1 **egg, lightly beaten**
- 1 **can (14½ ounces) Italian diced tomatoes, undrained**
- 1 **can (8 ounces) no-salt-added tomato sauce**
- 1 **teaspoon Italian seasoning**

1. Cook the pasta according to package directions to al dente; drain and rinse in cold water. In a large skillet, cook the beef, onion and green pepper over medium heat until meat is no longer pink; drain. In a large bowl, combine the ricotta cheese, 1 cup Italian cheese blend, Parmesan cheese, pesto, egg and half of the beef mixture.

EASY BEEF-STUFFED SHELLS

2. In a small bowl, combine the tomatoes, tomato sauce and Italian seasoning. Spread ¾ cup into a 13-in x 9-in. baking dish coated with cooking spray. Spoon cheese mixture into pasta shells; place in baking dish. Combine remaining beef mixture and tomato mixture; spoon over shells. Sprinkle with the remaining cheese. Cover and refrigerate overnight.

3. Remove from the refrigerator 30 minutes before baking. Cover and bake at 350° for 40 minutes. Uncover; bake 5-10 minutes longer or until cheese is melted.

PER SERVING *295 cal., 12 g fat (5 g sat. fat), 70 mg chol., 436 mg sodium, 23 g carb., 2 g fiber, 22 g pro.* **Diabetic Exchanges:** *3 lean meat, 1½ starch, 1 fat.*

Whiskey Sirloin Steak

Tender and slightly sweet from the marinade, this juicy steak boasts wonderful flavor with hardly any prep. Serve with potatoes and veggies for a satisfyingly healthy meal.

—TASTE OF HOME TEST KITCHEN

PREP: 10 MIN. + MARINATING
BROIL: 15 MIN.
MAKES: 4 SERVINGS

- ¼ cup whiskey or apple cider
- ¼ cup reduced-sodium soy sauce
- 1 tablespoon sugar
- 1 garlic clove, thinly sliced
- ½ teaspoon ground ginger
- 1 beef top sirloin steak (1 inch thick and 1 pound)

1. In a large resealable plastic bag, combine the first five ingredients; add the beef. Seal bag and turn to coat; refrigerate for 8 hours or overnight.
2. Drain and discard marinade. Place the beef on a broiler pan coated with cooking spray. Broil 4-6 in. from the heat for 7-8 minutes on each side or until the meat reaches desired doneness (for medium-rare, a thermometer should read 145°; medium, 160°; well-done, 170°).
PER SERVING *168 cal., 5 g fat (2 g sat. fat), 46 mg chol., 353 mg sodium, 2 g carb., trace fiber, 25 g pro.* **Diabetic Exchange:** *3 lean meat.*

Italian Beef Barley Stew

I'm a fan of soups that can be made ahead and also freeze well. This one meets both of those criteria and is a winner with meat and potato lovers.

—JACQUELINE KLOESS IOWA CITY, IA

PREP: 30 MIN. • **COOK:** 1¾ HOURS
MAKES: 10 SERVINGS (3½ QUARTS)

- 1 boneless beef chuck roast (2 pounds), cut into ¾-inch cubes
- 3 medium onions, coarsely chopped
- 4 celery ribs, thinly sliced
- 3 medium carrots, halved lengthwise and thinly sliced
- 2 medium potatoes, peeled and cubed
- 2 garlic cloves, minced
- 1 can (46 ounces) tomato juice
- 1 can (28 ounces) diced tomatoes, undrained
- 1 bay leaf
- 1½ teaspoons dried marjoram
- 1½ teaspoons dried thyme
- ½ teaspoon salt
- ¼ teaspoon coarsely ground pepper
- ½ cup medium pearl barley

1. In a Dutch oven coated with cooking spray, cook beef and onions over medium heat until meat is no longer pink; drain. Stir in the celery, carrots and potatoes. Cook and stir 5 minutes or until crisp-tender. Add the garlic; cook 1 minute longer.
2. Stir in tomato juice, tomatoes, bay leaf and seasonings. Bring to a boil. Stir in barley. Reduce heat; cover and simmer for 1¼ to 1½ hours or until the meat and barley are tender.
3. Discard bay leaf. Serve desired amount. Cool remaining soup; transfer to freezer containers. Freeze for up to 3 months.
TO USE FROZEN SOUP *Thaw in the refrigerator overnight. Place in a saucepan and heat through.*
PER SERVING *281 cal., 9 g fat (3 g sat. fat), 59 mg chol., 636 mg sodium, 30 g carb., 6 g fiber, 22 g pro.* **Diabetic Exchanges:** *3 lean meat, 2 starch.*

ITALIAN BEEF BARLEY STEW

**FAMILY-FAVORITE
MEAT LOAF**

Family-Favorite Meat Loaf

Combining ground beef with ground turkey is the key to this flavorful meat loaf. Horseradish adds just the right amount of zip. It has my husband's seal of approval!

—COLETTE GEROW RAYTOWN, MO

PREP: 15 MIN. • **BAKE:** 45 MIN.
MAKES: 6 SERVINGS

- ⅓ **cup egg substitute**
- 1 **can (6 ounces) tomato paste, divided**
- 2 **tablespoons Dijon mustard**
- 2 **teaspoons prepared horseradish, divided**
- ½ **cup quick-cooking oats**
- 1 **envelope onion soup mix**
- 1½ **teaspoons garlic powder**
- 1 **teaspoon steak seasoning**
- 1 **pound lean ground beef**
- ½ **pound lean ground turkey**
- 1 **teaspoon water**
- ½ **teaspoon sugar**

1. In a large bowl, combine the egg substitute, ½ cup tomato paste, mustard, 1 teaspoon horseradish, oats, soup mix, garlic powder and steak seasoning. Crumble beef and turkey over mixture and mix well.

2. Shape into a loaf and place in an 11-in. x 7-in. baking dish coated with cooking spray. Combine the water, sugar, remaining tomato paste and remaining horseradish; spread over meat loaf.

3. Bake, uncovered, at 350° 45-55 minutes or until a thermometer reads 165°. Drain if necessary.

NOTE *This recipe was tested with McCormick's Montreal Steak Seasoning. Look for it in the spice aisle.*

PER SERVING *250 cal., 10 g fat (3 g sat. fat), 76 mg chol., 763 mg sodium, 16 g carb., 3 g fiber, 24 g pro.* **Diabetic Exchanges:** *3 lean meat, 1 vegetable, 1 fat, ½ starch.*

Crab-Stuffed Filet Mignon

Save this one for a special occasion. Even though it's straight to prepare, it's worthy of a dinner celebration for two.

—**SHANE HARRIS** ABINGDON, VA

START TO FINISH: 30 MIN.
MAKES: 2 SERVINGS

- ½ cup lump crabmeat, drained
- 2 tablespoons shredded Parmesan cheese
- 1 tablespoon chopped green onion
- 1 teaspoon butter, melted
- 2 beef tenderloin steaks (6 ounces each)
- ¼ teaspoon salt
- ⅛ teaspoon pepper

1. In a small bowl, combine the crabmeat, cheese, onion and butter. Sprinkle steaks with salt and pepper. Cut a horizontal slit through each steak to within ½ in. of the opposite side, forming a pocket. Fill with ½ cup crab mixture. Secure with kitchen string if necessary.

2. Broil 4 in. from the heat for 7-9 minutes on each side or until meat reaches desired doneness (for medium-rare, a thermometer should read 145°; medium, 160°; well-done, 170°). Let stand for 5 minutes before serving.

PER SERVING *318 cal., 14 g fat (6 g sat. fat), 113 mg chol., 506 mg sodium, trace carb., trace fiber, 45 g pro.*

Nacho Beef Bake

For casual gatherings, this beefy comfort food is an easy way to feed a crowd. Only the person who makes it has to know it's been lightened up.

—**CARLA WEEKS** INDEPENDENCE, IA

PREP: 25 MIN. • **BAKE:** 20 MIN.
MAKES: 12 SERVINGS

- 1½ pounds lean ground beef (90% lean)
- 1 can (15 ounces) black beans, rinsed and drained
- ½ cup water
- 1 envelope reduced-sodium taco seasoning
- 2 tubes (8 ounces each) refrigerated reduced-fat crescent rolls
- 1 cup (8 ounces) reduced-fat sour cream
- 1 cup (4 ounces) shredded reduced-fat cheddar cheese
- 4 ounces baked nacho-flavored tortilla chips (about 2 cups), crushed
- 3 cups shredded lettuce
- 3 medium tomatoes, chopped

1. In a large skillet, cook beef over medium heat until the meat is no longer pink; drain. Add the beans, water and taco seasoning; mash slightly. Cook and stir for 4-5 minutes or until heated through; set aside.

2. Unroll crescent dough and press onto the bottom and up the sides of a 13-in. x 9-in. baking dish coated with cooking spray; seal seams and perforations. Spoon beef mixture over dough. Spread sour cream over beef mixture; sprinkle with cheese and chips.

3. Bake, uncovered, at 375° for 18-22 minutes or until cheese is melted. Top with lettuce and tomatoes. Serve immediately.

PER SERVING *357 cal., 15 g fat (6 g sat. fat), 41 mg chol., 728 mg sodium, 34 g carb., 3 g fiber, 20 g pro.*

NACHO BEEF BAKE

Sesame Beef Stir-Fry

Soy sauce and gingerroot add great flavor to this quick beef stir-fry. It couldn't be simpler to make, but it's definitely elegant enough to serve someone special.

—CHARLENE CHAMBERS

ORMOND BEACH, FL

START TO FINISH: 30 MIN.
MAKES: 2 SERVINGS

- 2 teaspoons cornstarch
- ½ cup reduced-sodium beef broth
- 4 teaspoons reduced-sodium soy sauce
- 1 tablespoon minced fresh gingerroot
- 1 garlic clove, minced
- ½ pound beef top sirloin steak, thinly sliced
- 2 teaspoons sesame seeds toasted, divided
- 2 teaspoons peanut or canola oil, divided
- 2 cups fresh broccoli florets
- 1 small sweet yellow pepper, julienned
- 1 cup hot cooked brown rice

SESAME BEEF
STIR-FRY

1. In a small bowl, combine the first five ingredients until blended; set aside.

2. In a large nonstick skillet or wok, stir-fry beef and 1 teaspoon sesame seeds in 1 teaspoon oil until the meat is no longer pink. Remove and keep warm.

3. Stir-fry broccoli in remaining oil for 2 minutes. Add the pepper; stir-fry 4-6 minutes longer or until vegetables are crisp-tender.

4. Stir cornstarch mixture and add to pan. Bring to a boil; cook and stir for 2 minutes or until thickened. Add beef; heat through. Serve with rice. Sprinkle with the remaining sesame seeds.

PER SERVING 363 cal., 12 g fat (3 g sat. fat), 47 mg chol., 606 mg sodium, 33 g carb., 5 g fiber, 31 g pro. *Diabetic Exchanges: 3 lean meat, 2 starch, 1 vegetable, 1 fat.*

Basil Burgers with Sun-Dried Tomato Mayonnaise

I often end up with a bumper crop of basil, and here's a favorite way to use some of it. These burgers have a wonderful Italian twist. And who can resist their gooey, cheesy centers and scrumptious topping?

—VIRGINIA KOCHIS SPRINGFIELD, VA

PREP: 25 MIN. • **GRILL:** 10 MIN.
MAKES: 6 SERVINGS

- ¼ cup sun-dried tomatoes (not packed in oil)
- 1 cup boiling water
- 1 cup fat-free mayonnaise
- 2 teaspoons Worcestershire sauce
- ¼ cup fresh basil leaves, coarsely chopped
- 2 teaspoons Italian seasoning
- 2 garlic cloves, minced
- ½ teaspoon pepper
- ¼ teaspoon salt
- 1½ pounds lean ground beef (90% lean)
- ¾ cup shredded part-skim mozzarella cheese
- 6 whole wheat hamburger buns, split
  Additional fresh basil leaves, optional

1. In a small bowl, combine the tomatoes and water. Let stand for 5 minutes; drain. In a food processor, combine mayonnaise and tomatoes; cover and process until blended. Chill until serving.

2. In a large bowl, combine the Worcestershire sauce, basil, Italian seasoning, garlic, pepper and salt. Crumble beef over mixture and mix well. Shape into 12 thin patties. Place 2 tablespoons cheese on six patties; top with remaining patties and press edges firmly to seal.

3. Moisten a paper towel with cooking oil; using long-handled tongs, lightly coat the grill rack. Grill burgers, covered, over medium heat or broil 4 in. from the heat for 5-7 minutes on each side or until a thermometer reads 160° and juices run clear. Serve on buns with the mayonnaise mixture and additional basil if desired.

PER SERVING 368 cal., 15 g fat (6 g sat. fat), 83 mg chol., 816 mg sodium, 30 g carb., 5 g fiber, 30 g pro. *Diabetic Exchanges: 4 lean meat, 2 starch, ½ fat.*

South of the Border Sirloin

Marinated in beer and jalapenos, these steaks have a mild heat the whole family will love! They're topped with veggies, bread crumbs and cheese for an appetizing look. But they're so easy to prepare!

—GILDA LESTER MILLSBORO, DE

PREP: 15 MIN. + MARINATING
BROIL: 5 MIN.
MAKES: 4 SERVINGS

- 1 bottle (12 ounces) light or nonalcoholic beer
- 1 medium onion, chopped
- 3 garlic cloves, minced
- 1 tablespoon chili powder
- 1 teaspoon salt
- 1 teaspoon pepper
- 1 beef top sirloin steak (1 pound)

TOPPING

- 2 large onions, thinly sliced
- 5 teaspoons olive oil, divided
- 2 jalapeno peppers, seeded and minced
- 1 medium sweet red pepper, julienned
- 3 garlic cloves, minced
- 3 tablespoons dry bread crumbs
- 3 tablespoons shredded reduced-fat cheddar cheese

1. In a large resealable plastic bag, combine the first six ingredients. Cut steak into four serving-size pieces; place in bag. Seal the bag and turn to coat; refrigerate for up to 2 hours.
2. Meanwhile, in a large ovenproof skillet, cook onions in 2 teaspoons oil over medium heat for 15-20 minutes or until onions are golden brown, stirring occasionally. Add peppers and garlic; cook 4 minutes longer. Remove and keep warm.

3. Drain and discard marinade. In the same skillet over medium heat, cook steak in 2 teaspoons oil for 3-4 minutes on each side or until meat reaches desired doneness (for medium-rare, a thermometer should read 145°; medium, 160°; well-done, 170°).
4. Spoon onion mixture over steaks. In a small bowl, combine the bread crumbs, cheese and remaining oil; sprinkle over tops. Broil 3-4 in. from the heat for 2-3 minutes or until golden brown.

NOTE *Wear disposable gloves when cutting hot peppers; the oils can burn skin. Avoid touching your face.*
PER SERVING *280 cal., 12 g fat (3 g sat. fat), 50 mg chol., 228 mg sodium, 15 g carb., 3 g fiber, 28 g pro.* **Diabetic Exchanges:** *3 lean meat, 2 vegetable, 1 fat.*

My Take on Mom's Meat Loaf

Here's a lower-in-fat-and-salt take on my mother's original recipe. I use fresh ingredients like garlic, mushrooms and onions for dried onion soup mix and garlic powder. It's still hearty and tastes like home.

—BRENDA MOEHRINGER GANSEVOORT, NY

PREP: 20 MIN. • **BAKE:** 35 MIN. + STANDING
MAKES: 4 SERVINGS

- 1 egg white
- 1 tablespoon steak sauce
- 1 tablespoon Worcestershire sauce
- 5 medium fresh mushrooms, finely chopped
- ½ cup seasoned bread crumbs
- ⅓ cup finely chopped sweet onion
- 2 tablespoons grated Parmesan cheese
- 2 garlic cloves, minced

MY TAKE ON MOM'S MEAT LOAF

- 1 teaspoon dried sage leaves
- ½ teaspoon pepper
- ⅛ teaspoon salt
- 1 pound lean ground beef (90% lean)
  Barbecue sauce, optional

1. In a large bowl, combine the first 11 ingredients. Crumble the beef over mixture and mix well. Shape into a loaf; place in an 11-in. x 7-in. baking dish coated with cooking spray.
2. Bake, uncovered, at 350° for 35-40 minutes or until no pink remains and a thermometer reads 160°. Let stand for 10 minutes before slicing. Drizzle with the barbecue sauce if desired.

PER SERVING *264 cal., 11 g fat (4 g sat. fat), 71 mg chol., 503 mg sodium, 15 g carb., 1 g fiber, 26 g pro.* **Diabetic Exchanges:** *3 lean meat, 1 starch, 1 fat.*

Feta Stuffed Peppers

One of my favorite meals when I was younger was a recipe my mother made called Quick Chili Rice Casserole. I put a Greek spin on it and stuffed it in a pepper. It works great paired with a garden salad and fresh bread.

—SACHA MORGAN WOODSTOCK, GA

PREP: 35 MIN. • **BAKE:** 30 MIN.
MAKES: 3 SERVINGS

- 3 **large green peppers**
- ½ **pound lean ground beef (90% lean)**
- 1 **small onion, chopped**
- 1 **can (14½ ounces) diced tomatoes, undrained**
- 2 **cups chopped fresh spinach**
- ¾ **cup uncooked whole wheat orzo pasta**
- 2 **tablespoons minced fresh oregano or 2 teaspoons dried oregano**
- ¼ **teaspoon salt**
- ¼ **teaspoon pepper**
- 6 **tablespoons crumbled feta cheese**

1. Cut peppers in half lengthwise and remove seeds. In a Dutch oven, cook peppers in boiling water for 3-5 minutes. Drain and rinse in cold water; invert onto paper towels.

2. In a large skillet, cook beef and onion over medium heat until meat is no longer pink. Stir in the tomatoes, spinach, orzo, oregano, salt and pepper. Bring to a boil. Reduce heat; cover and simmer for 5-7 minutes or until orzo is tender.

3. Spoon into the peppers. Place in an 11-in. x 7-in. baking dish coated with cooking spray. Cover and bake at 350° for 30-35 minutes or until peppers are tender.

4. Sprinkle with cheese; bake 5 minutes longer or until the cheese is softened.

PER SERVING *369 cal., 10 g fat (4 g sat. fat), 55 mg chol., 567 mg sodium, 46 g carb., 13 g fiber, 26 g pro.* ***Diabetic Exchanges:*** *3 starch, 2 lean meat, ½ fat.*

FETA STUFFED PEPPERS

Tender Salsa Beef

This is my Mexican-style twist on comfort food. To keep it kid-friendly, use mild salsa.

—**STACIE STAMPER** NORTH WILKESBORO, NC

PREP: 15 MIN. • **COOK:** 8 HOURS
MAKES: 8 SERVINGS

- 1½ **pounds beef stew meat, cut into ¾-inch cubes**
- 2 **cups salsa**
- 1 **tablespoon brown sugar**
- 1 **tablespoon reduced-sodium soy sauce**
- 1 **garlic clove, minced**
- 4 **cups hot cooked brown rice**

In a 3-qt. slow cooker, combine the beef, salsa, brown sugar, soy sauce and garlic. Cover and cook on low for 8-10 hours or until meat is tender. Using a slotted spoon, serve beef with rice.

PER SERVING 259 cal., 7 g fat (2 g sat. fat), 53 mg chol., 356 mg sodium, 28 g carb., 2 g fiber, 19 g pro. **Diabetic Exchanges:** 2 starch, 2 lean meat.

Drain the Fat

Draining ground beef in a colander after it's cooked prevents your tacos, sloppy joes or pitas from getting too greasy. To remove even more fat, blot the meat with paper towels after draining.

HEARTY PITA TACOS

FAST FIX
Hearty Pita Tacos

Our 9-year-old daughter enjoys helping us make these tasty tacos and enjoys eating them even more. We find that the leftover beef mixture makes an excellent taco salad for lunch the next day.

—**JAMIE VALOCCHI** MESA, AZ

START TO FINISH: 30 MIN.
MAKES: 6 SERVINGS

- 1 **pound lean ground beef (90% lean)**
- 1 **small sweet red pepper, chopped**
- 2 **green onions, chopped**
- 1 **can (16 ounces) kidney beans, rinsed and drained**
- ¾ **cup frozen corn**
- ⅔ **cup taco sauce**
- 1 **can (2¼ ounces) sliced ripe olives, drained**
- ½ **teaspoon garlic salt**
- ¼ **teaspoon onion powder**
- ¼ **teaspoon dried oregano**
- ¼ **teaspoon paprika**
- ¼ **teaspoon pepper**
- 6 **whole wheat pita pocket halves**
- 6 **tablespoons shredded reduced-fat cheddar cheese**
  Sliced avocado and additional taco sauce, optional

1. In a large skillet, cook the beef, red pepper and onions over medium heat until meat is no longer pink; drain. Stir in the beans, corn, taco sauce, olives and seasonings; heat through.
2. Spoon ¾ cup beef mixture into each pita half. Sprinkle with the cheese. Serve with avocado and additional taco sauce if desired.

PER SERVING 339 cal., 10 g fat (4 g sat. fat), 52 mg chol., 787 mg sodium, 38 g carb., 8 g fiber, 26 g pro. **Diabetic Exchanges:** 3 lean meat, 2½ starch.

ITALIAN BURRITOS

Italian Burritos

No beans about it...beef, cheese, garlic and sauce are stuffed inside these baked burritos. My family is very picky, so I came up with these to satisfy everyone—and it really worked!

—DONNA HOLTER CENTENNIAL, CO

PREP: 20 MIN. • **BAKE:** 20 MIN.
MAKES: 8 SERVINGS

- 1 **pound lean ground beef (90% lean)**
- 1 **cup marinara sauce**
- ½ **cup shredded part-skim mozzarella cheese**
- ¼ **cup grated Parmesan cheese**
- ¼ **teaspoon garlic powder**
- 8 **whole wheat tortillas (8 inches), warmed**

1. In a large skillet, cook beef over medium heat until no longer pink; drain. Stir in the marinara, cheeses and garlic powder.

2. Spoon ⅓ cup filling off center on each tortilla. Fold sides and ends over filling and roll up. Place on a baking sheet coated with cooking spray.

3. Bake at 375° for 18-20 minutes or until heated through and bottoms are lightly browned.

PER SERVING *275 cal., 10 g fat (3 g sat. fat), 42 mg chol., 326 mg sodium, 26 g carb., 3 g fiber, 18 g pro.* **Diabetic Exchanges: 2 starch, 2 lean meat.**

FAST FIX

Beefy Tomato Rice Skillet

I put this together one day with what I had on hand. It's quick on busy nights or in the summer when we're camping.

—ELLYN GRAEBERT YUMA, AZ

START TO FINISH: 25 MIN.
MAKES: 6 SERVINGS

- 1 **pound ground beef**
- 1 **cup chopped celery**
- ⅔ **cup chopped onion**
- ½ **cup chopped green pepper**
- 1 **can (11 ounces) whole kernel corn, drained**
- 1 **can (10¾ ounces) condensed tomato soup, undiluted**
- 1 **cup water**
- 1 **teaspoon Italian seasoning**
- 1 **cup uncooked instant rice**

1. In a large skillet over medium heat, cook the beef, celery, onion and pepper until the meat is no longer pink and vegetables are tender; drain.

2. Add the corn, soup, water and Italian seasoning; bring to a boil. Stir in rice; cover and remove from the heat. Let stand for 10 minutes or until rice is tender.

PER SERVING *266 cal., 7 g fat (3 g sat. fat), 37 mg chol., 506 mg sodium, 30 g carb., 2 g fiber, 17 g pro.* **Diabetic Exchanges: 2 lean meat, 2 vegetable, 1 starch, 1 fat.**

Hearty Beef Ravioli

FAST FIX

In this fun family-friendly supper, we add our favorite taco toppings to a bowl of beefy ravioli. It's effortless for kids to customize their favorite fixings.
—TASTE OF HOME TEST KITCHEN

START TO FINISH: 30 MIN.
MAKES: 6 SERVINGS

- 1 package (25 ounces) frozen beef ravioli
- ½ pound extra-lean ground beef (95% lean)
- 1 medium green pepper, chopped
- 1 can (14½ ounces) no-salt-added diced tomatoes
- 1 can (8 ounces) no-salt-added tomato sauce
- 2 tablespoons reduced-sodium taco seasoning
- ¾ cup shredded reduced-fat cheddar cheese
- 1 can (2¼ ounces) sliced ripe olives, drained

1. Cook the ravioli according to package directions.
2. Meanwhile, in a large nonstick skillet, cook the beef and green pepper over medium heat until meat is no longer pink. Stir in the tomatoes, tomato sauce and taco seasoning. Bring to a boil. Reduce heat; simmer, uncovered, for 5-7 minutes or until slightly thickened.
3. Drain the pasta. Serve with sauce. Sprinkle each serving with 2 tablespoons cheese and about 1 tablespoon olives.
PER SERVING *375 cal., 10 g fat (5 g sat. fat), 44 mg chol., 695 mg sodium, 49 g carb., 4 g fiber, 21 g pro.*

Grilled Red Chili Steak

C FAST FIX

This super-simple recipe turns regular steak into a mouthwatering entree. I like it best with ground ancho chili powder and a little salsa on the side.
—MARY RELYEA CANASTOTA, NY

START TO FINISH: 30 MIN.
MAKES: 4 SERVINGS

- 3 tablespoons chili powder
- 2 teaspoons brown sugar
- 2 teaspoons pepper
- 2 garlic cloves, minced
- ½ teaspoon salt
- ½ teaspoon dried oregano
- ¼ teaspoon ground cumin
- 1 pound beef top sirloin steak
- Salsa

1. Combine the first seven ingredients; rub over steak.
2. Grill steak, covered, over medium heat for 5-7 minutes on each side or until meat reaches desired doneness (for medium-rare, a thermometer should read 145°; medium, 160°; well-done, 170°). Let stand for 10 minutes before slicing. Serve with salsa.
PER SERVING *160 cal., 6 g fat (2 g sat. fat), 64 mg chol., 269 mg sodium, 4 g carb., 2 g fiber, 22 g pro.* **Diabetic Exchanges:** *3 lean meat, ½ fat.*

GRILLED RED CHILI STEAK

FAST FIX ▶

Easy Cuban Picadillo

My girlfriend gave me this delicious recipe years ago. I've made it ever since for family and friends, and they all love it. My daughter says it's the best dish I make and loves to take leftovers to school for lunch the next day.

—MARIE WIELGUS WAYNE, NJ

START TO FINISH: 30 MIN.
MAKES: 4 SERVINGS

- 1 **pound lean ground beef (90% lean)**
- 1 **small green pepper, chopped**
- ¼ **cup chopped onion**
- 1 **can (8 ounces) tomato sauce**
- ½ **cup sliced pimiento-stuffed olives**
- ¼ **cup raisins**
- 1 **tablespoon cider vinegar**
- 2 **cups hot cooked rice**

In a large nonstick skillet, cook the beef, pepper and onion over medium heat until meat is no longer pink; drain. Stir in the tomato sauce, olives, raisins and vinegar. Cook for 5-6 minutes or until raisins are plumped. Serve with rice.

PER SERVING *354 cal., 12 g fat (3 g sat. fat), 56 mg chol., 697 mg sodium, 36 g carb., 2 g fiber, 25 g pro.* **Diabetic Exchanges:** *3 lean meat, 1½ starch, 1 vegetable, 1 fat, ½ fruit.*

Light Mexican Casserole

A must-try dinner: Here's a healthy layered casserole using whole wheat tortillas, lean beef and more veggies than traditional recipes.

—TASTE OF HOME TEST KITCHEN

PREP: 30 MIN. • **BAKE:** 25 MIN.
MAKES: 6 SERVINGS

- 1 **pound extra-lean ground beef (95% lean)**
- 1 **medium onion, chopped**
- 1 **medium green pepper, chopped**
- ¾ **cup water**
- 1 **tablespoon all-purpose flour**
- 1 **tablespoon hot chili powder**
- 1 **teaspoon garlic powder**
- ½ **teaspoon ground cumin**
- ½ **teaspoon ground coriander**
- ¼ **teaspoon salt**
- 1 **can (16 ounces) refried beans**
- ½ **cup salsa**
- 4 **whole wheat tortillas (8 inches)**
- 1 **cup frozen corn**
- ¾ **cup shredded sharp cheddar cheese**
  Shredded lettuce and chopped tomatoes, optional

1. In a large nonstick skillet, cook the beef, onion and green pepper over medium heat until meat is no longer pink. Stir in the water, flour, chili powder, garlic powder, cumin, coriander and salt. Bring to a boil. Reduce heat; simmer, uncovered, for 5-6 minutes or until thickened.

2. In a small bowl, combine beans and salsa. Place two tortillas in a round 2½-qt. baking dish coated with cooking spray. Layer with half of the beef mixture, bean mixture and corn; repeat layers. Top with the cheese.

3. Bake, uncovered, at 350° for 25-30 minutes or until heated through and the cheese is melted. Let stand for 5 minutes before cutting. Serve with lettuce and tomatoes if desired.

PER SERVING *367 cal., 11 g fat (5 g sat. fat), 64 mg chol., 657 mg sodium, 39 g carb., 8 g fiber, 26 g pro.* **Diabetic Exchanges:** *3 lean meat, 2½ starch, 1 vegetable, ½ fat.*

LIGHT MEXICAN CASSEROLE

EASY CUBAN PICADILLO

Slow-Cooked Caribbean Pot Roast

I put this dish together throughout the fall and winter seasons, but considering how simple it is to prepare, it should be taken advantage of year-round!

—JENN TIDWELL FAIR OAKS, CA

PREP: 30 MIN. • **COOK:** 6 HOURS
MAKES: 10 SERVINGS

- 2 medium sweet potatoes, cubed
- 2 large carrots, sliced
- ¼ cup chopped celery
- 1 boneless beef chuck roast (2½ pounds)
- 1 tablespoon canola oil
- 1 large onion, chopped
- 2 garlic cloves, minced
- 1 tablespoon all-purpose flour
- 1 tablespoon sugar
- 1 tablespoon brown sugar
- 1 teaspoon ground cumin
- ¾ teaspoon salt
- ¾ teaspoon ground coriander
- ¾ teaspoon chili powder
- ½ teaspoon dried oregano
- ⅛ teaspoon ground cinnamon
- ¾ teaspoon grated orange peel
- ¾ teaspoon baking cocoa
- 1 can (15 ounces) tomato sauce

1. Place the potatoes, carrots and celery in a 5-qt. slow cooker. In a large skillet, brown meat in oil on all sides. Transfer the meat to the slow cooker.
2. In the same skillet, saute onion in drippings until tender. Add the garlic; cook 1 minute longer. Combine the flour, sugar, brown sugar, seasonings, orange peel and cocoa. Stir in tomato sauce; add to skillet and heat through. Pour over the beef.
3. Cover and cook on low for 6-8 hours or until beef and vegetables are tender.

PER SERVING *278 cal., 12 g fat (4 g sat. fat), 74 mg chol., 453 mg sodium, 16 g carb., 3 g fiber, 25 g pro.* **Diabetic Exchanges:** *3 lean meat, 1 starch, 1 vegetable, ½ fat.*

SLOW-COOKED
CARIBBEAN POT ROAST

SAVORY TURKEY POTPIES
PAGE 164

**JANICE MENTZER'S
CITRUS GRILLED TURKEY CUTLETS**
PAGE 150

**ERIN HAMANN'S
CHICKEN CAESAR DELUXE PIZZA**
PAGE 158

**BRANDI CASTILLO'S
SLOW-COOKED SOUTHWEST
CHICKEN** *PAGE 165*

Chicken & Turkey

If you suspect your chicken or turkey dinner is stuck in a rut, start here to **perk up your poultry.** No matter the featured bird, these **recipes are as irresistible** as they are healthy. Dig in!

Chevre-Stuffed Chicken with Apricot Glaze

My original version of this recipe used several tablespoons of butter. Now with one tablespoon of oil and a few more tweaks, this rich and filling entree is under 350 calories.

—**DAVID DAHLMAN** CHATSWORTH, CA

PREP: 20 MIN. • **COOK:** 20 MIN.
MAKES: 2 SERVINGS

- 2 **boneless skinless chicken breast halves (6 ounces each)**
- ¼ **teaspoon salt**
- ¼ **teaspoon pepper**
- 2 **tablespoons goat cheese**
- 2 **tablespoons part-skim ricotta cheese**
- 4 **tablespoons chopped shallots, divided**
- 1 **teaspoon olive oil**
- ⅔ **cup reduced-sodium chicken broth**
- 2 **tablespoons apricot spreadable fruit**
- 1 **tablespoon lemon juice**
- 1 **teaspoon spicy brown mustard**
- 1 **teaspoon minced fresh parsley**

1. Flatten chicken to ¼-in. thickness; sprinkle with salt and pepper. Mix goat cheese, ricotta and 1 tablespoon shallots; spread over the center of each chicken breast. Roll up and secure with toothpicks.
2. In a nonstick skillet, brown chicken in oil on all sides. Remove; keep warm.
3. In the same skillet, saute remaining shallots until tender. Stir in the broth, spreadable fruit, lemon juice and mustard. Bring to a boil; cook until liquid is reduced by half.
4. Return chicken to the pan; cover and cook for 6-7 minutes or until a no longer pink. Discard toothpicks. Serve chicken with cooking liquid. Sprinkle with parsley.
PER SERVING *340 cal., 12 g fat (5 g sat. fat), 110 mg chol., 695 mg sodium, 16 g carb., trace fiber, 41 g pro.*

F S C
Roast Turkey Breast with Rosemary Gravy

A velvety gravy coats this remarkably tender and juicy turkey breast that's perfect for a holiday get-together.

—**REBECCA CLARK** WARRIOR, AL

PREP: 20 MIN.
BAKE: 1¾ HOURS + STANDING
MAKES: 18 SERVINGS (1⅓ CUPS GRAVY)

- 2 **medium apples, sliced**
- 1½ **cups sliced leeks (white portion only)**
- 2¼ **cups reduced-sodium chicken broth, divided**
- 1 **bone-in turkey breast (6 pounds)**
- 1 **tablespoon canola oil**
- 2 **teaspoons minced fresh rosemary, divided**
- 3 **tablespoons reduced-fat butter**
- ¼ **cup all-purpose flour**

1. Preheat oven to 325°. Arrange apples and leeks in a roasting pan; add 1 cup broth. Place turkey breast over apple mixture. In a small bowl, combine oil and 1½ teaspoons rosemary. With fingers, carefully loosen skin from the turkey breast; rub rosemary mixture under the skin. Secure skin to underside of breast with toothpicks.
2. Bake, uncovered, 1¾ to 2¼ hours or until a thermometer reads 170°, basting every 30 minutes. Cover loosely with foil if turkey browns too quickly. Remove turkey from oven; tent with foil. Let stand 15 minutes before carving, reserving ¼ cup pan juices. Discard apples and leeks.
3. In a small saucepan, melt butter; add flour and remaining rosemary until blended, stirring constantly. Skim fat from pan juices. Gradually add pan juices and remaining broth to saucepan. Bring to a boil. Cook and stir for 1 minute or until thickened. Serve with turkey.
NOTE *This recipe was tested with Land O'Lakes light stick butter.*
PER SERVING *151 cal., 3 g fat (1 g sat. fat), 81 mg chol., 136 mg sodium, 2 g carb., trace fiber, 29 g pro.* **Diabetic Exchange:** *4 lean meat.*

Turkey Stroganoff with Spaghetti Squash

My twin sister and I came up with this entree after we both successfully lost weight but still wanted to indulge in comfort food. Spaghetti squash is a fantastic healthy alternative to pasta, and we use it in many recipes.

—COURTNEY VARELA ALISO VIEJO, CA

PREP: 25 MIN. • **COOK:** 15 MIN.
MAKES: 6 SERVINGS

- 1 medium spaghetti squash (about 4 pounds)
- 1 pound lean ground turkey
- 2 cups sliced fresh mushrooms
- 1 medium onion, chopped
- 2 garlic cloves, minced
- ½ cup white wine or beef stock
- 3 tablespoons cornstarch
- 2 cups beef stock
- 2 tablespoons Worcestershire sauce
- 1 tablespoon Montreal steak seasoning
- 1 teaspoon minced fresh thyme or ¼ teaspoon dried thyme
- ¼ cup half-and-half cream
  Grated Parmesan cheese and minced fresh parsley, optional

1. Cut squash in half lengthwise; discard seeds. Place squash cut side down on a microwave-safe plate. Microwave, uncovered, on high for 15-18 minutes or until tender.

2. Meanwhile, in a large nonstick skillet, cook the turkey, mushrooms and onion over medium heat until turkey is no longer pink; drain. Add the garlic; cook 1 minute longer. Stir in the wine.

3. Combine cornstarch and stock until smooth. Add to pan. Stir in the Worcestershire sauce, steak seasoning and thyme. Bring to a boil; cook and stir for 2 minutes or until thickened. Reduce heat. Stir in the cream and heat through.

4. When squash is cool enough to handle, use a fork to separate strands. Serve with turkey mixture. Sprinkle with cheese and parsley if desired.

PER SERVING *246 cal., 9 g fat (3 g sat. fat), 65 mg chol., 677 mg sodium, 25 g carb., 4 g fiber, 17 g pro.* **Diabetic Exchanges:** *2 lean meat, 1½ starch.*

Coconut Curry Chicken

My husband and I love this yummy dish! It's a breeze to prepare in the slow cooker, and it tastes just like a meal you'd have at your favorite Indian or Thai restaurant.

—ANDI KAUFFMAN BEAVERCREEK, OR

PREP: 20 MIN. • **COOK:** 5 HOURS
MAKES: 4 SERVINGS

- 2 medium potatoes, peeled and cubed
- 1 small onion, chopped
- 4 boneless skinless chicken breast halves (4 ounces each)
- 1 cup light coconut milk
- 4 teaspoons curry powder
- 1 garlic clove, minced
- 1 teaspoon reduced-sodium chicken bouillon granules
- ¼ teaspoon salt
- ¼ teaspoon pepper
- 2 cups hot cooked rice
- ¼ cup thinly sliced green onions
  Raisins, flaked coconut and chopped unsalted peanuts, optional

1. Place potatoes and onion in a 3- or 4-qt. slow cooker. In a large nonstick skillet coated with cooking spray, brown chicken on both sides.

2. Transfer to slow cooker. In a small bowl, combine the coconut milk, curry, garlic, bouillon, salt and pepper; pour over the chicken. Cover and cook on low for 5-6 hours or until the meat is tender.

3. Serve the chicken and sauce with rice; sprinkle with green onions. Garnish with raisins, coconut and peanuts if desired.

PER SERVING *396 cal., 11 g fat (7 g sat. fat), 63 mg chol., 309 mg sodium, 43 g carb., 3 g fiber, 27 g pro.* **Diabetic Exchanges:** *3 lean meat, 2½ starch, 2 fat.*

COCONUT CURRY CHICKEN

TURKEY STROGANOFF WITH SPAGHETTI SQUASH

Italian Chicken and Peppers

I put this chicken recipe together one day when I had leftover peppers and wanted something easy. To my delight, the taste reminded me of pizza—something I love but can no longer eat! It's great with steamed broccoli.

—BRENDA NOLEN SIMPSONVILLE, SC

PREP: 20 MIN. • **COOK:** 4 HOURS
MAKES: 6 SERVINGS

- 6 **boneless skinless chicken breast halves (4 ounces each)**
- 1 **jar (24 ounces) garden-style spaghetti sauce**
- 1 **medium onion, sliced**
- ½ **each small green, sweet yellow and red peppers, julienned**
- ¼ **cup grated Parmesan cheese**
- 2 **garlic cloves, minced**
- 1 **teaspoon dried oregano**
- 1 **teaspoon dried basil**
- ½ **teaspoon salt**
- ¼ **teaspoon pepper**
- 4½ **cups uncooked spiral pasta**
  Shaved Parmesan cheese, optional

1. Place chicken in a 3-qt. slow cooker. In a large bowl, combine the spaghetti sauce, onion, peppers, cheese, garlic, oregano, basil, salt and pepper. Pour over chicken. Cover and cook on low for 4-5 hours or until a thermometer reads 170°.
2. Cook pasta according to package directions; drain. Serve with chicken and sauce. Top with shaved Parmesan cheese if desired.
PER SERVING *396 cal., 7 g fat (2 g sat. fat), 70 mg chol., 770 mg sodium, 50 g carb., 5 g fiber, 32 g pro.*

Spinach-Walnut Stuffed Chicken

For just 300 calories, you'd be surprised at how much flavor is tucked inside these chicken breasts. The toasted walnut coating adds a delicious crunch.

—KERI CAPUANO NARRAGANSETT, RI

PREP: 20 MIN. • **BAKE:** 25 MIN.
MAKES: 4 SERVINGS

- ½ **cup finely chopped onion**
- ½ **cup finely chopped fresh mushrooms**
- ¼ **cup finely chopped celery**
- 2 **garlic cloves, minced**
- 2½ **teaspoons olive oil**
- 1 **package (10 ounces) frozen chopped spinach, thawed and squeezed dry**
- ¼ **cup crumbled Gorgonzola cheese**
- 4 **boneless skinless chicken breast halves (6 ounces each)**
- ¼ **teaspoon salt**
- ¼ **teaspoon pepper**
- 1 **egg white**
- ¼ **cup ground walnuts**

1. In a small skillet, saute the onion, mushrooms, celery and garlic in oil until tender. Stir in spinach and cheese; remove from the heat.
2. Cut a lengthwise slit through the thickest part of each chicken breast; fill with spinach mixture. Sprinkle with salt and pepper. Place egg white and walnuts in separate shallow bowls. Dip one side of chicken in egg white, then in walnuts.
3. Place in an 11-in. x 7-in. baking dish coated with cooking spray. Bake, uncovered, at 350° for 25-30 minutes or until chicken juices run clear.
PER SERVING *300 cal., 12 g fat (3 g sat. fat), 100 mg chol., 398 mg sodium, 7 g carb., 3 g fiber, 40 g pro.* **Diabetic Exchanges:** *5 lean meat, 2 fat, 1 vegetable.*

SPINACH-WALNUT STUFFED CHICKEN

ITALIAN RESTAURANT CHICKEN

F C Citrus Grilled Turkey Cutlets

My family enjoys this turkey recipe year-round, but it's especially nice in summer as an alternative to grilled chicken. Add a green salad, grilled veggies and some crusty bread for a great dinner.

—**JANICE MENTZER** SHARPSBURG, MD

PREP: 15 MIN. + MARINATING
GRILL: 5 MIN.
MAKES: 4 SERVINGS

- 2 **tablespoons each lemon, lime and orange juices**
- 1 **tablespoon minced fresh cilantro**
- 1 **tablespoon canola oil**
- 1 **tablespoon honey**
- 1 **small garlic clove, minced**
- ½ **teaspoon salt**
- ½ **teaspoon chili powder**
- ¼ **teaspoon ground cumin**
- ¼ **teaspoon pepper**
- 1 **package (17.6 ounces) turkey breast cutlets**

1. In a large resealable plastic bag, combine the juices, cilantro, oil, honey, garlic and seasonings; add turkey. Seal bag and turn to coat; refrigerate 2 hours.
2. Drain and discard the marinade. Moisten a paper towel with cooking oil. Using long-handled tongs, lightly coat the grill rack.
3. Grill turkey, covered, over medium heat or broil 4 in. from heat 2-4 minutes on each side or until no longer pink.
PER SERVING *160 cal., 2 g fat (trace sat. fat), 77 mg chol., 173 mg sodium, 3 g carb., trace fiber, 31 g pro.* **Diabetic Exchanges:** *4 lean meat, ½ fat.*

C Italian Restaurant Chicken

We call this Pollo della Trattoria. It's a favorite with family and friends. While the chicken and sauce cook, I make pasta to serve with it.

—**PATRICIA NIEH** PORTOLA VALLEY, CA

PREP: 25 MIN. • **BAKE:** 50 MIN.
MAKES: 6 SERVINGS

- 1 **broiler/fryer chicken (3 pounds), cut up and skin removed**
- ½ **teaspoon salt**
- ¼ **teaspoon pepper**
- 2 **tablespoons olive oil**
- 1 **small onion, finely chopped**
- ¼ **cup finely chopped celery**
- ¼ **cup finely chopped carrot**
- 3 **garlic cloves, minced**
- ½ **cup dry red wine or reduced-sodium chicken broth**
- 1 **can (28 ounces) crushed tomatoes**
- 1 **bay leaf**
- 1 **teaspoon minced fresh rosemary or ¼ teaspoon dried rosemary, crushed**
- ¼ **cup minced fresh basil**

1. Preheat oven to 325°. Sprinkle chicken with salt and pepper. In an ovenproof Dutch oven, brown chicken in oil in batches. Remove; keep warm.
2. In same pan, saute onion, celery, carrot and garlic in pan drippings until tender. Add the wine, stirring to loosen browned bits from pan. Stir in tomatoes, bay leaf, rosemary and chicken; bring to a boil.
3. Cover and bake 50-60 minutes or until juices run clear. Discard bay leaf; sprinkle with basil.
PER SERVING *254 cal., 11 g fat (2 g sat. fat), 73 mg chol., 442 mg sodium, 12 g carb., 3 g fiber, 27 g pro.* **Diabetic Exchanges:** *3 lean meat, 2 vegetable, 1 fat.*

Indonesian Peanut Chicken

Here's a great make-ahead dish! I cut up fresh chicken, put it in a bag with the remaining slow-cooker ingredients and freeze. To cook, just remove the bag a day ahead to thaw in the fridge, then pour all the contents into the slow cooker.

—**SARAH NEWMAN** MAHTOMEDI, MN

PREP: 15 MIN. • **COOK:** 4 HOURS
MAKES: 6 SERVINGS

- 1½ **pounds boneless skinless chicken breasts, cut into 1-inch cubes**
- ⅓ **cup chopped onion**
- ⅓ **cup water**
- ¼ **cup reduced-fat creamy peanut butter**
- 3 **tablespoons chili sauce**
- ¼ **teaspoon salt**
- ¼ **teaspoon cayenne pepper**
- ¼ **teaspoon pepper**
- 3 **cups hot cooked brown rice**
- 6 **tablespoons chopped salted peanuts**
- 6 **tablespoons chopped sweet red pepper**

1. Place chicken in a 4-qt. slow cooker. In a small bowl, combine the onion, water, peanut butter, chili sauce, salt, cayenne and pepper; pour over chicken. Cover and cook on low for 4-6 hours or until chicken is no longer pink.
2. Shred meat with two forks and return to slow cooker; heat through. Serve with rice. Sprinkle with peanuts and red pepper.
PER SERVING *353 cal., 12 g fat (2 g sat. fat), 63 mg chol., 370 mg sodium, 31 g carb., 3 g fiber, 31 g pro.* **Diabetic Exchanges:** *3 lean meat, 2 starch, 2 fat.*

Turkey Pasta Toss

I served this pasta once for a church supper, and it was a big hit. I often prepare it at home without the sausage because we try to eat meatless two to three times a week.

—**HEATHER SAVAGE** CORYDON, IN

PREP: 15 MIN. • **COOK:** 20 MIN.
MAKES: 6 SERVINGS

- 3 **cups uncooked penne pasta**
- 2 **Italian turkey sausage links, casings removed**
- 1 **large sweet yellow pepper, cut into ½-inch strips**
- 1 **tablespoon olive oil**
- 6 **garlic cloves, minced**
- 4 **plum tomatoes, cut into 1-inch chunks**
- 20 **pitted ripe olives, halved**
- ¼ **cup minced fresh basil**
- ¼ **teaspoon crushed red pepper flakes**
- ¼ **teaspoon salt**
- ¼ **cup shredded Romano cheese**

1. Cook pasta according to package directions. Meanwhile, crumble sausage into a large skillet. Cook over medium heat until meat is no longer pink; drain and keep warm.
2. In the same skillet, saute pepper in oil until crisp-tender. Add garlic; cook 1 minute longer. Stir in the tomatoes, olives, basil, pepper flakes, salt and reserved sausage. Drain pasta. Stir into skillet and heat through. Sprinkle with cheese.
PER SERVING *249 cal., 9 g fat (2 g sat. fat), 24 mg chol., 480 mg sodium, 32 g carb., 3 g fiber, 12 g pro.* **Diabetic Exchanges:** *2 starch, 1 medium-fat meat, ½ fat.*

TURKEY PASTA TOSS

C FAST FIX ▸
Chicken Thighs with Shallots & Spinach

This moist and tender chicken comes complete with its own creamy and flavorful vegetable side! It makes a pretty presentation and goes together in no time flat for a nutritious weeknight meal.

—GENNA JOHANNES
WRIGHTSTOWN, WI

START TO FINISH: 30 MIN.
MAKES: 6 SERVINGS

- 6 boneless skinless chicken thighs (about 1½ pounds)
- ½ teaspoon seasoned salt
- ½ teaspoon pepper
- 1½ teaspoons olive oil
- 4 shallots, thinly sliced
- ⅓ cup white wine or reduced-sodium chicken broth
- ¼ cup fat-free sour cream
- ¼ teaspoon salt
- 1 package (10 ounces) fresh spinach

1. Sprinkle chicken with seasoned salt and pepper. In a large nonstick skillet coated with cooking spray, heat oil over medium heat. Add chicken; cook 6 minutes on each side or until a thermometer reads 165°. Remove from pan; keep warm.

2. In same pan, cook and stir shallots until tender. Add wine, sour cream and salt. Bring to a boil; cook and stir 2-3 minutes or until sauce is slightly thickened. Add spinach; cook and stir just until spinach is wilted. Serve with the chicken.

PER SERVING *225 cal., 10 g fat (2 g sat. fat), 77 mg chol., 338 mg sodium, 8 g carb., 1 g fiber, 24 g pro.* **Diabetic Exchanges:** *3 lean meat, 1½ fat, 1 vegetable.*

C
Prosciutto Chicken in Wine Sauce

Last year, I decided to grow basil, sage and thyme. The scent of sage is very enticing to me, so I included it in this recipe. The rest just happened.

—LORRAINE CALAND SHUNIAH, ON

PREP: 25 MIN. • **COOK:** 30 MIN.
MAKES: 6 SERVINGS

- 1 broiler/fryer chicken (3 pounds), cut up and skin removed
- ½ teaspoon salt
- ¼ teaspoon pepper
- 1 tablespoon olive oil
- 1 tablespoon butter
- 1 cup white wine or reduced-sodium chicken broth
- 4 thin slices prosciutto or deli ham, chopped
- 1 shallot, chopped
- 1 tablespoon fresh sage or 1 teaspoon dried sage leaves
- 1 garlic clove, minced

1. Sprinkle chicken with salt and pepper. In a large nonstick skillet coated with cooking spray, brown chicken on all sides in oil and butter.

2. Add the remaining ingredients, stirring to loosen browned bits. Bring to a boil. Reduce heat; cover and simmer for 20-25 minutes or until chicken juices run clear. Remove chicken and keep warm. Bring sauce to a boil; cook for 10-12 minutes or until liquid is reduced to ¾ cup. Serve with chicken.

PER SERVING *231 cal., 11 g fat (4 g sat. fat), 87 mg chol., 456 mg sodium, 2 g carb., trace fiber, 27 g pro.* **Diabetic Exchanges:** *4 lean meat, 1 fat.*

CHICKEN THIGHS WITH SHALLOTS & SPINACH

Spice-Rubbed Turkey

A neighbor served this turkey several years ago. My family was impressed, and they now request I make them the lemon-filled dish ever since!

—**SUSAN GREISHAW** ARCHER, FL

PREP: 20 MIN.
BAKE: 3½ HOURS + STANDING
MAKES: 28 SERVINGS

- 6 **teaspoons salt**
- 1¼ **teaspoons cayenne pepper**
- 1 **teaspoon pepper**
- ½ **teaspoon garlic powder**
- ½ **teaspoon chili powder**
- 1 **turkey (14 pounds)**
- 2 **tablespoons olive oil**
- 5 **small lemons**
- 2 **medium onions, cut into wedges**

1. In a small bowl combine the first five ingredients. With fingers, carefully loosen skin from turkey; rub half the spice mixture under the skin.
2. Brush the turkey with oil. Rub remaining spice mixture over turkey. Place lemons inside the neck and body cavity. Tuck wings under turkey; tie drumsticks together.
3. Arrange onions in a shallow roasting pan coated with cooking

Self-Basting

(top tip)

Self-basting turkeys are injected with a solution that includes broth, water, salt and seasoning. Most frozen turkeys are self-basting, while fresh turkeys are not. A 4-ounce serving of self-basting turkey has about 250 mg sodium compared to 40 mg without solution.

spray. Place the turkey, breast side up, over onions.
4. Bake, uncovered, at 325° for 3½ to 4 hours or until a thermometer inserted in thigh reads 180°, basting occasionally with pan drippings. Cover loosely with foil if turkey browns too quickly. Cover and let stand for 20 minutes before carving.
5. Remove lemons from cavity. When cool enough to handle, halve lemons and squeeze juice over turkey if desired. Discard onions.
PER SERVING *208 cal., 7 g fat (2 g sat. fat), 86 mg chol., 586 mg sodium, 2 g carb., trace fiber, 33 g pro.* **Diabetic Exchange:** *4 lean meat.*

Chicken with Artichokes

Artichokes and a splash of white wine lend distinctive flavors to this chicken and turn an easy dish into something special.

—**TASTE OF HOME TEST KITCHEN**

PREP: 10 MIN. • **COOK:** 35 MIN.
MAKES: 4 SERVINGS

- ½ **teaspoon salt**
- ⅛ **teaspoon pepper**
- 4 **boneless skinless chicken breast halves (4 ounces each)**
- 3 **teaspoons canola oil, divided**
- 1 **medium onion, thinly sliced**
- 3 **garlic cloves, minced**
- ½ **cup white wine or reduced-sodium chicken broth**
- ½ **cup reduced-sodium chicken broth**
- 1 **can (14 ounces) water-packed artichoke hearts, rinsed, drained and coarsely chopped**

1. Combine salt and pepper; sprinkle over the chicken. In a large nonstick skillet coated with cooking spray, cook the chicken in 2 teaspoons oil for 4-5

CHICKEN WITH ARTICHOKES

minutes on each side or until lightly browned. Remove and keep warm.
2. In the same skillet, cook onion and garlic in remaining oil for 3-4 minutes or until onions are tender. Stir in wine and chicken broth, stirring to loosen any browned bits from pan. Bring to a boil. Add the chicken. Reduce heat; simmer, uncovered, for 10-15 minutes or until the chicken juices run clear. Remove the chicken; keep warm.
3. Add artichokes to pan. Return to a boil. Reduce heat; simmer, uncovered, for 8-12 minutes or until liquid is reduced by half. Serve with chicken.
PER SERVING *230 cal., 6 g fat (1 g sat. fat), 63 mg chol., 678 mg sodium, 11 g carb., 1 g fiber, 26 g pro.* **Diabetic Exchanges:** *3 lean meat, 2 vegetable, 1 fat.*

Texan Ranch Chicken Casserole

I'm happy this Texan Ranch Chicken Casserole recipe was passed down to me because every time I make it, people rave about it. It's not too hot, so spice lovers can add jalapenos for more heat. I also love that it freezes well.

—KENDRA DOSS COLORADO SPRINGS, CO

PREP: 25 MIN. • **BAKE:** 30 MIN.
MAKES: 8 SERVINGS

- 1 large onion, finely chopped
- 2 celery ribs, finely chopped
- 1 medium green pepper, finely chopped
- 1 medium sweet red pepper, finely chopped
- 1 tablespoon canola oil
- 1 garlic clove, minced
- 3 cups cubed cooked chicken breast
- 1 can (10¾ ounces) reduced-fat reduced-sodium condensed cream of celery soup, undiluted
- 1 can (10¾ ounces) reduced-fat reduced-sodium condensed cream of chicken soup, undiluted
- 1 can (10 ounces) diced tomatoes and green chilies, undrained
- 1 tablespoon chili powder
- 12 corn tortillas (6 inches), cut into 1-inch strips
- 2 cups (8 ounces) shredded reduced-fat cheddar cheese, divided

1. In a large nonstick skillet coated with cooking spray, saute the onion, celery and peppers in oil until crisp-tender. Add the garlic; cook 1 minute longer. Stir in the chicken, soups, tomatoes and chili powder.
2. Line the bottom of a 3-qt. baking dish with half of the tortilla strips; top with half of the chicken mixture and 1 cup cheese. Repeat layers. Bake, uncovered, at 350° for 30-35 minutes or until bubbly.

PER SERVING *329 cal., 12 g fat (5 g sat. fat), 65 mg chol., 719 mg sodium, 31 g carb., 3 g fiber, 26 g pro.* **Diabetic Exchanges:** *3 lean meat, 1½ starch, 1 vegetable, 1 fat.*

FAST FIX ▶
Chicken & Spinach Pasta

One of my favorite things about this recipe is that the sauce is thick enough to eat without the pasta. I like to make a double batch of the chicken and freeze the leftovers.

—PAMELA ZIEMER HUTCHINSON, MN

START TO FINISH: 30 MIN.
MAKES: 4 SERVINGS

- 1½ cups uncooked medium pasta shells
- 1 medium onion, chopped
- 1 large portobello mushroom, chopped
- 2 garlic cloves, minced
- 1 teaspoon olive oil
- 1 tablespoon all-purpose flour
- 1 cup fat-free milk
- ½ cup reduced-sodium chicken broth

CHICKEN & SPINACH PASTA

- 2½ cups cubed cooked chicken breast
- 1 package (10 ounces) frozen chopped spinach, thawed and squeezed dry
- 6 tablespoons shredded Parmesan cheese, divided
- 1 teaspoon lemon juice
- ¼ teaspoon pepper
- ¼ teaspoon crushed red pepper flakes

1. Cook pasta according to package directions. Meanwhile, in a large saucepan, saute the onion, mushroom and garlic in oil until tender. Stir in flour until blended; gradually add milk and broth. Bring to a boil; cook and stir for 2 minutes or until thickened.
2. Add chicken, spinach, 3 tablespoons cheese, lemon juice, pepper and pepper flakes; heat through.
3. Drain the pasta; toss with the chicken mixture. Sprinkle with the remaining cheese.

PER SERVING *396 cal., 7 g fat (2 g sat. fat), 74 mg chol., 337 mg sodium, 44 g carb., 5 g fiber, 40 g pro.* **Diabetic Exchanges:** *5 lean meat, 2 starch, 1 vegetable, 1 fat.*

TEXAN RANCH CHICKEN CASSEROLE

Almond Chicken & Strawberry-Balsamic Sauce

I made this entree many years ago for a contest and it won the grand prize! I've been making it ever since, and it's still one of my favorite ways to prepare chicken.

—**VIRGINIA ANTHONY** JACKSONVILLE, FL

PREP: 20 MIN. • **COOK:** 20 MIN.
MAKES: 4 SERVINGS

- ½ **cup panko (Japanese) bread crumbs**
- ⅓ **cup unblanched almonds, coarsely ground**
- ½ **teaspoon salt**
- ¼ **teaspoon pepper**
- 4 **boneless skinless chicken breast halves (4 ounces each)**
  Butter-flavored cooking spray
- 3 **teaspoons canola oil, divided**
- ¼ **cup chopped shallots**
- ⅓ **cup reduced-sodium chicken broth**
- ⅓ **cup strawberry preserves**
- 3 **tablespoons balsamic vinegar**
- 1 **tablespoon minced fresh rosemary or 1 teaspoon dried rosemary, crushed**
- 1 **package (9 ounces) fresh baby spinach**

1. In a large resealable plastic bag, combine the bread crumbs, almonds, salt and pepper. Add chicken, one piece at a time, and shake to coat.
2. In a large nonstick skillet coated with butter-flavored spray, cook chicken in 2 teaspoons oil over medium heat for 4-5 minutes on each side or until juices run clear. Remove and keep warm.
3. In the same pan, cook the shallots in the remaining oil until tender. Stir in the broth, preserves, vinegar and rosemary. Bring to a boil. Reduce heat;

simmer for 5-6 minutes or until sauce is thickened.
4. Meanwhile, in a large saucepan, bring ½ in. of water to a boil. Add spinach; cover and boil for 3-5 minutes or until wilted. Drain; serve with chicken and sauce.
PER SERVING *349 cal., 13 g fat (2 g sat. fat), 63 mg chol., 476 mg sodium, 31 g carb., 3 g fiber, 29 g pro.*

FAST FIX
Waldorf Turkey Pitas

Living in New York City means not having a lot of time to prepare meals. This is quick, easy and healthy, making it ideal for my lifestyle.

—**KEVIN SOBOTKA** STATEN ISLAND, NY

START TO FINISH: 15 MIN.
MAKES: 4 SERVINGS

- 2 **cups cubed cooked turkey breast**
- 2 **celery ribs, finely chopped**
- 1 **medium tart apple, diced**
- 1 **cup seedless red grapes, halved**
- ½ **cup fat-free mayonnaise**
- 2 **ounces fresh mozzarella cheese, diced**
- 8 **whole wheat pita pocket halves**
- 2 **cups fresh baby spinach**

In a large bowl, combine the first six ingredients. Line pita halves with spinach; fill with turkey mixture.
PER SERVING *363 cal., 7 g fat (3 g sat. fat), 75 mg chol., 626 mg sodium, 48 g carb., 7 g fiber, 30 g pro.*

WALDORF TURKEY PITAS

TURKEY SLOPPY JOES
FOR A CROWD

Turkey Sloppy Joes for a Crowd

While flipping through my mother's recipe box I came across this dish. Sometimes I'll serve it over vegetables, such as corn or green beans, but it's equally delicious on a bun.

—JULIE CLEMES ADRIAN, MI

PREP: 25 MIN. • **COOK:** 40 MIN.
MAKES: 16 SERVINGS

- 3 **pounds lean ground turkey**
- 3 **medium green peppers, chopped**
- 3 **medium onions, finely chopped**
- 2¼ **cups ketchup**
- ¾ **cup water**
- 3 **tablespoons white vinegar**
- 3 **tablespoons spicy brown mustard**
- 1 **jalapeno pepper, seeded and chopped**
- ½ **teaspoon pepper**
- 16 **whole wheat hamburger buns, split**

1. In a Dutch oven coated with cooking spray, cook the turkey, green peppers and onions over medium heat until the meat is no longer pink and vegetables are tender; drain.

2. Stir in the ketchup, water, vinegar, mustard, jalapeno and pepper. Bring to a boil. Reduce heat; cover and simmer for 20-30 minutes, stirring occasionally. Serve on buns.

NOTE *Wear disposable gloves when cutting hot peppers; the oils can burn skin. Avoid touching your face.*

PER SERVING *293 cal., 9 g fat (2 g sat. fat), 67 mg chol., 751 mg sodium, 35 g carb., 4 g fiber, 19 g pro.* **Diabetic Exchanges:** *2 starch, 2 lean meat.*

Chicken Noodle Casserole

I first saw the casserole when it was featured on a cooking show. Of course, I tweaked it to better suit our tastes.

—SYLVIA MCCRONE DANVILLE, IL

PREP: 20 MIN. • **BAKE:** 40 MIN.
MAKES: 8 SERVINGS

- 5 **cups uncooked egg noodles**
- 1 **cup frozen peas**
- 1 **celery rib, chopped**
- 1 **medium carrot, chopped**
- 4 **cups cubed cooked chicken breast**
- 1 **can (14¾ ounces) cream-style corn**
- 1 **can (10¾ ounces) reduced-fat reduced-sodium condensed cream of chicken soup, undiluted**
- 2 **cups (8 ounces) shredded reduced-fat Colby-Monterey Jack cheese, divided**
- 1 **small onion, chopped**
- ¼ **cup chopped green pepper**
- ¼ **cup chopped sweet red pepper**
- ¼ **teaspoon pepper**

1. In a large saucepan, cook noodles according to package directions, adding peas, celery and carrot during the last 5 minutes of cooking. Drain.

2. Stir in the chicken, corn, soup, 1 cup cheese, onion, green and red peppers and pepper. Transfer to a 13-in. x 9-in. baking dish coated with cooking spray.

3. Cover and bake at 350° for 30 minutes. Sprinkle with remaining cheese; bake 10 minutes longer or until cheese is melted.

PER SERVING *367 cal., 9 g fat (5 g sat. fat), 92 mg chol., 606 mg sodium, 37 g carb., 3 g fiber, 34 g pro.* **Diabetic Exchanges:** *4 lean meat, 2 starch, 1 vegetable.*

Balsamic Roast Chicken

Balsamic, wine and rosemary are classic flavors that work so well together. The chicken has all the makings for a special Sunday dinner with friends and family.

—TRACY TYLKOWSKI OMAHA, NE

PREP: 20 MIN.
BAKE: 2¼ HOURS + STANDING
MAKES: 12 SERVINGS
(1½ CUPS ONION SAUCE)

- 1 roasting chicken (6 to 7 pounds)
- 2 tablespoons minced fresh rosemary or 2 teaspoons dried rosemary, crushed
- 3 garlic cloves, minced
- 1 teaspoon salt
- 1 teaspoon pepper
- 2 medium red onions, chopped
- ½ cup dry red wine or reduced-sodium chicken broth
- ½ cup balsamic vinegar

1. Pat chicken dry. In a small bowl, combine the rosemary, garlic, salt and pepper; rub under skin of chicken. Place onions in a shallow roasting pan; top with chicken. Combine wine and balsamic vinegar; pour over chicken.
2. Bake, uncovered, at 350° for 2¼ to 2¾ hours or until a thermometer reads 180°, basting occasionally with pan juices. (Cover loosely with foil if chicken browns too quickly.)
3. Let stand for 15 minutes before carving. Remove and discard the skin before serving. Pour the onion sauce into a small bowl; skim fat. Serve with the chicken.

PER SERVING *182 cal., 7 g fat (2 g sat. fat), 77 mg chol., 275 mg sodium, 4 g carb., trace fiber, 25 g pro.* **Diabetic Exchange:** *4 lean meat.*

Sausage & Rice Stew

My husband loves sausage, so I find ways to serve it with healthy ingredients, like beans and spinach. I like to keep it colorful by adding red or yellow bell peppers or garnish with a fresh tomato and basil.

—KELLY YOUNG COCOA, FL

PREP: 20 MIN. • **COOK:** 30 MIN.
MAKES: 6 SERVINGS

- 1 package (14 ounces) smoked turkey kielbasa, halved lengthwise and sliced
- 1 large sweet onion, chopped
- 2 shallots, chopped
- 1 tablespoon chopped pickled jalapeno slices
- 3 garlic cloves, minced
- 1 tablespoon canola oil
- 2 cups water
- 1 can (14½ ounces) reduced-sodium chicken broth
- 2 cans (15 ounces each) white kidney or cannellini beans, rinsed and drained
- 1 cup uncooked long grain rice
- 1 teaspoon dried oregano
- 1 teaspoon dried thyme
- ½ teaspoon pepper
- 2 cups fresh baby spinach

1. In a Dutch oven, saute the kielbasa, onion, shallots, jalapeno and garlic in oil until onion is tender. Add water, broth, beans, rice and seasonings. Bring to a boil.
2. Reduce heat; cover and simmer for 15-20 minutes or until rice is tender. Stir in spinach. Cook 5 minutes longer or until spinach is wilted.

PER SERVING *369 cal., 7 g fat (2 g sat. fat), 47 mg chol., 1,162 mg sodium, 52 g carb., 7 g fiber, 22 g pro.*

top tip · Plan for Leftovers

Just think, if you serve the Balsamic Roast chicken (above) to a family of 4 tonight, you'll have a good amount of leftovers to make the Chicken Noodle Casserole on page 156 for dinner tomorrow night.

SAUSAGE & RICE STEW

Chicken Caesar Deluxe Pizza

This is my favorite pizza recipe! The trick is to use light Caesar dressing on the crust and fresh tomatoes for a pop of color.

—**ERIN HAMANN** REESEVILLE, WI

PREP: 30 MIN. + STANDING
BAKE: 30 MIN.
MAKES: 8 PIECES

- 1 **pound boneless skinless chicken breasts, cubed**
- 1 **teaspoon dried rosemary, crushed**
- 1 **tablespoon olive oil**
- 1¾ **cups all-purpose flour**
- 1 **cup whole wheat flour**
- 4 **teaspoons sugar**
- 1 **package (¼ ounce) quick-rise yeast**
- ¾ **teaspoon salt**
- 1 **teaspoon dried basil**

- 1¼ **cups warm water (120° to 130°)**
- ¾ **cup reduced-fat Caesar vinaigrette**
- 2 **cups fresh baby spinach**
- 1 **small green pepper, chopped**
- ½ **cup chopped fresh mushrooms**
- ⅓ **cup finely chopped onion**
- 1¾ **cups shredded part-skim mozzarella cheese**
- 4 **plum tomatoes, chopped**

1. In a large skillet over medium heat, cook chicken and rosemary in oil until chicken is no longer pink; set aside.

2. In a large bowl, combine 1¼ cups all-purpose flour, whole wheat flour, sugar, yeast, salt and basil. Add water; beat just until moistened. Stir in enough remaining all-purpose flour to form a soft dough (dough will be sticky). Turn onto a lightly floured surface; knead until smooth and elastic, about 5 minutes. Cover and rest for 10 minutes.

3. Press dough onto the bottom and up the sides of a 15-in. x 10-in. x 1-in. baking pan coated with cooking spray. Bake at 400° for 7-9 minutes or until lightly browned.

4. Spread vinaigrette over the crust. Layer with the spinach, green pepper, mushrooms, onion and chicken. Sprinkle with cheese and tomatoes. Bake for 20-25 minutes or until crust is golden brown and cheese is melted.

PER SERVING *358 cal., 11 g fat (4 g sat. fat), 47 mg chol., 794 mg sodium, 39 g carb., 4 g fiber, 24 g pro.* **Diabetic Exchanges:** *3 lean meat, 2½ starch, 1 fat.*

CHICKEN CAESAR
DELUXE PIZZA

Pretzel-Crusted Chicken

I often double the entree so we have leftovers the next day. It tastes just as good cold as it does hot!

—EILEEN KORECKO

HOT SPRINGS VILLAGE, AR

PREP: 20 MIN. • **BAKE:** 40 MIN.
MAKES: 6 SERVINGS

- 4 cups miniature pretzels
- 5 cooked bacon strips, coarsely chopped
- ½ cup grated Parmesan cheese
- 1 tablespoon dried parsley flakes
- 1 egg
- ½ cup light or nonalcoholic beer
- ⅓ cup all-purpose flour
- 1 teaspoon paprika
- ¼ teaspoon ground ginger
- ¼ teaspoon pepper
- 1 broiler/fryer chicken (3 pounds), cut up and skin removed

1. Place the pretzels, bacon, cheese and parsley in a food processor; cover and process until coarsely chopped. Transfer to a shallow bowl.
2. In another shallow bowl, whisk the egg, beer, flour and spices. Dip a few pieces of chicken at a time in beer mixture, then pretzel mixture. Place chicken in a 13-in. x 9-in. baking dish coated with cooking spray. Bake at 350° for 40-50 minutes or until chicken juices run clear.
PER SERVING 283 cal., 9 g fat (3 g sat. fat), 98 mg chol., 498 mg sodium, 19 g carb., 1 g fiber, 30 g pro. *Diabetic Exchanges: 4 lean meat, 1 starch, ½ fat.*

CREOLE-POACHED
CHICKEN BREASTS

Creole-Poached Chicken Breasts

Aside from a little veggie chopping, this one-dish dinner couldn't get much easier! A dash of cayenne adds some Creole-style heat to this hearty weeknight meal.

—TASTE OF HOME TEST KITCHEN

PREP: 15 MIN. • **COOK:** 30 MIN.
MAKES: 4 SERVINGS

- 2 medium onions, finely chopped
- 2 celery ribs, finely chopped
- 1 medium green pepper, diced
- 2 teaspoons canola oil
- 4 boneless skinless chicken breast halves (4 ounces each)
- 1 can (15 ounces) crushed tomatoes
- ½ cup reduced-sodium chicken broth
- 1 teaspoon dried thyme
- ¼ teaspoon salt
- ⅛ teaspoon cayenne pepper

1. In a large nonstick skillet coated with cooking spray, saute the onions, celery and pepper in oil until tender. Add the remaining ingredients. Bring to a boil; reduce the heat. Simmer, uncovered, for 10-15 minutes or until a thermometer reads 165°. Remove chicken; keep warm.
2. Return the cooking juices to a boil. Reduce heat; simmer, uncovered, for 8-10 minutes or until most of sauce is evaporated. Serve with chicken.
PER SERVING 220 cal., 5 g fat (1 g sat. fat), 63 mg chol., 432 mg sodium, 18 g carb., 5 g fiber, 26 g pro. *Diabetic Exchanges: 3 lean meat, 1 starch.*

Aromatic Fennel Chicken

When you prepare my chicken for the first time, you'll know exactly how it got its name. Sizzling bacon along with sauteing fennel, onions and garlic will have your family begging for the first taste.

—REBECCA HUNT SANTA PAULA, CA

PREP: 35 MIN. • **COOK:** 50 MIN.
MAKES: 6 SERVINGS

- 4 bacon strips, chopped
- 1 broiler/fryer chicken (3½ to 4 pounds), cut up, skin removed
- ½ teaspoon salt
- ½ teaspoon pepper
- 2 fennel bulbs, sliced
- 2 medium onions, chopped
- 6 garlic cloves, minced
- ¾ cup white wine or reduced-sodium chicken broth
- ¼ cup lemon juice
- 1 tablespoon grated lemon peel
- 2 bay leaves
- 2 teaspoons dried thyme
   Pinch cayenne pepper
- 3 tablespoons capers, drained

1. In a large nonstick skillet, cook bacon over medium heat until crisp. Using a slotted spoon, remove bacon to paper towels; drain, reserving 1 tablespoon drippings.

2. Sprinkle chicken with salt and pepper. Brown chicken on all sides in reserved drippings; remove and keep warm. Add fennel and onions to the pan; cook and stir for 3-4 minutes or until onions are tender. Add garlic; cook 1 minute longer.

3. Stir in the wine, lemon juice and peel, bay leaves, thyme and cayenne. Return chicken to the pan. Bring to a boil. Reduce heat; cover and simmer for 20-25 minutes or until chicken juices run clear. Remove chicken and keep warm.

4. Cook fennel mixture, uncovered, for 8-10 minutes or until slightly thickened, stirring occasionally. Stir in capers and reserved bacon. Discard bay leaves. Serve with chicken.

PER SERVING *290 cal., 12 g fat (4 g sat. fat), 92 mg chol., 520 mg sodium, 13 g carb., 4 g fiber, 31 g pro. Diabetic Exchanges: 4 lean meat, 2 vegetable, 1 fat.*

AROMATIC FENNEL CHICKEN

Sweet and Sour Turkey Meatballs

I'm always looking for recipes that are big on flavor but quick and easy to prepare, with little cleanup. This one has it all. And it's my son's favorite lunch or dinner.

—MICHELE ORTHNER LETHBRIDGE, AB

PREP: 50 MIN. • **COOK:** 25 MIN.
MAKES: 6 SERVINGS

- 2 large carrots, chopped
- 1 large onion, chopped
- 1 medium green pepper, chopped
- 1 tablespoon olive oil
- 1 can (15 ounces) tomato sauce
- 1 can (14½ ounces) reduced-sodium chicken broth
- 1 can (8 ounces) unsweetened crushed pineapple, undrained
- ¼ cup packed brown sugar
- ¼ cup white vinegar
- ¼ cup ketchup
- 1 egg, beaten
- ¼ cup fat-free milk
- 1 slice white bread, torn into small pieces
- ½ cup shredded zucchini
- ½ teaspoon salt
- ½ teaspoon garlic powder
- ½ teaspoon pepper
- 1 pound lean ground turkey
- 2 cups uncooked instant brown rice

1. In a Dutch oven coated with cooking spray, saute the carrots, onion and green pepper in oil until tender. Add tomato sauce, broth, pineapple, brown sugar, vinegar and ketchup. Bring to a boil. Reduce heat; simmer, uncovered, for 10 minutes.

2. Meanwhile, in a large bowl, mix the egg, milk, bread, zucchini, salt, garlic powder and pepper. Crumble turkey over mixture and mix well. Shape into 2-in. balls. Carefully add to tomato mixture. Cover and simmer for 15-20 minutes or until meatballs are no longer pink.

3. Add rice. Bring to a boil. Reduce heat; cover and simmer for 5 minutes or until liquid is absorbed. Let stand for 5 minutes. Fluff with a fork.

PER SERVING *389 cal., 11 g fat (2 g sat. fat), 95 mg chol., 991 mg sodium, 53 g carb., 4 g fiber, 21 g pro.*

GARDEN CHICKEN CACCIATORE

C
Garden Chicken Cacciatore

When I have company, I take advantage of the slow cooker so I can spend time with my guests. Served with hot cooked pasta, green salad and a dry red wine, this is a wonderful dinner-party meal. Mangia!

—MARTHA SCHIRMACHER

STERLING HEIGHTS, MI

PREP: 15 MIN. • **COOK:** 8½ HOURS
MAKES: 12 SERVINGS

12 boneless skinless chicken thighs (about 3 pounds)
2 medium green peppers, chopped
1 can (14½ ounces) diced tomatoes with basil, oregano and garlic, undrained
1 can (6 ounces) tomato paste
1 medium onion, sliced
½ cup reduced-sodium chicken broth
¼ cup dry red wine or additional reduced-sodium chicken broth
3 garlic cloves, minced
¾ teaspoon salt
⅛ teaspoon pepper
2 tablespoons cornstarch
2 tablespoons cold water

1. Place chicken in a 4-qt. slow cooker. In a small bowl, combine the green peppers, tomatoes, tomato paste, onion, broth, wine, garlic, salt and pepper. Cover and cook on low for 8-10 hours or until chicken is tender.
2. Combine the cornstarch and water until smooth; gradually stir into the slow cooker. Cover and cook on high 30 minutes longer or until the sauce is thickened.

PER SERVING *207 cal., 9 g fat (2 g sat. fat), 76 mg chol., 410 mg sodium, 8 g carb., 1 g fiber, 23 g pro.* **Diabetic Exchanges:** *3 lean meat, 1 vegetable, ½ fat.*

FAST FIX
Chicken Fajita Pizza

Chicken Fajita Pizza has always been a hit with my kids. It's such a great way to sneak in extra vegetables.

—CARRIE SHAUB MOUNT JOY, PA

START TO FINISH: 30 MIN.
MAKES: 6 SERVINGS

1 package (13.8 ounces) refrigerated pizza crust
8 ounces boneless skinless chicken breasts, cut into thin strips
1 teaspoon canola oil, divided
1 medium onion, sliced
1 medium sweet red pepper, sliced
1 medium green pepper, sliced
1 teaspoon chili powder
½ teaspoon ground cumin
1 garlic clove, minced
¼ cup chunky salsa
2 cups (8 ounces) shredded reduced-fat Mexican cheese blend
1 tablespoon minced fresh cilantro
Sour cream and additional salsa, optional

1. Unroll the dough into a 15-in. x 10-in. x 1-in. baking pan coated with cooking spray; flatten the dough and build up edges slightly. Bake at 425° for 8-10 minutes or until the edges are lightly browned.
2. Meanwhile, in a large nonstick skillet coated with cooking spray, cook the chicken over medium heat in ½ teaspoon oil for 4-6 minutes or until no longer pink; remove and keep warm.
3. In the same pan, saute the onion, peppers, chili powder and cumin in remaining oil until crisp-tender. Add garlic; cook 1 minute longer. Stir in salsa and chicken.
4. Sprinkle half of the cheese over prepared crust; top with chicken mixture and remaining cheese. Bake for 8-10 minutes or until crust is golden brown and cheese is melted. Sprinkle with cilantro. Serve with sour cream and additional salsa if desired.

PER SERVING *351 cal., 12 g fat (4 g sat. fat), 48 mg chol., 767 mg sodium, 38 g carb., 2 g fiber, 25 g pro.* **Diabetic Exchanges:** *3 lean meat, 2 starch, 1 vegetable, ½ fat.*

CHICKEN FAJITA PIZZA

QUICK TURKEY
SPAGHETTI

Quick Turkey Spaghetti

My family never tires of this versatile entree. We can have it once a week, and it's different each time! I sometimes omit the turkey for a meatless meal, change up the veggies or use my own tomato sauce.
—**MARY LOU MOELLER** WOOSTER, OH

PREP: 15 MIN. • **COOK:** 25 MIN.
MAKES: 4 SERVINGS

- 1 **pound lean ground turkey**
- 1 **small green pepper, chopped**
- ½ **cup sliced fresh mushrooms**
- ¼ **cup chopped onion**
- 1 **can (15 ounces) tomato sauce**
- 6 **ounces uncooked multigrain spaghetti, broken into 2-inch pieces**
- ¾ **cup water**
- ¼ **teaspoon garlic salt**
  Grated Parmesan cheese, optional

1. In a large nonstick skillet coated with cooking spray, cook the turkey, pepper, mushrooms and onion over medium heat until meat is no longer pink and vegetables are crisp-tender.
2. Stir in the tomato sauce, spaghetti, water and garlic salt. Bring to a boil. Reduce heat; cover and simmer for 15-20 minutes or until spaghetti and vegetables are tender. Garnish with cheese if desired.
PER SERVING *357 cal., 10 g fat (3 g sat. fat), 90 mg chol., 728 mg sodium, 36 g carb., 4 g fiber, 30 g pro.* **Diabetic Exchanges:** *3 lean meat, 2 starch, 1 vegetable.*

S C
Balsamic Chicken Breasts

Balsamic Chicken Breasts are a quick go-to dish of mine. I typically round them out with tossed salad and a whole wheat roll for a satisfying weeknight meal.
—**DENISE JOHANOWICZ** MADISON, WI

PREP: 15 MIN. • **COOK:** 20 MIN.
MAKES: 4 SERVINGS

- ¼ **cup all-purpose flour**
- ½ **teaspoon pepper**
- ⅛ **teaspoon salt**
- 4 **boneless skinless chicken breast halves (4 ounces each)**
- 1 **tablespoon canola oil**
- 1 **small onion, thinly sliced**
- ¼ **cup water**
- 2 **tablespoons balsamic vinegar**
- ½ **teaspoon dried thyme**
- ⅛ **teaspoon dried rosemary, crushed**

1. In a large resealable plastic bag, combine the flour, pepper and salt. Add chicken, one piece at a time, and shake to coat.
2. In a large nonstick skillet coated with cooking spray, cook chicken in oil over medium heat for 4-5 minutes on each side or until juices run clear. Remove and keep warm.
3. In the same pan, cook onion until tender. Add water, stirring to loosen browned bits. Add the vinegar, thyme and rosemary; cook and stir for 3-4 minutes or until sauce is slightly thickened. Serve with chicken.
PER SERVING *194 cal., 6 g fat (1 g sat. fat), 63 mg chol., 131 mg sodium, 9 g carb., 1 g fiber, 24 g pro.* **Diabetic Exchanges:** *3 lean meat, 1 fat, ½ starch.*

Chicken with Garden Salsa

Fresh chilies vary greatly in taste and price. A fruity serrano gives this supper real Mexican flavor, but jalapenos cost less and are more commonly available. To save time, use canned tomatoes and corn in the salsa.

—**MARY RELYEA** CANASTOTA, NY

START TO FINISH: 30 MIN.
MAKES: 4 SERVINGS

- ½ **cup lime juice**
- 1 **tablespoon olive oil**
- ½ **teaspoon garlic salt**
- ½ **teaspoon coarsely ground pepper**
- 4 **boneless skinless chicken breast halves (4 ounces each)**
- 1 **cup frozen corn, thawed**
- 1 **medium tomato, chopped**
- 1 **serrano pepper, seeded and chopped**
- 1 **green onion, cut into ½-inch pieces**
- ¼ **teaspoon ground cumin**
- 2 **slices Monterey Jack or pepper jack cheese, halved**

1. In a small bowl, combine the lime juice, oil, garlic salt and pepper. Set aside 5 tablespoons. Pour remaining lime juice mixture into a resealable plastic bag; add chicken. Seal and turn to coat; let stand at room temperature for 10 minutes.

2. Meanwhile, in a small bowl, mix the corn, tomato, pepper, green onion, cumin and 3 tablespoons reserved lime juice mixture. Cover and chill.

3. Drain and discard marinade from chicken. Moisten a paper towel with cooking oil. Using long-handled tongs, and lightly coat the grill rack. Grill, covered, over medium heat or broil 4 in. from heat for 5-6 minutes on each side or until a thermometer reads 165°, basting twice with the remaining lime juice mixture.

4. Top with cheese; grill or broil 1-2 minutes longer or until the cheese is melted. Serve with salsa.

NOTE *Wear disposable gloves when cutting hot peppers; the oils can burn skin. Avoid touching your face.*

PER SERVING *239 cal., 9 g fat (3 g sat. fat), 74 mg chol., 276 mg sodium, 13 g carb., 2 g fiber, 28 g pro.* **Diabetic Exchanges:** *3 lean meat, 1 starch, 1 fat.*

Gingered Chicken Thighs

Here is a chicken recipe that was born from my desire to develop a time-saving, easy-on-the-budget entree with Asian flavor. It's a favorite at the girls' camp where I am the head cook. I usually serve it with rice prepared with coconut milk.

—**DEBBIE FLEENOR** MONTEREY, TN

PREP: 20 MIN. + MARINATING
BAKE: 20 MIN.
MAKES: 6 SERVINGS

- 2 **tablespoons ground ginger**
- 2 **tablespoons orange juice**
- 2 **tablespoons honey**
- 2 **tablespoons reduced-sodium soy sauce**
- 2 **teaspoons curry powder**
- 2 **garlic cloves, minced**
- ½ **teaspoon crushed red pepper flakes**
- 6 **boneless skinless chicken thighs (about 1½ pounds)**

PEANUT SAUCE

- 2 **tablespoons chicken broth**
- 2 **tablespoons orange juice**
- 1 **tablespoon reduced-fat creamy peanut butter**
- ½ **teaspoon ground ginger**

1. In a large resealable plastic bag, combine the first seven ingredients; add the chicken. Seal bag and turn to coat; refrigerate for up to 4 hours.

2. Drain and discard marinade. In a large skillet coated with cooking spray, brown chicken on each side. Transfer to an 11-in. x 7-in. baking dish coated with cooking spray. In a small bowl, whisk sauce ingredients; pour over chicken. Bake, uncovered, at 350° for 20-25 minutes or until no longer pink.

PER SERVING *199 cal., 9 g fat (2 g sat. fat), 76 mg chol., 200 mg sodium, 6 g carb., trace fiber, 22 g pro.* **Diabetic Exchanges:** *3 lean meat, ½ starch.*

GINGERED CHICKEN THIGHS

SAVORY TURKEY POTPIES

Savory Turkey Potpies

Who would ever suspect that a traditional potpie could be on the lighter side? My comforting entree promises to warm you up on winter's chilliest nights, without adding inches to your waistline.

—**JUDY WILSON** SUN CITY WEST, AZ

PREP: 25 MIN. • **BAKE:** 20 MIN.
MAKES: 8 SERVINGS

- 1 **small onion, chopped**
- ¼ **cup all-purpose flour**
- 3 **cups chicken stock**
- 3 **cups cubed cooked turkey breast**
- 1 **package (16 ounces) frozen peas and carrots**
- 2 **medium red potatoes, cooked and cubed**
- 3 **tablespoons minced fresh parsley**
- 1 **tablespoon minced fresh thyme**
- ¼ **teaspoon pepper**
- 1 **sheet refrigerated pie pastry**
  Additional fresh parsley or thyme leaves, optional
- 1 **egg**
- 1 **teaspoon water**
- ½ **teaspoon kosher salt**

1. In a Dutch oven coated with cooking spray, saute onion until tender. In a small bowl, whisk flour and stock until smooth; gradually stir into Dutch oven. Bring to a boil; cook and stir 2 minutes or until thickened. Remove from heat. Add turkey, peas and carrots, potatoes, parsley, thyme and pepper; stir gently.

2. Preheat oven to 425°. Divide turkey mixture among eight 10-oz. ramekins. On a lightly floured surface, unroll pastry. Cut out eight 3-in. circles. Gently press parsley into pastries if desired. Place over turkey mixture. Beat egg and water; brush over tops. Sprinkle with salt.

3. Place ramekins on a baking sheet. Bake 20-25 minutes or until crusts are golden brown.

PER SERVING 279 cal., 9 g fat (3 g sat. fat), 77 mg chol., 495 mg sodium, 28 g carb., 3 g fiber, 22 g pro. **Diabetic Exchanges:** 2 starch, 2 lean meat, ½ fat.

Curried Chicken Rice Soup

The original recipe for my soup called for twice as much butter and used full-fat evaporated milk. This lighter version is still rich and creamy, and it's lower in sodium than most soups.

—**REBECCA COOK** HELOTES, TX

PREP: 15 MIN. • **COOK:** 20 MIN.
MAKES: 11 SERVINGS (2¾ QUARTS)

- ¼ **cup butter, cubed**
- 2 **large carrots, finely chopped**
- 2 **celery ribs, finely chopped**
- 1 **small onion, finely chopped**
- ¾ **cup plus 2 tablespoons all-purpose flour**
- 1 **teaspoon seasoned salt**
- 1 **teaspoon curry powder**
- 2 **cans (12 ounces each) fat-free evaporated milk**
- 1 **cup half-and-half cream**
- 4½ **cups reduced-sodium chicken broth**
- 3 **cups cubed cooked chicken breast**
- 2 **cups cooked brown rice**

1. In a Dutch oven, melt butter. Add the carrots, celery and onion; saute for 2 minutes. Sprinkle with flour; stir until blended. Stir in seasoned salt and curry. Gradually add milk and cream. Bring to a boil; cook and stir for 2 minutes or until thickened.

2. Gradually add the broth. Stir in the chicken and rice; return to a boil. Reduce the heat; simmer, uncovered, for 10 minutes or until the vegetables are tender.

PER SERVING 263 cal., 8 g fat (5 g sat. fat), 54 mg chol., 524 mg sodium, 26 g carb., 2 g fiber, 20 g pro. **Diabetic Exchanges:** 2 lean meat, 1 starch, 1 fat, ½ fat-free milk.

CURRIED CHICKEN RICE SOUP

SLOW-COOKED
SOUTHWEST CHICKEN

Slow-Cooked Southwest Chicken

Mildly spiced, this Southwestern-inspired stew is kid-friendly, but can be kicked up for heat-lovers with a touch of hot sauce or topped with sliced jalapenos.

—BRANDI CASTILLO SANTA MARIA, CA

PREP: 15 MIN. • **COOK:** 6 HOURS
MAKES: 6 SERVINGS

- 2 **cans (15 ounces each) black beans, rinsed and drained**
- 1 **can (14½ ounces) reduced-sodium chicken broth**
- 1 **can (14½ ounces) diced tomatoes with mild green chilies, undrained**
- ½ **pound boneless skinless chicken breast**
- 1 **jar (8 ounces) chunky salsa**
- 1 **cup frozen corn**
- 1 **tablespoon dried parsley flakes**
- 1 **teaspoon ground cumin**
- ¼ **teaspoon pepper**
- 3 **cups hot cooked rice**

1. In a 2- or 3-qt. slow cooker, mix the beans, broth, tomatoes, chicken, salsa, corn and seasonings. Cover and cook on low for 6-8 hours or until a thermometer reads 170°.

2. Shred chicken with two forks and return to slow cooker; heat through. Serve with rice.

PER SERVING *320 cal., 1 g fat (trace sat. fat), 21 mg chol., 873 mg sodium, 56 g carb., 8 g fiber, 19 g pro.*

FAST FIX

Effortless Alfredo Pizza

Here's a lighter, scrumptious twist for pizza night. It makes great use of convenience products, boosting flavor and zip with wholesome turkey, nutty fontina cheese and red pepper flakes.

—BRITTNEY HOUSE LOCKPORT, IL

START TO FINISH: 20 MIN.
MAKES: 6 SLICES

- 1 **package (10 ounces) frozen chopped spinach, thawed and squeezed dry**
- 1 **cup shredded cooked turkey breast**
- 2 **teaspoons lemon juice**
- ¼ **teaspoon salt**
- ¼ **teaspoon pepper**
- 1 **prebaked 12-inch pizza crust**
- 1 **garlic clove, peeled and halved**
- ½ **cup reduced-fat Alfredo sauce**
- ¾ **cup shredded fontina cheese**
- ½ **teaspoon crushed red pepper flakes**

1. Preheat oven to 450°. In a large bowl, mix the first five ingredients until blended.

2. Place crust on an ungreased 12-in. pizza pan; rub with cut sides of garlic. Discard garlic. Spread Alfredo sauce over crust. Top with the spinach mixture, cheese and pepper flakes. Bake 8-12 minutes or until the crust is lightly browned.

PER SERVING *302 cal., 10 g fat (4 g sat. fat), 45 mg chol., 756 mg sodium, 33 g carb., 1 g fiber, 20 g pro.* **Diabetic Exchanges:** *2 starch, 2 lean meat, ½ fat.*

TURKEY WITH SAUSAGE STUFFING

Simple Chicken Tagine

I like to sprinkle the tagine with toasted almonds or cashews and serve it with hot couscous. Cinnamon and apricots add a delectable flavor, which makes the stew taste like you spent all day in the kitchen!

—**ANGELA BUCHANAN** LONGMONT, CO

PREP: 15 MIN. • **COOK:** 6 HOURS
MAKES: 6 SERVINGS

- 2¼ **pounds bone-in chicken thighs, skin removed**
- 1 **large onion, chopped**
- 2 **medium carrots, sliced**
- ¾ **cup unsweetened apple juice**
- 1 **garlic clove, minced**
- 1 **teaspoon salt**
- ½ **teaspoon ground cinnamon**
- ½ **teaspoon pepper**
- 1 **cup chopped dried apricots**
  Hot cooked couscous

1. Place the chicken, onion and carrots in a 3- or 4-qt. slow cooker coated with cooking spray. In a small bowl, combine the apple juice, garlic, salt, cinnamon and pepper; pour over the vegetables.

2. Cover and cook on low for 6-8 hours or until chicken is tender.

3. Remove chicken from slow cooker; shred meat with two forks. Skim fat from cooking juices; stir in the apricots. Return shredded chicken to slow cooker; heat though. Serve with the couscous.

PER SERVING *279 cal., 10 g fat (3 g sat. fat), 87 mg chol., 497 mg sodium, 23 g carb., 3 g fiber, 25 g pro.* **Diabetic Exchanges:** *3 lean meat, 1 vegetable, 1 fruit.*

Turkey with Sausage Stuffing

Years ago a lady shared this dish with me. Since the first time I served it to my family, they were addicted and it became our turkey recipe of choice. We just love it.

—**ALMA WINBERRY** GREAT FALLS, MT

PREP: 30 MIN.
BAKE: 3 HOURS + STANDING
MAKES: 24 SERVINGS (12 CUPS STUFFING)

- 2 **pounds Italian turkey sausage links, casings removed**
- 6 **cups chopped cabbage**
- 3 **medium carrots, shredded**
- 2 **celery ribs, chopped**
- ⅓ **cup chopped onion**
- 3 **cups stuffing mix**
- 3 **cups seasoned stuffing cubes**
- 1 **cup reduced-sodium chicken broth**
- 6 **tablespoons egg substitute**
- ¼ **cup half-and-half cream**
- ½ **teaspoon poultry seasoning**
- ½ **teaspoon pepper**
- ⅛ **teaspoon salt**
- 1 **turkey (12 pounds)**

1. In a large nonstick skillet coated with cooking spray, cook the sausage, cabbage, carrots, celery and onion over medium heat until meat is no longer pink and vegetables are tender.

2. Transfer to a large bowl; stir in the stuffing mix, stuffing cubes, broth, egg substitute, cream, poultry seasoning, pepper and salt.

3. Just before baking, loosely stuff turkey with 4 cups of stuffing. Place remaining stuffing in a 13-in. x 9-in. baking dish coated with cooking spray; refrigerate until ready to bake. Skewer the turkey openings closed; tie drumsticks together.

4. Place breast side up on a rack in a roasting pan. Bake, uncovered, at 325° for 3 to 3½ hours or until a thermometer inserted in the thigh reads 180° for the turkey and 165° for the stuffing, basting occasionally with pan drippings. Cover loosely with foil if turkey browns too quickly.

5. Cover and bake additional stuffing for 25-30 minutes. Uncover; bake 10 minutes longer or until lightly browned. Cover turkey and let stand for 20 minutes before removing the stuffing and carving the turkey.

PER SERVING *317 cal., 10 g fat (3 g sat. fat), 109 mg chol., 568 mg sodium, 12 g carb., 1 g fiber, 41 g pro.* **Diabetic Exchanges:** *5 lean meat, 1 starch.*

Mediterranean Turkey Potpies

Your clan will rave over my wonderful, stick-to-the-ribs potpies with a Mediterranean twist. The leftovers from our big holiday turkey are always used to make this recipe. I think my family enjoys the potpies more than the original feast!

—MARIE RIZZIO INTERLOCHEN, MI

PREP: 30 MIN. • **BAKE:** 20 MIN.
MAKES: 6 SERVINGS

- 2 medium onions, thinly sliced
- 2 teaspoons olive oil
- 3 garlic cloves, minced
- 3 tablespoons all-purpose flour
- 1¼ cups reduced-sodium chicken broth
- 1 can (14½ ounces) no-salt-added diced tomatoes, undrained
- 2½ cups cubed cooked turkey breast
- 1 can (14 ounces) water-packed artichoke hearts, rinsed, drained and sliced
- ½ cup pitted ripe olives, halved
- ¼ cup sliced pepperoncini
- 1 tablespoon minced fresh oregano or 1 teaspoon dried oregano
- ¼ teaspoon pepper

CRUST
- 1 loaf (1 pound) frozen pizza dough, thawed
- 1 egg white
- 1 teaspoon minced fresh oregano or ¼ teaspoon dried oregano

1. In a Dutch oven, saute onions in oil until tender. Add the garlic; cook 1 minute longer. In a small bowl, whisk the flour and broth until smooth; gradually stir into onion mixture. Stir in tomatoes. Bring to a boil; cook and stir for 2 minutes or until thickened.
2. Remove from the heat. Add turkey, artichokes, olives, pepperoncini, oregano and pepper; stir gently.

Divide turkey mixture among six 10-oz. ramekins.
3. Roll out 2 ounces dough to fit each ramekin (reserve remaining dough for another use). Cut slits in dough; place over the filling. Press to seal the edges. Combine the egg white and oregano; brush over dough.
4. Place ramekins on a baking sheet. Bake at 425° for 18-22 minutes or until crusts are golden brown.
PER SERVING *326 cal., 4 g fat (1 g sat. fat), 50 mg chol., 699 mg sodium, 43 g carb., 3 g fiber, 26 g pro.* **Diabetic Exchanges:** *2 starch, 2 lean meat, 2 vegetable, ½ fat.*

F
Zesty Mexican Chicken

A hint of lime juice helps tame the heat of spicy chicken breasts with crunchy vegetables. And because it's all prepared in the slow cooker, you and your kitchen will stay cool, too!

—MICHELLE SHELDON
MIDDLETOWN, DE

PREP: 15 MIN. • **COOK:** 3 HOURS
MAKES: 6 SERVINGS

- 6 boneless skinless chicken breast halves (4 ounces each)
- 1 can (14½ ounces) diced tomatoes, undrained
- 1 large onion, chopped
- 1 medium green pepper, chopped
- 3 garlic cloves, minced
- 2 tablespoons lime juice
- 1 tablespoon hot pepper sauce
- ¼ teaspoon salt
- ¼ teaspoon pepper
- 3 cups hot cooked rice

1. Place chicken in a 4-qt. slow cooker coated with cooking spray. In a large bowl, combine the tomatoes, onion, green pepper, garlic, lime juice, pepper sauce, salt and pepper. Pour over chicken.
2. Cover and cook on low for 3-4 hours or until chicken is tender. Serve with rice.
PER SERVING *256 cal., 3 g fat (1 g sat. fat), 63 mg chol., 257 mg sodium, 30 g carb., 2 g fiber, 26 g pro.* **Diabetic Exchanges:** *3 lean meat, 1½ starch, 1 vegetable.*

ZESTY MEXICAN CHICKEN

Lasagna Deliziosa

My family loves this lasagna. We often serve it as a birthday dinner. I've lightened it up a lot from the original, but no one can tell the difference.

—HEATHER O'NEILL TROY, OH

PREP: 45 MIN.
BAKE: 50 MIN. + STANDING
MAKES: 12 SERVINGS

- 9 uncooked lasagna noodles
- 1 package (19½ ounces) Italian turkey sausage links, casings removed
- ½ pound lean ground beef (90% lean)
- 1 large onion, chopped
- 2 garlic cloves, minced
- 1 can (28 ounces) diced tomatoes, undrained
- 1 can (12 ounces) tomato paste
- ¼ cup water
- 2 teaspoons sugar
- 1 teaspoon dried basil
- ½ teaspoon fennel seed
- ¼ teaspoon pepper
- 1 egg, lightly beaten
- 1 carton (15 ounces) reduced-fat ricotta cheese
- 1 tablespoon minced fresh parsley
- ½ teaspoon salt
- 2 cups (8 ounces) shredded part-skim mozzarella cheese
- ¾ cup grated Parmesan cheese

1. Cook noodles according to package directions. Meanwhile, in a Dutch oven, cook the sausage, beef and onion over medium heat until meat is no longer pink. Add garlic; cook 1 minute longer. Drain.

2. Stir in the tomatoes, tomato paste, water, sugar, basil, fennel and pepper. Bring to a boil. Reduce heat; cover and simmer for 15-20 minutes, stirring occasionally.

3. In a small bowl, combine the egg, ricotta cheese, parsley and salt. Drain the noodles and rinse in cold water. Spread 1 cup meat sauce into a 13-in. x 9-in. baking dish coated with cooking spray. Top with three noodles, 2 cups meat sauce, ⅔ cup ricotta cheese mixture, ⅔ cup mozzarella and ¼ cup Parmesan. Repeat layers twice.

4. Cover and bake at 375° for 40 minutes. Uncover; bake 10-15 minutes longer or until bubbly. Let stand for 10 minutes before cutting.

PER SERVING *323 cal., 12 g fat (5 g sat. fat), 79 mg chol., 701 mg sodium, 28 g carb., 4 g fiber, 25 g pro.* **Diabetic Exchanges:** *3 lean meat, 2 vegetable, 1 starch, 1 fat.*

LASAGNA DELIZIOSA

FAST FIX

Chicken Stir-Fry with Noodles

Stock up on chicken thighs for budget-friendly dinners. This rich and creamy entree comes together in 30 minutes for a nutritious weeknight meal.

—BEVERLY NORRIS EVANSTON, WY

START TO FINISH: 30 MIN.
MAKES: 4 SERVINGS

CHICKEN STIR-FRY WITH NOODLES

- 8 ounces uncooked whole wheat spaghetti
- 1 head bok choy (16 ounces)
- 1 pound boneless skinless chicken breasts, cubed
- 2 tablespoons canola oil, divided
- 1 celery rib, sliced
- ½ cup chopped green pepper
- ½ cup chopped sweet red pepper
- ⅓ cup chopped onion
- 6 tablespoons reduced-sodium teriyaki sauce

1. Cook the spaghetti according to package directions; drain.

2. Meanwhile, cut off and discard root end of bok choy. Cut leaves from the stalks; coarsely chop and set aside. Cut stalks into 1-in. pieces.

3. In a large skillet or wok, stir-fry chicken in 1 tablespoon oil until no longer pink. Remove and keep warm.

4. Stir-fry the bok choy stalks, celery, peppers and onion in remaining oil for 4 minutes. Add bok choy leaves; stir-fry 2-4 minutes longer or until vegetables are crisp-tender. Stir in the teriyaki sauce. Add the chicken and spaghetti; heat through.

PER SERVING *434 cal., 11 g fat (1 g sat. fat), 63 mg chol., 623 mg sodium, 53 g carb., 9 g fiber, 35 g pro.*

Grilled Chicken with Barley

Our taste testers described this dish as simply amazing, for its fresh flavors, generous portion size and a super healthy combo of colorful veggies and nutty barley.

—TASTE OF HOME TEST KITCHEN

PREP: 20 MIN. + MARINATING
COOK: 50 MIN.
MAKES: 4 SERVINGS

- ¼ cup lemon juice
- 1 tablespoon plus 1 teaspoon canola oil, divided
- 2 garlic cloves, minced
- 1 teaspoon dried oregano
- ½ teaspoon dried basil
- 4 boneless skinless chicken breast halves (4 ounces each)
- 1 can (14½ ounces) reduced-sodium chicken broth
- ½ cup medium pearl barley
- ¼ teaspoon salt
- 1 medium carrot, chopped
- 1 small sweet red pepper, chopped
- 3 green onions, thinly sliced
- ¼ teaspoon pepper

1. In a small bowl, combine the lemon juice, 1 tablespoon oil, garlic, oregano and basil. Pour 2 tablespoons of the marinade into a large resealable plastic bag; add the chicken. Seal bag and turn to coat; refrigerate for 1 hour. Cover and refrigerate the remaining marinade.

2. In a large saucepan, bring broth to a boil. Stir in barley and salt. Reduce heat; cover and simmer for 45-50 minutes or until tender. In a small nonstick skillet, saute carrot and red pepper in remaining oil until crisp-tender. Add onions and pepper; saute 2-3 minutes longer or until tender. Stir vegetables and reserved marinade into cooked barley.

3. Drain and discard marinade. Moisten a paper towel with cooking oil. Using long-handled tongs, lightly coat the grill rack. Grill the chicken, covered, over medium heat or broil 4 in. from the heat for 4-7 minutes on each side or until a thermometer reads 165°. Serve with barley mixture.

PER SERVING *270 cal., 7 g fat (1 g sat. fat), 63 mg chol., 514 mg sodium, 25 g carb., 5 g fiber, 28 g pro.* **Diabetic Exchanges:** *3 lean meat, 1½ starch, 1 fat.*

Southwest Turkey Bulgur Dinner

In the past few years, I've been trying to incorporate more whole grains in our dinners. Bulgur is one of my favorite grains to work with because of its fast cooking time. Besides being high in fiber and rich in minerals, it has a mild taste that my kids enjoy.

—MARIA VASSEUR VALENCIA, CA

PREP: 15 MIN. • **COOK:** 30 MIN.
MAKES: 4 SERVINGS

- 8 ounces lean ground turkey
- 1 small onion, chopped
- 1 garlic clove, minced
- 1 can (16 ounces) kidney beans, rinsed and drained
- 1 can (14½ ounces) diced tomatoes with mild green chilies
- 1½ cups water
- ½ cup frozen corn
- 1 tablespoon chili powder
- 1 teaspoon ground cumin
- ¼ teaspoon pepper
- ⅛ teaspoon salt
- 1 cup bulgur

TOPPING
- ½ cup fat-free plain Greek yogurt
- 1 tablespoon finely chopped green onion
- 1 tablespoon minced fresh cilantro

1. In a large nonstick skillet coated with cooking spray, cook the turkey and onion over medium heat until meat is no longer pink. Add garlic; cook 1 minute longer.

2. Stir in the beans, tomatoes, water, corn, chili powder, cumin, pepper and salt. Bring to a boil. Stir in the bulgur. Reduce heat; cover and simmer for 13-18 minutes or until the bulgur is tender.

3. Remove from the heat; let stand 5 minutes. Fluff with a fork. Meanwhile, in a small bowl, combine the yogurt, green onion and cilantro. Serve with turkey mixture.

PER SERVING *387 cal., 6 g fat (1 g sat. fat), 45 mg chol., 628 mg sodium, 59 g carb., 14 g fiber, 27 g pro.*

SOUTHWEST TURKE
BULGUR DINN

**GRILLED PORK
TENDERLOIN SATAY** *PAGE 180*

**LOUISE WATKINS'
BARBECUES FOR THE BUNCH**

PAGE 173

**ROBIN HAAS'
CUBAN-STYLE PORK
SANDWICHES** *PAGE 178*

**TAHNIA FOX'S
PORK MEDALLIONS IN MUSTARD
SAUCE** *PAGE 182*

Pork

It's no wonder **pork is one of the most commonly consumed meats** in the world. Whether you're craving Asian, Cuban or Italian, or simply **looking for new ways to dress up a pork chop**, there's a recipe for you in this chapter.

C FAST FIX
Elegant Pork Marsala

Wine and fresh mushrooms lend elegance to this simple reinvention of an Italian classic. If you don't have Marsala wine, just use reduced-sodium chicken broth in its place.
—**KIM GILLIS** HIGH FALLS, NY

START TO FINISH: 30 MIN.
MAKES: 6 SERVINGS

- 5 teaspoons cornstarch
- ⅔ cup reduced-sodium chicken broth
- ⅓ cup whole wheat flour
- ½ teaspoon pepper
- 6 boneless pork loin chops (4 ounces each)
- 1 tablespoon olive oil
- 2 cups sliced fresh mushrooms
- ⅓ cup chopped onion
- 2 turkey bacon strips, diced
- ¼ teaspoon minced garlic
- 1 cup Marsala wine or additional reduced-sodium chicken broth

1. In a small bowl, mix cornstarch and broth until smooth; set aside.
2. Place flour and pepper in a large resealable plastic bag. Add pork, a few pieces at a time, and shake to coat. In a large nonstick skillet coated with cooking spray, cook chops in oil for 4-5 minutes on each side or until a thermometer reads 145°. Remove and keep warm.

3. In the same skillet, saute the mushrooms, onion and bacon in drippings for 3 minutes or until bacon is crisp-tender. Add the garlic; cook 1 minute longer. Add wine, stirring to loosen browned bits from pan.
4. Stir cornstarch mixture; add to the pan. Bring to a boil; cook and stir for 2 minutes or until slightly thickened. Serve with pork.
PER SERVING *232 cal., 10 g fat (3 g sat. fat), 60 mg chol., 161 mg sodium, 7 g carb., 1 g fiber, 24 g pro.* **Diabetic Exchanges:** *3 lean meat, ½ starch, ½ fat.*

Meat Loaf from the Slow Cooker

Being busy with my job, I've fallen in love with my slow cooker. This is one of my personal favorites for an easy meat loaf.
—**LAURA BURGESS** MOUNT VERNON, SD

PREP: 25 MIN. • **COOK:** 3 HOURS
MAKES: 8 SERVINGS

- ½ cup tomato sauce
- ½ cup egg substitute
- ¼ cup ketchup
- 1 teaspoon Worcestershire sauce
- 1 small onion, chopped
- ⅓ cup crushed saltines (about 10 crackers)
- ¾ teaspoon minced garlic
- ½ teaspoon seasoned salt
- ⅛ teaspoon seasoned pepper
- 1½ pounds lean ground beef (90% lean)
- ½ pound reduced-fat bulk pork sausage

SAUCE
- ½ cup ketchup
- 3 tablespoons brown sugar
- ¾ teaspoon ground mustard
- ¼ teaspoon ground nutmeg

1. Cut three 25-in. x 3-in. strips of heavy-duty foil; crisscross so they resemble spokes of a wheel. Place strips on the bottom and up the sides of a 4- or 5-qt. slow cooker. Coat strips with cooking spray.
2. In a large bowl, combine the first nine ingredients. Crumble beef and sausage over mixture and mix well (mixture will be moist). Shape into a loaf. Place meat loaf in the center of the strips.
3. In a small bowl, combine the sauce ingredients. Spoon over the meat loaf. Cover; cook on low 3-4 hours or until no pink remains and a thermometer reads 160°. Using foil strips as handles, remove the meat loaf to a platter.
PER SERVING *267 cal., 12 g fat (5 g sat. fat), 72 mg chol., 740 mg sodium, 16 g carb., trace fiber, 23 g pro.* **Diabetic Exchanges:** *3 lean meat, 1 starch, ½ fat.*

Chipotle Mustard Pork Tenderloin

Heat from the chipotle really comes through, and mustard-lovers are sure to savor this fun, quick-fix dinner. But you might want to keep a pitcher of iced tea or ice-cold lemonade within reach.

—LINDA FOREMAN LOCUST GROVE, OK

PREP: 15 MIN. + MARINATING
GRILL: 25 MIN.
MAKES: 4 SERVINGS

- ½ cup honey Dijon mustard
- ⅓ cup minced fresh cilantro
- ¼ cup lime juice
- 1 tablespoon minced chipotle pepper in adobo sauce
- 2 garlic cloves, minced
- ½ teaspoon ground cumin
- ¼ teaspoon salt
- ⅛ teaspoon ground cinnamon
- 1 pork tenderloin (1 pound)
  Chopped honey-roasted peanuts, optional

1. In a small bowl, combine the first eight ingredients. Pour ½ cup marinade into a large resealable plastic bag; add the pork. Seal bag and turn to coat; refrigerate for 8 hours or overnight. Cover and refrigerate remaining marinade.

2. Drain and discard marinade from pork. Moisten a paper towel with cooking oil. Using long-handled tongs, lightly coat the grill rack. Grill pork, covered, over indirect medium-hot heat for 25-40 minutes or until a thermometer reads 145°. Let stand for 5 minutes before slicing.

3. Heat reserved mustard mixture; brush over pork before serving. Sprinkle with peanuts if desired.
PER SERVING *191 cal., 6 g fat (2 g sat. fat), 64 mg chol., 366 mg sodium, 13 g carb., 1 g fiber, 24 g pro.* **Diabetic Exchanges:** *3 lean meat, 1 starch.*

Ham & Asparagus Casserole

I love to try out new recipes on my family. I'm always looking for ways to incorporate some of my favorite vegetables in with my main dishes, and this one was a success!

—RACHEL KOWASIC VALRICO, FL

PREP: 25 MIN. • **BAKE:** 25 MIN.
MAKES: 4 SERVINGS

- 3¾ cups uncooked yolk-free whole wheat noodles
- 2½ cups cut fresh asparagus (1-inch pieces)
- 1 medium onion, chopped
- 1 tablespoon reduced-fat butter
- ¼ cup all-purpose flour
- ½ teaspoon dried thyme
- ⅛ teaspoon pepper
- 1 cup fat-free milk
- 1 cup reduced-sodium chicken broth
- 1 tablespoon lemon juice
- 1½ cups cubed fully cooked lean ham
- ¼ cup minced fresh parsley
- ⅓ cup french-fried onions
- 2 tablespoons shredded Parmesan cheese

HAM & ASPARAGUS CASSEROLE

1. Cook noodles according to package directions. Meanwhile, in a large saucepan, bring 2 cups of water to a boil. Add asparagus. Cover and cook for 3-5 minutes or until crisp-tender; drain and set aside.

2. In a large skillet, saute the chopped onion in butter until tender. Combine the flour, thyme and pepper; gradually whisk in milk and broth until smooth. Add milk mixture to the skillet. Bring to a boil; cook and stir for 1-2 minutes or until thickened. Remove from the heat; stir in lemon juice.

3. Drain noodles; add ham, parsley, sauce and asparagus. Transfer to a 13-in. x 9-in. baking dish coated with cooking spray. Top with fried onions and cheese.

4. Cover and bake at 350° for 20 minutes or until bubbly. Uncover and bake 5-10 minutes longer or until golden brown.
NOTE *This recipe was tested with Land O'Lakes light stick butter.*
PER SERVING *343 cal., 8 g fat (3 g sat. fat), 27 mg chol., 946 mg sodium, 50 g carb., 7 g fiber, 22 g pro.*

CHIPOTLE MUSTARD PORK TENDERLOIN

Pork Chops with Apricot Glaze

This quick recipe is fantastic! The seasonings add just the right amount of flavor, and the apricot preserves offer a touch of sweetness. The glaze is also tasty on grilled chicken.

—**KATHY HARDING** RICHMOND, MO

START TO FINISH: 30 MIN.
MAKES: 6 SERVINGS

- 1½ teaspoons ground ginger
- 1 teaspoon salt
- ½ teaspoon garlic powder
- ½ teaspoon pepper
- 6 boneless pork loin chops (6 ounces each)
- 1 cup apricot preserves
- 2 tablespoons hoisin sauce
- ½ teaspoon crushed red pepper flakes
- 2 green onions, chopped
- 3 tablespoons chopped unsalted peanuts

1. Mix ginger, salt, garlic powder and pepper; rub onto both sides of chops. In a small saucepan, combine the preserves, hoisin sauce and pepper flakes; cook and stir over medium heat until blended. Reserve ½ cup for brushing chops after grilling.
2. Moisten a paper towel with cooking oil. Using long-handled tongs, rub on grill rack to coat lightly. Grill pork, covered, over medium heat or broil 4 in. from heat 4-5 minutes on each side or until a thermometer reads 145°, basting frequently with remaining sauce during the last 4 minutes of cooking. Let stand 5 minutes before serving. Brush chops with reserved sauce; sprinkle with green onions and peanuts.
PER SERVING 399 cal., 12 g fat (4 g sat. fat), 82 mg chol., 549 mg sodium, 39 g carb., 1 g fiber, 34 g pro.

Barbecues for the Bunch

When I worked full-time, this was an easy way to have dinner ready when I got home. It's fall-apart tender and makes enough to freeze for another night.
—**LOUISE WATKINS** LONG KEY, FL

PREP: 25 MIN. • **COOK:** 6 HOURS
MAKES: 16 SERVINGS

- 2 pounds beef top sirloin steak, cubed
- 1½ pounds boneless pork loin roast, cubed
- 2 large onions, chopped
- ¾ cup chopped celery
- 1 can (6 ounces) tomato paste
- ½ cup packed brown sugar
- ¼ cup cider vinegar
- ¼ cup chili sauce
- 2 tablespoons Worcestershire sauce
- 1 tablespoon ground mustard
- 16 hamburger buns, split

1. In a 5-qt. slow cooker, combine the beef, pork, onions and celery. In a small bowl, combine the tomato paste, brown sugar, vinegar, chili sauce, Worcestershire sauce and mustard. Pour over meat mixture.
2. Cover and cook on high for 6-8 hours or until meat is very tender. Shred meat in the slow cooker with two forks. With a slotted spoon, serve ½ cup meat mixture on each bun.
PER SERVING 297 cal., 7 g fat (2 g sat. fat), 53 mg chol., 336 mg sodium, 34 g carb., 2 g fiber, 24 g pro. *Diabetic Exchanges: 3 lean meat, 2 starch.*

BARBECUES FOR THE BUNCH

CRUMB-CRUSTED
PORK ROAST WITH
ROOT VEGETABLES

Crumb-Crusted Pork Roast with Root Vegetables

Perfect for fall, this homey meal combines sweet roasted veggies with a savory crumb-coated roast. It's the kind of dinner that makes an ordinary weeknight feel like a special occasion.

—TASTE OF HOME TEST KITCHEN

PREP: 25 MIN.
BAKE: 1½ HOURS + STANDING
MAKES: 8 SERVINGS

- 1 boneless pork loin roast (2 to 3 pounds)
- 4½ teaspoons honey
- 1 tablespoon molasses
- 1½ teaspoons spicy brown mustard
- 2 teaspoons rubbed sage
- 1 teaspoon dried thyme
- 1 teaspoon dried rosemary, crushed
- ½ cup soft whole wheat bread crumbs
- 2 tablespoons grated Parmesan cheese
- 1 large celery root, peeled and cubed
- 1 large rutabaga, peeled and cubed
- 1 large sweet potato, peeled and cubed
- 1 large onion, cut into wedges
- 2 tablespoons canola oil
- ½ teaspoon salt
- ¼ teaspoon pepper

1. Preheat oven to 350°. Place roast on a rack in a shallow roasting pan coated with cooking spray. In a small bowl, mix honey, molasses and mustard; brush over roast.

2. In a large bowl, mix sage, thyme and rosemary. In a small bowl, toss bread crumbs with Parmesan cheese and 2 teaspoons herb mixture; press onto roast.

3. Add vegetables, oil, salt and pepper to remaining herb mixture; toss to coat. Arrange vegetables around roast.

4. Roast 1½ to 1¾ hours or until a thermometer inserted in the roast reads 145°. Remove from pan; let stand 10 minutes before slicing. Serve with vegetables.

PER SERVING *302 cal., 10 g fat (2 g sat. fat), 57 mg chol., 313 mg sodium, 29 g carb., 5 g fiber, 25 g pro.* ***Diabetic Exchanges:*** *3 lean meat, 2 starch, ½ fat.*

Pork Chop Skillet

My husband and I enjoy this quick supper on busy days when there's little time to cook. It satisfies our meat-and-potato cravings, and leftovers (if there are any) taste even better the next day!

—SUSAN BLAIR STERLING, MI

PREP: 15 MIN. • **COOK:** 30 MIN.
MAKES: 4 SERVINGS

- 4 **medium red potatoes, cubed**
- ½ **cup water**
- 1¼ **cups fresh baby carrots**
- 2 **celery ribs, coarsely chopped**
- 1 **medium onion, cut into wedges**
- 4 **boneless pork loin chops
  (4 ounces each)**
- 1 **tablespoon canola oil**

SAUCE

- 1 **can (10¾ ounces) condensed
  tomato soup, undiluted**
- ½ **cup water**
- 1 **teaspoon dried thyme**
- 1 **teaspoon Worcestershire sauce**
- ¼ **teaspoon pepper**
- 1½ **teaspoons all-purpose flour**
- 2 **tablespoons cold water**

1. Place the potatoes and water in a microwave-safe dish; cover and microwave on high for 3 minutes. Add the carrots, celery and onion; cook 4-6 minutes longer or until vegetables are crisp-tender. Drain.
2. In a large skillet over medium heat, brown pork chops in oil on both sides. Top with vegetables.
3. Combine the soup, water, thyme, Worcestershire sauce and pepper; pour over the top. Bring to a boil. Reduce heat; cover and simmer for 20-25 minutes or until meat and vegetables are tender. Remove chops and vegetables; keep warm.
4. Combine the flour and cold water until smooth; gradually stir into the sauce. Bring to a boil; cook and stir for 2 minutes or until thickened. Serve with chops and vegetables.
NOTE *This recipe was tested in a 1,100-watt microwave.*
PER SERVING *360 cal., 10 g fat (3 g sat. fat), 55 mg chol., 548 mg sodium, 40 g carb., 5 g fiber, 26 g pro.* **Diabetic Exchanges:** *3 lean meat, 2 starch, 1 vegetable, ½ fat*

SPINACH-ALMOND SALAD

C **FAST FIX**

Spinach-Almond Salad

My favorite salad combines power-packed spinach, a good source of vitamins A and K, with other veggies, lean meat and crunchy heart-healthy almonds. The combination of ingredients goes well with a light Asian dressing.

—MARY ANN KIEFFER LAWRENCE, KS

START TO FINISH: 10 MIN.
MAKES: 4 SERVINGS

- 1 **package (6 ounces) fresh baby
  spinach**
- 2 **cups cubed cooked pork**
- 1 **cup bean sprouts**
- 2 **medium carrots, thinly sliced**
- ½ **cup sliced fresh mushrooms**
- ¼ **cup sliced almonds, toasted**
- ½ **cup reduced-fat sesame ginger
  salad dressing**

In a large bowl, combine the first six ingredients. Divide among four salad plates; drizzle each serving with 2 tablespoons salad dressing. Serve immediately.
PER SERVING *244 cal., 11 g fat (3 g sat. fat), 63 mg chol., 500 mg sodium, 12 g carb., 3 g fiber, 24 g pro.* **Diabetic Exchanges:** *3 lean meat, 1 vegetable, 1 fat, ½ starch.*

C FAST FIX
Secret Ingredient Saucy Chops

Coffee, steak sauce, molasses and chocolate are combined with garlic and thyme to create a thick, savory sauce that drapes over these juicy chops.

—TASTE OF HOME TEST KITCHEN

START TO FINISH: 30 MIN.
MAKES: 4 SERVINGS

- 4 **bone-in pork loin chops (7 ounces each)**
- ½ **teaspoon salt**
- ½ **teaspoon pepper**
- 1 **tablespoon canola oil**
- ¾ **cup strong brewed coffee**
- 2 **tablespoons steak sauce**
- 1 **tablespoon molasses**
- ¼ **teaspoon garlic powder**
- ¼ **teaspoon dried thyme**
- 1 **ounce semisweet chocolate, chopped**

1. Sprinkle pork chops with salt and pepper. In a large nonstick skillet, cook chops in oil over medium heat for 4-6 minutes on each side or until a thermometer reads 145°. Remove and keep warm.

2. Add coffee, steak sauce, molasses, garlic powder and thyme to the pan. Bring to a boil; cook until liquid is reduced by half. Whisk in chocolate until melted. Return pork chops to pan; heat through.

PER SERVING *295 cal., 14 g fat (5 g sat. fat), 86 mg chol., 500 mg sodium, 10 g carb., 1 g fiber, 31 g pro.* **Diabetic Exchanges:** *4 lean meat, 1 fat, ½ starch.*

Italian Pulled Pork Sandwiches

Enjoy all the flavors of classic Italian sausage sandwiches with a healthier alternative that uses spicy and tender pulled pork.

—**DELLARIO LIA** MIDDLEPORT, NY

PREP: 20 MIN. • **COOK:** 8 HOURS
MAKES: 12 SERVINGS

- 1 **tablespoon fennel seed, crushed**
- 1 **tablespoon steak seasoning**
- 1 **teaspoon cayenne pepper, optional**
- 1 **boneless pork shoulder butt roast (3 pounds)**
- 1 **tablespoon olive oil**
- 2 **medium green or sweet red peppers, thinly sliced**
- 2 **medium onions, thinly sliced**
- 1 **can (14½ ounces) diced tomatoes, undrained**
- 12 **whole wheat hamburger buns, split**

1. In a small bowl, combine the fennel seed, steak seasoning and cayenne if desired. Cut roast in half. Rub the seasoning mixture over pork. In a large skillet, brown roast in oil on all sides. Place in a 4- or 5-qt. slow cooker. Add the peppers, onions and tomatoes; cover and cook on low for 7-9 hours or until meat is tender.

2. Remove roast; cool slightly. Skim fat from cooking juices. Shred pork with two forks and return to slow cooker; heat through. Using a slotted spoon, place ½ cup meat mixture on each bun.

NOTE *This recipe was tested with McCormick's Montreal Steak Seasoning. Look for it in the spice aisle.*
PER SERVING *288 cal., 8 g fat (2 g sat. fat), 56 mg chol., 454 mg sodium, 27 g carb., 5 g fiber, 26 g pro.* **Diabetic Exchanges:** *3 lean meat, 2 starch.*

SECRET INGREDIENT
SAUCY CHOPS

SC Cajun Orange Pork Chops

My husband and I are very busy but we try to be conscious of calories. This dish is perfect for us because it's quick, delicious and easy on the waistline.

—**PATRICIA HARMON** BADEN, PA

PREP: 15 MIN. + MARINATING
GRILL: 10 MIN.
MAKES: 4 SERVINGS

- ½ cup orange juice
- 2 green onions, chopped
- 2 tablespoons orange marmalade
- 2 garlic cloves, minced
- 1 teaspoon Cajun seasoning
- 4 boneless pork loin chops (4 ounces each)

1. In a small bowl, combine the first five ingredients. Pour ⅓ cup marinade into a large resealable bag; add the pork. Seal bag and turn to coat; refrigerate for 8 hours or overnight. Cover and refrigerate remaining marinade for sauce.
2. In a small saucepan, bring reserved marinade to a boil. Reduce heat; simmer, uncovered, for 5-7 minutes or until thickened. Keep warm.
3. Discard marinade. Moisten a paper towel with cooking oil. Using long-handled tongs, lightly coat the grill

top tip No Bones About It

The recommended serving size of pork is 3 ounces of cooked meat. Start with 4 ounces of boneless, raw pork to yield 3 ounces of cooked pork, keeping in mind a 3-ounce serving is about the same size as a deck of cards.

LIGHT HAM TETRAZZINI

rack. Grill pork, covered, over medium heat or broil 4-5 in. from the heat for 4-5 minutes on each side or until a thermometer reads 145°. Let meat stand for 5 minutes before serving. Brush with sauce.

PER SERVING *183 cal., 6 g fat (2 g sat. fat), 55 mg chol., 138 mg sodium, 8 g carb., trace fiber, 22 g pro.* **Diabetic Exchanges:** *3 lean meat, ½ starch.*

Light Ham Tetrazzini

This creamy pasta is an easy way to serve a hungry crowd. If you're bringing this tetrazzini to a potluck, cook and add the spaghetti to the slow cooker just before heading to the gathering.

—**SUSAN BLAIR** STERLING, MI

PREP: 15 MIN. • **COOK:** 4 HOURS
MAKES: 10 SERVINGS

- 2 cans (10¾ ounces each) reduced-fat reduced-sodium condensed cream of mushroom soup, undiluted
- 2 cups sliced fresh mushrooms
- 2 cups cubed fully cooked ham
- 1 cup fat-free evaporated milk
- ¼ cup white wine or water
- 2 teaspoons prepared horseradish
- 1 package (14½ ounces) uncooked multigrain spaghetti
- 1 cup shredded Parmesan cheese

1. In a 5-qt. slow cooker, combine the soup, mushrooms, ham, milk, wine and horseradish. Cover and cook on low for 4 hours.
2. Cook the spaghetti according to package directions; drain. Add the spaghetti and cheese to slow cooker; toss to coat.

PER SERVING *279 cal., 5 g fat (2 g sat. fat), 26 mg chol., 734 mg sodium, 37 g carb., 4 g fiber, 20 g pro.* **Diabetic Exchanges:** *2½ starch, 1 lean meat, ½ fat.*

PORK

Cuban-Style Pork Sandwiches

Loaded with tangy flavor, this is a lighter version of a favorite restaurant-style sandwich. If you don't have a panini press, tuck the sandwiches under the broiler until the bread is browned and the cheese is melted.

—ROBIN HAAS CRANSTON, RI

PREP: 20 MIN.
COOK: 6 HOURS + STANDING
MAKES: 10 SERVINGS

- 1 large onion, cut into wedges
- ¾ cup reduced-sodium chicken broth
- 1 cup minced fresh parsley
- 7 garlic cloves, minced and divided
- 2 tablespoons cider vinegar
- 1 tablespoon plus 1½ teaspoons lemon juice, divided
- 2 teaspoons ground cumin
- 1 teaspoon ground mustard
- 1 teaspoon dried oregano
- ½ teaspoon salt
- ½ teaspoon pepper
- 1 boneless pork shoulder butt roast (3 to 4 pounds)
- 1¼ cups fat-free mayonnaise
- 2 tablespoons Dijon mustard
- 10 whole wheat hamburger buns, split
- 1¼ cups (5 ounces) shredded reduced-fat Swiss cheese
- 1 medium onion, thinly sliced and separated into rings
- 2 whole dill pickles, sliced

1. Place onion wedges and broth in a 5-qt. slow cooker. In a small bowl, combine the parsley, 5 garlic cloves, vinegar, 1 tablespoon lemon juice, cumin, mustard, oregano, salt and pepper; rub over pork. Add to slow cooker. Cover and cook on low for 6-8 hours or until meat is tender.

2. Remove meat; let stand for 10 minutes before slicing. In another small bowl, combine the mayonnaise, mustard and remaining garlic and lemon juice; spread over buns. Layer bun bottoms with pork, cheese, sliced onion and pickles; replace tops.

3. Cook on a panini maker or indoor grill for 2-3 minutes or until buns are browned and cheese is melted.

PER SERVING *415 cal., 18 g fat (6 g sat. fat), 90 mg chol., 943 mg sodium, 32 g carb., 5 g fiber, 33 g pro.*

CUBAN-STYLE PORK SANDWICHES

Teriyaki Pork Kabobs

Soy sauce, garlic and ginger add Asian zing to this quick dish and help make it delicious without a lot of added fat.

—EDIE DESPAIN LOGAN, UT

PREP: 20 MIN. • **GRILL:** 15 MIN.
MAKES: 4 SERVINGS

- 4½ teaspoons cornstarch
- 1 tablespoon brown sugar
- 1 can (14½ ounces) reduced-sodium beef broth
- 2 tablespoons reduced-sodium soy sauce
- 2 garlic cloves, minced
- ¼ teaspoon ground ginger

TERIYAKI PORK KABOBS

- 1 pork tenderloin (1 pound), cut into 1-inch cubes
- 16 medium fresh mushrooms
- 1 large red onion, cut into wedges
- 8 cherry tomatoes
  Hot cooked rice, optional

1. In a small saucepan, combine the cornstarch and brown sugar. Stir in the broth, soy sauce, garlic and ginger until blended. Bring to a boil; cook and stir for 2 minutes or until thickened. Set aside half of the sauce for serving; keep warm.

2. On eight metal or soaked wooden skewers, alternately thread the pork, mushrooms and onion. Grill, covered, over medium heat for 10-15 minutes or until meat is no longer pink, basting frequently with remaining sauce and turning once.

3. Place a tomato on the end of each kabob. Grill 1-2 minutes longer or until tomatoes are heated through, turning occasionally. Serve with reserved sauce and rice if desired.

PER SERVING *210 cal., 4 g fat (1 g sat. fat), 65 mg chol., 539 mg sodium, 16 g carb., 2 g fiber, 27 g pro.* **Diabetic Exchanges:** *3 lean meat, 2 vegetable, ½ starch.*

Glazed Pork Chops with Corn Bread Dressing

Baking the pork chops with the stuffing allows parts of the stuffing to crisp up, adding a tasty texture to this homey casserole. The slightly sweet glaze on top perfectly coats the pork, so every bite is sweet, savory and scrumptious.

—DAWN KLOMAN WATERTOWN, WI

PREP: 10 MIN. • **BAKE:** 25 MIN.
MAKES: 6 SERVINGS

1¼ cups reduced-sodium chicken broth
¾ cup chopped onion
¾ cup frozen corn
1 celery rib, chopped
    Dash cayenne pepper
3 cups crushed corn bread stuffing
6 boneless pork loin chops (6 ounces each)
2 tablespoons brown sugar
2 teaspoons spicy brown mustard

1. Preheat oven to 400°. In a large saucepan, bring broth, onion, corn, celery and cayenne to a boil. Remove from the heat; stir in stuffing.
2. Transfer to a 13-in. x 9-in. baking dish coated with cooking spray. Top with pork chops. Combine brown sugar and mustard; spread over chops. Bake, uncovered, 25-30 minutes or until a thermometer reads 145°. Let stand 5 minutes before serving.
PER SERVING *389 cal., 11 g fat (4 g sat. fat), 82 mg chol., 516 mg sodium, 33 g carb., 2 g fiber, 37 g pro.* **Diabetic Exchanges:** *5 lean meat, 2 starch, 1 fat.*

FAST FIX
Skewerless Stovetop Kabobs

My family loves this simple-to-do recipe so much, we never have any leftovers. It's also great on the grill.

—JENNIFER MITCHELL ALTOONA, PA

START TO FINISH: 30 MIN.
MAKES: 4 SERVINGS

---

1 pound pork tenderloin, cut into ¾-inch cubes
¾ cup fat-free Italian salad dressing, divided
2 large green peppers, cut into ¾-inch pieces
2 small zucchini, cut into ½-inch slices
½ pound medium fresh mushrooms, halved
1 large sweet onion, cut into wedges
1 cup cherry tomatoes
¼ teaspoon pepper
⅛ teaspoon seasoned salt

1. In a large nonstick skillet, saute pork in ¼ cup salad dressing until no longer pink. Remove and keep warm.
2. In the same pan, cook the peppers, zucchini, mushrooms, onion, tomatoes, pepper and seasoned salt in remaining salad dressing until the vegetables are tender. Return pork to skillet; heat through.
PER SERVING *236 cal., 5 g fat (2 g sat. fat), 65 mg chol., 757 mg sodium, 22 g carb., 4 g fiber, 27 g pro.* **Diabetic Exchanges:** *3 lean meat, 2 starch.*

SKEWERLESS STOVETOP KABOBS

Grilled Pork Tenderloin Satay

My dad used to make this often, pairing peanut butter and soy sauce for a great Asian-style entree. I frequently served it with roasted veggies and yellow rice.
—**GAYLE JEFFERSON** LAS VEGAS, NV

PREP: 25 MIN. • **GRILL:** 10 MIN.
MAKES: 8 SKEWERS (½ CUP SAUCE)

- 1 **small onion, chopped**
- ¼ **cup packed brown sugar**
- ¼ **cup water**
- 3 **tablespoons reduced-sodium soy sauce**
- 2 **tablespoons reduced-fat creamy peanut butter**
- 4½ **teaspoons canola oil**
- 2 **garlic cloves, minced**
- ¼ **teaspoon ground ginger**
- 1 **pork tenderloin (1 pound)**

1. In a small saucepan, bring the first eight ingredients to a boil. Reduce heat; simmer, uncovered, for 10-12 minutes or until thickened. Set aside ½ cup mixture for sauce.

2. Cut pork in half widthwise; cut each half into thin strips. Thread pork strips onto eight metal or soaked wooden skewers. Grill, uncovered, over medium-hot heat for 2-3 minutes on each side or until no longer pink, basting occasionally with remaining mixture. Serve with reserved sauce.

PER SERVING *287 cal., 12 g fat (2 g sat. fat), 63 mg chol., 549 mg sodium, 19 g carb., 1 g fiber, 26 g pro.* **Diabetic Exchanges:** *3 lean meat, 1½ fat, 1 starch.*

top tip | Calculating Cost

When shopping for pork, be sure to calculate the cost per serving. Some cuts seem more expensive but are a better choice because you're not paying for the bone. Divide the cost per pound by the number of servings per pound and then compare.

GRILLED PORK TENDERLOIN SATAY

CANADIAN PORK ROAST WITH GRAVY

S C

Canadian Pork Roast with Gravy

My son wanted something he could make in the slow cooker while he took his new girlfriend out for a bike ride on their second date. This is the meal I came up with for him.

—MARILYN MCCRORY CRESTON, BC

PREP: 20 MIN. • **COOK:** 5 HOURS
MAKES: 10 SERVINGS

- 1 **boneless whole pork loin roast (3 pounds)**
- ⅓ **cup maple syrup**
- 1 **tablespoon lemon juice**
- 1 **tablespoon Dijon mustard**
- 1 **garlic clove, minced**
- 2 **tablespoons cornstarch**
- ¼ **cup cold water**

1. Cut roast in half. Transfer to a 5-qt. slow cooker. Combine the syrup, lemon juice, mustard and garlic; pour over pork. Cover and cook on low for 5-6 hours or until meat is tender.

2. Remove meat to a serving platter; keep warm. Strain cooking juices; transfer 1 cup to a small saucepan. Combine cornstarch and water until smooth; stir into cooking juices. Bring to a boil; cook and stir for 2 minutes or until thickened. Slice the roast; serve with the gravy.

PER SERVING *205 cal., 6 g fat (2 g sat. fat), 68 mg chol., 76 mg sodium, 9 g carb., trace fiber, 26 g pro.* **Diabetic Exchanges:** *4 lean meat, ½ starch.*

C FAST FIX ▶

Pork Medallions in Mustard Sauce

Mustard and apple juice liven up lean pork tenderloin, creating a dish that's ideal for family or special guests.

—TAHNIA FOX TRENTON, MI

START TO FINISH: 30 MIN.
MAKES: 4 SERVINGS

- ½ cup reduced-sodium chicken broth
- 2 tablespoons thawed apple juice concentrate
- 4½ teaspoons stone-ground mustard
- 1 pound pork tenderloin, cut into ½-inch slices
- ¼ teaspoon salt
- ¼ teaspoon pepper
- 1 tablespoon olive oil
- 2 garlic cloves, minced
- 1 teaspoon cornstarch
- 2 tablespoons cold water
- 1 tablespoon minced fresh parsley

1. In a small bowl, mix the broth, juice concentrate and mustard; set aside.

2. Sprinkle pork with salt and pepper. In a large nonstick skillet, brown pork in oil. Remove and set aside.

3. Add garlic to the pan; saute for 1 minute. Add reserved broth mixture, stirring to loosen browned bits from pan. Bring to a boil. Reduce heat; simmer, uncovered, for 6-8 minutes or until liquid is reduced to about ⅓ cup.

4. Return pork to the pan; cover and cook over low heat for 3-4 minutes or until meat is no longer pink. Combine cornstarch and water until smooth; add to the pan. Bring to a boil; cook and stir for 2 minutes or until thickened. Sprinkle with parsley.

PER SERVING *193 cal., 7 g fat (2 g sat. fat), 63 mg chol., 356 mg sodium, 6 g carb., 1 g fiber, 23 g pro.* **Diabetic Exchanges:** *3 lean meat, ½ starch, ½ fat.*

HAM & SPINACH COUSCOUS

PORK MEDALLIONS IN MUSTARD SAUCE

FAST FIX ▶

Ham & Spinach Couscous

Here's a simple way to dress up couscous. The colorful, foolproof dish makes a lovely one-pot meal when time's tight.

—LISA SHANNON CULLMAN, AL

START TO FINISH: 20 MIN.
MAKES: 4 SERVINGS

- 2 cups water
- 1 cup chopped fully cooked ham
- 1 cup chopped fresh spinach
- ½ teaspoon garlic salt
- 1 cup uncooked couscous
- ¼ cup shredded cheddar cheese

In a large saucepan, combine the water, ham, spinach and garlic salt. Bring to a boil. Stir in the couscous. Remove from the heat; cover and let stand for 5-10 minutes or until water is absorbed. Fluff with a fork. Sprinkle with cheese.

PER SERVING *248 cal., 6 g fat (3 g sat. fat), 26 mg chol., 727 mg sodium, 36 g carb., 2 g fiber, 14 g pro.* **Diabetic Exchanges:** *2 starch, 1 lean meat, 1 fat.*

Tangy Pork Chops

Many years ago my nephew was working his way through college, and he sold me a knife collection. It came with a cookbook which included these chops. It's since become my signature entree for guests.

—MRS. THOMAS MAUST BERLIN, PA

PREP: 30 MIN. • **BAKE:** 20 MIN.
MAKES: 6 SERVINGS

- 6 bone-in pork loin chops (7 ounces each)
- 2 teaspoons canola oil
- 2 celery ribs, finely chopped
- 1 small onion, finely chopped
- 1 tablespoon butter
- ½ cup ketchup
- ¼ cup water
- 2 tablespoons cider vinegar
- 1 tablespoon brown sugar
- 1 tablespoon lemon juice
- 1 tablespoon Worcestershire sauce
- ¼ teaspoon salt
- ⅛ teaspoon pepper
- 1 small onion, thinly sliced
- 1 large green pepper, cut into rings

1. In a large nonstick skillet coated with cooking spray, brown chops in oil in batches. Transfer to a 13-in. x. 9-in. baking dish coated with cooking spray.
2. In the same pan, saute celery and chopped onion in butter until tender. Stir in ketchup, water, vinegar, brown sugar, lemon juice, Worcestershire sauce, salt and pepper. Bring to a boil. Reduce heat; cover and simmer for 15-20 minutes or until the sauce is slightly reduced.

3. Pour sauce over chops. Top with sliced onion and pepper rings. Cover and bake at 350° for 20-25 minutes or until a thermometer reads 145°. Let stand 5 minutes before serving.
PER SERVING *284 cal., 12 g fat (4 g sat. fat), 91 mg chol., 469 mg sodium, 12 g carb., 1 g fiber, 31 g pro. Diabetic Exchanges: 4 lean meat, 1 starch, ½ fat.*

FAST FIX
Creamy Ham Penne

Mixing spreadable cheese with whole wheat pasta, broccoli and fat-free milk for a pasta dinner is a healthier use of this convenience product than simply spreading it on crackers.

—BARBARA PLETZKE HERNDON, VA

START TO FINISH: 30 MIN.
MAKES: 4 SERVINGS

- 2 cups uncooked whole wheat penne pasta
- 2 cups fresh broccoli florets
- 1 cup fat-free milk
- 1 package (6½ ounces) reduced-fat garlic-herb spreadable cheese
- 1 cup cubed fully cooked ham
- ¼ teaspoon pepper

1. In a large saucepan, cook penne according to package directions, adding broccoli during the last 5 minutes of cooking; drain. Remove and set aside.
2. In the same pan, combine milk and spreadable cheese. Cook and stir over medium heat for 3-5 minutes or until cheese is melted. Add the ham, pepper and penne mixture; heat through.
PER SERVING *371 cal., 8 g fat (5 g sat. fat), 47 mg chol., 672 mg sodium, 49 g carb., 7 g fiber, 25 g pro.*

CREAMY HAM PENNE

SPICE-RUBBED HAM

Spice-Rubbed Ham

Now this is a ham—sweet and smoky, with just enough clove and ginger flavor to let you know you're in for a treat.

—SHARON TIPTON WINTER GARDEN, FL

PREP: 15 MIN.
BAKE: 3¼ HOURS + STANDING
MAKES: 24 SERVINGS

- 1 **fully cooked semi-boneless ham (8 to 10 pounds)**
- ½ **cup spicy brown mustard**
- ¼ **cup packed brown sugar**
- ¼ **teaspoon ground ginger**
- ¼ **teaspoon ground cinnamon**
  Whole cloves

1. Place ham on a rack in a shallow roasting pan. Score the surface of ham, making diamond shapes ½ in. deep. Mix the mustard, brown sugar, ginger and cinnamon; rub over surface of ham. Insert a clove in each diamond.
2. Bake, uncovered, at 325° for 1½ hours. Cover and bake 1¾ to 2 hours longer or until a thermometer reads 140°. Cover loosely with foil if ham browns too quickly. Discard cloves. Let the ham stand for 10 minutes before slicing.
PER SERVING *139 cal., 4 g fat (1 g sat. fat), 66 mg chol., 858 mg sodium, 3 g carb., trace fiber, 22 g pro.* **Diabetic Exchange:** *3 lean meat.*

C Cranberry-Glazed Pork Roast

Pork roast with a sweet-tart cranberry glaze has become a Sunday dinner tradition in my family. It's low in fat and calories, but it tastes like down-home comfort food.

—BETH BRANDENBURGER ROCHESTER, MN

PREP: 10 MIN.
COOK: 1 HOUR 20 MIN. + STANDING
MAKES: 16 SERVINGS

- 1 cup whole-berry cranberry sauce
- ¾ cup unsweetened apple juice
- ¾ cup barbecue sauce
- 1 teaspoon salt
- 1 tablespoon cornstarch
- 2 tablespoons cold water
- 1 boneless rolled pork loin roast (4 pounds)

1. In a small saucepan, combine the cranberry sauce, apple juice, barbecue sauce and salt. Bring to a boil. Reduce the heat; simmer, uncovered, for 10 minutes. Combine the cornstarch and water until smooth; stir into the cranberry mixture. Bring to a boil; cook and stir for 2 minutes or until thickened. Set aside 1 cup sauce.
2. Place roast in a shallow roasting pan. Bake, uncovered, at 350° for 1 hour. Spoon a third of the remaining glaze over pork. Bake 20-30 minutes longer or until a thermometer reads 145°, basting twice. Let stand for 10 minutes before slicing. Serve with reserved sauce.

PER SERVING *181 cal., 5 g fat (2 g sat. fat), 56 mg chol., 280 mg sodium, 10 g carb., trace fiber, 22 g pro.* **Diabetic Exchanges:** *3 lean meat, ½ starch*

CRANBERRY-GLAZED PORK ROAST

S C Pork Tenderloin with Cherry Relish

Pork tenderloin, one of the leanest sources of protein, is a smart, low-fat choice for an entree. The herb rub on the tenderloin keeps the flavor high and sodium low. Combined with a dried-cherry relish, rich in antioxidants, you'll have a fabulous, heart-healthy meal.

—TASTE OF HOME TEST KITCHEN

PREP: 10 MIN. + CHILLING • **COOK:** 25 MIN.
MAKES: 8 SERVINGS (1 CUP RELISH)

- 1 teaspoon garlic powder
- 1 teaspoon each dried oregano, tarragon and rosemary, crushed
- 2 pork tenderloins (1 pound each), trimmed

RELISH
- 1 large red onion, sliced
- 2 tablespoons olive oil
- 3 tablespoons sugar

PORK TENDERLOIN WITH CHERRY RELISH

- ½ cup dried cherries
- ¼ cup red wine vinegar
- ¼ teaspoon dried rosemary, crushed

1. In a small bowl, combine garlic powder and herbs; rub over pork. Cover and refrigerate for 30 minutes.
2. For relish, in a large saucepan, saute onion in oil until tender. Add sugar; cook and stir over medium heat for 10 minutes or until onion is browned. Add the cherries, vinegar and rosemary. Bring to a boil. Reduce the heat; cover and simmer for 10 minutes. Cool to room temperature.
3. Place pork on a rack in a foil-lined shallow roasting pan. Bake at 425° for 25-30 minutes or until a thermometer reads 165°. Let stand for 10 minutes before slicing. Serve with relish.

PER SERVING *217 cal., 7 g fat (2 g sat. fat), 63 mg chol., 46 mg sodium, 14 g carb., 1 g fiber, 23 g pro.* **Diabetic Exchanges:** *3 lean meat, ½ starch, ½ fruit, ½ fat.*

BALSAMIC-GLAZED
SALMON *PAGE 201*

**GREGG MAY'S
GRILLED TILAPIA WITH MANGO**

PAGE 190

**LIBBY WALP'S
HEARTY PAELLA**

PAGE 194

**EDIE DE SPAIN'S
SCALLOP KABOBS**

PAGE 196

Seafood

Decadent and healthful, these fish and seafood treasures bring together the best of both worlds. Dive in to discover **your new favorite.**

FAST FIX
Easy Crab Cakes

Canned crabmeat makes these delicate patties simple enough for busy weeknight dinners. For something different, try forming the crab mixture into four thick patties instead of eight cakes.

—**CHARLENE SPELOCK** APOLLO, PA

START TO FINISH: 25 MIN.
MAKES: 4 SERVINGS

- 2 cans (6 ounces each) crabmeat, drained, flaked and cartilage removed
- 1 cup seasoned bread crumbs, divided
- 1 egg, lightly beaten
- ¼ cup finely chopped green onions
- ¼ cup finely chopped sweet red pepper
- ¼ cup reduced-fat mayonnaise
- 1 tablespoon lemon juice
- ½ teaspoon garlic powder
- ⅛ teaspoon cayenne pepper
- 1 tablespoon butter

1. In a large bowl, combine the crab, ⅓ cup bread crumbs, egg, onions, red pepper, mayonnaise, lemon juice, garlic powder and cayenne.
2. Divide mixture into eight portions; shape into 2-in. balls. Roll in the remaining bread crumbs. Flatten to ½-in. thickness.
3. In a large nonstick skillet, cook crab cakes in butter for 3-4 minutes on each side or until golden brown.

PER SERVING *295 cal., 12 g fat (3 g sat. fat), 142 mg chol., 879 mg sodium, 23 g carb., 1 g fiber, 23 g pro.* **Diabetic Exchanges:** *3 lean meat, 1½ starch, 1½ fat.*

Colorful Shrimp Pad Thai

Bright, fresh veggie flavors, a splash of tart lime juice, the crunch of peanuts and a hint of heat make this healthy and beautiful shrimp stir-fry a real standout!

—**TASTE OF HOME TEST KITCHEN**

PREP: 30 MIN. • **COOK:** 15 MIN.
MAKES: 6 SERVINGS

- 6 ounces uncooked thick rice noodles
- ¼ cup rice vinegar
- 3 tablespoons reduced-sodium soy sauce
- 2 tablespoons sugar
- 2 tablespoons fish sauce or additional reduced-sodium soy sauce
- 1 tablespoon lime juice
- 2 teaspoons Thai chili sauce
- 1 teaspoon sesame oil
- ¼ teaspoon crushed red pepper flakes

STIR-FRY
- 1½ pounds uncooked medium shrimp, peeled and deveined
- 3 teaspoons sesame oil, divided
- 2 cups fresh snow peas
- 2 medium carrots, grated
- 2 garlic cloves, minced
- 2 eggs, lightly beaten
- 2 cups bean sprouts
- 2 green onions, chopped
- ¼ cup minced fresh cilantro
- ¼ cup unsalted dry roasted peanuts, chopped

1. Cook noodles according to package directions. Meanwhile, in a small bowl, combine the vinegar, soy sauce, sugar, fish sauce, lime juice, chili sauce, oil and pepper flakes until blended; set aside.
2. In a large nonstick skillet or wok, stir-fry shrimp in 2 teaspoons oil until shrimp turn pink; remove and keep warm. Stir-fry snow peas and carrots in remaining oil for 1-2 minutes. Add garlic, cook 1 minute longer or until vegetables are crisp-tender. Add eggs; cook and stir until set.
3. Drain noodles; add to shrimp mixture. Stir vinegar mixture and add to the skillet. Bring to a boil. Add shrimp mixture, bean sprouts and green onions; heat through. Sprinkle with cilantro and peanuts.

PER SERVING *352 cal., 10 g fat (2 g sat. fat), 208 mg chol., 955 mg sodium, 38 g carb., 4 g fiber, 28 g pro.* **Diabetic Exchanges:** *3 lean meat, 2 starch, 1 vegetable, 1 fat.*

Tangy Shrimp Kabobs

For these kabobs, an easy tomato-based mixture is used as a marinade and basting sauce to add just the right amount of sweet-sour taste to the shrimp, pineapple and veggies.

—PAT WAYMIRE YELLOW SPRINGS, OH

PREP: 25 MIN. + MARINATING
GRILL: 15 MIN.
MAKES: 6 SERVINGS

- 1 **can (20 ounces) unsweetened pineapple chunks**
- 1 **can (8 ounces) tomato sauce**
- ½ **cup fat-free Italian salad dressing**
- 4½ **teaspoons brown sugar**
- 1 **teaspoon prepared mustard**
- 1½ **pounds uncooked large shrimp, peeled and deveined**
- 12 **pearl onions**
- 1 **large sweet red pepper, cut into 1-inch pieces**
- 1 **large green pepper, cut into 1-inch pieces**
  Hot cooked rice, optional

1. Drain pineapple, reserving ¼ cup juice; set aside. In a small bowl, combine the tomato sauce, Italian dressing, brown sugar, mustard and reserved pineapple juice. Pour ¾ cup marinade into a large resealable plastic bag; add shrimp. Seal bag; turn to coat. Refrigerate for 3 hours, turning occasionally. Cover and refrigerate the remaining mixture for sauce.

2. In a Dutch oven, bring 6 cups water to a boil. Add the onions; boil for 2 minutes. Add the peppers and boil 2 minutes longer. Drain and rinse in cold water; peel onions. Refrigerate vegetables until ready to grill.

3. In a small saucepan, bring ¾ cup of reserved tomato sauce mixture to a boil. Reduce heat; simmer, uncovered, 5 minutes or until slightly thickened. Keep warm.

4. Drain and discard marinade from shrimp. On 12 metal or soaked wooden skewers, alternately thread shrimp and vegetables. Moisten a paper towel with cooking oil. Using long-handled tongs, lightly coat the grill rack.

5. Grill kabobs, covered, over medium heat or broil 4 in. from the heat for 3-5 minutes on each side or until shrimp turn pink, basting occasionally with the remaining tomato sauce mixture. Drizzle the kabobs with warm sauce. Serve with rice if desired.

PER SERVING *194 cal., 2 g fat (trace sat. fat), 138 mg chol., 474 mg sodium, 24 g carb., 3 g fiber, 20 g pro.* **Diabetic Exchanges:** *3 lean meat, 2 vegetable, 1 fruit.*

TANGY SHRIMP KABOBS

Apricot-Glazed Salmon with Herb Rice

Salmon lovers will really enjoy the nice and fruity-tasting fish with just the right amount of sweetness. If salmon is new to your family, this is a great way to introduce it to them.

—CHARLENE CHAMBERS
ORMOND BEACH, FL

PREP: 25 MIN. • **COOK:** 20 MIN.
MAKES: 6 SERVINGS

- 6 **salmon fillets (4 ounces each)**
- ¼ **teaspoon salt**

APRICOT-GLAZED SALMON WITH HERB RICE

- ⅛ **teaspoon pepper**
- ⅓ **cup white wine or reduced-sodium chicken broth**
- ⅓ **cup apricot spreadable fruit**
- ½ **teaspoon grated fresh gingerroot**
- 2 **cups reduced-sodium chicken broth**
- 1 **cup uncooked long grain rice**
- 2 **teaspoons butter**
- 2 **tablespoons chopped dried apricots**
- 2 **tablespoons minced fresh parsley**
- 1 **tablespoon minced chives**
- 1 **teaspoon minced fresh thyme or ¼ teaspoon dried thyme**
- 3 **tablespoons sliced almonds, toasted**

1. Place salmon in a 13-in. x 9-in. baking dish coated with cooking spray. Sprinkle with salt and pepper. In a small bowl, combine wine, spreadable fruit and ginger; spoon over salmon.

2. Bake at 375° for 15-20 minutes or until fish flakes easily with a fork.

3. Meanwhile, in a small saucepan, bring the broth, rice and butter to a boil. Reduce heat; cover and simmer for 10 minutes. Add apricots; cover and cook 5-8 minutes longer or until liquid is absorbed and rice is tender. Stir in the parsley, chives and thyme. Serve with salmon. Sprinkle each serving with almonds.

PER SERVING *408 cal., 15 g fat (3 g sat. fat), 70 mg chol., 369 mg sodium, 37 g carb., 1 g fiber, 27 g pro.*

F C
Baked Lobster Tails

Lobster tails always make a rich and filling entree, especially when served alongside steak. In this recipe, three lobster tails are cut in half to feed six people.

—TASTE OF HOME TEST KITCHEN

PREP: 15 MIN. • **BAKE:** 20 MIN.
MAKES: 6 SERVINGS

- 3 **lobster tails (8 to 10 ounces each)**
- 1 **cup water**
- 1 **tablespoon minced fresh parsley**
- ⅛ **teaspoon salt**
  Dash pepper
- 1 **tablespoon butter, melted**
- 2 **tablespoons lemon juice**
  Lemon wedges and additional melted butter, optional

1. Split lobster tails in half lengthwise. With cut side up and using scissors, cut along the edge of the shell to loosen the cartilage covering the tail meat from the shell; remove and discard cartilage.

2. Pour water into a 13-in. x 9-in. baking dish; place lobster tails in dish. Combine the parsley, salt and pepper; sprinkle over lobster. Drizzle with butter and lemon juice.

3. Bake, uncovered, at 375° for 20-25 minutes or until meat is firm and opaque. Serve with lemon wedges and melted butter if desired.

PER SERVING *120 cal., 3 g fat (1 g sat. fat), 113 mg chol., 405 mg sodium, 1 g carb., trace fiber, 21 g pro.*

C
Soy-Glazed Scallops

Lightly glazed and naturally buttery and sweet, these yummy broiled scallops are also a great source of B12 and heart-healthy minerals such as magnesium, helpful in keeping your heartbeat steady.

—APRIL KORANDO AVA, IL

PREP: 25 MIN. + MARINATING
BROIL: 5 MIN.
MAKES: 4 SERVINGS

- ¼ **cup lemon juice**
- 2 **tablespoons canola oil**
- 2 **tablespoons reduced-sodium soy sauce**
- 2 **tablespoons honey**
- 2 **garlic cloves, minced**
- ½ **teaspoon ground ginger**
- 12 **sea scallops (about 1½ pounds)**

1. In a small bowl, combine the first six ingredients. Pour ⅓ cup marinade into a large resealable plastic bag. Add the scallops; seal bag and turn to coat. Refrigerate for 20 minutes.

2. Place the remaining marinade in a small saucepan. Bring to a boil. Reduce the heat; simmer, uncovered, for 8-10 minutes or until marinade is slightly thickened.

3. Drain and discard marinade from scallops. Thread scallops onto four metal or soaked wooden skewers. Broil 4 in. from the heat for 2-4 minutes on each side or until the scallops are firm and opaque, basting occasionally with the remaining marinade.

PER SERVING *250 cal., 8 g fat (1 g sat. fat), 54 mg chol., 567 mg sodium, 15 g carb., trace fiber, 28 g pro.*
Diabetic Exchanges: *4 lean meat, 1 fat, ½ starch.*

SOY-GLAZED SCALLOPS

Grilled Tilapia with Mango

This is a different twist on tilapia that I created for my wife. She enjoyed the combination of mango with Parmesan. We like to eat this outside on the deck with a cold glass of iced tea.

—**GREGG MAY** COLUMBUS, OH

START TO FINISH: 20 MIN.
MAKES: 4 SERVINGS

- 4 **tilapia fillets (6 ounces each)**
- 1 **tablespoon olive oil**
- ½ **teaspoon salt**
- ½ **teaspoon dill weed**
- ¼ **teaspoon pepper**
- 1 **tablespoon grated Parmesan cheese**
- 1 **medium lemon, sliced**
- 1 **medium mango, peeled and thinly sliced**

1. Brush fillets with oil; sprinkle with salt, dill and pepper. Moisten a paper towel with cooking oil. Using long-handled tongs, lightly coat grill rack.

2. Grill tilapia, covered, over medium heat for 5 minutes. Turn tilapia; top with cheese, lemon and mango. Grill 4-6 minutes longer or until fish flakes easily with a fork.

PER SERVING *213 cal., 5 g fat (1 g sat. fat), 84 mg chol., 377 mg sodium, 10 g carb., 1 g fiber, 32 g pro.* ***Diabetic Exchanges:*** *5 lean meat, ½ fruit, ½ fat.*

C FAST FIX
Salmon Supreme with Ginger Soy Sauce

Served with asparagus, this is my go-to meal for Friday nights. It's light in calories and delicious, too.

—**AGNES WARD** STRATFORD, ON

START TO FINISH: 25 MIN.
MAKES: 4 SERVINGS

- 2 **tablespoons all-purpose flour**
- 1 **tablespoon cornstarch**
- 4 **salmon fillets (4 ounces each)**
- 1 **tablespoon canola oil**
- ⅓ **cup sherry or unsweetened apple juice**
- 2 **green onions, chopped**
- ¼ **cup minced fresh gingerroot**
- 3 **tablespoons reduced-sodium soy sauce**
- 2 **tablespoons honey**
- 1 **tablespoon balsamic vinegar**
- ½ **teaspoon garlic powder**

1. In a shallow bowl, combine flour and cornstarch. Dip fillets in flour mixture. In a large nonstick skillet coated with cooking spray, cook the salmon in oil over medium-high heat for 4-6 minutes on each side or until fish flakes easily with a fork. Remove and keep warm.

2. Add sherry, stirring to loosen the browned bits from the pan. Stir in the remaining ingredients; cook, stirring occasionally, for 2 minutes to allow flavors to blend. Serve with salmon.

PER SERVING *319 cal., 16 g fat (3 g sat. fat), 67 mg chol., 526 mg sodium, 15 g carb., trace fiber, 24 g pro.*

C FAST FIX
Pistachio-Crusted Fish Fillets

The crunchy crust on this fish dish is delicious, but it doesn't come close to breaking your New Year's resolutions. It's a fresh and fun way to reel in your family to the dinner table.

—**MARIE STUPIN** ROANOKE, VA

START TO FINISH: 25 MIN.
MAKES: 4 SERVINGS

- 1 **egg white, beaten**
- ½ **cup pistachios, finely chopped**
- ⅓ **cup dry bread crumbs**
- ¼ **cup minced fresh parsley**
- ½ **teaspoon pepper**
- ¼ **teaspoon salt**
- 4 **orange roughy fillets (6 ounces each)**
- 4 **teaspoons butter, melted**

1. Place egg white in a shallow bowl. Combine the pistachios, bread crumbs, parsley, pepper and salt in another shallow bowl. Dip fillets in egg white, then pistachio mixture.

2. Place fish on a baking sheet coated with cooking spray. Drizzle with butter. Bake at 450° for 8-10 minutes or until fish flakes easily with a fork.

PER SERVING *295 cal., 13 g fat (3 g sat. fat), 112 mg chol., 444 mg sodium, 11 g carb., 2 g fiber, 34 g pro.*

Salmon Sub

If you love salmon, consider trying your favorite salmon recipe with Alaskan black cod. Also known as sablefish, it has a naturally buttery flavor, rich texture and high Omega-3 oil content.

Mini Scallop Casseroles

Tiny and tender bay scallops take center stage in these miniature dishes. They're reminiscent of potpies, very creamy and packed with flavorful veggies in every bite.

—VIVIAN MANARY NEPEAN, ON

PREP: 30 MIN. • **BAKE:** 20 MIN.
MAKES: 4 SERVINGS

- 3 **celery ribs, chopped**
- 1 **cup sliced fresh mushrooms**
- 1 **medium green pepper, chopped**
- 1 **small onion, chopped**
- 2 **tablespoons butter**
- ⅓ **cup all-purpose flour**
- ¼ **teaspoon salt**
- ¼ **teaspoon pepper**
- 2 **cups fat-free milk**
- 1 **pound bay scallops**

TOPPING
- 1 **cup soft bread crumbs**
- 1 **tablespoon butter, melted**
- ¼ **cup shredded cheddar cheese**

1. In a large skillet, saute the celery, mushrooms, green pepper and onion in butter until tender. Stir in the flour, salt and pepper until blended; gradually add milk. Bring to a boil; cook and stir for 2 minutes or until thickened.

2. Reduce heat; add scallops. Cook, stirring occasionally, for 3-4 minutes or until scallops are firm and opaque.

3. Divide mixture among four 10-oz. ramekins or custard cups. In a small bowl, combine crumbs and butter; sprinkle over scallop mixture.

4. Bake, uncovered, at 350° for 15-20 minutes or until bubbly. Sprinkle with cheese; bake 5 minutes longer or until cheese is melted.

PER SERVING *332 cal., 12 g fat (7 g sat. fat), 70 mg chol., 588 mg sodium, 27 g carb., 2 g fiber, 28 g pro.* **Diabetic Exchanges:** *3 lean meat, 2 fat, 1 starch, 1 vegetable, ½ fat-free milk.*

Crab-Stuffed Manicotti

I love pasta, and my husband loves seafood. I combined them to create this meal, and he raved that it's the best ever.

—SONYA POLFLIET ANZA, CA

PREP: 25 MIN. • **BAKE:** 25 MIN.
MAKES: 2 SERVINGS

- 4 **uncooked manicotti shells**
- 1 **tablespoon butter**
- 4 **teaspoons all-purpose flour**
- 1 **cup fat-free milk**
- 1 **tablespoon grated Parmesan cheese**
- 1 **cup lump crabmeat, drained**
- ⅓ **cup reduced-fat ricotta cheese**
- ¼ **cup shredded part-skim mozzarella cheese**
- ¼ **teaspoon lemon-pepper seasoning**
- ¼ **teaspoon pepper**
- ⅛ **teaspoon garlic powder**
  Minced fresh parsley

1. Cook the manicotti according to package directions. In a small saucepan, melt butter. Stir in flour until smooth; gradually add milk. Bring to a boil; cook and stir for 2 minutes or until thickened. Remove from heat; stir in Parmesan cheese.

2. In a small bowl, combine the crab, ricotta cheese, mozzarella cheese, lemon-pepper, pepper and garlic powder. Drain manicotti; stuff with the crab mixture. Spread ¼ cup sauce in an 8-in. square baking dish coated with cooking spray. Top with stuffed manicotti. Pour the remaining sauce over top.

3. Cover and bake at 350° for 25-30 minutes or until heated through. Just before serving, sprinkle with parsley.

PER SERVING *359 cal., 12 g fat (7 g sat. fat), 98 mg chol., 793 mg sodium, 38 g carb., 1 g fiber, 26 g pro.* **Diabetic Exchanges:** *2 starch, 2 lean meat, 1 fat, ½ fat-free milk.*

MINI SCALLOP CASSEROLES

SHRIMP PICCATA PASTA

Crab Macaroni Casserole

Cold winter evenings are much more tolerable with this comforting casserole. Whole wheat macaroni boosts nutrition, while the melted cheese topping makes it creamy and so satisfying. We like it best with a veggie side.

—JASON EGNER EDGERTON, WI

PREP: 25 MIN. • **BAKE:** 20 MIN.
MAKES: 6 SERVINGS

- 2 **cups uncooked whole wheat elbow macaroni**
- 3 **tablespoons chopped onion**
- 2 **tablespoons butter**
- 3 **tablespoons all-purpose flour**
- 1½ **cups fat-free milk**
- 2 **cans (6 ounces each) lump crabmeat, drained**
- 1 **cup (8 ounces) reduced-fat sour cream**
- ½ **cup shredded Swiss cheese**
- ½ **teaspoon salt**
- ½ **teaspoon ground mustard**
- 1 **cup (4 ounces) shredded fat-free cheddar cheese, divided**

1. Cook macaroni according to package directions.
2. Meanwhile, in a large skillet, saute onion in butter until tender. Combine flour and milk until smooth; stir into pan. Bring to a boil; cook and stir for 1-2 minutes or until thickened. Remove from the heat. Drain the macaroni. Add the crabmeat, sour cream, Swiss cheese, salt, mustard, macaroni and ¼ cup cheddar cheese to the skillet.
3. Transfer to an 11-in. x 7-in. baking dish coated with cooking spray. Sprinkle with the remaining cheddar cheese. Bake, uncovered, at 350° for 20-25 minutes or until heated through.
PER SERVING *380 cal., 11 g fat (6 g sat. fat), 86 mg chol., 619 mg sodium, 38 g carb., 4 g fiber, 31 g pro.* **Diabetic Exchanges:** *3 lean meat, 2 starch, 1½ fat.*

FAST FIX
Shrimp Piccata Pasta

Want a quick, easy and wonderful way to serve shrimp? A light and tangy sauce spiked with capers makes this pasta an instant classic.

—CAROLE BESS WHITE PORTLAND, OR

START TO FINISH: 20 MIN.
MAKES: 4 SERVINGS

- 6 **ounces uncooked spaghetti**
- 2 **shallots, chopped**
- 1 **tablespoon olive oil**
- 1 **pound uncooked medium shrimp, peeled and deveined**
- 1 **jar (3 ounces) capers, drained**
- 3 **tablespoons lemon juice**
- ½ **teaspoon garlic powder**

1. Cook the spaghetti according to package directions. Meanwhile, in a large nonstick skillet, saute shallots in oil until tender. Add shrimp, capers, lemon juice and garlic powder; cook and stir for 5-6 minutes or until the shrimp turn pink.
2. Drain spaghetti; toss with the shrimp mixture.
PER SERVING *293 cal., 5 g fat (1 g sat. fat), 168 mg chol., 453 mg sodium, 37 g carb., 2 g fiber, 24 g pro.* **Diabetic Exchanges:** *3 lean meat, 2 starch, ½ fat.*

CRAB MACARONI CASSEROLE

Hearty Paella

I had paella for the first time in Spain. And it was so good, I've been on the quest to re-create the rich flavors of that dish ever since. We love the shrimp, chicken, veggie and olives in this make-at-home version.

—**LIBBY WALP** CHICAGO, IL

PREP: 25 MIN. • **COOK:** 30 MIN.
MAKES: 6 SERVINGS

- 1¼ pounds boneless skinless chicken breasts, cut into 1-inch cubes
- 1 tablespoon olive oil
- 1 cup uncooked long grain rice
- 1 medium onion, chopped
- 2 garlic cloves, minced
- 2¼ cups reduced-sodium chicken broth
- 1 can (14½ ounces) diced tomatoes, undrained
- 1 teaspoon dried oregano
- ½ teaspoon paprika
- ¼ teaspoon salt
- ¼ teaspoon pepper
- ⅛ teaspoon saffron threads
- ⅛ teaspoon ground turmeric
- 1 pound uncooked medium shrimp, peeled and deveined
- ¾ cup frozen peas
- 12 pimiento-stuffed olives
- 1 medium lemon, cut into six wedges

1. In a large skillet over medium heat, cook chicken in oil until no longer pink. Remove and keep warm. Add rice and onion to the pan; cook until rice is lightly browned and onion is tender, stirring frequently. Add garlic; cook 1 minute longer.

2. Stir in broth, tomatoes, oregano, paprika, salt, pepper, saffron and turmeric. Bring to a boil. Reduce heat to low; cover and cook for 10 minutes.

3. Add shrimp, peas and olives. Cover and cook 10 minutes longer or until rice is tender, shrimp turn pink and liquid is absorbed. Add chicken; heat through. Serve with lemon wedges.
PER SERVING *367 cal., 8 g fat (1 g sat. fat), 144 mg chol., 778 mg sodium, 36 g carb., 3 g fiber, 37 g pro.* **Diabetic Exchanges:** *5 lean meat, 2 starch, 1 vegetable, 1 fat.*

HEARTY PAELLA

C **FAST FIX**

Dilly Salmon Patties

Here's a quick and easy recipe with great dill taste. I like to serve these tender patties with a crisp side salad.

—**AERIAL RYAN** ACRA, NY

START TO FINISH: 25 MIN.
MAKES: 4 SERVINGS

- 2 eggs, lightly beaten
- 1 medium onion, finely chopped
- ¼ cup mashed potato flakes
- ¼ cup seasoned bread crumbs
- 1 garlic clove, minced
- ¼ teaspoon dill weed
- ¼ teaspoon pepper
- ⅛ teaspoon celery salt
- 1 can (14¾ ounces) salmon, drained, bones and skin removed
- 1 teaspoon olive oil

1. In a small bowl, combine the first eight ingredients. Crumble salmon over mixture and mix well. Shape into four patties.

2. In a large nonstick skillet coated with cooking spray, cook patties in oil over medium heat for 5 minutes on each side or until browned.
PER SERVING *265 cal., 12 g fat (3 g sat. fat), 152 mg chol., 761 mg sodium, 12 g carb., 1 g fiber, 27 g pro.*

Colorful Crab Stir-Fry

My love for seafood has carried over from childhood, when we used to fish together as a family. So I was happy to find this change-of-pace entree that combines stir-fry with seafood.

—LEE DENEAU LANSING, MI

START TO FINISH: 30 MIN.
MAKES: 4 SERVINGS

- 2 **teaspoons cornstarch**
- 1 **teaspoon chicken bouillon granules**
- ¾ **cup water**
- ½ **teaspoon reduced-sodium soy sauce**
- 1 **cup sliced fresh carrots**
- 1 **tablespoon canola oil**
- 1 **cup fresh or frozen snow peas**
- ½ **cup julienned sweet red pepper**
- 1 **teaspoon minced fresh gingerroot**
- 1 **teaspoon minced garlic**
- 1 **package (8 ounces) imitation crabmeat**
  Hot cooked rice, optional

1. In a small bowl, combine the cornstarch, bouillon, water and soy sauce until smooth; set aside. In a large skillet or wok, stir-fry carrots in oil. Add the peas, red pepper, ginger and garlic; stir-fry 1-2 minutes longer or until vegetables are crisp-tender.

2. Stir cornstarch mixture and gradually add to the pan. Bring to a boil; cook and stir for 2 minutes or until thickened. Add the crab; heat through. Serve with rice if desired.

PER SERVING *126 cal., 4 g fat (trace sat. fat), 7 mg chol., 562 mg sodium, 16 g carb., 2 g fiber, 7 g pro.* ***Diabetic Exchanges:*** *3 vegetable, 1 lean meat.*

COLORFUL CRAB
STIR-FRY

WALNUT GINGER SALMON

C
Walnut Ginger Salmon

Ginger comes through nicely in this easy marinade for salmon fillets. The addition of walnuts adds a toasty crunch.

—**BECKY WALCH** ORLAND, CA

PREP: 10 MIN. + MARINATING
BROIL: 10 MIN.
MAKES: 4 SERVINGS

- 1 tablespoon brown sugar
- 1 tablespoon Dijon mustard
- 1 tablespoon soy sauce
- 1 teaspoon ground ginger
- 4 skinless salmon fillets (4 ounces each)
- ¼ cup chopped walnuts

1. In a large resealable plastic bag, combine the brown sugar, mustard, soy sauce and ginger; add the salmon. Seal bag and turn to coat; refrigerate for 30 minutes, turning occasionally.
2. Drain and discard marinade. Place salmon on a foil-lined baking sheet coated with cooking spray. Broil 4-6 in. from the heat for 7-9 minutes or until fish flakes easily with a fork, sprinkling with walnuts during the last 2 minutes of cooking.
PER SERVING 270 cal., 17 g fat (3 g sat. fat), 67 mg chol., 292 mg sodium, 4 g carb., trace fiber, 25 g pro. **Diabetic Exchanges:** 3 medium-fat meat, 1 fat.

C
Scallop Kabobs

I'm always on the lookout for recipes that are lower in fat and heart-healthy, too, and these kabobs are just that. I serve them with a fruit salad and a light dessert.

—**EDIE DESPAIN** LOGAN, UT

PREP: 30 MIN. + MARINATING
GRILL: 10 MIN.
MAKES: 4 SERVINGS

- 3 tablespoons lemon juice
- 3 tablespoons reduced-sodium soy sauce
- 2 tablespoons canola oil
  Dash garlic powder
  Dash pepper
- 1½ pounds sea scallops
- 3 medium green peppers, cut into 1½-inch pieces
- 2 cups cherry tomatoes

1. In a small bowl, combine the first five ingredients. Pour ¼ cup into a large resealable plastic bag; add scallops. Seal bag and turn to coat; refrigerate for 20 minutes. Cover and refrigerate the remaining marinade for basting.
2. Meanwhile, in a large saucepan, bring 3 cups water to a boil. Add peppers; cover and boil for 2 minutes. Drain and immediately place peppers in ice water. Drain and pat dry.
3. Drain and discard marinade. On eight metal or soaked wooden skewers, alternately thread the tomatoes, scallops and peppers.
4. Moisten a paper towel with cooking oil. Using long-handled tongs, lightly coat grill rack. Grill, covered, over medium heat or broil 4 in. from the heat for 3-5 minutes on each side or until the scallops are firm and opaque, basting occasionally with reserved marinade.
PER SERVING 238 cal., 7 g fat (1 g sat. fat), 56 mg chol., 624 mg sodium, 13 g carb., 2 g fiber, 31 g pro. **Diabetic Exchanges:** 4 lean meat, 2 vegetable, 1 fat.

SCALLOP KABOBS

PAN-SEARED
SHRIMP

FAST FIX

Pan-Seared Shrimp

Garlic, parsley and wine punch up the buttery flavor of this simple shrimp dish and give it a decadent and special feel. It's party-pretty and perfect for guests!

—PATRICIA ZARTMAN YORK, PA

START TO FINISH: 30 MIN.
MAKES: 4 SERVINGS

- 1 **pound uncooked medium shrimp, peeled and deveined**
- 2 **garlic cloves, minced**
- 2 **tablespoons olive oil**
- ⅓ **cup white wine or reduced-sodium chicken broth**
- ½ **teaspoon seafood seasoning**
- 2 **cups hot cooked rice**
- 2 **tablespoons minced fresh parsley**

In a large skillet, saute shrimp and garlic in oil for 3 minutes. Add wine and seasoning; cook and stir 3-5 minutes longer or until the shrimp turn pink. Serve with rice; sprinkle with parsley.

PER SERVING *262 cal., 9 g fat (1 g sat. fat), 138 mg chol., 238 mg sodium, 24 g carb., trace fiber, 21 g pro. **Diabetic Exchanges:** 3 lean meat, 1½ starch, 1 fat.*

Shrimp Smarts

Most "fresh" shrimp in stores have actually been previously frozen and thawed. You might end up saving a few bucks by buying them from the freezer aisle instead. To quickly thaw, place shrimp in a colander under cold running water until thawed.

Mediterranean Shrimp Couscous

Shrimp couscous is a low-fat meal my family loves. It's light and elegant and all the flavors work really well together; you'll be proud to serve this dish.

—HEATHER CARROLL
COLORADO SPRINGS, CO

PREP: 20 MIN. • **COOK:** 25 MIN.
MAKES: 6 SERVINGS

- 1½ pounds uncooked medium shrimp, peeled and deveined
- 1 tablespoon chopped shallot
- 2 garlic cloves, minced
- 3 tablespoons olive oil, divided
- 1 cup chopped zucchini
- ½ cup white wine or reduced-sodium chicken broth
- ¼ cup chopped sun-dried tomatoes (not packed in oil)
- 2 tablespoons capers, drained
- 3 cups fresh baby spinach
- 1½ cups reduced-sodium chicken broth
- 1½ cups uncooked couscous
- 2 tablespoons lemon juice
- 2 tablespoons balsamic vinegar
- ½ cup crumbled feta cheese, divided
- ½ teaspoon dried oregano
- ¼ teaspoon salt
- ¼ teaspoon pepper

1. In a large skillet, saute the shrimp, shallot and garlic in 1 tablespoon oil until shrimp turn pink. Remove and keep warm.

2. In the same skillet, cook and stir the zucchini, wine, tomatoes and capers until zucchini is tender. Add spinach; cook just until wilted. Add broth and bring to a boil. Stir in couscous. Cover and remove from the heat; let stand for 5 minutes or until the liquid is absorbed. Fluff with a fork.

3. Whisk the lemon juice, vinegar and remaining oil; add to the pan. Stir in ¼ cup feta cheese, the seasonings and reserved shrimp mixture; cook and stir over low heat until heated through. Sprinkle with the remaining cheese.

PER SERVING 385 cal., 11 g fat (2 g sat. fat), 143 mg chol., 619 mg sodium, 41 g carb., 3 g fiber, 28 g pro. *Diabetic Exchanges: 3 lean meat, 2½ starch, 2 fat.*

MEDITERRANEAN SHRIMP COUSCOUS

COMPANY-READY CRUSTED SALMON

Company-Ready Crusted Salmon

My husband had high cholesterol so I created this heart-healthy recipe. Now I serve it to guests all the time...even fish-haters have asked for the recipe!

—SUSAN ROBENSON HOT SPRINGS, AR

PREP: 20 MIN. • **BAKE:** 20 MIN.
MAKES: 6 SERVINGS

- 2 packages (6 ounces each) fresh baby spinach
- 1 salmon fillet (1½ pounds)
- 1 teaspoon olive oil
- 3 tablespoons honey
- 3 tablespoons Dijon mustard
- ¼ cup cornflakes
- 2 tablespoons sliced almonds
- 2 tablespoons chopped pecans
- ¼ cup fat-free mayonnaise
  Hot cooked couscous, optional

1. Place spinach in a 13-in. x 9-in. baking dish coated with cooking spray; top with salmon. Drizzle oil over spinach.

2. Combine honey and mustard. Remove 2 tablespoons mixture; brush over salmon. Place the cornflakes, almonds and pecans in a small food processor; cover and process until ground. Press onto salmon. Stir mayonnaise into remaining honey mixture; refrigerate until serving.

3. Bake, uncovered, at 450° for 18-22 minutes or until fish flakes easily with a fork. Drizzle with reserved sauce. Serve with couscous if desired.

PER SERVING 296 cal., 15 g fat (3 g sat. fat), 68 mg chol., 381 mg sodium, 15 g carb., 2 g fiber, 25 g pro.

Poached Salmon with Dill Sauce

The sauce is what makes the salmon shine. It's simply excellent, with a fresh dill and mustard flavor, and it drapes beautifully over the poached fish.

—PATTI SHERMAN SCHENECTADY, NY

PREP: 25 MIN. • **COOK:** 10 MIN.
MAKES: 4 SERVINGS

- 2 cups water
- 1 cup white wine or reduced-sodium chicken broth
- 1 medium onion, chopped
- ¼ cup chopped celery
- 4 salmon fillets (4 ounces each)

SAUCE
- ¼ cup reduced-fat sour cream
- ¼ cup plain yogurt
- 2 teaspoons snipped fresh dill
- 1½ teaspoons Dijon mustard
- ¼ teaspoon salt
  Dash hot pepper sauce

1. In a large nonstick skillet, combine the water, wine, onion and celery. Bring to a boil. Reduce heat; add the salmon and poach, uncovered, for 5-10 minutes or until fish is firm and flakes easily with a fork.

2. Meanwhile, in a small bowl, combine the sauce ingredients. Serve with salmon.

PER SERVING *239 cal., 14 g fat (4 g sat. fat), 74 mg chol., 277 mg sodium, 2 g carb., trace fiber, 24 g pro.*

Lightened-Up Gumbo

You'll get a generous portion of meat and veggies in our authentic-tasting gumbo. Don't worry...the sauce has a moderate amount of heat.

—TASTE OF HOME TEST KITCHEN

PREP: 30 MIN. • **COOK:** 20 MIN.
MAKES: 6 SERVINGS

- ½ cup all-purpose flour
- 3 cups reduced-sodium chicken broth
- 1 small onion, chopped
- 1 celery rib, chopped
- 1 small green pepper, chopped
- 1 tablespoon canola oil
- 2 garlic cloves, minced
- 8 ounces smoked turkey sausage, sliced
- 1 cup frozen sliced okra
- 2 bay leaves
- 1 teaspoon Creole seasoning
- ¼ teaspoon salt
- ¼ teaspoon pepper
- 1 pound uncooked medium shrimp, peeled and deveined
- 1 cup cubed cooked chicken breast
- 3 cups cooked brown rice

1. In a large skillet over medium-high heat, cook and stir the flour for 6-7 minutes or until light brown in color. Immediately transfer to a small bowl; whisk in broth until smooth.

2. In the same skillet, saute the onion, celery and green pepper in oil until tender. Add garlic; cook 1 minute longer. Stir flour mixture; add to the pan. Bring to a boil; cook and stir for 2 minutes or until thickened.

3. Add the sausage, okra, bay leaves, Creole seasoning, salt and pepper. Simmer, uncovered, for 4-5 minutes or until okra is tender. Stir in the shrimp and chicken. Cook and stir 5-6 minutes longer or until shrimp turn pink. Discard bay leaves. Serve with rice.

PER SERVING *336 cal., 7 g fat (1 g sat. fat), 134 mg chol., 981 mg sodium, 35 g carb., 3 g fiber, 31 g pro.* **Diabetic Exchanges:** *4 lean meat, 2 starch, ½ fat.*

LIGHTENED-UP GUMBO

CREAMY TUNA-
NOODLE CASSEROLE

Favorite Jambalaya

Our lower-in-sodium version of jambalaya is not only saucy and yummy, it's got all the great flavors you know and love in low-country cuisine.

—TASTE OF HOME TEST KITCHEN

PREP: 20 MIN. • **COOK:** 25 MIN.
MAKES: 6 SERVINGS

- ½ **pound boneless skinless chicken breasts, cubed**
- ¼ **pound smoked turkey sausage, halved lengthwise and sliced**
- 1 **large onion, chopped**
- 1 **medium green pepper, chopped**
- 1 **celery rib, chopped**
- 1 **tablespoon canola oil**
- 2 **garlic cloves, minced**
- 2 **cans (14½ ounces each) no-salt-added diced tomatoes, undrained**
- 1 **bay leaf**
- 1 **teaspoon Cajun seasoning**
- 1 **teaspoon dried thyme**
- ¼ **teaspoon cayenne pepper**
- ¼ **teaspoon pepper**
- 1 **pound uncooked medium shrimp, peeled and deveined**
- 3 **cups hot cooked brown rice**

1. In a nonstick Dutch oven, saute the chicken, sausage, onion, green pepper and celery in oil until the chicken is no longer pink. Add the garlic; cook 1 minute longer. Stir in the tomatoes, bay leaf, Cajun seasoning, thyme, cayenne and pepper.
2. Bring to a boil. Reduce heat; cover and simmer for 15 minutes. Add the shrimp; cook 5-6 minutes longer or until shrimp turn pink. Discard bay leaf. Serve with rice.
PER SERVING *302 cal., 6 g fat (1 g sat. fat), 125 mg chol., 450 mg sodium, 34 g carb., 5 g fiber, 27 g pro.* **Diabetic Exchanges:** *3 lean meat, 2 vegetable, 1 starch.*

Creamy Tuna-Noodle Casserole

Tuna is an excellent standby when you need supper on the table in a hurry. You'll love this casserole packed with peas, peppers and onions. Not fond of tuna? Try substituting chicken.

—**EDIE DESPAIN** LOGAN, UTAH

PREP: 25 MIN. • **BAKE:** 25 MIN.
MAKES: 6 SERVINGS

- 5 **cups uncooked egg noodles**
- 1 **can (10¾ ounces) reduced-fat reduced-sodium condensed cream of mushroom soup, undiluted**
- 1 **cup (8 ounces) fat-free sour cream**
- ⅔ **cup grated Parmesan cheese**
- ⅓ **cup 2% milk**
- ¼ **teaspoon salt**
- 2 **cans (5 ounces each) light water-packed tuna, drained and flaked**
- 1 **cup frozen peas, thawed**
- ¼ **cup finely chopped onion**
- ¼ **cup finely chopped green pepper**

TOPPING
- ½ **cup soft bread crumbs**
- 1 **tablespoon butter, melted**

1. Cook the noodles according to package directions.
2. Meanwhile, in a large bowl, mix soup, sour cream, cheese, milk and salt. Stir in the tuna, peas, onion and pepper. Drain the noodles; add to the soup mixture.
3. Transfer to an 11-in. x 7-in. baking dish coated with cooking spray. Combine the topping ingredients; sprinkle over the casserole. Bake, uncovered, at 350° for 25-30 minutes or until bubbly.
PER SERVING *340 cal., 8 g fat (4 g sat. fat), 63 mg chol., 699 mg sodium, 41 g carb., 3 g fiber, 25 g pro.* **Diabetic Exchanges:** *3 starch, 2 lean meat, ½ fat.*

Salmon Grilled in Foil

Steaming in its own juices makes the salmon incredibly tender. A little curry adds a punch that's perfectly balanced by onion and tomato.

—MERIDETH BERKOVICH THE DALLES, OR

START TO FINISH: 20 MIN.
MAKES: 4 SERVINGS

- 4 **salmon fillets (4 ounces each)**
- 1 **teaspoon garlic powder**
- 1 **teaspoon lemon-pepper seasoning**
- 1 **teaspoon curry powder**
- ½ **teaspoon salt**
- 1 **small onion, cut into rings**
- 2 **medium tomatoes, seeded and chopped**

1. Place salmon, skin side down, on a double thickness of heavy-duty foil (about 18 in. x 12 in.). Combine the garlic powder, lemon-pepper, curry and salt; sprinkle over salmon. Top with onion and tomatoes. Fold foil over fish and seal tightly.

2. Grill, covered, over medium heat for 10-15 minutes or until fish flakes easily with a fork. Open foil carefully to allow steam to escape.

PER SERVING *232 cal., 13 g fat (3 g sat. fat), 67 mg chol., 482 mg sodium, 5 g carb., 1 g fiber, 24 g pro.*

Balsamic-Glazed Salmon

In this simple treatment for baked salmon, garlic and oregano blend nicely with a honey-balsamic glaze and the fish turns out scrumptious every time.

—MARY LOU TIMPSON COLORADO CITY, AZ

PREP: 20 MIN. • **BAKE:** 15 MIN.
MAKES: 6 SERVINGS

- 4 **garlic cloves, minced**
- 1 **teaspoon olive oil**
- ⅓ **cup balsamic vinegar**
- 4 **teaspoons Dijon mustard**
- 1 **tablespoon white wine or water**
- 1 **tablespoon honey**
- ¼ **teaspoon salt**
- ¼ **teaspoon pepper**
- 6 **salmon fillets (4 ounces each)**
- 1 **tablespoon minced fresh oregano or 1 teaspoon dried oregano**

1. Preheat oven to 425°. Line a 15-in.x 10-in x 1-in. baking pan with foil; coat foil with cooking spray. Set aside.

2. In a small saucepan, saute garlic in oil until tender. Stir in the vinegar, mustard, wine, honey, salt and pepper. Bring to a boil. Reduce heat; simmer, uncovered, 3-5 minutes or until the sauce is slightly thickened. Set aside 2 tablespoons for basting.

3. Place fillets on prepared pan. Brush with sauce and sprinkle with oregano. Bake, uncovered, 15-18 minutes or until the salmon flakes easily with a fork. Brush with the reserved sauce before serving.

PER SERVING *243 cal., 13 g fat (3 g sat. fat), 67 mg chol., 249 mg sodium, 7 g carb., trace fiber, 23 g pro.*

BALSAMIC-GLAZED SALMON

SAUCY VEGETABLE TOFU
PAGE 214

**SCARLETT ELROD'S
FOUR-CHEESE BAKED PENNE**

PAGE 206

**JACQUELINE CORREA'S
ENCHILADA PIE**

PAGE 205

**MARY HAAS'
GRILLED PORTOBELLO BURGERS**

PAGE 211

Vegetarian

Many familes **opt to enjoy meatless entrees** several times a week.
Here you'll find dozens of protein-packed dinners **suitable for any occassion.**

Lactose-Free Veggie-Stuffed Shells

I converted traditional stuffed shells into a saucy, lactose-free and vegan entree to meet the needs of my family. It so delicious it's hard to believe there's no cheese.

—**KIMBERLY HAMMOND** KINGWOOD, TX

PREP: 30 MIN. • **BAKE:** 35 MIN.
MAKES: 12 SERVINGS

- 1 **package (12 ounces) jumbo pasta shells**
- ½ **pound sliced fresh mushrooms**
- 1 **medium onion, chopped**
- 1 **tablespoon olive oil**
- 4 **garlic cloves, minced**
- 1 **package (12.3 ounces) silken extra-firm tofu**
- 3 **tablespoons lemon juice**
- 1 **package (10 ounces) frozen chopped spinach, thawed and squeezed dry**
- 1 **can (3.8 ounces) sliced ripe olives, drained**
- 3 **tablespoons minced fresh basil**
- ½ **teaspoon salt**
- ⅛ **teaspoon pepper**
- 1 **jar (24 ounces) meatless spaghetti sauce**
- ¼ **cup pine nuts**

1. Cook pasta according to package directions; drain. Meanwhile, in a large skillet, saute mushrooms and onion in oil until tender. Add garlic; cook 1 minute longer.

2. In a large bowl, mash tofu with lemon juice. Stir in the spinach, olives, basil, salt and pepper. Add to the mushroom mixture; heat through. Spoon into shells.

3. Spread 1 cup spaghetti sauce in a 13-in. x 9-in. baking dish coated with cooking spray. Arrange shells over sauce; top with remaining sauce. Sprinkle with pine nuts.

4. Cover and bake at 375° for 30 minutes. Uncover; bake 5-10 minutes longer or until bubbly.

PER SERVING *198 cal., 5 g fat (1 g sat. fat), trace chol., 485 mg sodium, 32 g carb., 4 g fiber, 9 g pro. **Diabetic Exchanges:** 1½ starch, 1 lean meat, 1 vegetable, 1 fat.*

FAST FIX

Cheese Tortellini with Tomatoes and Corn

Fresh corn and basil make this dish taste like summer. I think it's a good one to bring to picnics or gatherings, and it's easy to double if needed.

—**SALLY MALONEY** DALLAS, GA

START TO FINISH: 25 MIN.
MAKES: 4 SERVINGS

- 1 **package (9 ounces) refrigerated cheese tortellini**
- 1 **package (16 ounces) frozen corn, thawed or 3⅓ cups fresh corn**
- 2 **cups cherry tomatoes, quartered**
- ¼ **cup thinly sliced green onions**
- ¼ **cup minced fresh basil**
- 2 **tablespoons grated Parmesan cheese**
- 4 **teaspoons olive oil**
- ¼ **teaspoon garlic powder**
- ⅛ **teaspoon pepper**

1. In a Dutch oven, cook tortellini according to package directions, adding the corn during the last 5 minutes of cooking. Drain and rinse in cold water.

2. In a large serving bowl, combine tortellini mixture and remaining ingredients; toss to coat.

PER SERVING *366 cal., 12 g fat (4 g sat. fat), 30 mg chol., 286 mg sodium, 57 g carb., 5 g fiber, 14 g pro.*

CHEESE TORTELLINI WITH TOMATOES AND CORN

Fiery Stuffed Poblanos

I love Southwest-inspired cuisine, but since it's often laden with fatty meat and cheese, I tend to steer clear. As a future dietitian, I try to come up with healthy twists on recipes. That's how my stuffed chili dish was born.

—AMBER MASSEY ARGYLE, TX

PREP: 50 MIN. + STANDING • **BAKE:** 20 MIN.
MAKES: 8 SERVINGS

- 8   poblano peppers
- 1   can (15 ounces) black beans, rinsed and drained
- 1   medium zucchini, chopped
- 1   small red onion, chopped
- 4   garlic cloves, minced
- 1   can (15¼ ounces) whole kernel corn, drained
- 1   can (14½ ounces) fire-roasted diced tomatoes, undrained
- 1   cup cooked brown rice
- 1   tablespoon ground cumin
- 1   to 1½ teaspoons ground ancho chili pepper
- ¼   teaspoon salt
- ¼   teaspoon pepper
- 1   cup (4 ounces) shredded reduced-fat Mexican cheese blend, divided
- 3   green onions, chopped
- ½   cup reduced-fat sour cream

1. Broil peppers 3 in. from the heat until skins blister, about 5 minutes. With tongs, rotate peppers a quarter turn. Broil and rotate until all sides are blistered and blackened. Immediately place peppers in a large bowl; cover and let stand for 20 minutes.

2. Meanwhile, in a small bowl, coarsely mash beans; set aside. In a large nonstick skillet coated with cooking spray, cook and stir zucchini and onion until tender. Add garlic; cook 1 minute longer. Add the corn, tomatoes, rice, seasonings and beans. Remove from the heat; stir in ½ cup cheese. Set aside.

3. Peel off and discard charred skins from poblanos. Cut a lengthwise slit down each pepper, leaving the stem intact; remove membranes and seeds. Fill each pepper with ⅔ cup filling.

4. Place peppers in a 13-in. x 9-in. baking dish coated with cooking spray. Bake, uncovered, at 375° for 18-22 minutes or until heated through, sprinkling with green onions and remaining cheese during last 5 minutes of baking. Garnish with sour cream.

PER SERVING *223 cal., 5 g fat (2 g sat. fat), 15 mg chol., 579 mg sodium, 32 g carb., 7 g fiber, 11 g pro.* **Diabetic Exchanges:** *2 vegetable, 1 starch, 1 lean meat, 1 fat.*

FIERY STUFFED POBLANOS

Veggie Bean Tacos

In the summer when fresh corn and just-picked tomatoes are in season, authentic Mexican dishes like this leave you wanting that next bite. My personal preference is to serve them with a slice of lime to squeeze over the avocado.

—TONYA BURKHARD DAVIS, IL

PREP: 20 MIN. • **COOK:** 20 MIN.
MAKES: 6 SERVINGS

- 2   cups fresh corn
- 2   tablespoons canola oil, divided
- 4   medium tomatoes, seeded and chopped
- 3   small zucchini, chopped
- 1   large red onion, chopped
- 3   garlic cloves, minced
- 1   cup black beans, rinsed and drained
- 1   teaspoon minced fresh oregano or ¼ teaspoon dried oregano
- ½   teaspoon salt
- ¼   teaspoon pepper
- 12 corn tortillas (6 inches), warmed
- ¾   cup shredded Monterey Jack cheese
- ¼   cup salsa verde
- 1   medium ripe avocado, peeled and thinly sliced
     Reduced-fat sour cream, optional

1. In a large skillet, saute corn in 1 tablespoon oil until lightly browned. Remove and keep warm. In the same skillet, saute tomatoes, zucchini and onion in remaining oil until tender. Add garlic; cook 1 minute longer. Stir in the beans, oregano, salt, pepper and corn; heat through.

2. Divide filling among tortillas. Top with cheese, salsa, avocado and sour cream if desired.

PER SERVING *378 cal., 16 g fat (4 g sat. fat), 13 mg chol., 517 mg sodium, 52 g carb., 10 g fiber, 13 g pro.*

Enchilada Pie

Stacked with layers of beans, vegetables and cheese, this mile-high pie makes for a fun fiesta night with the family. Who would have guessed it all comes together in the slow cooker?

—**JACQUELINE CORREA** LANDING, NJ

PREP: 40 MIN. • **COOK:** 4 HOURS
MAKES: 8 SERVINGS

- 1 package (12 ounces) frozen vegetarian meat crumbles
- 1 cup chopped onion
- ½ cup chopped green pepper
- 2 teaspoons canola oil
- 1 can (16 ounces) kidney beans, rinsed and drained
- 1 can (15 ounces) black beans, rinsed and drained
- 1 can (10 ounces) diced tomatoes and green chilies, undrained
- ½ cup water
- 1½ teaspoons chili powder
- ½ teaspoon ground cumin
- ¼ teaspoon pepper
- 6 whole wheat tortillas (8 inches)
- 2 cups (8 ounces) shredded reduced-fat cheddar cheese

1. Cut three 25-in. x 3-in. strips of heavy-duty foil; crisscross so they resemble spokes of a wheel. Place strips on the bottom and up the sides of a 5-qt. slow cooker. Coat strips with cooking spray.

2. In a large saucepan, cook the meat crumbles, onion and green pepper in oil until the vegetables are tender. Stir in both cans of beans, tomatoes, water, chili powder, cumin and pepper. Bring to a boil. Reduce the heat; simmer, uncovered, for 10 minutes.

3. In prepared slow cooker, layer about a cup of bean mixture, one tortilla and ⅓ cup cheese. Repeat layers five times. Cover and cook on low for 4-5 hours or until heated

ENCHILADA PIE

through and cheese is melted.

4. Using foil strips as handles, remove the pie to a platter.

NOTE *Vegetarian meat crumbles are a nutritious protein source made from soy. Look for them in the natural foods freezer section.*

PER SERVING *367 cal., 11 g fat (4 g sat. fat), 20 mg chol., 818 mg sodium, 41 g carb., 9 g fiber, 25 g pro.* **Diabetic Exchanges:** *3 starch, 2 lean meat, 1 fat.*

FAST FIX
Spinach Quesadillas

I adapted this dish from one of my cookbooks, using reduced-fat ingredients to make it lighter. It's a family favorite and my favorite...especially when I need something quick.

—**PAM KAISER** MANSFIELD, MO

START TO FINISH: 20 MIN.
MAKES: 6 SERVINGS

- 4 cups fresh baby spinach
- 4 green onions, chopped
- 1 small tomato, chopped
- 2 tablespoons lemon juice
- 1 teaspoon ground cumin
- ¼ teaspoon garlic powder
- 1 cup (4 ounces) shredded reduced-fat Monterey Jack cheese or Mexican cheese blend
- ¼ cup reduced-fat ricotta cheese
- 6 flour tortillas (6 inches)
- ¼ cup fat-free sour cream

1. In a large nonstick skillet, cook the spinach, onions, tomato, lemon juice, cumin and garlic powder over medium heat until spinach is wilted. Remove from the heat; stir in cheeses.

2. Divide spinach mixture evenly among three tortillas. Top with remaining tortillas. Cook in a large skillet coated with cooking spray over low heat for 1-2 minutes on each side or until heated through. Cut each quesadilla into four wedges. Serve with sour cream.

PER SERVING *178 cal., 8 g fat (3 g sat. fat), 18 mg chol., 422 mg sodium, 19 g carb., 1 g fiber, 10 g pro.* **Diabetic Exchanges:** *1 starch, 1 lean meat, 1 fat.*

FOUR-CHEESE BAKED PENNE

Four-Cheese Baked Penne

Rich and cheesy with a slight heat from pepper flakes, you don't miss the meat in this protein-packed pasta.

—SCARLETT ELROD NEWNAN, GA

PREP: 30 MIN. + COOLING • **BAKE:** 20 MIN.
MAKES: 6 SERVINGS

- 4 **cups uncooked whole wheat penne pasta**
- 1 **medium onion, chopped**
- 2 **teaspoons olive oil**
- 4 **garlic cloves, minced**
- 1 **can (15 ounces) crushed tomatoes**
- 1 **can (8 ounces) tomato sauce**
- 3 **tablespoons minced fresh parsley or 1 tablespoon dried parsley flakes**
- 1 **teaspoon dried oregano**
- 1 **teaspoon dried rosemary, crushed**
- ½ **teaspoon crushed red pepper flakes**
- ¼ **teaspoon pepper**
- 1½ **cups (12 ounces) 2% cottage cheese**
- 1¼ **cups (5 ounces) shredded part-skim mozzarella cheese, divided**
- 1 **cup part-skim ricotta cheese**
- ¼ **cup grated Parmesan cheese**

1. Cook penne according to package directions.

2. Meanwhile, in a large skillet, saute onion in oil until tender. Add garlic; cook 1 minute longer. Stir in the tomatoes, tomato sauce, parsley, oregano, rosemary, pepper flakes and pepper. Bring to a boil. Remove from the heat; cool for 15 minutes.

3. Drain penne; add to sauce. Stir in the cottage cheese, ½ cup mozzarella and all of the ricotta. Transfer to a 13-in. x 9-in. baking dish coated with cooking spray. Top with Parmesan cheese and remaining mozzarella.

4. Bake, uncovered, at 400° for 20-25 minutes or until bubbly.

PER SERVING 523 cal., 12 g fat (6 g sat. fat), 37 mg chol., 682 mg sodium, 72 g carb., 11 g fiber, 32 g pro.

Curried Tofu with Rice

Tofu takes center stage in this bold dish with lots of curry and cilantro flavor. And the whole supper comes together in one skillet.

—CRYSTAL JO BRUNS ILIFF, CO

PREP: 15 MIN. • **COOK:** 20 MIN.
MAKES: 4 SERVINGS

- 1 **package (12.3 ounces) extra-firm tofu, drained and cubed**
- 1 **teaspoon seasoned salt**
- 1 **tablespoon canola oil**
- 1 **small onion, chopped**
- 3 **garlic cloves, minced**
- ½ **cup light coconut milk**
- ¼ **cup minced fresh cilantro**
- 1 **teaspoon curry powder**
- ¼ **teaspoon salt**
- ¼ **teaspoon pepper**
- 2 **cups cooked brown rice**

1. Sprinkle the tofu with seasoned salt. In a large nonstick skillet coated with cooking spray, saute tofu in oil until lightly browned. Remove and keep warm.

2. In the same skillet, saute onion and garlic for 1-2 minutes or until crisp-tender. Stir in coconut milk, cilantro, curry, salt and pepper. Bring to a boil. Reduce heat; simmer, uncovered, for 4-5 minutes or until sauce is slightly thickened. Stir in tofu; heat through. Serve with rice.

PER SERVING 240 cal., 11 g fat (3 g sat. fat), 0 chol., 540 mg sodium, 27 g carb., 3 g fiber, 10 g pro. *Diabetic Exchanges:* 1½ starch, 1 medium-fat meat, 1 fat.

Eggplant Parmesan

Because my recipe calls for baking the eggplant instead of frying it, it's much healthier but still tasty!

—LACI HOOTEN MCKINNEY, TX

PREP: 40 MIN. • COOK: 25 MIN.
MAKES: 8 SERVINGS

- 3 eggs, beaten
- 2½ cups panko (Japanese) bread crumbs
- 3 medium eggplants, cut into ¼-inch slices
- 2 jars (4½ ounces each) sliced mushrooms, drained
- ½ tsp dried basil
- ⅛ teaspoon dried oregano
- 2 cups (8 ounces) shredded part-skim mozzarella cheese
- ½ cup grated Parmesan cheese
- 1 jar (28 ounces) spaghetti sauce

1. Place eggs and bread crumbs in separate shallow bowls. Dip eggplant in eggs, then coat in crumbs. Place on baking sheets coated with cooking spray. Bake at 350° for 15-20 minutes or until tender and golden brown, turning once.
2. In a small bowl, combine the mushrooms, basil and oregano. In another small bowl, combine mozzarella and Parmesan cheeses.
3. Spread ½ cup sauce into a 13-in. x 9-in. baking dish coated with cooking spray. Layer with a third of the mushroom mixture, eggplant, ¾ cup sauce and a third of the cheese mixture. Repeat layers twice.
4. Bake, uncovered, at 350° for 25-30 minutes or until heated through and cheese is melted.
PER SERVING 305 cal., 12 g fat (5 g sat. fat), 102 mg chol., 912 mg sodium, 32 g carb., 9 g fiber, 18 g pro. Diabetic Exchanges: 2 starch, 2 vegetable, 1 medium-fat meat.

FAST FIX ▶

Vegetarian Stuffed Peppers

My favorite appliance is my slow cooker, and I use it more than anyone I know. I love the convenience of walking in the door and having a meal ready to go. For recipes like my slow-cooked stuffed peppers, you don't have to worry about boiling the peppers first and preparing the filling separately.

—MICHELLE GURNSEY LINCOLN, NE

PREP: 15 MIN. • COOK: 3 HOURS
MAKES: 4 SERVINGS

- 4 medium sweet red peppers
- 1 can (15 ounces) black beans, rinsed and drained
- 1 cup (4 ounces) shredded pepper jack cheese
- ¾ cup salsa
- 1 small onion, chopped
- ½ cup frozen corn
- ⅓ cup uncooked converted long grain rice
- 1¼ teaspoons chili powder
- ½ teaspoon ground cumin
  Reduced-fat sour cream, optional

1. Cut tops off the peppers and remove seeds; set aside. In a large bowl, combine the beans, cheese, salsa, onion, corn, rice, chili powder and cumin; spoon into peppers. Place in a 5-qt. slow cooker coated with cooking spray.
2. Cover and cook on low for 3-4 hours or until peppers are tender and filling is heated through. Serve with sour cream if desired.
PER SERVING 317 cal., 10 g fat (5 g sat. fat), 30 mg chol., 565 mg sodium, 43 g carb., 8 g fiber, 15 g pro. Diabetic Exchanges: 2 starch, 2 lean meat, 2 vegetable, 1 fat.

EGGPLANT PARMESAN

Spinach Cheese Manicotti

Cream cheese and cottage cheese beef up the filling and give this lasagna-like dish a creamy base. With generous serving portions, you'll get 5 grams of fiber and 25 grams of protein.

—**JULIE LOWER** KATY, TX

PREP: 55 MIN. • **BAKE:** 55 MIN.
MAKES: 7 SERVINGS

- 1 **large onion, chopped**
- 2 **garlic cloves, minced**
- 1 **tablespoon olive oil**
- 3 **cans (8 ounces each) no-salt-added tomato sauce**
- 2 **cans (6 ounces each) tomato paste**
- 1½ **cups water**
- ½ **cup dry red wine or vegetable broth**
- 2 **tablespoons Italian seasoning**
- 2 **teaspoons sugar**
- 2 **teaspoons dried oregano**

FILLING

- 1 **package (8 ounces) fat-free cream cheese**
- 1¼ **cups (10 ounces) 2% cottage cheese**
- 1 **package (10 ounces) frozen chopped spinach, thawed and squeezed dry**
- ¼ **cup grated Parmesan cheese**
- 2 **eggs, lightly beaten**
- ½ **teaspoon salt**
- 1 **package (8 ounces) manicotti shells**
- 1 **cup (4 ounces) shredded part-skim mozzarella cheese**

1. In a large saucepan, saute onion and garlic in oil until tender. Stir in the tomato sauce, tomato paste, water, wine, Italian seasoning, sugar and oregano. Bring to a boil. Reduce heat; simmer, uncovered, for 15-20 minutes, stirring occasionally.

2. Meanwhile, for filling, in a large bowl, beat cream cheese until smooth. Stir in the cottage cheese, spinach, Parmesan cheese, eggs and salt.

3. Stuff cream cheese mixture into uncooked manicotti shells. Spread 1 cup sauce into a 13-in. x 9-in. baking dish coated with cooking spay. Arrange manicotti over sauce. Pour remaining sauce over top.

4. Cover and bake at 350° for 50-55 minutes or until pasta is tender. Uncover; sprinkle with mozzarella cheese. Bake 5-10 minutes longer or until cheese is melted.

PER SERVING *389 cal., 9 g fat (4 g sat. fat), 80 mg chol., 722 mg sodium, 50 g carb., 5 g fiber, 25 g pro.*

SPINACH CHEESE MANICOTTI

Grilled Veggie Pizza

I created my terrific pizza one summer as a way to use up vegetables from our garden. Grilling the veggies first brings out their sizzling flavors. For a different taste, try sprinkling olives or pine nuts over the top before adding the cheese.

—SUSAN MARSHALL

COLORADO SPRINGS, CO

PREP: 30 MIN. • **BAKE:** 10 MIN.
MAKES: 6 SERVINGS

- 8 **small fresh mushrooms, halved**
- 1 **small zucchini, cut into ¼-inch slices**
- 1 **small sweet yellow pepper, sliced**
- 1 **small sweet red pepper, sliced**
- 1 **small onion, sliced**
- 1 **tablespoon white wine vinegar**
- 1 **tablespoon water**
- 4 **teaspoons olive oil, divided**
- 2 **teaspoons minced fresh basil or ½ teaspoon dried basil**
- ¼ **teaspoon salt**
- ¼ **teaspoon pepper**
- 1 **prebaked 12-inch thin whole wheat pizza crust**
- 1 **can (8 ounces) pizza sauce**
- 2 **small tomatoes, chopped**
- 2 **cups (8 ounces) shredded part-skim mozzarella cheese**

1. In a large bowl, mix mushrooms, zucchini, peppers, onion, vinegar, water, 3 teaspoons oil and seasonings. Transfer to a grill wok or basket. Grill, covered, over medium heat for 8-10 minutes or until tender, stirring once.
2. Prepare grill for indirect heat. Brush crust with remaining oil; spread with pizza sauce. Top with grilled vegetables, tomatoes and cheese. Grill, covered, over indirect medium heat for 10-12 minutes or until edges are lightly browned and cheese is melted. Rotate pizza halfway through cooking to ensure evenly browned crust.

GRILLED VEGGIE PIZZA

NOTE *If you don't have a grill wok or basket, use a disposable foil pan. Poke holes in the bottom of the pan with a meat fork to allow liquid to drain.*
PER SERVING *274 cal., 11 g fat (5 g sat. fat), 22 mg chol., 634 mg sodium, 30 g carb., 5 g fiber, 17 g pro.* **Diabetic Exchanges:** *2 starch, 2 medium-fat meat, 1 vegetable.*

Keep Basil Green

If using fresh basil as a garnish, be sure to cut it just before serving to prevent it from getting brown.

ZUCCHINI BURGERS

Penne with Kale and Onion

My husband hates kale, but I love it. When I swapped it into a favorite penne with spinach recipe, it was so delicious, he asked for seconds!

—KIMBERLY HAMMOND KINGWOOD, TX

PREP: 15 MIN. • **COOK:** 20 MIN.
MAKES: 6 SERVINGS

- 1 medium onion, sliced
- 2 tablespoons olive oil, divided
- 8 garlic cloves, thinly sliced
- 3 cups uncooked penne pasta
- 6 cups chopped fresh kale
- ½ teaspoon salt

1. In a large skillet, cook onion in 1 tablespoon oil over medium heat for 15-20 minutes or until onion is golden brown, stirring frequently and adding the garlic during the last 2 minutes of cooking time.

2. Meanwhile, in a large saucepan, cook the penne according to package directions. In a Dutch oven, bring 1 in. of water to a boil. Add the kale; cover and cook for 10-15 minutes or until tender; drain.

3. Drain the penne; drizzle with the remaining oil. Stir the salt, penne and kale into onion mixture; heat through.

PER SERVING *191 cal., 5 g fat (1 g sat. fat), 0 chol., 206 mg sodium, 31 g carb., 2 g fiber, 6 g pro.* **Diabetic Exchanges:** *1½ starch, 1 vegetable, 1 fat.*

Zucchini Burgers

The patties for this omelet-like veggie burger hold together well while cooking and are hearty enough to serve without buns. I like to make them in summer with fresh-picked zucchini.

—KIMBERLY DANEK PINKSON

SAN ANSELMO, CA

PREP: 20 MIN. • **COOK:** 5 MIN./BATCH
MAKES: 4 SERVINGS

- 2 cups shredded zucchini
- 1 medium onion, finely chopped
- ½ cup dry bread crumbs
- 2 eggs, lightly beaten
- ⅛ teaspoon salt
  Dash cayenne pepper
- 3 hard-cooked egg whites, chopped
- 2 tablespoons canola oil
- 4 whole wheat hamburger buns, split
- 4 lettuce leaves
- 4 slices tomato
- 4 slices onion

1. In a sieve or colander, drain the zucchini, squeezing to remove excess liquid. Pat dry. In a small bowl, mix the zucchini, onion, bread crumbs, eggs, salt and cayenne. Gently stir in cooked egg whites.

2. Heat 1 tablespoon oil in a large nonstick skillet over medium-low heat. Drop batter by scant ⅔ cupfuls into oil; press lightly to flatten. Fry in batches until golden brown on both sides, using remaining oil as needed.

3. Serve on buns with lettuce, tomato and onion.

PER SERVING *314 cal., 12 g fat (2 g sat. fat), 106 mg chol., 467 mg sodium, 40 g carb., 6 g fiber, 13 g pro.* **Diabetic Exchanges:** *2 starch, 1½ fat, 1 lean meat, 1 vegetable.*

Grilled Portobello Burgers

Tastes like a bistro-style grilled cheese, but eats like a hearty burger—meet the new cheese-bello.

—**MARY HAAS** HEWITT, NJ

START TO FINISH: 25 MIN.
MAKES: 4 SERVINGS

- 4 **large portobello mushrooms (4 to 4½ inches), stems removed**
- 6 **tablespoons reduced-fat balsamic vinaigrette, divided**
- 4 **slices red onion**
- 1 **cup roasted sweet red peppers, drained**
- 4 **slices fresh mozzarella cheese**
- 4 **kaiser rolls, split**
- ¼ **cup fat-free mayonnaise**

1. Brush the mushrooms with 4 tablespoons vinaigrette. Grill mushrooms and onion, covered, over medium heat for 3-4 minutes on each side or until tender. Top mushrooms with red peppers, onion and cheese. Grill, covered, 2-3 minutes longer or until the cheese is melted. Grill the rolls, uncovered, for 1-2 minutes or until toasted.

2. Spread the roll bottoms with the mayonnaise and drizzle with the remaining vinaigrette. Top with mushrooms; replace roll tops.

PER SERVING *354 cal., 12 g fat (4 g sat. fat), 17 mg chol., 979 mg sodium, 42 g carb., 3 g fiber, 15 g pro.* **Diabetic Exchanges:** *2 starch, 1 medium-fat meat, 1 vegetable, 1 fat.*

Freezer Veggie Burgers

I try to limit our intake of red meat to once a week, so I'm happy my family likes these burgers. They freeze well so you can make a batch and cook as needed. We like how the outside gets a little crispy.

—**ELAINE SOLOCHIER** CONCORD, NC

PREP: 25 MIN. + FREEZING • **BAKE:** 30 MIN.
MAKES: 6 SERVINGS

- 1 **can (16 ounces) kidney beans, rinsed and drained**
- ½ **cup old-fashioned oats**
- 2 **tablespoons ketchup**
- ½ **cup finely chopped fresh mushrooms**
- 1 **medium onion, finely chopped**
- 1 **medium carrot, shredded**
- 1 **small sweet red pepper, finely chopped**
- 2 **garlic cloves, minced**
- ½ **teaspoon salt**
- ⅛ **teaspoon white pepper**
- 6 **hamburger buns, split**
- 6 **lettuce leaves**
- 6 **slices tomato**

Place the beans, oats and ketchup in a food processor; cover and pulse until blended. Transfer to a small bowl; stir in vegetables, garlic and seasonings. Shape into six 3-in. patties; wrap each in plastic wrap and freeze.

TO USE FROZEN BURGERS *Unwrap burgers and place on a baking sheet coated with cooking spray. Bake at 350° for 30 minutes or until heated through, turning once. Serve on buns with lettuce and tomato.*

PER SERVING *241 cal., 3 g fat (1 g sat. fat), 0 chol., 601 mg sodium, 45 g carb., 7 g fiber, 11 g pro.* **Diabetic Exchanges:** *2½ starch, 1 lean meat, 1 vegetable.*

GRILLED PORTOBELLO BURGERS

Zesty Light Tacos

A complete protein with black beans and brown rice, this colorful entree is perfect for when I'm feeding vegetarians. If you need to cut down on sodium, use reduced-sodium beans and tomatoes.

—MAUREEN MACK MILWAUKEE, WI

PREP: 15 MIN. • **COOK:** 50 MIN.
MAKES: 8 SERVINGS

- 1 cup uncooked brown rice
- 1 medium red onion, halved and sliced
- 1 medium green pepper, thinly sliced
- 1 tablespoon canola oil
- 1 can (15 ounces) black beans, rinsed and drained
- 1 can (14½ ounces) diced tomatoes with mild green chilies, undrained
- ½ cup frozen corn
- ½ cup taco sauce
- 1 teaspoon chili powder
- ¾ teaspoon cayenne pepper
- 8 whole wheat tortillas (8 inches), warmed

Optional toppings: shredded lettuce, chopped tomatoes, pickled jalapeno slices, shredded reduced-fat cheddar cheese and reduced-fat sour cream

1. Cook rice according to package directions. Meanwhile, in a large nonstick skillet, saute onion and pepper in oil until tender. Stir in the beans, tomatoes, corn, taco sauce, chili powder and cayenne; heat through. Stir in cooked rice.

2. Spoon ¾ cup mixture down the center of each tortilla. Add toppings if desired.

PER SERVING *326 cal., 6 g fat (trace sat. fat), 0 chol., 565 mg sodium, 57 g carb., 7 g fiber, 10 g pro.*

BEAN & PINEAPPLE
SOFT TACOS

ZESTY LIGHT TACOS

FAST FIX

Bean & Pineapple Soft Tacos

The sweet and spicy filling in these scrumptious soft tacos is a refreshing change from basic ground beef or chicken. I think the best side dish for them is a fresh fruit salad with melon, mango, papaya and a splash of lime juice.

—TRISHA KRUSE EAGLE, ID

START TO FINISH: 30 MIN.
MAKES: 10 SERVINGS

- 1 can (15 ounces) black beans, rinsed and drained
- 1 large onion, chopped
- 1 medium sweet red pepper, chopped
- 1 tablespoon olive oil
- 1 can (20 ounces) unsweetened pineapple tidbits, drained
- 1 jar (16 ounces) salsa
- 1 can (4 ounces) chopped green chilies
- ¼ cup minced fresh cilantro
- 10 whole wheat tortillas (8 inches), warmed
     Sliced avocado, shredded lettuce, chopped tomatoes, shredded reduced-fat cheddar cheese and reduced-fat sour cream, optional

1. Mash half of the beans; set aside.

2. In a large skillet, saute onion and red pepper in oil until tender. Add the pineapple, salsa, chilies, mashed beans and remaining beans; heat through. Stir in cilantro.

3. Place ½ cup filling on one side of each tortilla. Add toppings of your choice; fold in half. Serve immediately.

PER SERVING *236 cal., 4 g fat (trace sat. fat), 0 chol., 479 mg sodium, 40 g carb., 5 g fiber, 7 g pro.* **Diabetic Exchanges:** *1½ starch, 1 lean meat, 1 vegetable, ½ fruit, ½ fat.*

Curried Quinoa and Chickpeas

If you're a fan of curry seasoning and want to cook more with quinoa, this is a must-try recipe. Orange juice and raisins are a wonderful addition to this dish.

—**SUZANNE BANFIELD** BASKING RIDGE, NJ

PREP: 15 MIN. • **COOK:** 25 MIN.
MAKES: 4 SERVINGS

- 1½ cups water
- ½ cup orange juice
- 1 can (15 ounces) chickpeas or garbanzo beans, rinsed and drained
- 2 medium tomatoes, seeded and chopped
- 1 medium sweet red pepper, julienned
- 1 cup quinoa, rinsed
- 1 small red onion, finely chopped
- ½ cup raisins
- 1 teaspoon curry powder
- ½ cup minced fresh cilantro

1. In a large saucepan, bring water and orange juice to a boil. Stir in the chickpeas, tomatoes, red pepper, quinoa, onion, raisins and curry. Return to a boil. Reduce heat; cover and simmer for 15-20 minutes or until liquid is absorbed.

2. Remove from the heat; fluff with a fork. Sprinkle with cilantro.

NOTE *Look for quinoa in the cereal, rice or organic food aisle.*

PER SERVING *355 cal., 5 g fat (trace sat. fat), 0 chol., 155 mg sodium, 70 g carb., 9 g fiber, 12 g pro.*

Black Bean Veggie Burritos

Sweet potatoes give these baked burritos a seasonal twist. Stuffed with beans, veggies and cheesy goodness, one burrito yields a generous portion that promises to fill up each family member.

—**CARISSA SUMNER** WASHINGTON, WA DC

PREP: 30 MIN. • **BAKE:** 25 MIN.
MAKES: 8 SERVINGS

- 1 large sweet potato, peeled and cut into ½-inch cubes
- 1 medium onion, finely chopped
- 1 tablespoon water
- 1 can (15 ounces) black beans, rinsed and drained
- 1 cup frozen corn
- 1 medium green pepper, chopped
- 2 tablespoons lemon juice
- 3 garlic cloves, minced
- 1 tablespoon chili powder
- 2 teaspoons dried oregano
- 1 teaspoon ground cumin
- 8 whole wheat tortillas (8 inches), warmed
- 2 cups (8 ounces) shredded Monterey Jack cheese
- ½ cup fat-free plain yogurt
- ½ cup salsa

1. In a microwave-safe bowl, mix the sweet potato, onion and water. Cover; microwave on high for 4-5 minutes or until potato is almost tender. Stir in the beans, corn, green pepper, lemon juice, garlic and seasonings.

2. Spoon a heaping ½ cup filling off center on each tortilla. Sprinkle with ¼ cup cheese. Fold sides and ends over filling and roll up.

3. Place seam side down in a 13-in. x 9-in. baking dish coated with cooking spray. Cover and bake at 350° for 25-30 minutes or until heated through. Serve with yogurt and salsa.

PER SERVING *362 cal., 12 g fat (5 g sat. fat), 25 mg chol., 505 mg sodium, 47 g carb., 7 g fiber, 16 g pro.*

BLACK BEAN VEGGIE BURRITOS

VEGETARIAN

VEGETARIAN TEX-MEX PEPPERS

Vegetarian Tex-Mex Peppers

Folks who enjoy stuffed peppers will enjoy my Tex-Mex twist. The filling holds together well and has a good amount of heat to fit well with the sweetness of the peppers.

—**CELE KNIGHT** NACOGDOCHES, TX

PREP: 20 MIN. • **BAKE:** 45 MIN.
MAKES: 4 SERVINGS

- 4 **large green peppers**
- 2 **eggs, beaten**
- 2 **cups cooked brown rice**
- 1 **cup frozen vegetarian meat crumbles**
- 1 **cup canned black beans, rinsed and drained**
- ½ **teaspoon pepper**
- ¼ **teaspoon hot pepper sauce**
- ¼ **teaspoon ground cardamom, optional**
- 1 **can (14½ ounces) diced tomatoes, drained**
- 1 **can (10 ounces) diced tomatoes and green chilies**
- 1 **can (8 ounces) no-salt-added tomato sauce**
- ½ **cup shredded Colby cheese**

1. Cut peppers in half lengthwise and remove seeds. Discard stems. In a large Dutch oven, cook peppers in boiling water for 3-5 minutes. Drain and rinse in cold water; set aside.
2. In a large bowl, combine the eggs, rice, meat crumbles, beans, pepper, pepper sauce and cardamom if desired. Spoon into peppers. Place in a 13-in. x 9-in. baking dish coated with cooking spray.
3. In a small bowl, combine the diced tomatoes, tomatoes and green chilies, and tomato sauce. Spoon over the peppers. Cover and bake at 350° for 40-45 minutes or until a thermometer reads 160°. Sprinkle with the cheese; bake 5 minutes longer or until cheese is melted.
NOTE *Vegetarian meat crumbles are a nutritious protein source made from soy. Look for them in the natural foods freezer section.*
PER SERVING *364 cal., 9 g fat (4 g sat. fat), 119 mg chol., 769 mg sodium, 53 g carb., 11 g fiber, 19 g pro.*

FAST FIX
Saucy Vegetable Tofu

This is my daughter Tonya's favorite meal. Sometimes we make it with rigatoni and call it Riga-Tonya. Either way, it's a great, quick way to prepare your kids some yummy vegetables.

—**SANDRA ECKERT** POTTSTOWN, PA

START TO FINISH: 20 MIN.
MAKES: 6 SERVINGS

- 8 **ounces uncooked whole wheat spiral pasta**
- 1 **large onion, coarsely chopped**
- 1 **large green or sweet red pepper, coarsely chopped**
- 1 **medium zucchini, halved lengthwise and sliced**
- 1 **tablespoon olive oil**
- 1 **package (16 ounces) firm tofu, drained and cut into ½-inch cubes**
- 2 **cups meatless spaghetti sauce**

1. Cook pasta according to package directions. Meanwhile, in a large skillet, saute the onion, pepper and zucchini in oil until crisp-tender.
2. Stir in tofu and spaghetti sauce; heat through. Drain pasta; serve with tofu mixture.
PER SERVING *274 cal., 7 g fat (1 g sat. fat), 0 chol., 380 mg sodium, 41 g carb., 7 g fiber, 14 g pro.* **Diabetic Exchanges:** *2 starch, 2 lean meat, 1 vegetable, ½ fat.*

SAUCY VEGETABLE TOFU

Pumpkin Lasagna

I especially like this comforting fall dish because it's vegetarian. Even friends who aren't big fans of pumpkin are surprised by this delectable lasagna! Canned pumpkin and no-cook noodles make it a cinch to prepare, any time of year.

—**TAMARA HURON** NEW MARKET, AL

PREP: 25 MIN. • **BAKE:** 55 MIN. + STANDING
MAKES: 6 SERVINGS

- ½ **pound sliced fresh mushrooms**
- 1 **small onion, chopped**
- ½ **teaspoon salt, divided**
- 2 **teaspoons olive oil**
- 1 **can (15 ounces) solid-pack pumpkin**
- ½ **cup half-and-half cream**
- 1 **teaspoon dried sage leaves Dash pepper**
- 9 **no-cook lasagna noodles**
- 1 **cup reduced-fat ricotta cheese**
- 1 **cup (4 ounces) shredded part-skim mozzarella cheese**
- ¾ **cup shredded Parmesan cheese**

1. In a skillet, saute the mushrooms, onion and ¼ teaspoon salt in oil until tender; set aside. In a small bowl, combine the pumpkin, cream, sage, pepper and remaining salt.

2. Spread ½ cup pumpkin sauce in an 11-in. x 7-in. baking dish coated with cooking spray. Top with three noodles (noodles will overlap slightly). Spread ½ cup pumpkin sauce to edges of noodles. Top with half of mushroom mixture, ½ cup ricotta, ½ cup mozzarella and ¼ cup Parmesan cheese. Repeat layers. Top with remaining noodles and sauce.

3. Cover and bake at 375° for 45 minutes. Uncover; sprinkle with remaining Parmesan cheese. Bake 10-15 minutes longer or until cheese is melted. Let stand for 10 minutes before cutting.

PUMPKIN LASAGNA

PER SERVING *310 cal., 12 g fat (6 g sat. fat), 36 mg chol., 497 mg sodium, 32 g carb., 5 g fiber, 17 g pro.* **Diabetic Exchanges:** *2 starch, 2 fat, 1 lean meat.*

Vegetable-Stuffed Portobellos

Usually portobellos take the place of hamburger patties in burgers, but in this open-faced sandwich, they take the place of buns. My family loves this tasty, healthful dinner, and it's ready in no time.

—**ELIZABETH DOSS** CALIFORNIA CITY, CA

PREP: 20 MIN. • **BROIL:** 15 MIN.
MAKES: 4 SERVINGS

- 1 **can (15 ounces) white kidney or cannellini beans, rinsed and drained**
- 2 **tablespoons olive oil, divided**
- 1 **tablespoon water**
- 1 **teaspoon dried rosemary, crushed**
- 1 **garlic clove, peeled and halved**
- ¼ **teaspoon salt**
- ¼ **teaspoon pepper**
- 4 **large portobello mushrooms (4 to 4½ inches), stems removed**
- 1 **medium sweet red pepper, finely chopped**
- 1 **medium red onion, finely chopped**
- 1 **medium zucchini, finely chopped**
- ½ **cup shredded pepper Jack cheese**

1. In a food processor, combine beans, 1 tablespoon oil, water, rosemary, garlic, salt and pepper. Cover and process until pureed; set aside.

2. Place mushrooms on a broiler pan coated with cooking spray. Broil 4 in. from the heat for 6-8 minutes on each side or until mushrooms are tender.

3. Meanwhile, in a small nonstick skillet coated with cooking spray, saute the red pepper, red onion and zucchini in remaining oil until tender.

4. Spread about ⅓ cup reserved bean mixture over each mushroom; top with ½ cup vegetable mixture. Sprinkle with the cheese. Broil 2-3 minutes longer or until the cheese is melted.

PER SERVING *252 cal., 12 g fat (4 g sat. fat), 15 mg chol., 378 mg sodium, 26 g carb., 7 g fiber, 11 g pro.* **Diabetic Exchanges:** *2 lean meat, 2 vegetable, 1 starch, 1 fat.*

Vegetable Pad Thai

Classic flavors of Thailand abound in this fragrant entree featuring peanuts, tofu and noodles. Once it's all tossed together in the pan, the fettuccine absorbs the cooking sauce, making a tasty dish.

—**SARA LANDRY** BROOKLINE, MA

PREP: 25 MIN. • **COOK:** 15 MIN.
MAKES: 6 SERVINGS

- 1 **package (12 ounces) whole wheat fettuccine**
- ¼ **cup rice vinegar**
- 3 **tablespoons reduced-sodium soy sauce**
- 2 **tablespoons brown sugar**
- 2 **tablespoons fish sauce or additional reduced-sodium soy sauce**
- 1 **tablespoon lime juice**
- Dash Louisiana-style hot sauce
- 1 **package (12 ounces) extra-firm tofu, drained and cut into ½-inch cubes**
- 3 **teaspoons canola oil, divided**
- 2 **medium carrots, grated**
- 2 **cups fresh snow peas, halved**
- 3 **garlic cloves, minced**
- 2 **eggs, lightly beaten**
- 2 **cups bean sprouts**
- 3 **green onions, chopped**
- ½ **cup minced fresh cilantro**
- ¼ **cup unsalted peanuts, chopped**

1. Cook the fettuccine according to package directions. Meanwhile, in a bowl, combine vinegar, soy sauce, brown sugar, fish sauce, lime juice and hot sauce until smooth; set aside.

2. In a large skillet or wok, stir-fry tofu in 2 teaspoons oil until golden brown. Remove and keep warm.

3. Stir-fry carrots and snow peas in remaining oil for 1-2 minutes. Add garlic, cook 1 minute longer or until vegetables are crisp-tender. Add eggs; cook and stir until set.

4. Drain the pasta; add to vegetable mixture. Stir vinegar mixture and add to the skillet. Bring to a boil. Add the tofu, bean sprouts and onions; heat through. Sprinkle with the cilantro and peanuts.

PER SERVING *383 cal., 11 g fat (2 g sat. fat), 71 mg chol., 806 mg sodium, 61 g carb., 10 g fiber, 18 g pro.*

VEGETABLE PAD THAI

SPAGHETTI SQUASH
WITH BALSAMIC
VEGETABLES
AND TOASTED PINE NUTS

Spaghetti Squash with Balsamic Vegetables and Toasted Pine Nuts

To save time prep the veggies while the squash is cooking in the microwave. You can have a satisfying low-carb and low-fat meal on the table quickly.

—DEANNA MCDONALD KALAMAZOO, MI

PREP: 20 MIN. • **COOK:** 15 MIN.
MAKES: 6 SERVINGS

- 1 **medium spaghetti squash (about 4 pounds)**
- 1 **cup chopped carrots**
- 1 **small red onion, halved and sliced**
- 1 **tablespoon olive oil**
- 4 **garlic cloves, minced**
- 1 **can (15½ ounces) great northern beans, rinsed and drained**
- 1 **can (14½ ounces) diced tomatoes, drained**
- 1 **can (14 ounces) water-packed artichoke hearts, rinsed, drained and halved**
- 1 **medium zucchini, chopped**
- 3 **tablespoons balsamic vinegar**
- 2 **teaspoons minced fresh thyme or ½ teaspoon dried thyme**
- ¼ **teaspoon salt**
- ¼ **teaspoon pepper**
- ½ **cup pine nuts, toasted**

1. Cut the squash in half lengthwise; discard seeds. Place squash cut side down on a microwave-safe plate. Microwave, uncovered, on high 15-18 minutes or until tender.

2. Meanwhile, in a large nonstick skillet, saute the carrots and onion in oil until tender. Add the garlic; cook 1 minute. Stir in the beans, tomatoes, artichokes, zucchini, vinegar, thyme, salt and pepper. Cook and stir over medium heat 8-10 minutes or until heated through.

3. When squash is cool enough to handle, use a fork to separate strands. Serve with bean mixture. Sprinkle with pine nuts.

PER SERVING *275 cal., 10 g fat (1 g sat. fat), 0 chol., 510 mg sodium, 41 g carb., 10 g fiber, 11 g pro.* **Diabetic Exchanges:** *2½ starch, 1½ fat, 1 lean meat.*

Vegetarian Sloppy Joes

You won't miss the meat in my version of sloppy joes. It tastes like the classic recipe but is lower in fat and a great option for vegetarians.

—LINDA WINTER OAK HARBOR, WA

START TO FINISH: 25 MIN.
MAKES: 6 SERVINGS

- 2 **teaspoons butter**
- 1 **small onion, finely chopped**
- 1 **package (12 ounces) frozen vegetarian meat crumbles**
- ½ **teaspoon pepper**
- 2 **tablespoons all-purpose flour**
- ⅔ **cup ketchup**
- 1 **can (8 ounces) no-salt-added tomato sauce**
- 6 **hamburger buns, split and toasted**

1. In a large nonstick skillet coated with cooking spray, melt butter over medium-high heat. Add onion; cook and stir until tender. Stir in meat crumbles and pepper; heat through.
2. Sprinkle flour over mixture and stir until blended. Stir in ketchup and

tomato sauce. Bring to a boil; cook and stir 1-2 minutes or until thickened. Serve on buns.

NOTE *Vegetarian meat crumbles are a nutritious protein source made from soy. Look for them in the natural foods freezer section.*

PER SERVING *273 cal., 6 g fat (2 g sat. fat), 4 mg chol., 815 mg sodium, 39 g carb., 5 g fiber, 15 g pro.* **Diabetic Exchanges:** *2½ starch, 2 lean meat.*

VEGETARIAN SLOPPY JOES

Black Bean Burgers with Chipotle Slaw

We like to eat meatless at least one day a week, so I keep cans of various beans in the pantry for quick meals like this one.

—DEBORAH BIGGS OMAHA, NE

PREP: 25 MIN. + CHILLING • **COOK:** 10 MIN.
MAKES: 4 SERVINGS

- 1 **can (15 ounces) black beans, rinsed and drained**
- 6 **tablespoons panko (Japanese) bread crumbs**
- ¼ **cup finely chopped onion**
- ¼ **cup finely chopped sweet red pepper**
- ¼ **cup minced fresh cilantro**
- 2 **egg whites, lightly beaten**
- 1 **garlic clove, minced**
- ¼ **teaspoon salt**
- 2 **tablespoons red wine vinegar**
- 1 **tablespoon plus 4 teaspoons olive oil, divided**
- 1 **tablespoon minced chipotle pepper in adobo sauce**
- 1½ **teaspoons sugar**
- 2¼ **cups coleslaw mix**
- 2 **green onions, chopped**
- 4 **whole wheat hamburger buns, split**

1. In a large bowl, mash beans. Add the panko, onion, red pepper, cilantro, egg whites, garlic and salt; mix well.

BLACK BEAN BURGERS WITH CHIPOTLE SLAW

Shape bean mixture into four patties; refrigerate for 30 minutes.
2. Meanwhile, in a small bowl, whisk the vinegar, 1 tablespoon oil, chipotle pepper and sugar; stir in coleslaw mix and onions. Chill until serving.
3. In a large nonstick skillet, cook burgers in remaining oil over medium heat for 3-5 minutes on each side or until a thermometer reads 160°. Serve on buns with slaw.

PER SERVING *327 cal., 10 g fat (1 g sat. fat), 0 chol., 635 mg sodium, 48 g carb., 9 g fiber, 12 g pro.* **Diabetic Exchanges:** *3 starch, 1½ fat, 1 lean meat.*

top tip Just Add Beans

Did you know that one cup of black beans offers 15 grams of fiber? According to researchers at Tulane University, adding beans to four dishes a week could cut your risk of heart disease by 22 percent.

Vegetarian Chili Ole!

I combine ingredients for this hearty chili the night before, start my trusty slow cooker in the morning and come home to a rich, spicy meal at night!

—MARJORIE AU HONOLULU, HI

PREP: 35 MIN. • **COOK:** 6 HOURS
MAKES: 7 SERVINGS

- 1 **can (16 ounces) kidney beans, rinsed and drained**
- 1 **can (15 ounces) black beans, rinsed and drained**
- 1 **can (14½ ounces) diced tomatoes, undrained**
- 1½ **cups frozen corn**
- 1 **large onion, chopped**
- 1 **medium zucchini, chopped**
- 1 **medium sweet red pepper, chopped**
- 1 **can (4 ounces) chopped green chilies**
- 1 **ounce Mexican chocolate, chopped**
- 1 **cup water**
- 1 **can (6 ounces) tomato paste**
- 1 **tablespoon cornmeal**
- 1 **tablespoon chili powder**
- ½ **teaspoon salt**
- ½ **teaspoon dried oregano**
- ½ **teaspoon ground cumin**
- ¼ **teaspoon hot pepper sauce, optional**
    Optional toppings: diced tomatoes, chopped green onions and crumbled queso fresco

1. In a 4-qt. slow cooker, combine the first nine ingredients. Combine the water, tomato paste, cornmeal, chili powder, salt, oregano, cumin and pepper sauce if desired until smooth; stir into slow cooker. Cover and cook on low for 6-8 hours or until vegetables are tender.

2. Serve with toppings of your choice.
PER SERVING *216 cal., 1 g fat (trace sat. fat), 0 chol., 559 mg sodium, 43 g carb., 10 g fiber, 11 g pro.* **Diabetic Exchanges:** *2½ starch, 1 lean meat.*

VEGETARIAN CHILI OLE!

SHRIMP FETTUCCINE ALFREDO
PAGE 231

CAROLINE SHIVELY'S
SOUTHWEST STEAK QUESADILLAS
PAGE 227

JACKIE TERMONT'S
ZESTY MARINATED PORK CHOPS
PAGE 225

NANCY ZIMMERMAN'S
BLACK FOREST CAKE
PAGE 228

Family Menus

See what other **health-conscious families** are cooking up for their loved ones and learn how to create **a healthy meal plan that works for you**—even on your busiest nights.

When time's tight and temptation is around every corner, **sticking with a wholesome meal plan** can feel overwhelming. Make it less daunting with a little help from those who do it regularly. In this chapter you'll meet five home cooks who learned to **balance busy schedules and healthy living** by sneaking in a few weekly workouts and maintaining a nutritious, practical diet. See what they're cooking for their families and **use these tips as a guide** to start a meal plan that works for yours.

VEGGIE TOSSED SALAD
PAGE 230

- **Make a list** of the days and times you need meals. Review your family's calendar and think about which meals you'll have time to cook and which ones you'll need to make ahead.
- **Ask your family** for meal ideas, choose your recipes and a make a grocery list.
- **Consider doubling your favorite dinner** and freezing one for later.
- **Plan for leftovers.** Make extra chicken, fish, meat or pork to use in another recipe the next day.

Katie Wollgast
Florissant, MO

Getting healthy and staying that way doesn't have to be hard. All it takes is smart choices in the kitchen and a little daily activity. For Katie Wollgast of Florissant, Missouri, this means growing her own produce, choosing healthy foods and staying in shape with daily workouts. "This definitely involves sticking to an exercise plan," she notes.

"My routine started in high school. I alternate stretching and strength training six mornings a week, and I take a 3-mile walk every evening. I love walking by myself or with my parents, who are walkers, too. It's a pleasant way to spend time with them at the end of each day."

Along with exercise, Katie also has a history of lightening dishes. "My mom was a good cook, who used lots of garden foods and fresh fruits. When I 'took over the kitchen,' I continued much of what she had done. I found that, in general, many recipes called for ingredients that weren't really needed, so I started lightening them right away."

Sausage and Pumpkin Pasta

My family really enjoys this meal. Cubed leftover turkey may be substituted for sausage. Just add to the skillet with the cooked pasta.

PREP: 20 MIN. • **COOK:** 15 MIN.
MAKES: 4 SERVINGS

- 2 cups uncooked multigrain bow tie pasta
- ½ pound Italian turkey sausage links, casings removed
- ½ pound sliced fresh mushrooms
- 1 medium onion, chopped
- 4 garlic cloves, minced
- 1 cup reduced-sodium chicken broth
- 1 cup canned pumpkin
- ½ cup white wine or additional reduced-sodium chicken broth
- ½ teaspoon rubbed sage
- ¼ teaspoon salt
- ¼ teaspoon garlic powder
- ¼ teaspoon pepper
- ¼ cup grated Parmesan cheese
- 1 tablespoon dried parsley flakes

1. Cook the pasta according to package directions.

2. Meanwhile, in a large nonstick skillet coated with cooking spray, cook the sausage, mushrooms and onion over medium heat until meat is no longer pink. Add garlic; cook 1 minute longer. Stir in the broth, pumpkin, wine, sage, salt, garlic powder and pepper. Bring to a boil. Reduce heat; simmer, uncovered, for 5-6 minutes or until slightly thickened.

3. Drain pasta; add to the skillet and heat through. Just before serving, sprinkle with cheese and parsley.

PER SERVING *348 cal., 9 g fat (2 g sat. fat), 38 mg chol., 733 mg sodium, 42 g carb., 7 g fiber, 23 g pro.* **Diabetic Exchanges:** *2½ starch, 2 lean meat, 1 vegetable, ½ fat.*

S **FAST FIX**
Easy Tossed Salad

Apples, almonds and cranberries provide amazing crunch and nutrition galore in this easy five-ingredient salad.

START TO FINISH: 10 MIN.
MAKES: 4 SERVINGS

- 8 cups torn mixed salad greens
- 1 large apple, sliced
- ½ cup sliced almonds, toasted
- ½ cup dried cranberries
- ½ cup fat-free poppy seed salad dressing

In a salad bowl, combine the salad greens, apple, almonds and cranberries. Drizzle with dressing; toss to coat. Serve immediately.

PER SERVING *210 cal., 6 g fat (1 g sat. fat), 5 mg chol., 109 mg sodium, 36 g carb., 6 g fiber, 5 g pro.*

SAUSAGE AND PUMPKIN PASTA
EASY TOSSD SALAD

EGGNOG CAKE

Eggnog Cake

We think the cake is scrumptious! During the holidays, I actually buy eggnog to freeze so I can make this year-round.

PREP: 25 MIN. • **BAKE:** 20 MIN. + COOLING
MAKES: 8 SERVINGS

- ¾ cup reduced-fat eggnog
- ¼ cup sugar
- 2 tablespoons canola oil
- 2 tablespoons unsweetened applesauce
- 1 egg
- 1½ cups all-purpose flour
- 2 teaspoons baking powder
- ½ teaspoon salt
- ¼ teaspoon ground nutmeg
- ¼ cup golden raisins
- 2 tablespoons chopped pecans

TOPPING

- ¼ cup packed brown sugar
- 2 tablespoons all-purpose flour
- ½ teaspoon ground nutmeg
- 1 tablespoon cold butter
- 2 tablespoons chopped pecans
- 2 cups reduced-fat vanilla ice cream, optional

1. In a large bowl, beat the eggnog, sugar, oil, applesauce and egg until well blended. In a small bowl, combine the flour, baking powder, salt and nutmeg; gradually beat into eggnog mixture until blended. Stir in raisins and pecans. Pour into a 9-in. round baking pan coated with cooking spray.

2. For topping, in a small bowl, combine the brown sugar, flour and nutmeg. Cut in butter until crumbly. Stir in pecans; sprinkle over batter.

3. Bake at 350° for 20-25 minutes or until a toothpick inserted near the center comes out clean. Cool for 10 minutes before removing from pan to a wire rack to cool completely. Serve with ice cream if desired.

NOTE *This recipe was tested with commercially prepared eggnog.*

PER SERVING *255 cal., 9 g fat (2 g sat. fat), 48 mg chol., 285 mg sodium, 39 g carb., 1 g fiber, 5 g pro.*

Jackie Termont
Ruther Glen, VA

When work began invading Jackie Termont's personal life, it turned out to be a good thing. "I went back to school and became a registered dietitian," says the Ruther Glen, Virginia, cook.

"I started lightening recipes and wanted to eat healthier and lose a few pounds. It was a gradual change, but I've been doing it for so long that it just comes naturally now," Jackie explains.

Though she doesn't follow a special diet, Jackie does pay attention to what she eats. "It's more fun for me when I don't have to worry if the food is potentially unhealthy," she says. "But I love food, and I think everything can be worked into a diet if you're careful about how much and how often you eat."

She has a balanced approach when it

comes to exercise, too—working out 4 days a week with weights, elliptical trainers and the treadmill.

She also does yoga twice a week and tries to walk or ride her bike on other days. "I just feel better after working out, like I've accomplished something good for myself," she says.

When not at the gym, Jackie can often be found at home, baking. To keep things lighter, she opts for reduced-fat and low-sugar ingredients. "However, I don't generally use totally fat-free dairy because I think you need some fat to make it palatable."

Jackie's menu is the perfect example of her eating philosophy—it relies on lean, nutritious ingredients, with the slightest touch of indulgence. Just dig into her heavenly Strawberry-Banana Graham Pudding to see what we mean!

F
Strawberry-Banana Graham Pudding

I add in more fruit to get a little closer to all those servings you need every day. You can also try using different puddings and fruits to change up the recipe.

PREP: 20 MIN. + CHILLING
MAKES: 12 SERVINGS

- 9 whole reduced-fat cinnamon graham crackers
- 1¾ cups cold fat-free milk
- 1 package (1 ounce) sugar-free instant cheesecake or vanilla pudding mix
- 1 large firm banana, sliced
- ½ teaspoon lemon juice
- 2 cups sliced fresh strawberries, divided
- 2½ cups reduced-fat whipped topping, divided
  Mint sprigs, optional

1. Line the bottom of a 9-in. square pan with 4½ graham crackers and set aside.
2. In a small bowl, whisk milk and pudding mix for 2 minutes. Let stand for 2 minutes or until soft-set. Place banana slices in another small bowl; toss with lemon juice. Stir bananas and 1 cup strawberries into pudding. Fold in 1¾ cups whipped topping.
3. Spread half of pudding over the graham crackers; repeat layers. Cover and refrigerate overnight. Refrigerate the remaining berries and whipped topping. Just before serving, top with the remaining berries and topping. Garnish with mint if desired.
PER SERVING *117 cal., 2 g fat (2 g sat. fat), 1 mg chol., 171 mg sodium, 23 g carb., 1 g fiber, 2 g pro.* **Diabetic Exchanges:** *1 starch, ½ fruit.*

F
Roasted Veggie Orzo

My sister inspired this recipe. I added a few more spices, but the concept is hers. It's easy to vary, and it's a simple way to add veggies to your diet.

PREP: 25 MIN. • **BAKE:** 20 MIN.
MAKES: 8 SERVINGS

- 1½ cups fresh mushrooms, halved
- 1 medium zucchini, chopped
- 1 medium sweet yellow pepper, chopped
- 1 medium sweet red pepper, chopped
- 1 small red onion, cut into wedges
- 1 cup cut fresh asparagus (1-inch pieces)
- 1 tablespoon olive oil
- 1 teaspoon each dried oregano, thyme and rosemary, crushed
- ½ teaspoon salt
- 1¼ cups uncooked orzo pasta
- ¼ cup crumbled feta cheese

1. Place vegetables in a 15-in. x 10-in. x 1-in. baking pan coated with cooking spray. Drizzle with oil and sprinkle with seasonings; toss to coat. Bake at 400° for 20-25 minutes or until tender, stirring occasionally.
2. Meanwhile, cook orzo according to package directions. Drain; transfer to a serving bowl. Stir in the roasted vegetables. Sprinkle with cheese.
PER SERVING *164 cal., 3 g fat (1 g sat. fat), 2 mg chol., 188 mg sodium, 28 g carb., 3 g fiber, 6 g pro.* **Diabetic Exchanges:** *1½ starch, 1 vegetable, ½ fat.*

S C

Zesty Marinated Pork Chops

My husband loves pork chops, and they're a good source of lean protein. It's easy to spice them up with fun, new seasonings.

PREP: 15 MIN. + MARINATING
COOK: 10 MIN.
MAKES: 6 SERVINGS

- ¼ **cup balsamic vinegar**
- 2 **tablespoons white wine or reduced-sodium chicken broth**
- 4 **teaspoons olive oil, divided**
- 1 **teaspoon chili powder**
- ½ **teaspoon prepared horseradish**
- ¼ **teaspoon dill weed**
- ¼ **teaspoon garlic powder**
- ¼ **teaspoon salt**
- 6 **boneless pork loin chops (4 ounces each)**

1. In a large resealable plastic bag, combine the vinegar, wine, 1 teaspoon oil, chili powder, horseradish, dill, garlic powder and salt. Add the pork chops; seal bag and turn to coat. Refrigerate for eight hours or overnight, turning occasionally.

2. Drain and discard marinade. In a large nonstick skillet over medium heat, cook chops in remaining oil for 4-5 minutes on each side or until a thermometer reads 145°. Remove from heat and let stand for 5 minutes.
PER SERVING *183 cal., 10 g fat (3 g sat. fat), 55 mg chol., 61 mg sodium, 1 g carb., trace fiber, 22 g pro.* **Diabetic Exchanges:** *3 lean meat, ½ fat.*

ZESTY MARINATED PORK CHOPS
AND ROASTED VEGGIE ORZO

Caroline Shively
c/o Eva Synalovski
New York, NY

Eating well and exercising can be daunting, but imagine if you had to do it while capturing the effects of a hurricane or as one of the few Westerners at the voting polls during Iraq's first election. Welcome to the life of Caroline Shively, a correspondent for FOX News. Her work places her in the middle of historic events—including covering the 2008 election—but Caroline's home life in Alexandria, Virginia, includes more typical things, such as cooking, spending time with her husband and playing tennis.

"I cook a lot when I'm home," Caroline says. "Kitchen time is fun for my husband, Robb, and me. Our schedules don't always allow us to see each other during the week,

so we talk and catch up while cooking." The Kentucky native turns to the recipes she grew up with for inspiration. "A lot of my cooking comes from my mom," she says. "My husband jokes that I can't make a meal without calling her!"

In addition to spending time in the kitchen, the couple enjoys exercising together, too, and learning to mesh eating habits didn't come as naturally at the start. "My husband loves to grill," says Caroline. "At first, he tended to cook fattier things, and I joked I was going to weigh too much if he kept feeding me cheeseburgers. Since then, we've learned to compromise—he still grills but now picks leaner meats." The dishes she offers here feature grilled steak and an easy leftover plan the couple appreciates.

SOUTHWEST STEAK SALAD

C FAST FIX
Southwest Steak Salad
With its tangy combination of lemon juice and balsamic vinegar dressing, this sweet and crunchy salad makes the perfect bed for savory slices of Southwest Steak.

START TO FINISH: 15 MIN.
MAKES: 4 SERVINGS

- ¼ cup minced fresh cilantro
- 3 tablespoons balsamic vinegar
- 2 tablespoons water
- 1 tablespoon lemon juice
- 1 tablespoon olive oil
- 1 package (5 ounces) spring mix salad greens
- 1 small red onion, chopped
- 1 each small green, sweet red and yellow peppers, chopped
- 1 cooked Southwest Flank Steak, thinly sliced

In a small bowl, whisk the first five ingredients; set aside. In a large bowl, combine the salad greens, onion and peppers. Drizzle with dressing; toss to coat. Divide among four plates. Heat steak if desired; place over salads.
PER SERVING *252 cal., 13 g fat (4 g sat. fat), 54 mg chol., 274 mg sodium, 9 g carb., 3 g fiber, 24 g pro.*

C
Southwest Steak
My husband and I came up with this together as something lighter to make on the grill. Lime juice tenderizes the steak while garlic, chili powder and red pepper flakes kick things up a bit.

PREP: 15 MIN. + MARINATING
GRILL: 10 MIN.
MAKES: 8 SERVINGS

- ¼ cup lime juice
- 6 garlic cloves, minced
- 4 teaspoons chili powder
- 4 teaspoons canola oil
- 1 teaspoon salt
- 1 teaspoon crushed red pepper flakes
- 1 teaspoon pepper
- 2 beef flank steaks (1 pound each)

1. In a large resealable plastic bag, combine the first seven ingredients; add beef. Seal bag and turn to coat; refrigerate for 4 hours or overnight.

2. Drain and discard marinade. Moisten a paper towel with cooking oil. Using long-handled tongs, lightly coat the grill rack. Grill beef, covered, over medium heat or broil 4 in. from the heat for 5-7 minutes on each side or until the meat reaches desired doneness (for medium-rare, a thermometer should read 145°; medium, 160°; well-done, 170°).

3. Let stand for 5 minutes; thinly slice across the grain.
PER SERVING *187 cal., 10 g fat (4 g sat. fat), 54 mg chol., 259 mg sodium, 2 g carb., trace fiber, 22 g pro.* **Diabetic Exchanges:** *3 lean meat, 1 fat.*

Southwest Steak Quesadillas

Colorful peppers and onions make this fantastic dish look as great as it tastes. As an added bonus, folding over one larger tortilla (instead of using two smaller ones) saves you a few grams of fat.

START TO FINISH: 30 MIN.
MAKES: 4 SERVINGS

- 1 **each small green, sweet red and yellow peppers, finely chopped**
- 1 **small red onion, finely chopped**
- 4 **fat-free flour tortillas (10 inches)**
- ½ **cup shredded reduced-fat cheddar cheese**
- 1 **cooked Southwest Steak, chopped**
- ¼ **cup minced fresh cilantro**
- 2 **tablespoons chopped seeded jalapeno pepper**
  Salsa, guacamole and reduced-fat sour cream, optional

1. In a large nonstick skillet coated with cooking spray, cook and stir the peppers and onion over medium-high heat until tender. Transfer to a bowl.
2. Coat the same skillet with cooking spray; add one tortilla. Sprinkle 2 tablespoons cheese over half of tortilla. Top with a fourth of the steak, ⅓ cup pepper mixture, 1 tablespoon cilantro and 1½ teaspoons jalapeno.
3. Fold over and cook over low heat for 1-2 minutes on each side or until cheese is melted; remove. Repeat for the remaining quesadillas, spraying pan as needed. Cut into wedges; serve with salsa, guacamole and sour cream if desired.

NOTE *Wear disposable gloves when cutting hot peppers; the oils can burn skin. Avoid touching your face.*
PER SERVING *379 cal., 13 g fat (6 g sat. fat), 64 mg chol., 772 mg sodium, 35 g carb., 3 g fiber, 30 g pro.*

SOUTHWEST STEAK QUESADILLAS

Nancy Zimmerman
Cape May Courthouse, NJ

They say being active keeps you healthy, and Nancy Zimmerman proves it's true. Between her job, pets (including 18 ducks!) and hobbies, this Cape May Court House, New Jersey, resident keeps busy. "I work part-time helping Christian radio stations, volunteer at the local rescue mission, farm and play volleyball and softball with my husband, Ken," she writes.

"I also enjoy photography and chatting with friends on tasteofhome.com."

To fit a workout into her hectic schedule, Nancy begins her day by running or weight training, a routine she started 16 years ago. "I exercise first thing in the morning, so I don't get sidetracked." She attributes exercising and eating right to improving her sports performance and keeping trim.

1. In a large bowl, beat the cherry juice, sugar, applesauce, oil, eggs, vinegar and vanilla until well blended.
2. In a large bowl, combine the flour, cocoa, baking soda and salt; gradually beat into the cherry juice mixture until blended.
3. Pour into a 13-in. x 9-in. baking pan coated with cooking spray. Bake at 350° for 35-40 minutes or until a toothpick inserted near the center comes out clean. Cool completely on a wire rack.
4. In a small bowl, whisk milk and pudding mix for 2 minutes. Let stand for 2 minutes or until soft-set. Frost top of cake with pudding. Cover and refrigerate for 15 minutes. Top with pie filling. Chill until serving. Serve with whipped topping.
PER SERVING 186 cal., 3 g fat (trace sat. fat), 18 mg chol., 272 mg sodium, 36 g carb., 1 g fiber, 3 g pro.

Black Forest Cake

Applesauce is used to keep this version of Black Forest Cake light and healthy. Now, even people who are on a diet can enjoy a slice of rich chocolate decadence!

PREP: 40 MIN. • **BAKE:** 35 MIN. + COOLING
MAKES: 24 SERVINGS

- 2 cups cherry juice blend
- 1¾ cups sugar
- ½ cup unsweetened applesauce
- ¼ cup canola oil
- 2 eggs
- 2 tablespoons cider vinegar
- 3 teaspoons vanilla extract
- 3 cups all-purpose flour
- ⅓ cup baking cocoa
- 2 teaspoons baking soda
- 1 teaspoon salt
- 1½ cups cold fat-free milk
- 1 package (1.4 ounces) sugar-free instant chocolate pudding mix
- 1 can (20 ounces) reduced-sugar cherry pie filling
- 1½ cups frozen fat-free whipped topping, thawed

BLACK FOREST CAKE

Cool Down

Patience is definitely a virtue when cooling a cake. The cake should be no warmer than room temperature when frosting. If the frosting or topping is spread over the cake while it is still warm, the frosting will soften and soak into the cake. The end results will be disappointing.

Spicy Vegetable Chili

This chili makes a great comforting meal on cool nights. I love dipping bread into it.

PREP: 25 MIN. • **COOK:** 35 MIN.
MAKES: 8 SERVINGS (2 QUARTS)

- 1 **medium onion, chopped**
- 1 **medium carrot, thinly sliced**
- 1 **medium green pepper, chopped**
- ½ **pound sliced fresh mushrooms**
- 1 **small zucchini, sliced**
- 1 **tablespoon olive oil**
- 4 **garlic cloves, minced**
- 1 **can (28 ounces) diced tomatoes, undrained**
- 2 **cans (16 ounces each) kidney beans, rinsed and drained**
- 2 **cans (8 ounces each) no-salt-added tomato sauce**
- 1 **can (4 ounces) chopped green chilies**
- 3 **tablespoons chili powder**
- 3 **teaspoons dried oregano**
- 2 **teaspoons ground cumin**
- 2 **teaspoons paprika**
- ¼ **teaspoon crushed red pepper flakes**
- 1 **tablespoon white wine vinegar**
  Minced fresh cilantro and fat-free sour cream, optional

1. In a Dutch oven, saute the onion, carrot, pepper, mushrooms and zucchini in oil until tender. Add garlic; cook 1 minute longer. Add tomatoes, beans, tomato sauce, green chilies and seasonings. Bring to a boil. Reduce the heat; simmer, uncovered, for 35 minutes, stirring occasionally.
2. Stir in vinegar. Serve in soup bowls; garnish each with cilantro and sour cream if desired.
PER SERVING *195 cal., 3 g fat (trace sat. fat), 0 chol., 423 mg sodium, 35 g carb., 11 g fiber, 10 g pro.* ***Diabetic Exchanges:*** *2 starch, 1 lean meat.*

SPICY VEGETABLE CHILI

RUSTIC OAT BRAN BREAD

Rustic Oat Bran Bread

A rustic bread like this goes perfectly with any meal. It's slightly sweet from the honey with a soft inside and chewy crust.

PREP: 30 MIN. + RISING
BAKE: 20 MIN. + COOLING
MAKES: 1 LOAF (12 WEDGES)

- 2¼ to 2¾ **cups all-purpose flour**
- ⅓ **cup oat bran**
- 1 **package (¼ ounce) active dry yeast**
- 1¼ **teaspoons salt**
- 1 **cup water**
- 2 **tablespoons honey**
- 1 **tablespoon cornmeal**

1. In a large bowl, combine 1 cup flour, oat bran, yeast and salt. In a small saucepan, heat water and honey to 120°-130°. Add to dry ingredients; beat just until moistened. Stir in enough remaining flour to form a stiff dough (dough will be sticky).
2. Turn onto a lightly floured surface; knead until smooth and elastic, about 6-8 minutes. Place in a bowl coated with cooking spray, turning once to coat the top. Cover and let rise in a warm place until doubled, about 30 minutes.
3. Punch down dough. Turn onto a lightly floured surface. Shape into a round loaf. Place on a baking sheet coated with cooking spray and sprinkled with the cornmeal. Cover and let rise until nearly doubled, about 30 minutes. With a sharp knife, make three diagonal slashes across top of the loaf.
4. Bake at 400° for 20-25 minutes or until golden brown. Remove from the baking sheet to wire rack to cool.
PER SERVING *107 cal., trace fat (trace sat. fat), 0 chol., 247 mg sodium, 23 g carb., 1 g fiber, 3 g pro.* ***Diabetic Exchange:*** *1½ starch.*

Evelyn Slade
Fruita, CO

Sometimes transitioning into a healthy lifestyle is as easy as taking a few steps in the right direction. "I don't have a set fitness routine," says Evelyn Slade of Fruita, Colorado. "I just strive to get in 10,000 steps each day and ride a bike or do yard work."

That keep-it-simple attitude carries into her cooking, as Evelyn, a school administrator, looks for quick-to-make meals low in sodium and calories. "I began cooking healthy several years ago to maintain my weight, keep my blood pressure in check and help my husband, Norm, lose weight. It was a gradual process, and friends and family responded well. I often make meals for the teachers at work, and I never get complaints!"

Along with keeping menus light, Evelyn also adds as many fruits and veggies as possible. "I purchase locally grown produce in the summer and fall—I think it tastes better—and work it into sides and main courses." With its garden-fresh goodness and easy preparation, the dinner Evelyn shares here is reason enough to take a healthy step toward supper tonight!

WHOLE WHEAT BREAD

F
Whole Wheat Bread

To make this bread, I tweaked an old recipe to include more nutritious ingredients. It comes out soft and tender every time!

PREP: 10 MIN. • **BAKE:** 3 HOURS + COOLING
MAKES: 1 LOAF (2 POUNDS, 16 SLICES)

- 1 cup water
- 1 egg
- 2 tablespoons canola oil
- 2 cups bread flour
- 1 cup whole wheat flour
- ½ cup oat flour
- ½ cup nonfat dry milk powder
- 3 tablespoons sugar
- 1½ teaspoons salt
- 1 package (¼ ounce) active dry yeast

In bread machine pan, place all ingredients in order suggested by manufacturer. Select basic bread setting. Choose crust color and loaf size if available. Bake according to bread machine directions (check dough after 5 minutes of mixing; add 1 to 2 tablespoons of water or flour if needed).

DILL WHOLE WHEAT BREAD *Add 2 teaspoons dill weed with the salt.*
NOTE *As a substitute for 1 cup oat flour, process 1¼ cups quick-cooking or old-fashioned oats until finely ground.*
PER SERVING *131 cal., 3 g fat (trace sat. fat), 14 mg chol., 246 mg sodium, 23 g carb., 2 g fiber, 5 g pro.*

C FAST FIX
Veggie Tossed Salad

This simple salad delivers a dose of veggies and great fresh flavors. Feel free to try it with your favorite dressing.

START TO FINISH: 10 MIN.
MAKES: 4 SERVINGS

- 1½ cups torn romaine
- 1½ cups fresh baby spinach
- ¾ cup sliced fresh mushrooms
- ¾ cup grape tomatoes
- ½ cup sliced cucumber
- ⅓ cup sliced ripe olives
- 1 tablespoon grated Parmesan cheese
- ¼ cup reduced-fat Italian salad dressing

In a large bowl, combine the first seven ingredients. Add salad dressing; toss to coat.

PER SERVING *62 cal., 4 g fat (1 g sat. fat), 1 mg chol., 245 mg sodium, 5 g carb., 2 g fiber, 2 g pro. **Diabetic Exchanges:** 1 vegetable, 1 fat.*

Shrimp Fettuccine Alfredo

This has always been a favorite, so when I started cooking healthier, I tried different ways to lighten it. Less butter and fat-free half-and-half worked well, along with using a little flour to thicken the sauce.

START TO FINISH: 30 MIN.
MAKES: 4 SERVINGS

- 6 ounces uncooked fettuccine
- 2 tablespoons butter
- 4½ teaspoons all-purpose flour
- 1 cup fat-free half-and-half
- 1 pound cooked medium shrimp, peeled and deveined
- ⅓ cup grated Parmesan cheese
- ½ teaspoon salt
- 2 tablespoons minced fresh parsley

Cook fettuccine according to package directions. Meanwhile, in a large saucepan, melt butter. Stir in flour until smooth; gradually add half-and-half. Bring to a boil; cook and stir for 1 minute or until thickened. Drain fettuccine; stir into pan. Stir in the shrimp, cheese and salt; heat through. Sprinkle with parsley before serving.

PER SERVING *397 cal., 11 g fat (5 g sat. fat), 193 mg chol., 670 mg sodium, 39 g carb., 2 g fiber, 34 g pro.*

SHRIMP FETTUCCINE ALFREDO

BAKED BANANA BOATS
PAGE 233

**KIM FORNI'S
SAUSAGE SPINACH PASTA BAKE**
PAGE 237

**MICHELE MCHENRY'S
WAFFLE SANDWICH**
PAGE 242

**JESSICA LEVINSON'S
BAKED APPLE SURPRISE**
PAGE 250

Kid Friendly

Parents, when the table becomes a **battleground between picky palates**, turn to these **family-pleasing recipes** that will inspire your kids to **choose good-for-you foods**.

S FAST FIX
Baked Banana Boats

Kids can make their own banana boats with custom toppings. We use different berries and honey or peanut butter instead of chocolate chips. They're also good topped with crushed graham crackers or granola—whatever your family likes.

—**REBEKAH VIERS** TAYLORS, SC

START TO FINISH: 20 MIN.
MAKES: 4 SERVINGS

- 4 medium bananas, unpeeled
- ½ cup unsweetened crushed pineapple, drained
- ¼ cup granola without raisins
- ¼ cup chopped pecans
- 4 teaspoons miniature semisweet chocolate chips

1. Cut each banana lengthwise about ½ in. deep, leaving ½ in. uncut at both ends. Place each banana on a 12-in. square of foil; crimp and shape foil around bananas so they sit flat. Gently pull each banana peel open, forming a pocket. Fill pockets with pineapple, granola, pecans and chocolate chips.
2. Place on a baking sheet. Bake at 350° for 10-12 minutes or until chips are softened.
PER SERVING *220 cal., 8 g fat (1 g sat. fat), 0 chol., 4 mg sodium, 40 g carb., 5 g fiber, 4 g pro.*

Four-Cheese Baked Ziti

For me, a day without pasta is like a day without sunshine! I think this dish is a best friend to busy cooks, vegetarian cooks and cooks with kids. Everyone loves it.

—**DIANE NEMITZ** LUDINGTON, MI

PREP: 30 MIN. • **BAKE:** 10 MIN.
MAKES: 8 SERVINGS

- 1 cup chopped onion
- ½ cup chopped green pepper
- ½ cup shredded carrots
- 2 garlic cloves, minced
- 2 cans (14½ ounces each) Italian diced tomatoes
- 1 can (15 ounces) crushed tomatoes
- 1 cup vegetable broth
- ⅛ teaspoon crushed red pepper flakes
- 8 ounces uncooked ziti or small tube pasta
- 1 cup (8 ounces) part-skim ricotta cheese
- ½ cup shredded provolone cheese
- ¼ cup loosely packed basil leaves, thinly sliced
- 1 cup (4 ounces) shredded part-skim mozzarella cheese
- ¼ cup grated Parmesan cheese

1. In a large nonstick skillet coated with cooking spray, cook the onion, green pepper and carrots until crisp-tender. Add the garlic; cook 1 minute longer. Stir in the tomatoes, broth and pepper flakes; bring to a boil. Reduce heat; simmer, uncovered, for 15 minutes.
2. Cook ziti according to package directions; drain. Stir in the vegetable mixture, ricotta cheese, provolone cheese and basil.
3. Transfer to a 13-in. x 9-in. baking dish coated with cooking spray. Sprinkle with mozzarella and Parmesan cheeses. Bake, uncovered, at 425° for 10-15 minutes or until heated through and cheese is melted.
PER SERVING *286 cal., 8 g fat (5 g sat. fat), 24 mg chol., 806 mg sodium, 39 g carb., 3 g fiber, 16 g pro.* ***Diabetic Exchanges:*** *3 vegetable, 1½ starch, 1 lean meat, 1 fat.*

FOUR-CHEESE BAKED ZITI

Sausage Pizza

Go ahead and make two of these fully-loaded pizzas and keep one in the freezer for busy nights. If making them for kids, try using a less-spicy sausage, such as chicken or turkey sausage.

—TASTE OF HOME TEST KITCHEN

PREP: 20 MIN. • **BAKE:** 15 MIN.
MAKES: 8 SLICES

- 1 loaf (1 pound) frozen bread dough, thawed
- ¾ pound bulk hot Italian sausage
- ½ cup sliced onion
- ½ cup sliced fresh mushrooms
- ½ cup chopped green pepper
- ½ cup pizza sauce
- 2 cups (8 ounces) shredded part-skim mozzarella cheese

1. With greased fingers, pat dough onto an ungreased 12-in. pizza pan. Prick dough thoroughly with a fork. Bake at 400° for 10-12 minutes or until lightly browned. Meanwhile, in a large skillet, cook the sausage, onion, mushrooms and green pepper over medium heat until the sausage is no longer pink; drain.

2. Spread pizza sauce over crust. Top with sausage mixture; sprinkle with cheese. Bake at 400° for 12-15 minutes or until golden brown. Or wrap pizza and freeze for up to 2 months.

TO USE FROZEN PIZZA *Unwrap and place on a pizza pan; thaw in the refrigerator. Bake at 400° for 18-22 minutes or until golden brown.*

PER SERVING *311 cal., 11 g fat (4 g sat. fat), 39 mg chol., 754 mg sodium, 33 g carb., 2 g fiber, 20 g pro.* **Diabetic Exchanges:** *2 starch, 1½ lean meat, 1½ fat.*

Pizza Joes

If you're tired of same old, boring sloppy joes, here's a tasty twist! These messy, kid-friendly sandwiches have a definite pizza flavor your family will love, but be sure to serve them with a fork!

—**CONNIE PETTIT** LOGAN, OH

START TO FINISH: 30 MIN.
MAKES: 6 SERVINGS

- 1 pound lean ground beef (90% lean)
- 1 medium onion, chopped
- ¼ cup chopped green pepper
- 1 jar (14 ounces) pizza sauce
- 3 ounces sliced turkey pepperoni (about 50 slices), chopped
- ½ teaspoon dried basil
- ¼ teaspoon dried oregano
- 6 hamburger buns, split
- 6 tablespoons shredded part-skim mozzarella cheese

1. In a large nonstick skillet, cook the beef, onion and pepper over medium heat until meat is no longer pink. Drain if necessary. Stir in the pizza sauce, pepperoni and herbs. Bring to a boil. Reduce heat; cover and simmer for 10 minutes.

2. Spoon ⅔ cup beef mixture onto each bun; sprinkle with cheese. Place on a baking sheet. Broil 3-4 in. from the heat for 1 minute or until cheese is melted. Replace tops.

PER SERVING *329 cal., 11 g fat (4 g sat. fat), 59 mg chol., 825 mg sodium, 29 g carb., 3 g fiber, 26 g pro.*

SAUSAGE PIZZA

HAMBURGER NOODLE CASSEROLE

Hamburger Noodle Casserole

People have a hard time believing this homey and hearty casserole uses lighter ingredients. The taste is so rich and creamy...what a great weeknight meal!

—**MARTHA HENSON** WINNSBORO, TX

PREP: 30 MIN. • **BAKE:** 35 MIN.
MAKES: 10 SERVINGS

- 5 **cups uncooked yolk-free noodles**
- 1¼ **pounds lean ground beef (90% lean)**
- 2 **garlic cloves, minced**
- 3 **cans (8 ounces each) tomato sauce**
- ½ **teaspoon sugar**
- ½ **teaspoon salt**
- ⅛ **teaspoon pepper**
- 1 **package (8 ounces) reduced-fat cream cheese**
- 1 **cup reduced-fat ricotta cheese**
- ¼ **cup fat-free sour cream**
- 3 **green onions, thinly sliced, divided**
- ⅔ **cup shredded reduced-fat cheddar cheese**

1. Cook noodles according to package directions. Meanwhile, in a large nonstick skillet over medium heat, cook beef until no longer pink. Add garlic; cook 1 minute longer. Drain. Stir in the tomato sauce, sugar, salt and pepper; heat through. Drain the noodles; stir into beef mixture.

2. In a small bowl, beat the cream cheese, ricotta cheese and sour cream until blended. Stir in half of the onions.

3. Spoon half of the noodle mixture into a 13-in. x 9-in. baking dish coated with cooking spray. Top with the cheese mixture and the remaining noodle mixture.

4. Cover and bake at 350° for 30 minutes. Uncover; sprinkle with cheddar cheese. Bake 5-10 minutes longer or until heated through and cheese is melted. Sprinkle with the remaining onions.

PER SERVING *290 cal., 12 g fat (7 g sat. fat), 56 mg chol., 650 mg sodium, 23 g carb., 2 g fiber, 22 g pro.* **Diabetic Exchanges:** *2 lean meat, 1½ starch, 1 fat.*

Chicken Marinara with Pasta

My preteen son, Logan, and I created this simple but very good dish. It was the first meal he made all by himself (with supervision, of course). Best of all, it was a real hit with the friends he invited for dinner.

—JOANIE FUSON INDIANAPOLIS, IN

PREP: 20 MIN. + MARINATING
COOK: 20 MIN.
MAKES: 6 SERVINGS

- 1½ pounds boneless skinless chicken breasts
- ½ cup reduced-fat Italian salad dressing
- 1 medium onion, chopped
- 1 tablespoon olive oil
- 2 garlic cloves, minced
- 1 can (15 ounces) crushed tomatoes
- 1 can (14½ ounces) diced tomatoes, undrained
- 1 tablespoon minced fresh parsley or 1 teaspoon dried parsley flakes
- 1 teaspoon minced fresh oregano or ¼ teaspoon dried oregano
- 1 teaspoon brown sugar
- ¼ teaspoon salt
- ¼ teaspoon pepper
- 9 ounces uncooked whole wheat spaghetti
- ¼ cup grated Parmesan cheese
- 6 tablespoons shredded part-skim mozzarella cheese

1. Flatten chicken to ½-in. thickness; place in a large resealable plastic bag. Add salad dressing. Seal bag and turn to coat; refrigerate for 30 minutes.
2. Meanwhile, in a large nonstick skillet coated with cooking spray, saute onion in oil until tender. Add garlic; cook 1 minute longer. Stir in the tomatoes, parsley, oregano, brown sugar, salt and pepper. Bring to a boil. Reduce heat; simmer, uncovered, for 10-15 minutes or until slightly thickened, stirring occasionally.
3. Drain and discard marinade. Using long-handled tongs, moisten a paper towel with cooking oil and lightly coat the grill rack. Grill chicken, covered, over medium heat or broil 4 in. from the heat for 4-6 minutes on each side or until no longer pink. When chicken is cool enough to handle, cut into ¼-in. strips.
4. Meanwhile, cook the spaghetti according to package directions. Stir the Parmesan cheese into sauce. Drain the spaghetti. Serve with the chicken and sauce; sprinkle with the mozzarella cheese.
PER SERVING *389 cal., 8 g fat (2 g sat. fat), 70 mg chol., 438 mg sodium, 44 g carb., 8 g fiber, 35 g pro.* **Diabetic Exchanges:** *4 lean meat, 2 starch, 2 vegetable.*

CHICKEN MARINARA
WITH PASTA

Honey Mustard Carrots

I brought this recipe back with me from Sonoma, California, where bees are raised everywhere. It works with any honey, but sage honey is my favorite.

—TRISHA KRUSE EAGLE, ID

START TO FINISH: 20 MIN.
MAKES: 10 SERVINGS

- 4 packages (10 ounces each) julienned carrots
- ½ cup honey
- ¼ cup honey mustard
- 4 teaspoons butter
- ½ teaspoon salt

1. Place 1 in. of water in a large saucepan; add carrots. Bring to a boil. Reduce heat; cover and simmer for 3-4 minutes or until crisp-tender. Drain and set aside.
2. In a small saucepan, combine the remaining ingredients. Bring to a boil; cook and stir for 2-3 minutes or until slightly thickened. Pour over carrots; heat through.
PER SERVING *125 cal., 2 g fat (1 g sat. fat), 4 mg chol., 259 mg sodium, 28 g carb., 3 g fiber, 1 g pro.* **Diabetic Exchanges:** *2 vegetable, 1 starch, ½ fat.*

top tip

Empowering Young Cooks

Don't be afraid to let your little ones help make dinner. When kids can see what's going in their food and know that they helped select it, it's almost a sure thing they're going to like it.

Sausage Spinach Pasta Bake

I've made this pasta many times and in different ways over the years. I've swapped in other meats, such as chicken sausage, veal or ground pork, and added in summer squash, zucchini, green beans and mushrooms, depending on what I have. Fresh herbs also perk up the flavor.

—**KIM FORNI** CLAREMONT, NH

PREP: 35 MIN. • **BAKE:** 25 MIN.
MAKES: 10 SERVINGS

- 1 **package (16 ounces) whole wheat spiral pasta**
- 1 **pound Italian turkey sausage links, casings removed**
- 1 **medium onion, chopped**
- 5 **garlic cloves, minced**
- 1 **can (28 ounces) crushed tomatoes**
- 1 **can (14½ ounces) diced tomatoes, undrained**
- 1 **teaspoon dried oregano**
- 1 **teaspoon dried basil**
- ¼ **teaspoon pepper**
- 1 **package (10 ounces) frozen chopped spinach, thawed and squeezed dry**
- ½ **cup half-and-half cream**
- 2 **cups (8 ounces) shredded part-skim mozzarella cheese**
- ½ **cup grated Parmesan cheese**

1. Cook the pasta according to package directions.
2. Meanwhile, in a large skillet, cook turkey and onion over medium heat until meat is no longer pink. Add garlic. Cook 1 minute longer; drain. Stir in tomatoes, oregano, basil and pepper. Bring to a boil. Reduce heat; simmer, uncovered, for 10 minutes.
3. Drain pasta; stir into the turkey mixture. Add spinach and cream; heat through. Transfer to a 13-in. x 9-in. baking dish coated with cooking spray. Sprinkle with the cheeses. Bake,

SAUSAGE SPINACH PASTA BAKE

uncovered, at 350° for 25-30 minutes or until golden brown.
PER SERVING *377 cal., 11 g fat (5 g sat. fat), 50 mg chol., 622 mg sodium, 45 g carb., 8 g fiber, 25 g pro.* ***Diabetic Exchanges:*** *3 lean meat, 2 starch, 2 vegetable, ½ fat.*

C
Baked Chicken Cordon Bleu

With only six ingredients, this simple take on Chicken Cordon Bleu is a family favorite. Your kids will love the ham and cheese filling.

—**SARAH CHRISTENSON** SAN DIEGO, CA

PREP: 15 MIN. • **BAKE:** 35 MIN.
MAKES: 4 SERVINGS

- 4 **boneless skinless chicken breast halves (6 ounces each)**
- ¼ **teaspoon salt**
- ¼ **teaspoon pepper**
- 4 **thin slices prosciutto or deli ham**
- ½ **cup shredded Asiago cheese**
- ¼ **cup seasoned bread crumbs**

1. Flatten chicken to ¼-in. thickness; sprinkle with salt and pepper. Top each with the prosciutto and cheese. Roll up and tuck in ends; secure with toothpicks.
2. Transfer to an 11-in. x 7-in. baking dish coated with cooking spray. Sprinkle with the bread crumbs. Bake, uncovered, at 350° for 35-45 minutes or until juices run clear.
PER SERVING *291 cal., 10 g fat (4 g sat. fat), 119 mg chol., 645 mg sodium, 6 g carb., trace fiber, 43 g pro.* ***Diabetic Exchanges:*** *6 lean meat, ½ fat.*

Barbecued Turkey Sandwiches

With just a handful of pantry ingredients, it's easy to turn leftover turkey or chicken into tasty barbecue sandwiches—a quick and casual meal that kids will love.

—BARBARA SMITH COLUMBUS, OH

START TO FINISH: 25 MIN.
MAKES: 6 SERVINGS

- ¼ cup chopped onion
- 1 tablespoon butter
- 3 cups shredded cooked turkey
- ½ cup water
- ½ cup ketchup
- ¼ cup red wine vinegar
- 1 tablespoon sugar
- 2 teaspoons Worcestershire sauce
- 1 teaspoon prepared mustard
- 1 teaspoon paprika
- 6 kaiser rolls, split

In a large nonstick skillet, saute onion in butter until tender. Add the turkey, water, ketchup, vinegar, sugar, Worcestershire sauce, mustard and paprika. Bring to a boil. Reduce heat;

BARBECUED TURKEY SANDWICHES

simmer, uncovered, for 15 minutes or until sauce is thickened. Serve on rolls.

PER SERVING *340 cal., 8 g fat (3 g sat. fat), 56 mg chol., 637 mg sodium, 39 g carb., 2 g fiber, 27 g pro.* **Diabetic Exchanges:** *3 lean meat, 2½ starch, ½ fat.*

Zesty Dill Tuna Sandwiches

I absolutely love tuna salad. With this recipe, I brought together all of my favorite things to make what I think is the best tuna salad sandwich ever.

—JENNY DUBINSKY INWOOD, WV

START TO FINISH: 15 MIN.
MAKES: 2 SERVINGS

- 1 can (5 ounces) light water-packed tuna, drained
- ¼ cup reduced-fat mayonnaise
- 1 tablespoon grated Parmesan cheese
- 1 tablespoon sweet pickle relish
- 1 tablespoon minced fresh parsley
- 1 teaspoon spicy brown mustard
- ¼ teaspoon dill weed
- ⅛ teaspoon onion powder
- ⅛ teaspoon curry powder
- ⅛ teaspoon garlic powder
- 4 slices whole wheat bread

In a small bowl, combine the first 10 ingredients. Spread over two slices of bread. Top with remaining bread.

PER SERVING *346 cal., 13 g fat (3 g sat. fat), 34 mg chol., 877 mg sodium, 29 g carb., 4 g fiber, 27 g pro.* **Diabetic Exchanges:** *3 lean meat, 2 starch, 1½ fat.*

ZESTY DILL TUNA SANDWICHES

Open-Faced Ham and Apple Melts

Serve these as a homework snack or light lunch. The yummy melts mix sweet apple crunch, hearty ham and tangy Dijon flavor wonderfully.

—SALLY MALONEY DALLAS, GA

START TO FINISH: 15 MIN.
MAKES: 4 SERVINGS

- 2 whole wheat English muffins, split
- 2 teaspoons Dijon mustard
- 4 slices deli ham
- ½ medium apple, thinly sliced
- 2 slices reduced-fat Swiss cheese, halved

1. Place English muffin halves cut side up on a baking sheet. Broil 4-6 in. from the heat for 2-3 minutes or until golden brown.

2. Spread with mustard. Top with ham, apple slices and cheese. Broil 3-4 minutes longer or until the cheese is melted.

PER SERVING *130 cal., 3 g fat (1 g sat. fat), 14 mg chol., 429 mg sodium, 17 g carb., 3 g fiber, 10 g pro.*

Chicken Casserole Supreme

On a cold day what better dish to serve for dinner than my satisfying chicken casserole? It gets even better the next day! I added apples and raisins and feel they really set this apart from other dishes.

—JUDY WILSON SUN CITY WEST, AZ

PREP: 40 MIN. • **BAKE:** 20 MIN.
MAKES: 6 SERVINGS

- 1 cup reduced-sodium chicken broth
- 1 medium apple, peeled and chopped
- ½ cup golden raisins
- 1 tablespoon butter
- 1 package (6 ounces) reduced-sodium stuffing mix
- 1 pound boneless skinless chicken breasts, cubed
- ¼ teaspoon salt
- ¼ teaspoon pepper
- 1 cup sliced fresh mushrooms
- 1 small onion, chopped
- 1 tablespoon olive oil
- 3 garlic cloves, minced
- 1½ cups (12 ounces) fat-free sour cream
- 1 can (10¾ ounces) reduced-fat reduced-sodium condensed cream of mushroom soup, undiluted
- 4 cups frozen broccoli florets, thawed

1. In a large saucepan, combine the broth, apple and raisins. Bring to a boil. Reduce heat; simmer, uncovered, for 3-4 minutes or until the apple is tender. Stir in butter and stuffing mix. Remove from the heat; cover and let stand for 5 minutes.

2. Sprinkle chicken with salt and pepper. In a large skillet, cook the chicken, mushrooms and onion in oil over medium heat until chicken is no longer pink. Add garlic; cook 1 minute longer. Remove from the heat. Stir in sour cream and soup.

3. Transfer to a 13-in. x 9-in. baking dish coated with cooking spray. Layer with broccoli and stuffing mixture. Bake, uncovered, at 350° for 20-25 minutes or until heated through.

PER SERVING *390 cal., 8 g fat (2 g sat. fat), 59 mg chol., 771 mg sodium, 52 g carb., 3 g fiber, 26 g pro.*

CHICKEN CASSEROLE SUPREME

Lasagna Corn Carne

My grandkids always ask me to make this dish, which is sort of like chili in a pan. I came up with the recipe one day using ingredients I had on hand and it was an instant hit!

—MARY LOU WILLS LA PLATA, MD

PREP: 30 MIN. • **BAKE:** 45 MIN. + STANDING
MAKES: 12 SERVINGS

- 1 **pound lean ground beef (90% lean)**
- 1 **jar (16 ounces) salsa**
- 1 **can (16 ounces) kidney beans, rinsed and drained**
- 1 **can (14¾ ounces) cream-style corn**
- 1 **large onion, chopped**
- 1 **medium green pepper, chopped**
- 1 **celery rib, chopped**
- 3 **garlic cloves, minced**
- 1 **tablespoon minced fresh basil or 1 teaspoon dried basil**
- 1 **teaspoon salt**
- 1 **teaspoon chili powder**
- 12 **lasagna noodles, cooked, rinsed and drained**
- 2 **cups (8 ounces) shredded part-skim mozzarella cheese**
- ½ **cup grated Parmesan cheese**

1. In a large skillet, cook beef over medium heat until no longer pink; drain. Add the salsa, beans, vegetables, garlic and seasonings. Bring to a boil. Reduce the heat; cover and simmer for 15 minutes.

2. Spread a fourth of the meat sauce in a 13-in. x 9-in. baking dish coated with cooking spray; top with four noodles. Repeat layers once. Top with half of the remaining sauce; sprinkle with half of the cheeses. Layer with remaining noodles, sauce and cheeses.

3. Cover and bake at 350° for 30 minutes. Uncover; bake 15-20 minutes longer or until heated through. Let stand for 15 minutes before cutting.

PER SERVING *292 cal., 8 g fat (4 g sat. fat), 37 mg chol., 674 mg sodium, 36 g carb., 4 g fiber, 20 g pro.* **Diabetic Exchanges:** *2½ starch, 2 lean meat.*

LASAGNA CON CARNE

Pizza Snacks

Since pizza is a big favorite with my teenagers, I like to keep these crispy snacks on hand. Loaded with toppings, they go right from the freezer to the oven with little time and effort. And they're always gone in minutes.

—RUBY WILLIAMS BOGALUSA, LA

PREP: 10 MIN. + FREEZING
MAKES: 10 SNACKS

- ½ **cup shredded cheddar cheese**
- ½ **cup shredded part-skim mozzarella cheese**
- 1 **jar (4½ ounces) sliced mushrooms, drained**
- ⅓ **cup chopped pepperoni**
- ⅓ **cup mayonnaise**
- ¼ **cup chopped onion**
- 3 **tablespoons chopped ripe olives**
- 5 **English muffins, split**

In a large bowl, combine the first seven ingredients. Spread over cut side of each muffin half. Cover and freeze for up to 2 months.

TO USE FROZEN SNACKS *Place on an ungreased baking sheet. Bake at 350° for 20 minutes or until the cheese is melted.*

PER SERVING *187 cal., 12 g fat (4 g sat. fat), 17 mg chol., 395 mg sodium, 15 g carb., 1 g fiber, 6 g pro.*

Penne Beef Bake

I had ground beef and veggies on hand so I came up with this pizza-flavored casserole. I never expected my family to love it so much. It's a good way to sneak in some extra veggies for the kids.

—JENNIFER WISE SELINSGROVE, PA

PREP: 35 MIN. • **BAKE:** 25 MIN.
MAKES: 8 SERVINGS

- 1 **package (12 ounces) whole wheat penne pasta**
- 1 **pound lean ground beef (90% lean)**
- 2 **medium zucchini, finely chopped**
- 1 **large green pepper, finely chopped**
- 1 **small onion, finely chopped**
- 1 **jar (24 ounces) meatless spaghetti sauce**
- 1½ **cups reduced-fat Alfredo sauce**
- 1 **cup (4 ounces) shredded part-skim mozzarella cheese, divided**
- ¼ **teaspoon garlic powder**

PENNE BEEF BAKE

1. Cook penne according to package directions. Meanwhile, in a Dutch oven, cook the beef, zucchini, pepper and onion over medium heat until meat is no longer pink; drain. Stir in the spaghetti sauce, Alfredo sauce, ½ cup mozzarella cheese and garlic powder. Drain penne; stir into the meat mixture.

2. Transfer to a 13-in. x 9-in. baking dish coated with cooking spray. Cover and bake at 375° for 20 minutes. Sprinkle with remaining mozzarella cheese. Bake, uncovered, 3-5 minutes longer or until cheese is melted.
PER SERVING *395 cal., 12 g fat (6 g sat. fat), 62 mg chol., 805 mg sodium, 45 g carb., 7 g fiber, 25 g pro.* ***Diabetic Exchanges:*** *3 starch, 2 lean meat, 1 fat.*

Potluck Sloppy Joes

For a change of pace, consider swapping out the green pepper in these tasty sloppy joes for an Anaheim, if available. Long and lighter in color than a bell pepper, Anaheim peppers have just a hint of a bite.

—RICK BOLTE MONTCLAIR, CA

PREP: 30 MIN. • **COOK:** 15 MIN.
MAKES: 12 SERVINGS

- 3 **pounds lean ground turkey**
- 3 **celery ribs, chopped**
- 2 **medium onions, chopped**
- 1 **large green pepper, chopped**
- 1¾ **cups ketchup**
- 1 **can (8 ounces) no-salt-added tomato sauce**
- 3 **tablespoons all-purpose flour**
- 3 **tablespoons sugar**
- 3 **tablespoons cider vinegar**
- 1 **tablespoon prepared mustard**
- 12 **whole wheat hamburger buns, split and toasted**

1. In a large nonstick skillet, cook the turkey, celery, onions and pepper over medium heat until meat is no longer pink; drain.

2. Stir in the ketchup, tomato sauce, flour, sugar, vinegar and mustard. Bring to a boil. Reduce heat; cover and simmer for 10-15 minutes or until heated through. Spoon ⅔ cup turkey mixture onto each bun.

3. Or, cool the turkey mixture and freeze in freezer containers for up to 3 months.

TO USE FROZEN TURKEY MIXTURE
Thaw in the refrigerator; place in a saucepan and heat through. Spoon ⅔ cup turkey mixture onto each bun.
PER SERVING *360 cal., 11 g fat (3 g sat. fat), 90 mg chol., 785 mg sodium, 41 g carb., 4 g fiber, 24 g pro.* ***Diabetic Exchanges:*** *3 lean meat, 2½ starch.*

BIRD'S NEST
BREAKFAST CUPS

FAST FIX

Waffle Sandwich

Keep 'em going right through to lunchtime with this quick and hefty breakfast sandwich idea!

—**MICHELE MCHENRY** BELLINGHAM, WA

START TO FINISH: 20 MIN.
MAKES: 1 SERVING

- 1 slice Canadian bacon
- 1 egg
- 1 green onion, chopped
- 2 frozen low-fat multigrain waffles
- 1 tablespoon shredded reduced-fat cheddar cheese
  Sliced tomato, optional

1. In a nonstick skillet coated with cooking spray, cook Canadian bacon over medium-high heat 1-2 minutes on each side or until lightly browned. Remove and keep warm.
2. In a small bowl, whisk egg and green onion; add to the same pan. Cook and stir until egg is thickened and no liquid egg remains.
3. Meanwhile, prepare waffles according to package directions. Place one waffle on a plate. Top with Canadian bacon, scrambled egg, cheese and, if desired, tomato. Top with remaining waffle.

PER SERVING *261 cal., 10 g fat (3 g sat. fat), 223 mg chol., 733 mg sodium, 30 g carb., 3 g fiber, 16 g pro.* **Diabetic Exchanges:** *2 starch, 2 medium-fat meat*

FAST FIX

Scrambled Egg Wraps

This tasty morning meal, which also makes a fast dinner, will fill your family up with protein and veggies. Try using flavored wraps to jazz things up.

—**JANE SHAPTON** IRVINE, CA

START TO FINISH: 20 MIN.
MAKES: 6 SERVINGS

- 1 medium sweet red pepper, chopped
- 1 medium green pepper, chopped
- 2 teaspoons canola oil
- 5 plum tomatoes, seeded and chopped
- 6 eggs
- ½ cup soy milk
- ¼ teaspoon salt
- 6 flour tortillas (8 inches), warmed

1. In a large nonstick skillet, saute peppers in oil until tender. Add tomatoes; saute 1-2 minutes longer.
2. Meanwhile, in a large bowl, whisk the eggs, soy milk and salt. Reduce heat to medium; add egg mixture to skillet. Cook and stir until eggs are completely set. Spoon ⅔ cup mixture down the center of each tortilla; roll up.

PER SERVING *258 cal., 10 g fat (2 g sat. fat), 212 mg chol., 427 mg sodium, 30 g carb., 1 g fiber, 12 g pro.* **Diabetic Exchanges:** *1½ starch, 1 lean meat, 1 vegetable, 1 fat.*

C **FAST FIX**

Bird's Nest Breakfast Cups

I make this often for guests because it's so easy and is such a fun presentation. The original recipe called for regular bacon and eggs, so I changed it to lighten it up.

—**ARIS GONZALEZ** DELTONA, FL

START TO FINISH: 30 MIN.
MAKES: 6 SERVINGS

- 12 turkey bacon strips
- 1½ cups egg substitute
- 6 tablespoons shredded reduced-fat Mexican cheese blend
- 1 tablespoon minced fresh parsley

1. In a large skillet, cook bacon over medium heat for 2 minutes on each side or until partially set but not crisp. Coat six muffin cups with cooking spray; wrap two bacon strips around the inside of each cup. Fill each with ¼ cup egg substitute; top with cheese.
2. Bake at 350° for 18-20 minutes or until set. Cool for 5 minutes before removing from the pan. Sprinkle with the parsley.

PER SERVING *120 cal., 7 g fat (2 g sat. fat), 30 mg chol., 515 mg sodium, 2 g carb., trace fiber, 12 g pro.* **Diabetic Exchange:** *2 lean meat.*

WAFFLE SANDWICH

Isaiah's Gingerbread Pancakes with Apple Slaw

Perfect for weekend mornings, these gingery pancakes are served with a sweet slaw. Use decaf coffee for kids and swap pears for apples to change things up.

—SILVANA NARDONE BROOKLYN, NY

PREP: 25 MIN. • **COOK:** 5 MIN./BATCH
MAKES: 10 SERVINGS (3 CUPS SLAW)

- 2 cups gluten-free pancake mix
- 2 tablespoons brown sugar
- 1 tablespoon baking cocoa
- 1½ teaspoons ground ginger
- 1 teaspoon pumpkin pie spice
- ½ teaspoon baking soda
- 2 eggs, separated
- 1 cup rice milk
- ½ cup plus 1 tablespoon brewed coffee, room temperature
- 2 tablespoons canola oil
- 1 tablespoon molasses

SLAW
- 3 medium apples, grated
- ½ cup chopped pecans, toasted
- ¼ cup golden raisins
- 2 tablespoons lemon juice
- 1 tablespoon honey
  Maple syrup, warmed

1. In a large bowl, combine the first six ingredients. Combine the egg yolks, rice milk, coffee, oil and molasses; add to dry ingredients just until moistened. In a small bowl, beat egg whites on medium speed until stiff peaks form. Fold into batter.
2. Pour batter by scant ¼ cupfuls onto a hot griddle coated with cooking spray; turn when bubbles form on top. Cook until second side is golden brown.
3. Meanwhile, in a small bowl, combine the apples, pecans, raisins, lemon juice and honey. Serve with pancakes and syrup.

ISAIAH'S GINGERBREAD PANCAKES WITH APPLE SLAW

NOTE *Read all ingredient labels for possible gluten content prior to use. Ingredient formulas can change, and production facilities vary among brands. If you're concerned that your brand may contain gluten, contact the company.*
PER SERVING *225 cal., 8 g fat (1 g sat. fat), 42 mg chol., 231 mg sodium, 36 g carb., 2 g fiber, 3 g pro.* **Diabetic Exchanges:** *1½ starch, 1½ fat, ½ fruit.*

S **FAST FIX**
Pumpkin Pie Oatmeal

I made this oatmeal because I love pumpkin pie and wanted it for the first meal of the day. You can use reduced-fat or fat-free milk instead of soy milk, and it will be just as creamy.

—AMBER RIFE COLUMBUS, OH

START TO FINISH: 15 MIN.
MAKES: 2 SERVINGS

- 1 cup water
- 1 cup vanilla soy milk
- 1 cup old-fashioned oats
- ½ cup canned pumpkin
- ¼ teaspoon pumpkin pie spice
- 2 tablespoons sugar
- ¼ teaspoon vanilla extract
  Dried cranberries, optional

1. In a small saucepan, combine the water, milk, oats, pumpkin and pie spice. Bring to a boil; cook and stir for 5 minutes.
2. Remove from the heat; stir in sugar and vanilla. Sprinkle with cranberries if desired.

PER SERVING *268 cal., 5 g fat (trace sat. fat), 0 chol., 51 mg sodium, 49 g carb., 6 g fiber, 10 g pro.*

C FAST FIX

Baked Veggie Chips

As a snack or side, I like to serve homemade veggie chips with assorted sauces for dipping, such as light ranch dressing, light sour cream or ketchup. But they're delicious all on their own.

—**CHRISTINE SCHENHER** SAN CLEMENTE, CA

START TO FINISH: 30 MIN.
MAKES: 7 SERVINGS

- ½ **pound fresh beets (about 2 medium)**
- 1 **medium potato**
- 1 **medium sweet potato**
- 1 **medium parsnip**
- 2 **tablespoons canola oil**
- 2 **tablespoons grated Parmesan cheese**
- ½ **teaspoon salt**
- ½ **teaspoon garlic powder**
- ½ **teaspoon dried oregano**
  Dash pepper

1. Peel vegetables and cut into ⅛-inch slices. Place in a large bowl. Drizzle with oil. Combine remaining ingredients; sprinkle over vegetables and toss to coat.

2. Arrange in a single layer on racks in two ungreased 15-in. x 10-in. x 1-in. baking pans. Bake at 375° for 15-20 minutes or until golden brown, turning once.

PER SERVING *108 cal., 5 g fat (1 g sat. fat), 1 mg chol., 220 mg sodium, 15 g carb., 2 g fiber, 2 g pro.* **Diabetic Exchanges:** *1 starch, 1 fat.*

Chili Tortilla Bake

A homestyle Tex-Mex casserole is all it takes to gather the whole family around the dinner table. With popular flavors and a bubbly cheese topping, you won't have to worry about leftovers.

—**CELINE WELDY** CAVE CREEK, AZ

PREP: 20 MIN. • **BAKE:** 25 MIN.
MAKES: 6 SERVINGS

- 1 **pound extra-lean ground beef (95% lean)**
- 2 **cans (8 ounces each) no-salt-added tomato sauce**
- 1 **can (15 ounces) black beans, rinsed and drained**
- 1 **cup frozen corn**
- 1 **can (4 ounces) chopped green chilies**
- 2 **tablespoons dried minced onion**
- 2 **tablespoons chili powder**
- 1 **teaspoon ground cumin**
- ½ **teaspoon garlic powder**
- ½ **teaspoon dried oregano**
- 6 **whole wheat tortillas (8 inches)**
- 1 **cup (4 ounces) shredded reduced-fat cheddar cheese**

1. In a large skillet, cook beef over medium heat until no longer pink. Stir in the tomato sauce, beans, corn, green chilies, onion, chili powder, cumin, garlic powder and oregano; heat through.

2. In an 11-in. x 7-in. baking dish coated with cooking spray, layer half of the tortillas, beef mixture and cheese. Repeat layers. Bake, uncovered, at 350° for 25-30 minutes or until bubbly.

PER SERVING *413 cal., 11 g fat (4 g sat. fat), 56 mg chol., 590 mg sodium, 47 g carb., 8 g fiber, 28 g pro.*

CHILI TORTILLA BAKE

BAKED VEGGIE CHIPS

Honey-Soy Pork Chops

Summer is always a special time for relaxed and casual meals, for patriotic holidays and picnics in the great outdoors. These pork chops are ideal for such occasions.

—**EDIE DESPAIN** LOGAN, UTAH

PREP: 10 MIN. + MARINATING
GRILL: 10 MIN.
MAKES: 4 SERVINGS

- ¼ **cup lemon juice**
- ¼ **cup honey**
- 2 **tablespoons reduced-sodium soy sauce**
- 1 **tablespoon sherry or unsweetened apple juice**
- 2 **garlic cloves, minced**
- 4 **boneless pork loin chops (4 ounces each)**

1. In a small bowl, combine the first five ingredients. Pour ½ cup into a large resealable plastic bag; add pork chops. Seal bag and turn to coat; refrigerate for 2-3 hours. Cover and refrigerate remaining marinade for basting.

2. Drain and discard marinade. Moisten a paper towel with cooking oil; using long-handled tongs, lightly coat the grill rack.

3. Grill pork, covered, over medium heat or broil 4-5 in. over the heat for 4-5 minutes on each side or until a thermometer reads 145°, basting frequently with remaining marinade. Let meat stand for 5 minutes before serving.

PER SERVING *176 cal., 6 g fat (2 g sat. fat), 55 mg chol., 132 mg sodium, 6 g carb., trace fiber, 22 g pro.* **Diabetic Exchange:** *3 lean meat.*

Broccoli-Cauliflower Cheese Bake

Adding Swiss and mozzarella cheeses is a surefire way to get the family to eat more vegetables. If serving this dish to kids, you can leave out the cayenne pepper.

—**JENN TIDWELL** FAIR OAKS, CA

PREP: 35 MIN. • **BAKE:** 20 MIN.
MAKES: 16 SERVINGS

- 7 **cups fresh cauliflowerets**
- 6 **cups fresh broccoli florets**
- 3 **tablespoons butter**
- ⅓ **cup all-purpose flour**
- 1½ **teaspoons spicy brown mustard**
- ¾ **teaspoon salt**
- ¼ **teaspoon ground nutmeg**
- ¼ **teaspoon cayenne pepper**
- ¼ **teaspoon pepper**
- 3¾ **cups fat-free milk**
- 1½ **cups (6 ounces) shredded part-skim mozzarella cheese, divided**
- 1½ **cups (6 ounces) shredded Swiss cheese, divided**

1. Place cauliflower and broccoli in a Dutch oven; add 1 in. of water. Bring to a boil. Reduce heat; cover and simmer for 3-5 minutes or until crisp-tender. Drain; transfer to a 13-in. x 9-in. baking dish coated with cooking spray.

2. In small saucepan, melt the butter. Stir in the flour, mustard, salt, nutmeg, cayenne and pepper until smooth; gradually add the milk. Bring to a boil; cook and stir for 1-2 minutes or until thickened.

3. Stir in 1¼ cups each mozzarella and Swiss cheeses, stirring until melted. Pour over vegetables. Bake, uncovered, at 400° for 15-20 minutes or until bubbly. Sprinkle with remaining cheeses. Bake 5 minutes longer or until golden brown.

PER SERVING *132 cal., 7 g fat (4 g sat. fat), 22 mg chol., 252 mg sodium, 9 g carb., 2 g fiber, 9 g pro.* **Diabetic Exchanges:** *1 high-fat meat, 1 vegetable.*

HONEY-SOY PORK CHOPS

KID FRIENDLY

FAST FIX
Coconut-Crusted Turkey Strips

These coconut-crusted turkey strips with a plum dipping sauce are just the thing to serve for a light supper. My granddaughter made them last year, and they were a big hit.

—AGNES WARD STRATFORD, ON

START TO FINISH: 30 MIN.
MAKES: 6 SERVINGS

- 2 egg whites
- 2 teaspoons sesame oil
- ½ cup flaked coconut, toasted
- ½ cup dry bread crumbs
- 2 tablespoons sesame seeds, toasted
- ½ teaspoon salt
- 1½ pounds turkey breast tenderloins, cut into ½-inch strips
  Cooking spray

DIPPING SAUCE
- ½ cup plum sauce
- ⅓ cup unsweetened pineapple juice
- 1½ teaspoons prepared mustard
- 1 teaspoon cornstarch

1. In a shallow bowl, whisk egg whites and oil. In another shallow bowl, combine the coconut, bread crumbs, sesame seeds and salt. Dip the turkey in the egg mixture, then coat with the coconut mixture.

2. Place on baking sheets coated with cooking spray; spritz the turkey with cooking spray. Bake at 425° for 4-6 minutes on each side or until golden brown and juices run clear.

3. Meanwhile, in a small saucepan, combine the sauce ingredients. Bring to a boil; cook and stir for 2 minutes or until thickened. Serve with the turkey strips.

PER SERVING 278 cal., 8 g fat (3 g sat. fat), 56 mg chol., 519 mg sodium, 22 g carb., 1 g fiber, 30 g pro. **Diabetic Exchanges:** 3 lean meat, 1 starch, ½ fat.

PORK CHOPS WITH APRICOT SAUCE

C FAST FIX
Pork Chops with Apricot Sauce

The apricot preserves bring a very special flavor to the pork chops. I serve it with good old corn bread, which can be made in advance and tastes great with this meal.

—PATRICIA SWART GALLOWAY, NJ

START TO FINISH: 30 MIN.
MAKES: 6 SERVINGS

- 6 boneless pork loin chops (6 ounces each)
- ½ teaspoon garlic pepper blend
- 1 tablespoon olive oil
- 1 cup sugar-free apricot preserves
- 1 tablespoon minced chives
- ¼ teaspoon salt

1. Sprinkle pork with garlic pepper blend. In a large nonstick skillet coated with cooking spray, brown chops in oil on each side.

2. Combine the preserves, chives and salt; spoon over chops. Reduce heat; cover and cook for 5-6 minutes or until a thermometer reads 145°. Let meat stand for 5 minutes before serving. Serve with sauce.

PER SERVING 273 cal., 12 g fat (4 g sat. fat), 82 mg chol., 169 mg sodium, 13 g carb., trace fiber, 33 g pro. **Diabetic Exchanges:** 5 lean meat, 1 starch, ½ fat.

COCONUT-CRUSTED TURKEY STRIPS

Mini Mediterranean Pizzas

I was on a mini-pizza kick and had already served up Mexican and Italian variations, so I opted for a Mediterranean version and came up with these.

—**JENNY DUBINSKY** INWOOD, WV

PREP: 30 MIN. • **BAKE:** 5 MIN.
MAKES: 4 SERVINGS

- 8 ounces lean ground beef (90% lean)
- ¼ cup finely chopped onion
- 2 garlic cloves, minced
- 1 can (8 ounces) tomato sauce
- 1 teaspoon minced fresh rosemary or ¼ teaspoon dried rosemary, crushed
- 2 whole wheat pita breads (6 inches), cut in half horizontally
- 1 medium tomato, seeded and chopped
- ½ cup fresh baby spinach, thinly sliced
- 12 Greek pitted olives, thinly sliced
- ½ cup shredded part-skim mozzarella cheese
- ¼ cup crumbled feta cheese

1. In a large nonstick skillet coated with cooking spray, cook the beef, onion and garlic over medium heat for 5-6 minutes or until meat is no longer pink; drain. Stir in tomato sauce and rosemary; bring to a boil. Reduce heat; simmer, uncovered, for 6-9 minutes or until thickened.

2. Place pita halves, cut side up, on a baking sheet. Top with meat mixture, tomato, spinach and olives. Sprinkle with cheeses. Bake at 400° for 4-6 minutes or until cheeses are melted.

PER SERVING 287 cal., 12 g fat (5 g sat. fat), 47 mg chol., 783 mg sodium, 25 g carb., 4 g fiber, 21 g pro. *Diabetic Exchanges: 2 lean meat, 1½ starch, 1 fat.*

MINI MEDITERRANEAN PIZZAS

FAST FIX
Black Bean 'n' Corn Quesadillas

The best part about my quesadillas is that they bake in the oven so all of them are ready at the same time. Plus, they make vegetables irresistible!

—**SUSAN FRANKLIN** LITTLETON, CO

START TO FINISH: 25 MIN.
MAKES: 6 SERVINGS

- 1 can (15 ounces) black beans, rinsed and drained, divided
- 1 small onion, finely chopped
- 2 teaspoons olive oil
- 1 can (11 ounces) Mexicorn, drained
- 1 teaspoon chili powder
- 1 teaspoon ground cumin
- 1 package (6 ounces) fresh baby spinach
- 8 flour tortillas (8 inches)
- ¾ cup shredded reduced-fat Monterey Jack cheese or Mexican cheese blend

1. In a small bowl, mash 1 cup beans with a fork. In a large skillet, saute onion in oil until tender. Add the corn, chili powder, cumin, mashed beans and remaining beans; cook and stir until heated through. Stir in spinach just until wilted.

2. Place two tortillas on an ungreased baking sheet; spread each with a rounded ½ cup of the bean mixture. Sprinkle each with 3 tablespoons of the cheese; top with another tortilla. Repeat.

3. Bake at 400° for 8-10 minutes or until the cheese is melted. Cut each quesadilla into six wedges. Serve warm.

PER SERVING 358 cal., 9 g fat (3 g sat. fat), 10 mg chol., 900 mg sodium, 56 g carb., 5 g fiber, 15 g pro.

Apple-Raisin Baked Oatmeal

I make this recipe often for our seven children. It's economical, and the kids love different variations of it.

—CHRISTINA SMEAL FAIRMONT, WV

PREP: 20 MIN. • **BAKE:** 35 MIN.
MAKES: 6 SERVINGS

- 3 cups old-fashioned oats
- ½ cup packed brown sugar
- 2 teaspoons baking powder
- 1½ teaspoons ground cinnamon
- ½ teaspoon salt
- ⅛ teaspoon ground nutmeg
- 2 eggs
- 2 cups fat-free milk
- 1 medium apple, chopped
- ⅓ cup raisins
- ⅓ cup chopped walnuts
  Additional fat-free milk, optional

1. In a large bowl, combine the first six ingredients. Whisk eggs and milk; stir into dry ingredients until blended. Let stand for 5 minutes. Stir in the apple, raisins and walnuts.

2. Transfer to an 8-in. square baking dish coated with cooking spray. Bake, uncovered, at 350° for 35-40 minutes or until edges are lightly browned and a thermometer reads 160°. Serve with additional milk if desired.

PER SERVING *349 cal., 9 g fat (1 g sat. fat), 72 mg chol., 397 mg sodium, 60 g carb., 5 g fiber, 12 g pro.*

CRUNCHY PEANUT BUTTER APPLE DIP

APPLE-RAISIN BAKED OATMEAL

S C FAST FIX

Crunchy Peanut Butter Apple Dip

A neighbor gave this dip to my mom and she always made it for us in the fall during apple season. Now I carry on the tradition and make it for my own children.

—JULI MEYERS HINESVILLE, GA

START TO FINISH: 10 MIN.
MAKES: 2½ CUPS

- 1 carton (8 ounces) reduced-fat spreadable cream cheese
- 1 cup creamy peanut butter
- ¼ cup fat-free milk
- 1 tablespoon brown sugar
- 1 teaspoon vanilla extract
- ½ cup chopped unsalted peanuts
  Apple slices

In a small bowl, beat the first five ingredients until blended. Stir in peanuts. Serve with apple slices. Refrigerate leftovers.

PER SERVING *2 tablespoons dip equals 126 cal., 10 g fat (3 g sat. fat), 5 mg chol., 115 mg sodium, 5 g carb., 1 g fiber, 5 g pro.*

Fun-on-the-Run Snack Mix

My gang loves this snack mix and have no idea they're eating cranberries. It's a great healthy snack for picnics or hikes.

—CARRIE HUBBARD BUENA VISTA, CO

START TO FINISH: 5 MIN.
MAKES: 8 CUPS

- 2 **cups Wheat Chex**
- 2 **cups miniature fish-shaped crackers**
- 2 **cups pretzel sticks**
- 1 **cup salted peanuts**
- 1 **cup dried cranberries**

In a large bowl, combine the cereal, crackers, pretzels, peanuts and cranberries. Store in an airtight container.
PER SERVING *½ cup equals 143 cal., 6 g fat (1 g sat. fat), 0 chol., 207 mg sodium, 20 g carb., 2 g fiber, 4 g pro.*
Diabetic Exchanges: 1 starch, 1 fat.

SNACKIN' GRANOLA

FUN-ON-THE-RUN
SNACK MIX

Snackin' Granola

Granola's a popular treat with my family, and this one couldn't be easier to prepare. I flavor it with lots of tasty, good-for-you ingredients. It's perfect to send in bag lunches or to serve after school. I've also used it as an in-the-car treat when we take family vacations.

—MARLENE MOHR CINCINNATI, OH

PREP: 15 MIN. • **BAKE:** 25 MIN. + COOLING
MAKES: 7 CUPS

- 2⅔ **cups flaked coconut**
- 1 **cup quick-cooking oats**
- ¼ **cup packed brown sugar**
- ¼ **cup raisins or chopped pitted dried plums**
- ¼ **cup chopped dried apricots**
- 2 **tablespoons sesame seeds**
- ¼ **cup canola oil**
- ¼ **cup honey**
- ¼ **cup semisweet chocolate chips or M&M's**

1. In a large metal bowl, combine the first six ingredients. In a small saucepan, bring the oil and honey just to a boil. Immediately remove from the heat; pour over coconut mixture, stirring to coat evenly.
2. Spread in an ungreased 13-in. x 9-in. baking pan. Bake at 325° for 25 minutes, stirring several times. Pour onto waxed paper to cool. Sprinkle with chocolate chips or M&M's. Store in an airtight container.
PER SERVING *¼ cup equals 106 cal., 6 g fat (3 g sat. fat), 0 chol., 25 mg sodium, 13 g carb., 1 g fiber, 1 g pro.*

F Baked Apple Surprise

To make these apples even more appealing to young ones, use Brie cheese instead of blue. It helps to bake the apples in a muffin tin so they don't roll around.

—JESSICA LEVINSON NYACK, NY

PREP: 10 MIN. • **BAKE:** 35 MIN.
MAKES: 2 SERVINGS

- 2 **medium apples**
- 2 **tablespoons crumbled blue cheese, divided**
- 2 **tablespoons quick-cooking oats**
- 2 **tablespoons bran flakes**
- 1 **tablespoon golden raisins**
- 1 **tablespoon raisins**
- 1 **tablespoon brown sugar**

1. Cut the apples in half lengthwise; remove cores. Place in an ungreased 8-in. square baking dish. Fill each half with 1 teaspoon blue cheese.
2. In a small bowl, combine the oats, bran flakes, golden raisins, raisins and brown sugar; spoon into apples. Top with the remaining cheese. Bake, uncovered, at 350° for 35-40 minutes or until tender.
PER SERVING *181 cal., 3 g fat (2 g sat. fat), 6 mg chol., 141 mg sodium, 39 g carb., 5 g fiber, 3 g pro.*

Rosemary Sweet Potato Fries

A local restaurant got me hooked on sweet potato fries. I started making them at home and experimented with different seasonings to match the flavor. I'm thrilled with my rosemary-kissed results!

—JACKIE GREGSTON HALLSVILLE, TX

PREP: 15 MIN. • **BAKE:** 30 MIN.
MAKES: 4 SERVINGS

- 3 **tablespoons olive oil**
- 1 **tablespoon minced fresh rosemary**
- 1 **garlic clove, minced**
- 1 **teaspoon cornstarch**
- ¾ **teaspoon salt**
- ⅛ **teaspoon pepper**
- 3 **large sweet potatoes, peeled and cut into ¼-inch julienned strips (about 2¼ pounds)**

1. In a large resealable plastic bag, combine the first six ingredients. Add sweet potatoes; shake to coat.
2. Arrange in a single layer on two 15-in. x 10-in. x 1-in. baking pans coated with cooking spray. Bake, uncovered, at 425° for 30-35 minutes or until tender and lightly browned, turning occasionally.
PER SERVING *256 cal., 10 g fat (1 g sat. fat), 0 chol., 459 mg sodium, 39 g carb., 5 g fiber, 3 g pro.*

ROSEMARY SWEET POTATO FRIES

F S Spiced Apple-Grape Juice

For some outdoor fun, we pour this spiced juiced into a thermos and take it with us. But it's also nice to cuddle up indoors while sipping on a cup of the warm cider.

—CLAIRE BEATTIE TORONTO, ON

PREP: 10 MIN. • **COOK:** 1 HOUR
MAKES: 8 SERVINGS

- 4 **cups white grape juice**
- 3 **cups unsweetened apple juice**
- 1 **cup water**
- 2 **cinnamon sticks (3 inches)**
- 12 **whole cloves**
- 8 **whole allspice**

1. In a large saucepan, combine the grape juice, apple juice and water. Place the cinnamon, cloves and allspice on a double thickness of cheesecloth; bring up corners of cloth and tie with string to form a bag. Add to the pan.
2. Bring to a boil. Reduce heat; simmer, uncovered, for 1 to 1½ hours or until flavors are blended. Discard spice bag. Serve warm in mugs.
PER SERVING *121 cal., trace fat (trace sat. fat), 0 chol., 10 mg sodium, 29 g carb., trace fiber, 1 g pro.*

BAKED APPLE SURPRISE

Kid-Pleasing Taco Pizza

Kids will love this quick-and-easy take on both tacos and pizza. And you'll love that it's healthful, full of flavor, and lower in fat and calories!

—**KIMBERLY THEOBALD** GALESBURG, IL

START TO FINISH: 30 MIN.
MAKES: 10 PIECES

- 1 **tube (13.8 ounces) refrigerated pizza crust**
- 1 **pound lean ground turkey**
- ¾ **cup water**
- 1 **envelope reduced-sodium taco seasoning**
- 1 **can (16 ounces) fat-free refried beans**
- 1½ **cups (6 ounces) shredded pizza cheese blend**
- 3 **medium tomatoes, chopped**
- 7 **cups shredded lettuce**
- 2 **cups crushed baked tortilla chip scoops**

1. Unroll crust into a 15-in. x 10-in. x 1-in. baking pan coated with cooking spray; flatten dough and build up edges slightly. Bake at 425° for 8-10 minutes or until edges are lightly browned.

2. Meanwhile, in a large nonstick skillet, cook turkey over medium heat until no longer pink; drain. Stir in the water and taco seasoning. Bring to a boil. Reduce heat; simmer, uncovered, for 5 minutes. Stir in refried beans until blended.

3. Spread turkey mixture over crust; sprinkle with the cheese. Bake at 425° for 5-7 minutes or until the cheese is melted. Top with tomatoes, lettuce and chips. Serve immediately.

PER SERVING *345 cal., 11 g fat (4 g sat. fat), 48 mg chol., 873 mg sodium, 42 g carb., 5 g fiber, 20 g pro.*

Egg- and Lactose-Free Chocolate Cupcakes

We wanted to make a super chocolaty dessert for kids with food allergies, and these little fudgy cakes turned out to be the perfect treat. The foil muffin liners worked like a charm and did not stick to the cupcake.

—**TASTE OF HOME TEST KITCHEN**

PREP: 20 MIN. • **BAKE:** 20 MIN. + COOLING
MAKES: 1½ DOZEN

- 2 **cups water**
- 1½ **cups sugar**
- ½ **cup unsweetened applesauce**
- ⅓ **cup canola oil**
- 3 **teaspoons vanilla extract**
- 3 **cups all-purpose flour**
- ½ **cup baking cocoa**
- 1¼ **teaspoons baking powder**
- 1 **teaspoon salt**
- ½ **teaspoon baking soda**

FROSTING

- ⅓ **cup lactose-free margarine, softened**
- 2 **cups confectioners' sugar**
- ⅓ **cup baking cocoa**
- 2 **tablespoons water**
- ¾ **teaspoon vanilla extract**

1. In a large bowl, beat the water, sugar, applesauce, oil and vanilla until well blended. In a small bowl, combine the flour, cocoa, baking powder, salt and baking soda; gradually beat into sugar mixture until blended.

2. Fill foiled-lined muffin cups three-fourths full. Bake at 350° for 18-22 minutes or until a toothpick inserted near the center comes out clean. Cool for 10 minutes before removing from pans to wire racks to cool completely.

3. In a small bowl, beat margarine until fluffy. Add the confectioners' sugar, cocoa, water and vanilla; beat until smooth. Frost cupcakes.

PER SERVING *275 cal., 8 g fat (1 g sat. fat), 0 chol., 234 mg sodium, 49 g carb., 1 g fiber, 3 g pro.*

EGG-AND LACTOSE-FREE
CHOCOLATE CUPCAKES

KID-PLEASING
TACO PIZZA

SHRIMP AND GRITS
PAGE 259

**DARCIE ZERNIAK'S
CREAMY MACARONI AND CHEESE**
PAGE 258

**MELISSA GLEASON'S
CHOCOLATE MINT LAYER CAKE**
PAGE 263

**HEATHER PRIVRATSKY'S
CAJUN CHICKEN PASTA**
PAGE 266

Makeovers

Do you want to make your own **family favorites a little healthier** but don't know how to begin? Here we give you the details on **how we've lightened a variety of foods**. You'll be able to pick up some tips and **apply them to your own recipes**.

Greek Chicken Penne

We love the bold flavors in Greek Chicken Penne—but not with almost 500 calories and 24 grams of fat per serving. We needed a lighter version we can feel good about eating.

—**SUSAN STETZEL** GAINESVILLE, NY

PREP: 20 MIN. • **COOK:** 20 MIN.
MAKES: 6 SERVINGS

- 2 **cups uncooked penne pasta**
- ½ **cup sun-dried tomatoes (not packed in oil)**
- 1½ **cups boiling water**
- 1 **large onion, chopped**
- 3 **tablespoons reduced-fat butter**
- ¼ **cup all-purpose flour**
- 1 **can (14½ ounces) reduced-sodium chicken broth**
- 3 **cups cubed cooked chicken breast**
- 1 **cup (4 ounces) crumbled feta cheese**
- 1 **cup water-packed artichoke hearts, rinsed, drained and chopped**
- ⅓ **cup Greek olives, sliced**
- 2 **tablespoons minced fresh parsley**
- ¼ **teaspoon Greek seasoning**

1. Cook pasta according to package directions. Meanwhile, place the tomatoes in a small bowl; add the boiling water. Cover and let stand for 5 minutes.

2. In a Dutch oven, saute onion in

GREEK CHICKEN PENNE

butter until tender. Stir in flour until blended; gradually add broth. Bring to a boil; cook and stir for 2 minutes or until thickened. Drain and chop tomatoes; add to the pan. Stir in remaining ingredients. Drain pasta; add to the pan and heat through.

NOTE *This recipe was tested with Land O'Lakes light stick butter.*
PER SERVING *343 cal., 11 g fat (5 g sat. fat), 71 mg chol., 813 mg sodium, 31 g carb., 3 g fiber, 30 g pro.*

↑ **MAKEOVER** / Calories: **343** / Fat: **11 g**

TRADITIONAL / Calories: **471** / Fat: **24 g**

WHAT WE DID Cutting back on the amount of butter and using reduced-fat butter shaved off 42 calories and 5 grams of fat per serving right off the bat. Then we swapped the marinated artichoke hearts with the water-packed version to cut an extra 32 calories. To make up for any lost flavors, we used a bag of sun-dried tomatoes that could be rehydrated in boiling water. Finally, we nixed the dark chicken meat and used only lean, white breast meat.

CARAMEL-PECAN
APPLE PIE

Caramel-Pecan Apple Pie

I lost 120 pounds and want my favorite pie to fit my new eating habits. This version better suits a healthy lifestyle and still delivers out-of-this-world apple tastiness.
—**RONDA DAVIS** KING, NC

PREP: 45 MIN. • **BAKE:** 55 MIN. + COOLING
MAKES: 8 SERVINGS

- 7 **cups sliced peeled tart apples**
- 1 **teaspoon lemon juice**
- 1 **teaspoon vanilla extract**
- ¼ **cup finely chopped pecans**
- ¼ **cup packed brown sugar**
- 2 **tablespoons sugar**
- 4½ **teaspoons ground cinnamon**
- 1 **tablespoon cornstarch**
- 1 **unbaked pastry shell (9 inches)**

TOPPING

- 2 **tablespoons all-purpose flour**
- 2 **tablespoons sugar**
- 2 **tablespoons cold butter**
- ¼ **cup finely chopped pecans**
- ¼ **cup caramel ice cream topping, room temperature**

1. In a large bowl, toss apples with lemon juice and vanilla. Combine the pecans, sugars, cinnamon and cornstarch; add to apple mixture and toss to coat. Pour into pastry shell.

2. In a small bowl, combine flour and sugar. Cut in butter until mixture resembles coarse crumbs. Stir in pecans. Sprinkle over filling.

3. Bake at 350° for 55-60 minutes or until filling is bubbly and topping is browned. Immediately drizzle with caramel topping. Cool on a wire rack.

PER SERVING *334 cal., 15 g fat (5 g sat. fat), 13 mg chol., 159 mg sodium, 50 g carb., 3 g fiber, 2 g pro.*

⬆ *MAKEOVER* / Calories: **334** / Fat: **15 g**

TRADITIONAL / Calories: **608** / Fat: **35 g**

WHAT WE DID Reducing the amount of pecans by 67 percent saved 51 calories and 5 grams of fat per serving but left just enough for satisfying crunch. Using a smaller amount of streusel topping saves an extra 141 calories and 10 grams of fat! The original recipe called for caramel topping on the bottom crust and melted butter over the pie filling. We eliminated these two steps (without detecting a taste difference) to save an extra 34 calories and more than 4 grams of fat per slice.

Ricotta Nut Torte

As a marathon-running dietitian, I enjoy indulging in an occasional dessert. But I'd like it much more if it wasn't so calorie-packed. This lightened-up option has lots of thin layers and a luscious frosting that make it a winning makeover.

—**SUZANNE RUNTZ** MOUNT PLEASANT, SC

PREP: 35 MIN. • **BAKE:** 20 MIN. + COOLING
MAKES: 16 SERVINGS

- 2 **cartons (15 ounces each) reduced-fat ricotta cheese**
- 1 **cup sugar**
- 1 **teaspoon vanilla extract**
- ⅓ **cup chopped pecans, toasted**
- 3 **milk chocolate candy bars (1.55 ounces each), grated**

BATTER

- ¼ **cup shortening**
- 1¼ **cups sugar**
- 2 **eggs**
- ½ **cup unsweetened applesauce**
- 1½ **teaspoons vanilla extract**
- 2½ **cups all-purpose flour**
- 2½ **teaspoons baking powder**
- 1 **teaspoon salt**
- 1¼ **cups fat-free milk**
- 1 **carton (8 ounces) frozen reduced-fat whipped topping, thawed**
  Whole hazelnuts and shaved chocolate, optional

1. Line three 8-in. round baking pans with waxed paper. Coat pans with cooking spray and sprinkle with flour; set aside.
2. For filling, in a small bowl, beat ricotta cheese and sugar until smooth; beat in vanilla. Fold in pecans and grated chocolate. Cover and chill.
3. Meanwhile, in a large bowl, beat shortening and sugar until crumbly, about 2 minutes. Add eggs, one at a time, beating well after each addition. Beat in applesauce and vanilla until well blended. Combine the flour, baking powder and salt; add to the creamed mixture alternately with milk, beating well after each addition.
4. Pour into prepared pans. Bake at 350° for 20-25 minutes or until a toothpick inserted near the center comes out clean. Cool for 10 minutes before removing from pans to wire racks to cool completely.
5. Cut each cake horizontally into two layers. Place bottom layer on a serving plate; spread with 1 cup filling. Repeat layers four times. Top with remaining cake layer.
6. Spread whipped topping over top and sides of cake. Garnish with hazelnuts and shaved chocolate if desired. Refrigerate until serving. Refrigerate leftovers.
PER SERVING *372 cal., 12 g fat (5 g sat. fat), 42 mg chol., 281 mg sodium, 57 g carb., 1 g fiber, 9 g pro.*

RICOTTA NUT TORTE

⬆ *MAKEOVER* / Calories: **372** / Fat: **12 g**
TRADITIONAL / Calories: **629** / Fat: **35 g**

WHAT WE DID To cut a significant amount of fat, we started by using reduced-fat ricotta instead of full fat and reduced the amount of pecans. Next we replaced a portion of the shortening with unsweetened applesauce and cut back on sugar. Eggs went down from three to two and fat-free milk took the place of whole. For the frosting, we chose a reduced-fat whipped topping instead of heavy whipping cream and confectioners' sugar.

MARBLED ORANGE FUDGE

F S C
Marbled Orange Fudge

Packed with orange flavor, marshmallow creme and white chocolate chips, this makeover is like eating an orange Creamsicle ice cream bar in amazing fudge form.

—JANA MOSES WEST LINN, OR

PREP: 30 MIN. + CHILLING
MAKES: ABOUT 2½ POUNDS

- 2½ cups sugar
- ⅔ cup evaporated milk
- ½ cup butter, cubed
- 1 package (10 to 12 ounces) white baking chips
- 1 jar (7 ounces) marshmallow creme
- 3 teaspoons orange extract
- 12 drops yellow food coloring
- 9 drops red food coloring

1. Line a 13-in. x 9-in. pan with foil and coat with cooking spray; set aside. In a small heavy saucepan, combine the sugar, evaporated milk and butter. Cook and stir over low heat until sugar is dissolved. Bring to a boil; cook and stir for 4 minutes. Remove from the heat; stir in chips and marshmallow creme until smooth.

2. Remove 1 cup and set aside. Add extract and food coloring to the remaining mixture; stir until blended. Pour into prepared pan. Pour reserved marshmallow mixture over the top; cut through mixture with a knife to swirl. Cover and refrigerate until set.

3. Using foil, lift fudge out of pan. Discard foil; cut fudge into 1-in. squares. Store in an airtight container in the refrigerator.

PER SERVING *45 cal., 2 g fat (1 g sat. fat), 3 mg chol., 10 mg sodium, 7 g carb., 0 fiber, trace pro.* **Diabetic Exchange:** *½ starch.*

⟶ **MAKEOVER** / Calories: **45** / Fat: **2 g** / Sat. Fat: **1 g** / Chol.: **3 mg**

TRADITIONAL / Calories: **109** / Fat: **3 g** / Sat. Fat: **2 g** / Chol.: **7 mg**

WHAT WE DID To cut calories by nearly 20 percent and fat by one third, we started by reducing the amount of sugar by ½ cup. We were able to replace the heavy cream without sacrificing texture by using evaporated milk, and we reduced the butter by half of a stick with no detectable difference in taste.

Coconut Cream Pie

Coconut Cream Pie is a dessert I can't live without, but it needed help with fat, cholesterol and calories. I want to learn how to keep all the yummy coconut while losing a lot of the bad stuff.

—**DIDI DESJARDINS** DARTMOUTH, MA

PREP: 35 MIN. • **BAKE:** 15 MIN. + CHILLING
MAKES: 8 SERVINGS

- 1 **cup sugar, divided**
- ⅓ **cup all-purpose flour**
  Dash salt
- 3 **cups fat-free milk**
- 2 **egg yolks, lightly beaten**
- 1¼ **cups flaked coconut, divided**
- 1 **teaspoon vanilla extract**
- ½ **teaspoon coconut extract**
- 1 **reduced-fat graham cracker crust**
  (8 inches)
- 1 **tablespoon cornstarch**
- ½ **cup water**
- 3 **egg whites**

1. In a large saucepan, mix ⅔ cup sugar, flour and salt. Stir in milk until smooth. Cook and stir over medium-high heat until thickened and bubbly. Remove from heat. Stir a small amount of hot filling into egg yolks; return all to the pan, stirring constantly. Bring to a gentle boil; cook and stir for 2 minutes. Remove from heat; stir in ¾ cup coconut and extracts.

2. Place crust on a baking sheet; add filling and set aside.

3. For meringue, combine cornstarch and remaining sugar in a small saucepan. Stir in water until smooth. Bring to a boil over medium heat, stirring constantly. Cook and stir for 2 minutes or until thickened and clear. In a bowl, beat egg whites until soft peaks form. Pour hot sugar mixture in a slow, steady stream into egg whites, beating constantly until stiff peaks form.

4. Spread meringue over hot filling, sealing edges to crust. Sprinkle with remaining coconut. Bake at 350° for 15-20 minutes or until meringue is golden brown. Cool on a wire rack. Refrigerate until chilled.

COCONUT CREAM PIE

PER SERVING *350 cal., 9 g fat (6 g sat. fat), 53 mg chol., 213 mg sodium, 59 g carb., 1 g fiber, 7 g pro.*

⚡ *MAKEOVER* / Calories: **350** / Fat: **9 g** / Chol.: **53 mg**

TRADITIONAL / Calories: **441** / Fat: **18 g** / Chol.: **123 mg**

WHAT WE DID Instead of a homemade pastry crust with 6 tablespoons of shortening, we substituted a store-bought, reduced-fat graham cracker crust, slashing 60 calories and 6 grams of fat per serving. We eliminated 2 egg yolks from the filling, cutting 51 mg of cholesterol. Finally, we replaced 2 percent milk with fat-free for a savings of 14 calories and 2 grams of fat per serving.

CREAMY MACARONI AND CHEESE

Creamy Macaroni and Cheese

Mac and cheese is just about the homiest dish around, but the fat and calories that come with it are not so necessary. Bring on this captivatingly creamy makeover!

—DARCIE ZERNIAK ONTARIO, NY

PREP: 20 MIN. • **BAKE:** 35 MIN.
MAKES: 7 SERVINGS

- 2 cups uncooked elbow macaroni
- ¼ cup butter, cubed
- ⅓ cup all-purpose flour
- 1½ cups fat-free milk
- ¼ cup reduced-sodium chicken broth
- 1 cup (8 ounces) fat-free sour cream
- ½ pound reduced-fat process cheese (Velveeta), cubed
- ¼ cup grated Parmesan cheese
- ½ teaspoon ground mustard
- ½ teaspoon pepper
- 2 cups (8 ounces) shredded reduced-fat cheddar cheese
  Minced chives, optional

1. Cook the macaroni according to package directions. Meanwhile, in a large saucepan, melt butter. Stir in flour until smooth. Gradually add milk and broth. Bring to a boil; cook and stir for 2 minutes or until thickened.
2. Reduce heat; stir in the sour cream, process cheese, Parmesan, mustard and pepper until smooth.
3. Drain macaroni; stir in cheddar cheese. Transfer to a 13-in. x 9-in. baking dish coated with cooking spray. Add cream sauce and mix well. Bake, uncovered, at 350° for 35-40 minutes or until bubbly. Sprinkle with the chives if desired.
PER SERVING *394 cal., 18 g fat (11 g sat. fat), 61 mg chol., 842 mg sodium, 37 g carb., 1 g fiber, 23 g pro.*

↗ *MAKEOVER* /	Calories: **394** /	Fat: **18 g** /	Sat. Fat: **11 g** /	Chol.: **61 mg**
TRADITIONAL /	Calories: **557** /	Fat: **38 g** /	Sat. Fat: **25 g** /	Chol.: **125 mg**

WHAT WE DID We decreased the amount of butter from ½ cup to ¼ cup to cut fat and calories. Using fat-free milk and sour cream keeps the creamy texture without added fat. For the cheese, we used reduced-fat shredded cheddar and reduced-fat Velveeta to make it even lighter.

Shrimp and Grits

I've tried over 25 recipes for Shrimp and Grits, and this is the best. After being lightened up to cut sodium and fat, it's still rich and smooth. This Southern tradition can be part of a healthy dinner rotation.

—**LIZABETH ELVINGTON** DILLON, SC

PREP: 30 MIN. • **COOK:** 15 MIN.
MAKES: 4 SERVINGS

- 1 can (14½ ounces) plus ½ cup reduced-sodium chicken broth, divided
- 2 cups water
- ¾ cup fat-free half-and-half
- 1 cup uncooked old-fashioned grits
- 2 center-cut bacon strips
- ¼ cup all-purpose flour
- ¼ teaspoon pepper
- 1 pound uncooked medium shrimp, peeled and deveined
- 1 cup sliced fresh mushrooms
- 4 green onions, chopped
- 2 garlic cloves, minced
- 2 tablespoons lemon juice
- ¾ teaspoon hot pepper sauce, divided
- ⅓ cup shredded sharp cheddar cheese
- ¼ cup grated Parmesan cheese
- 2 tablespoons reduced-fat butter
- ¼ teaspoon white pepper

1. In a large heavy saucepan, bring the can of broth, water and half-and-half to a boil. Slowly whisk in the grits. Reduce heat; cover and simmer for 15-20 minutes or until thickened, stirring occasionally.
2. Meanwhile, in a large nonstick skillet, cook bacon over medium heat until crisp. Remove to paper towels; drain, reserving drippings. Crumble bacon and set aside.
3. In a large resealable plastic bag, combine flour and pepper. Add shrimp, a few at a time, and shake to

SHRIMP AND GRITS

coat; set aside.
4. Saute mushrooms in the bacon drippings until tender. Add the onions, garlic and shrimp; cook and stir until shrimp turn pink. Stir in the lemon juice, ¼ teaspoon pepper sauce and remaining broth.
5. Stir the cheeses, butter, white pepper and remaining pepper sauce into the grits. Serve with shrimp mixture. Top with reserved bacon.
NOTE *This recipe was tested with Land O'Lakes light stick butter.*
PER SERVING *423 cal., 12 g fat (6 g sat. fat), 165 mg chol., 784 mg sodium, 46 g carb., 2 g fiber, 32 g pro.*

⬀ MAKEOVER	Cal.: 423	Fat: 12 g	Sat. Fat: 6 g	Sodium: 784 mg
TRADITIONAL	Cal.: 552	Fat: 25 g	Sat. Fat: 14 g	Sodium: 1,611 mg

WHAT WE DID The original's sodium and saturated fat were over the top. We started by decreasing the amount of cheese and using sharp cheddar for more flavor. We then eliminated added salt and used reduced-sodium chicken broth for a total savings of more than 800 mg per serving! To keep the creaminess in the grits but cut down on saturated fat, we replaced full-fat half-and-half with fat-free.

CORN PUDDING

Corn Pudding

My mother-in-law, Hazel, made this recipe for my husband when he was growing up. I learned how to make it, but with all that butter and cheese I knew it was high in fat and calories. This makeover version is just as comforting and one we'll serve for generations to come.

—ARLENE SPENCER OCONOMOWOC, WI

PREP: 15 MIN. • **BAKE:** 50 MIN.
MAKES: 12 SERVINGS

⅓ cup all-purpose flour
2 tablespoons sugar
1 cup fat-free milk
¾ cup egg substitute
1 tablespoon butter, melted
1 teaspoon salt
8 cups frozen corn, thawed
1 can (14¾ ounces) cream-style corn
1 cup (4 ounces) shredded sharp cheddar cheese

1. In a large bowl, combine flour and sugar. Whisk in milk, egg substitute, butter and salt. Stir in the corn, cream-style corn and cheese.
2. Pour into a 13-in. x 9-in. baking dish coated with cooking spray. Bake, uncovered, at 375° for 50-55 minutes or until a knife inserted near the center comes out clean.
PER SERVING *197 cal., 5 g fat (3 g sat. fat), 13 mg chol., 403 mg sodium, 35 g carb., 3 g fiber, 8 g pro.* **Diabetic Exchanges:** *2 starch, 1 fat.*

↗ *MAKEOVER* / Cal.: **197** / Fat: **5 g** / Chol.: **13 mg** / Sodium: **403 mg**

TRADITIONAL / Cal.: **285** / Fat: **10 g** / Chol.: **93 mg** / Sodium: **915 mg**

WHAT WE DID Cutting the butter in half, reducing the cheese by a third and substituting skim milk for whole milk significantly lowered the fat without sacrificing taste or texture. Replacing whole eggs with egg substitute slashed even more calories, and 80 mg cholesterol per serving. Finally, adding a can of creamed corn boosted the pudding's creaminess and enhanced the overall flavor.

Peanut Butter Bars

Peanut butter bars are a family favorite, but I needed to reduce the fat and sugar without compromising the tasty combination of chocolate and peanut butter. This lightened up adaptation is just as luscious as the original!

—LORI STEVENS RIVERTON, UTAH

PREP: 20 MIN. + CHILLING
BAKE: 20 MIN. + COOLING
MAKES: 3 DOZEN

- 1¾ cups reduced-fat creamy peanut butter, divided
- ⅓ cup butter, softened
- 1 cup packed brown sugar
- ¾ cup sugar
- 2 eggs
- ½ cup unsweetened applesauce
- 1 teaspoon vanilla extract
- 2 cups all-purpose flour
- 2 cups quick-cooking oats
- 1 teaspoon baking soda

FROSTING
- 4½ cups confectioners' sugar
- ⅓ cup fat-free milk
- ¼ cup baking cocoa
- ¼ cup butter, softened
- 1 teaspoon vanilla extract
- ½ teaspoon salt

1. In a large bowl, cream 1 cup peanut butter, butter, brown sugar and sugar until light and fluffy. Add eggs, one at a time, beating well after each addition. Beat in the applesauce and vanilla. Combine the flour, oats and baking soda; gradually add to the creamed mixture and mix well (batter will be thick).

2. Spread into a 15-in. x 10-in. x 1-in. baking pan coated with cooking spray. Bake at 350° for 18-22 minutes or until lightly browned. Cool on a wire rack for 10 minutes; spread with the remaining peanut butter. Cool to room temperature, then refrigerate for 30 minutes.

3. In a large bowl, beat frosting ingredients until light and fluffy. Spread over the peanut butter layer. Cut into bars.

PER SERVING *237 cal., 8 g fat (3 g sat. fat), 20 mg chol., 165 mg sodium, 38 g carb., 2 g fiber, 5 g pro.*

PEANUT BUTTER BARS

top tip

Fruit Purees

Applesauce is often used as a healthy stand-in for some of the oil or butter in a recipe. But other fruit, such as mashed bananas or canned pureed pears, peaches, apricots or plums, works just as well.

↗ MAKEOVER	Calories: **237**	Fat: **8 g**	Sat. Fat: **3 g**	Chol.: **20 mg**
TRADITIONAL	Calories: **321**	Fat: **16 g**	Sat. Fat: **6 g**	Chol.: **35 mg**

WHAT WE DID First we replaced some of the butter with unsweetened applesauce. Because of the natural sweetness in the applesauce, we were able to cut the amount of sugar by 25 percent. Then we substituted fat-free milk for whole in the frosting and 1¾ cups of reduced-fat peanut butter for 2½ cups of regular, saving 84 calories and 8 g fat per serving.

MAKEOVERS

BROCCOLI CHEDDAR
BRUNCH BAKE

C

Broccoli Cheddar Brunch Bake

I got this recipe from *Taste of Home* magazine years ago. It was sent in by Carol Strickland of Yuma, AZ. Looking for ways to cut calories and fat, I asked the *Taste of Home* Test Kitchen experts to help me revise the dish to make it healthier.

—**CARLA WEEKS** INDEPENDENCE, IA

PREP: 25 MIN. • **BAKE:** 40 MIN. + STANDING
MAKES: 12 SERVINGS

- 6 **tablespoons reduced-fat butter, cubed**
- 8 **cups chopped fresh broccoli**
- 1 **cup finely chopped onion**
- 6 **eggs, beaten**
- 1½ **cups egg substitute**
- 1½ **cups (6 ounces) shredded sharp cheddar cheese, divided**
- 1 **cup fat-free milk**
- 1 **cup half-and-half cream**
- 1 **teaspoon salt**
- 1 **teaspoon pepper**

1. In a Dutch oven, melt butter. Add the broccoli and onion; saute until crisp-tender. In a large bowl, combine the eggs, egg substitute, 1 cup cheese, milk, cream, salt and pepper. Stir in broccoli mixture. Pour into a 3-qt. baking dish coated with cooking spray.
2. Bake, uncovered, at 350° for 40-45 minutes or until a knife inserted near the center comes out clean. Sprinkle with remaining cheese. Let stand for 10 minutes before serving.
NOTE *This recipe was tested with Land O'Lakes light stick butter.*
PER SERVING *178 cal., 12 g fat (7 g sat. fat), 139 mg chol., 459 mg sodium, 7 g carb., 2 g fiber, 12 g pro.*

⬆ *MAKEOVER* / Calories: **178** / Fat: **12 g** / Sat. Fat: **7 g** / Chol.: **139 mg**

TRADITIONAL / Calories: **329** / Fat: **29 g** / Sat. Fat: **17 g** / Chol.: **289 mg**

WHAT WE DID Substituting reduced-fat butter for full-fat and cutting the original amount in half slashed 75 calories and 8 grams of fat per serving. Using 1 cup of half-and-half plus a cup of fat-free milk instead of 2 cups of heavy whipping cream saved 35 calories and 5 grams more of fat per serving. Replacing the dozen whole eggs with a half dozen, then making up the difference with egg substitute cut the cholesterol by more than 30 percent.

Chocolate Mint Layer Cake

I love chocolate mint cake but I know it's not good for me. Thanks for revamping my recipe without getting rid of the real whipped cream—my favorite part!

—MELISSA GLEASON SUGAR GROVE, IL

PREP: 30 MIN. • **BAKE:** 20 MIN. + CHILLING
MAKES: 16 SERVINGS

- ¼ cup butter, softened
- 1¼ cups sugar
- 2 eggs
- 1 container (2¼ ounces) prune baby food
- 1 teaspoon vanilla extract
- 1 cup all-purpose flour
- ¾ cup cake flour
- ½ cup baking cocoa
- 1 teaspoon baking soda
- ½ teaspoon salt
- 1¼ cups buttermilk

FILLING
- 1 cup heavy whipping cream
- 3 tablespoons confectioners' sugar
- ⅛ teaspoon mint extract
- 3 to 4 drops green food coloring, optional

ICING
- 1 cup (6 ounces) semisweet chocolate chips, melted and cooled
- ⅔ cup fat-free sour cream
- 1 teaspoon vanilla extract

1. Line two 9-in. round baking pans with waxed paper. Coat pans with cooking spray and sprinkle with flour; set aside.

2. In a large bowl, beat butter and sugar until crumbly, about 2 minutes. Add eggs, one at a time, beating well after each addition. Beat in baby food and vanilla. Combine the flours, cocoa, baking soda and salt; add to butter mixture alternately with buttermilk.

CHOCOLATE MINT
LAYER CAKE

3. Pour into prepared pans. Bake at 350° for 20-25 minutes or until a toothpick inserted near the center comes out clean. Cool for 10 minutes before removing from pans to wire racks to cool completely.

4. For filling, in a small bowl, beat the cream until it begins to thicken. Add confectioners' sugar and extract; beat until stiff peaks form. Beat in food coloring if desired. Place one cake layer on a serving plate; spread with filling. Top with second cake layer.

5. For icing, in a small bowl, combine the cooled chocolate, sour cream and vanilla. Spread over top and sides of cake. Refrigerate for at least 2 hours before serving.

PER SERVING *283 cal., 13 g fat (7 g sat. fat), 57 mg chol., 217 mg sodium, 40 g carb., 2 g fiber, 5 g pro.*

⬈ *MAKEOVER* / Calories: **283** / Fat: **13 g** / Chol.: **57 mg**
TRADITIONAL / Calories: **423** / Fat: **23 g** / Chol.: **85 mg**

WHAT WE DID We used prune baby food (other fruit purees like applesauce can be substituted) to replace some of the butter. Then we decreased the amount of sugar and eggs to cut calories and cholesterol. Using baking cocoa instead of melted unsweetened chocolate saved about 3.5 grams of fat per serving. To cut even more fat, we used buttermilk instead of whole milk.

POPPY SEED CHICKEN

Poppy Seed Chicken

Poppy Seed Chicken is traditionally a Southern dish and an amazingly delicious comfort food. But how do you make an ooey-gooey casserole filled with sour cream, cheese and butter into a light entree? This makeover dish proves it can be done.

—**CAROLYN KEESE** SENECA, SC

PREP: 10 MIN. • **BAKE:** 30 MIN.
MAKES: 6 SERVINGS

- 3 cups cubed cooked chicken breast
- 2 cans (10¾ ounces each) reduced-fat reduced-sodium condensed cream of chicken soup, undiluted
- 1 cup (8 ounces) reduced-fat sour cream
- 2 teaspoons poppy seeds
- 1 cup crushed reduced-fat butter-flavored crackers (about 25 crackers)
- 3 tablespoons reduced-fat butter, melted
- ⅓ cup grated Parmesan cheese

1. In a large bowl, combine the chicken, soup, sour cream and poppy seeds. In a small bowl, combine cracker crumbs and butter; set aside ½ cup for topping. Stir remaining crumbs into chicken mixture.

2. Transfer to an 11-in. x 7-in. baking dish coated with cooking spray. Top with reserved crumbs; sprinkle with cheese. Bake, uncovered, at 350° for 30-35 minutes or until bubbly.

PER SERVING *332 cal., 13 g fat (6 g sat. fat), 87 mg chol., 705 mg sodium, 23 g carb., trace fiber, 27 g pro.*

⊙ **MAKEOVER** / Cal.: **332** / Fat: **13 g** / Chol.: **87 mg** / Sodium: **705 mg**

TRADITIONAL / Cal.: **648** / Fat: **42 g** / Chol.: **138 mg** / Sodium: **1,260 mg**

WHAT WE DID The original recipe was very saucy, which meant we could cut down on the amount of butter and sour cream and replace them with reduced-fat versions. Using reduced-fat reduced-sodium soup helped us trim more fat and lower the total amount of sodium per serving by more than 500 mg. Finally, instead of using whole chicken, we chose chicken breast meat as a leaner option.

Lemon Streusel Muffins

These delightful muffins mimic the great coffee shop treats, but they use reduced-fat lemon yogurt and egg whites instead of whole eggs, making them lower in calories and fat!

—**CALVIN HWANG** LA MESA, CA

PREP: 20 MIN. • **BAKE:** 15 MIN.
MAKES: 1 DOZEN

- ¼ cup butter, softened
- ¾ cup sugar
- 2 egg yolks
- 1 teaspoon grated lemon peel
- 1 cup cake flour
- 1 cup all-purpose flour
- 1 teaspoon baking powder
- ½ teaspoon salt
- ¼ teaspoon baking soda
- ½ cup lemon juice
- ½ cup reduced-fat lemon yogurt
- 4 egg whites

STREUSEL
- 2 tablespoons all-purpose flour
- 2 tablespoons brown sugar
- ¼ teaspoon ground nutmeg
- 1 tablespoon cold butter
- ¼ cup chopped walnuts

1. In a large bowl, beat butter and sugar until crumbly. Beat in egg yolks and lemon peel. Combine the flours, baking powder, salt and baking soda; add to the butter mixture alternately with lemon juice and yogurt.

2. In a small bowl with clean beaters, beat egg whites until stiff peaks form. Fold into batter. Coat muffin cups with cooking spray or use paper liners; fill two-thirds full with batter.

3. For streusel, combine the flour, brown sugar and nutmeg; cut in butter until crumbly. Stir in walnuts.

Sprinkle over muffins. Bake at 375° for 15-20 minutes or until a toothpick inserted in the center comes out clean. Cool for 5 minutes before removing from pan to a wire rack.

PER SERVING *226 cal., 7 g fat (3 g sat. fat), 47 mg chol., 218 mg sodium, 36 g carb., 1 g fiber, 5 g pro.*

LEMON STREUSEL MUFFINS

top tip — Baking with Yogurt

Reduced-fat or fat-free yogurt can also replace milk in recipes for a creamier result. Simply substitute ¼ of the liquid with yogurt.

⬈ MAKEOVER	Calories: **226**	Fat: **7 g**	Sat. Fat: **3 g**	Chol.: **47 mg**
TRADITIONAL	Calories: **330**	Fat: **19 g**	Sat. Fat: **10 g**	Chol.: **111 mg**

WHAT WE DID The original recipe called for more than one cup of butter! We found that using ¼ cup instead worked just fine, and saved 92 calories and 10 grams of fat per muffin. However, to keep the muffins from drying out, we added reduced-fat lemon yogurt. We then cut the sugar down by a quarter without missing sweetness and removed 2 egg yolks to trim cholesterol.

CAJUN CHICKEN PASTA

Cajun Chicken Pasta

The first time I tasted this, I just had to have the recipe. But when I read over the ingredients, I knew it was loaded with fat and calories. So I sent the recipe to the *Taste of Home* Test Kitchen for a makeover. Now this rich and creamy pasta is a healthier dinnertime favorite.

—**HEATHER PRIVRATSKY** GREENFIELD, WI

PREP: 20 MIN. • **COOK:** 20 MIN.
MAKES: 6 SERVINGS

- 6 **boneless skinless chicken breast halves (4 ounces each)**
- 2 **tablespoons Cajun seasoning, divided**
- 2¼ **cups uncooked penne pasta**
- 1 **large onion, chopped**
- 2 **teaspoons olive oil**
- 2 **garlic cloves, minced**
- 1 **can (28 ounces) crushed tomatoes, drained**
- ¼ **teaspoon pepper**
- 1½ **cups half-and-half cream**

1. Rub chicken with 1 tablespoon Cajun seasoning. Moisten a paper towel with cooking oil; using long-handled tongs, lightly coat the grill rack. Grill chicken, covered, over medium heat or broil 4 in. from the heat for 4-7 minutes on each side or until a thermometer reads 165°; keep warm.

2. Meanwhile, in a large saucepan, cook pasta according to package directions. In a Dutch oven coated with cooking spray, saute onion in oil until crisp-tender. Add garlic and remaining Cajun seasoning; cook 1 minute longer. Stir in tomatoes and pepper.

3. Drain pasta; add to the onion mixture. Stir in cream; heat through (do not boil). Serve chicken with pasta.

PER SERVING *421 cal., 12 g fat (5 g sat. fat), 93 mg chol., 803 mg sodium, 45 g carb., 4 g fiber, 33 g pro.*

⊘ *MAKEOVER* / Calories: **421** / Fat: **12 g** / Sat. Fat: **5 g** / Chol.: **93 mg**

TRADITIONAL / Calories: **848** / Fat: **42 g** / Sat. Fat: **23 g** / Chol.: **186 mg**

WHAT WE DID Sauteing the onion and garlic in 2 teaspoons of olive oil rather than 3 tablespoons of butter cut 37 calories and 4 grams of fat per serving. Using 1½ cups of half-and-half instead of 2 cups of heavy whipping cream saved another 194 calories and 23 grams of fat. Cutting the Cajun seasoning in half reduced the sodium in each serving by a whopping 40 percent, but kept all the spicy flavor.

Frosted Banana Bars

I've made these banana bars many times, always with favorable comments and requests for the recipe. I'd love to find a way to reduce the calories and fat while keeping the flavor we all love so much.

—**SUSAN STUFF** MERCERSBURG, PA

PREP: 15 MIN. • **BAKE:** 20 MIN. + COOLING
MAKES: 3 DOZEN

- 3 tablespoons butter, softened
- 1½ cups sugar
- 2 eggs
- 1½ cups mashed ripe bananas (about 3 medium)
- ¼ cup unsweetened applesauce
- 1 teaspoon vanilla extract
- 2 cups all-purpose flour
- 1 teaspoon baking soda
  Dash salt

FROSTING

- 1 package (8 ounces) reduced-fat cream cheese
- ⅓ cup butter, softened
- 3 cups confectioners' sugar
- 2 teaspoons vanilla extract

1. In a large bowl, beat butter and sugar until crumbly, about 2 minutes. Add eggs, one at a time, beating well after each addition. Beat in the bananas, applesauce and vanilla. Combine the flour, baking soda and salt; stir into butter mixture just until blended.

2. Transfer to a 15-in. x 10-in. x 1-in. baking pan coated with cooking spray. Bake at 350° for 20-25 minutes or until a toothpick inserted near the center comes out clean. Cool in pan on a wire rack.

FROSTED BANANA BARS

3. For frosting, in a small bowl, beat cream cheese and butter until fluffy. Add confectioners' sugar and vanilla; beat until smooth. Frost the bars. Store in the refrigerator.

PER SERVING *149 cal., 4 g fat (3 g sat. fat), 23 mg chol., 89 mg sodium, 26 g carb., trace fiber, 2 g pro.* **Diabetic Exchanges:** *2 starch, 1 fat.*

⬆ MAKEOVER	Calories: **149**	Fat: **4 g**	Chol.: **23 mg**
TRADITIONAL	Calories: **202**	Fat: **8 g**	Chol.: **38 mg**

WHAT WE DID Using applesauce to replace some of the oil not only cut fat, but its flavor nicely complemented the bananas. Reducing the amount of sugar and eliminating one of the eggs also helped to lower calories and fat without sacrificing texture. For the frosting, reduced-fat cream cheese and less butter yielded a sweet and creamy topping that could have been mistaken for the original, only minus a significant percentage of fat.

ALMOND TORTE
PAGE 269

**JENNIFER RAFFERTY'S
CHOCOLATE CHIP CREAM CHEESE
BARS** *PAGE 275*

**JUDY SCHUT'S
RHUBARB-PINEAPPLE CRISP**
PAGE 276

**ANNE HENRY'S
CREAMY LEMON CHEESECAKE**
PAGE 279

Cakes, Pies & More

We wouldn't dream of publishing a cookbook without **our favorite cakes and pies**.
These lightened-up desserts are **among the most delicious**—right down to the last crumb.

Ⓢ Almond Torte

Reduced-fat sour cream, egg whites and applesauce lighten up this gorgeous torte, while a creamy custard filling provides irresistible richness. This flavor combo never goes out of season.

—**KATHY OLSEN** MARLBOROUGH, NH

PREP: 45 MIN. + CHILLING
BAKE: 25 MIN. + COOLING
MAKES: 16 SERVINGS

- ⅓ **cup sugar**
- 1 **tablespoon cornstarch**
- ½ **cup reduced-fat sour cream**
- 3 **egg yolks**
- 1 **tablespoon butter**
- 1 **teaspoon vanilla extract**
- ½ **teaspoon almond extract**

CAKE

- 4 **egg whites**
- ⅓ **cup butter, softened**
- 1½ **cups sugar, divided**
- 2 **egg yolks**
- ⅓ **cup fat-free milk**
- ¼ **cup unsweetened applesauce**
- 1 **teaspoon vanilla extract**
- 1 **cup cake flour**
- 1 **teaspoon baking powder**
- ⅛ **teaspoon salt**
- ½ **cup sliced almonds**
- ½ **teaspoon ground cinnamon**

1. In a double boiler or metal bowl over simmering water, constantly whisk the sugar, cornstarch, sour cream and egg yolks until mixture reaches 160° or is thick enough to coat the back of a spoon.

2. Remove from the heat; stir in butter and extracts until blended. Press waxed paper onto surface of custard. Refrigerate for several hours or overnight.

3. Place egg whites in a large bowl; let stand at room temperature for 30 minutes. Line two 8-in. round baking pans with waxed paper. Coat sides and paper with cooking spray; sprinkle with flour and set aside.

4. In a large bowl, beat butter and ½ cup sugar until blended, about 2 minutes. Add egg yolks; mix well. Beat in the milk, applesauce and vanilla (mixture may appear curdled). Combine the flour, baking powder and salt; add to butter mixture. Transfer to prepared pans; set aside.

5. Using clean beaters, beat egg whites on medium speed until soft peaks form. Gradually beat in remaining sugar, 2 tablespoons at a time, on high until stiff glossy peaks form and sugar is dissolved. Spread evenly over batter; sprinkle with almonds and cinnamon.

6. Bake at 350° for 25-30 minutes or until meringue is lightly browned. Cool in pans on wire racks for 10 minutes (meringue will crack). Loosen edges of cakes from pans with a knife. Using two large spatulas, carefully remove one cake to a serving plate, meringue side up; remove remaining cake to a wire rack, meringue side up. Cool cakes completely.

7. Carefully spread custard over cake on serving plate; top with remaining cake. Store in the refrigerator.

PER SERVING *215 cal., 8 g fat (4 g sat. fat), 79 mg chol., 99 mg sodium, 32 g carb., 1 g fiber, 4 g pro.* **Diabetic Exchanges:** *2 starch, 1 fat.*

 **Yolks & Whites**

To store unbroken egg yolks, place in a container and cover with water. Tightly cover and refrigerate for up to 4 days. Refrigerate egg whites in a tightly covered container for up to 4 days. Freeze egg whites in a tightly covered container for up to 1 year. To freeze egg yolks: for each ¼ cup of egg yolk, beat the yolks with ⅛ teaspoon salt or 1½ teaspoons corn syrup. Place in a tightly covered container for up to 1 year. Use the salted yolks in savory dishes and corn-syrup yolks in sweet recipes.

Quick Chocolate Snack Cake

S

I recently learned I'm diabetic. I never thought I'd be able to curb my sweet tooth until I made these cakey bars.

—ANGELA OELSCHLAEGER
TONGANOXIE, KS

PREP: 25 MIN. • **BAKE:** 20 MIN. + COOLING
MAKES: 18 SERVINGS

- ⅓ cup prune baby food or unsweetened applesauce
- 1 cup sugar
- ½ cup sugar blend
- ½ cup egg substitute
- ½ cup water
- ⅓ cup canola oil
- 1 teaspoon vanilla extract
- ¾ cup baking cocoa
- ⅔ cup all-purpose flour
- ⅔ cup whole wheat pastry flour
- ½ teaspoon baking soda
- ¼ teaspoon salt
- ½ cup semisweet chocolate chips

1. In a large bowl, beat the baby food, sugar, sugar blend, egg substitute, water, oil and vanilla until well blended. Combine the cocoa, flours, baking soda and salt; gradually beat into prune mixture until blended. Transfer to a 13-in. x 9-in. baking dish coated with cooking spray.

2. Bake at 350° for 20-25 minutes or until a toothpick inserted near the center comes out clean. Sprinkle with chips. Cool on a wire rack.

NOTE *This recipe was tested with Splenda sugar blend.*

PER SERVING *170 cal., 6 g fat (1 g sat. fat), 0 chol., 82 mg sodium, 29 g carb., 1 g fiber, 2 g pro.* **Diabetic Exchanges: 2 starch, 1 fat.**

Lactose-Free Chocolate Chip Cookies

S

Crispy edges and soft centers make these cookies irresistible. Refrigerating the dough one hour before baking will help the cookies maintain their shape and prevent them from spreading too much.

—SARAH ANN MANTHE BROOKFIELD, WI

PREP: 15 MIN. + CHILLING
BAKE: 15 MIN./BATCH
MAKES: 3 DOZEN

- 1 cup maple syrup
- ¾ cup sugar
- ½ cup canola oil
- ½ cup unsweetened applesauce
- 3½ teaspoons vanilla extract
- ¾ teaspoon molasses
- 3 cups all-purpose flour
- 3 teaspoons baking powder
- 1½ teaspoons baking soda
- ¾ teaspoon salt
- 1 package (10 ounces) dairy-free semisweet chocolate chips

1. In a large bowl, beat the syrup, sugar, oil, applesauce, vanilla and molasses until well blended. Combine the flour, baking powder, baking soda and salt; gradually add to syrup mixture and mix well. Stir in chocolate chips. Cover and refrigerate for 1 hour.

2. Drop by heaping tablespoonfuls 2 in. apart onto baking sheets lightly coated with cooking spray. Bake at 350° for 11-13 minutes or until the edges are lightly browned. Remove to wire racks.

NOTE *This recipe was tested with Enjoy Life semisweet chocolate chips.*

PER SERVING *147 cal., 6 g fat (2 g sat. fat), 0 chol., 136 mg sodium, 23 g carb., 1 g fiber, 2 g pro.* **Diabetic Exchanges: 1½ starch, 1 fat.**

QUICK CHOCOLATE SNACK CAKE

Cherry-Almond Streusel Tart

Brimming with fresh cherries and topped with a crunchy streusel, this tempting tart is a great way to end dinner on a sweet note. It's fast to fix, looks elegant and tastes delicious.

—**MARION LEE** MOUNT HOPE, ON

PREP: 20 MIN. • **BAKE:** 30 MIN. + COOLING
MAKES: 8 SERVINGS

> Pastry for single-crust pie
> (9 inches)
⅔ cup sugar
3 tablespoons cornstarch
> Dash salt
4 cups fresh tart cherries, pitted or frozen pitted tart cherries, thawed
⅛ teaspoon almond extract

TOPPING

¼ cup quick-cooking oats
3 tablespoons all-purpose flour
2 tablespoons brown sugar
1 tablespoon slivered almonds
2 tablespoons cold butter

1. Press pastry onto the bottom and up the sides of an ungreased 9-in. fluted tart pan with removable bottom; trim edges.
2. In a large saucepan, combine the sugar, cornstarch and salt. Stir in cherries; bring to a boil over medium heat, stirring constantly. Cook and stir for 1-2 minutes or until thickened. Remove from the heat; stir in extract. Pour into crust.
3. For topping, combine the oats, flour, brown sugar and almonds. Cut in butter until mixture resembles coarse crumbs. Sprinkle over filling. Bake at 350° for 30-35 minutes or until topping is golden brown. Cool on a wire rack.
PER SERVING *298 cal., 11 g fat (5 g sat. fat), 13 mg chol., 143 mg sodium, 49 g carb., 2 g fiber, 3 g pro.*

CHERRY-ALMOND STREUSEL TART

S C
Peanut Butter Granola Mini Bars

Kids and adults will flip over this wonderful, oaty sweet snack. With honey, peanut butter, brown sugar and two types of chips, what's not to love? All at less than 100 calories.

—**VIVIAN LEVINE** SUMMERFIELD, FL

PREP: 20 MIN. • **BAKE:** 15 MIN. + COOLING
MAKES: 3 DOZEN

½ cup reduced-fat creamy peanut butter
⅓ cup honey
1 egg
2 tablespoons canola oil
1 teaspoon vanilla extract
3½ cups old-fashioned oats
½ cup packed brown sugar
¾ teaspoon salt
⅓ cup peanut butter chips
⅓ cup miniature semisweet chocolate chips

1. In a large bowl, beat the peanut butter, honey, egg, oil and vanilla until blended. Combine the oats, brown sugar and salt; add to the peanut butter mixture and mix well. Stir in chips. (Batter will be sticky.)
2. Transfer to a 13-in. x 9-in. baking dish coated with cooking spray. Bake at 350° for 12-15 minutes or until set and edges are lightly browned. Cool on a wire rack. Cut into bars.
PER SERVING *93 cal., 4 g fat (1 g sat. fat), 6 mg chol., 76 mg sodium, 14 g carb., 1 g fiber, 3 g pro.* **Diabetic Exchanges:** *1 starch, 1 fat.*

Berry Patch Pie

Enjoy a gorgeous, made-for-summer pie with this mouthwatering recipe. Each bite bursts with sweet, juicy berries.

—TASTE OF HOME TEST KITCHEN

PREP: 30 MIN. + COOLING
MAKES: 8 SERVINGS

Pastry for single-crust pie (9 inches)
¾ cup sugar
¼ cup cornstarch
2 cups halved fresh strawberries
1½ cups fresh raspberries
1 cup fresh blackberries
1 cup fresh blueberries
1 tablespoon lemon juice

1. On a lightly floured surface, unroll pastry. Transfer to a 9-in. pie plate. Trim pastry to ½ in. beyond edge of plate; flute edges. Line unpricked pastry with a double thickness of heavy-duty foil. Bake at 450° for 8 minutes. Remove foil; bake 5-7 minutes longer or until golden brown. Cool on a wire rack.
2. Meanwhile, in a large saucepan, combine sugar and cornstarch. Stir in berries and lemon juice. Cook, stirring occasionally, over medium heat until mixture just comes to a boil; pour into prepared crust. Cool completely on a wire rack.
PER SERVING 250 cal., 7 g fat (3 g sat. fat), 5 mg chol., 101 mg sodium, 46 g carb., 4 g fiber, 2 g pro.

BERRY PATCH PIE

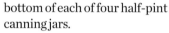

CRAN-ORANGE PIE IN A JAR

Cran-Orange Pie in a Jar

These individual pudding pies in a jar definitely don't skimp on filling, and they make a delicious craft activity for kids.

—TASTE OF HOME TEST KITCHEN

PREP: 20 MIN. + CHILLING
MAKES: 4 SERVINGS

1 cup graham cracker crumbs
2 tablespoons butter, melted
2 cups cold fat-free milk
1 package (1 ounce) sugar-free instant white chocolate pudding mix
½ teaspoon grated orange peel
½ cup whole-berry cranberry sauce

1. In a small bowl, combine cracker crumbs and butter. Press into the bottom of each of four half-pint canning jars.
2. In another bowl, whisk milk and pudding mix for 2 minutes. Stir in orange peel. Let stand for 2 minutes or until soft-set. Spoon over crusts. Top with cranberry sauce. Cover and refrigerate for at least 1 hour.
PER SERVING 253 cal., 8 g fat (4 g sat. fat), 18 mg chol., 439 mg sodium, 40 g carb., 1 g fiber, 6 g pro.

top tip Pie, Your Way

Using the Cran-Orange Pie in a Jar recipe and method as a base, experiment with different combinations of sugar-free puddings and fruit or jam toppings. Pistachio pudding and cherries? Butterscotch pudding with bananas? Lemon pudding with strawberry jam? Oh, the possibilities!

Pumpkin Pie Cupcakes

My family always asks for these cupcakes once fall starts. We just love the flavors of cinnamon and cloves.
—MELISSA STORY TREGO, WI

PREP: 30 MIN. • **BAKE:** 15 MIN. + COOLING
MAKES: 2 DOZEN

- 1¾ cups fresh or canned pumpkin
- ¾ cup sugar
- ¾ cup packed brown sugar
- ½ cup unsweetened applesauce
- ⅓ cup canola oil
- 2 eggs
- 2 egg whites
- 2⅔ cups all-purpose flour
- 2 teaspoons baking powder
- 2 teaspoons ground cinnamon
- 1 teaspoon baking soda
- 1 teaspoon salt
- ¼ teaspoon ground nutmeg
- ¼ teaspoon ground cloves

CINNAMON-CLOVE BUTTERCREAM
- ¼ cup butter, softened
- ¼ cup shortening
- 1¾ cups confectioners' sugar
- ¼ teaspoon ground cinnamon
- ⅛ teaspoon ground cloves
- ½ cup finely chopped walnuts

1. In a large bowl, beat the pumpkin, sugars, applesauce, oil, eggs and egg whites until well blended. Combine the flour, baking powder, cinnamon, baking soda, salt, nutmeg and cloves; gradually beat into pumpkin mixture until blended.

2. Fill foil-lined muffin cups two-thirds full. Bake at 350° for 15-20 minutes or until a toothpick inserted near the center comes out clean. Cool for 10 minutes before removing from pans to wire racks to cool completely.

3. In a small bowl, beat butter and shortening until fluffy. Add the confectioners' sugar, cinnamon and cloves; beat until smooth. Spread over cupcakes; sprinkle with walnuts.

PER SERVING *229 cal., 9 g fat (2 g sat. fat), 23 mg chol., 212 mg sodium, 35 g carb., 1 g fiber, 3 g pro.*

Peanut Butter Pies

I absolutely love peanut butter, and peanut butter pie is one of my favorite desserts. But I'm a registered dietitian, so I knew just how high my original recipe was in fat and calories. I finally made up a light version that meets my expectations.
—LISA VARNER EL PASO, TX

PREP: 15 MIN. + FREEZING
MAKES: 2 PIES (8 SERVINGS EACH)

- 1 package (8 ounces) fat-free cream cheese
- ¾ cup reduced-fat creamy peanut butter
- 1 can (14 ounces) fat-free sweetened condensed milk
- 1 teaspoon vanilla extract
- 1 carton (12 ounces) frozen fat-free whipped topping, thawed
- 2 reduced-fat graham cracker crusts (8 inches)
- ¼ cup chocolate syrup
- ¼ cup finely chopped unsalted peanuts

1. In a large bowl, beat cream cheese and peanut butter until smooth. Beat in milk and vanilla until blended. Fold in whipped topping. Pour into crusts. Cover and freeze for 8 hours or overnight.

2. Remove from freezer 10 minutes before serving. Drizzle with syrup and sprinkle with peanuts. Store leftovers in the freezer.

PER SERVING *305 cal., 8 g fat (2 g sat. fat), 4 mg chol., 285 mg sodium, 47 g carb., 1 g fiber, 9 g pro.*

PUMPKIN PIE CUPCAKES

Coconut-Streusel Pear Pie

I remember my mom making this pie when I was growing up. I make several while I have fresh pears from the family tree then freeze them for later.
—PAULA HOFFMAN PLAINVIEW, NE

PREP: 20 MIN. • **BAKE:** 20 MIN. + COOLING
MAKES: 8 SERVINGS

- Pastry for single-crust pie (9 inches)
- ⅓ cup sugar
- ¼ cup all-purpose flour
- ¼ teaspoon salt
- 6 cups sliced peeled fresh pears
- 1 tablespoon lemon juice

TOPPING
- 3 tablespoons sugar
- 3 tablespoons all-purpose flour
- 4½ teaspoons cold butter
- ⅓ cup flaked coconut

1. Line a 9-in. pie plate with pastry; trim and flute edges. In a large saucepan, combine the sugar, flour and salt. Add pears and lemon juice. Cook and stir over medium heat for 4-5 minutes or until thickened. Pour into pastry.
2. For topping, in a small bowl, combine sugar and flour. Cut in butter until crumbly. Stir in coconut; sprinkle over top. Bake at 400° for 20-25 minutes or until filling is bubbly and topping is lightly browned. Cool on a wire rack.
PER SERVING *306 cal., 11 g fat (6 g sat. fat), 11 mg chol., 200 mg sodium, 52 g carb., 4 g fiber, 2 g pro.*

COCONUT-STREUSEL PEAR PIE

Wonderful Carrot Cake

To lighten up my carrot cake I use less sugar and replace some of the oil with applesauce. I also substitute wheat flour for some of the white. But in my opinion, there's no alternative for real cream cheese in the frosting.
—BRENDA RANKHORN NEW MARKET, AL

PREP: 25 MIN. • **BAKE:** 40 MIN. + COOLING
MAKES: 24 SERVINGS

- ¾ cup sugar
- ¾ cup packed brown sugar
- 3 eggs
- ½ cup canola oil
- ½ cup unsweetened applesauce
- 1 teaspoon vanilla extract
- 1½ cups all-purpose flour
- ½ cup whole wheat flour
- 2 teaspoons baking powder
- 1 teaspoon salt
- 1 teaspoon ground cinnamon
- ½ teaspoon ground allspice
- ¼ teaspoon baking soda
- 3 cups finely shredded carrots
- ½ cup chopped walnuts

FROSTING
- 3 ounces cream cheese, softened
- 1 tablespoon fat-free milk
- 1 teaspoon vanilla extract
- 2½ cups confectioners' sugar
- Dash salt

WONDERFUL CARROT CAKE

1. In a large bowl, beat the sugars, eggs, oil, applesauce and vanilla until well blended. Combine the flours, baking powder, salt, cinnamon, allspice and baking soda; gradually beat into sugar mixture until blended. Stir in carrots and walnuts.
2. Pour into a 13-in. x 9-in. baking pan coated with cooking spray. Bake at 350° for 40-45 minutes or until a toothpick inserted near the center comes out clean. Cool completely on a wire rack.
3. For frosting, in a small bowl, beat the cream cheese, milk and vanilla until fluffy. Add the confectioners' sugar and salt; beat until smooth. Spread over top of the cake. Store in the refrigerator.
PER SERVING *223 cal., 8 g fat (1 g sat. fat), 30 mg chol., 183 mg sodium, 36 g carb., 1 g fiber, 3 g pro.*

Mocha Cheesecake Bars

So many cheesecake recipes are hard to make, but these bars are easy to whip up and don't require many ingredients.

—MARY WILHELM SPARTA, WI

PREP: 30 MIN. + CHILLING
MAKES: 24 SERVINGS

- 25 reduced-fat Oreo cookies,
- 3 tablespoons fat-free hot fudge ice cream topping
- 3 tablespoons butter, melted

FILLING

- 1 envelope unflavored gelatin
- ½ cup cold strong brewed coffee
- 2 packages (8 ounces each) reduced-fat cream cheese
- ¾ cup sugar
- 1 cup (8 ounces) reduced-fat sour cream
- 3 ounces bittersweet chocolate, melted and cooled
- 24 chocolate-covered coffee beans, optional

1. Place cookies in a food processor. Cover and pulse until fine crumbs form. Add fudge topping and butter; pulse just until blended. Press onto the bottom of a 13-in. x 9-in. dish coated with cooking spray. Refrigerate for 10 minutes.

2. Meanwhile, for filling, in a small saucepan, sprinkle gelatin over coffee; let stand for 1 minute. Heat over low heat, stirring until the gelatin is completely dissolved. Remove from the heat; set aside.

3. In a large bowl, beat cream cheese and sugar until smooth. Beat in the sour cream, chocolate and reserved coffee mixture until blended. Pour over crust. Cover and refrigerate for at least 4 hours or until firm.

4. Cut into bars. Garnish with coffee beans if desired. Refrigerate leftovers.

CHOCOLATE CHIP CREAM CHEESE BARS

PER SERVING *166 cal., 9 g fat (5 g sat. fat), 20 mg chol., 167 mg sodium, 20 g carb., 1 g fiber, 4 g pro.* **Diabetic Exchanges:** *2 fat, 1 starch.*

Chocolate Chip Cream Cheese Bars

Lower in fat and calories than you might guess, these sweet bars couldn't be easier to whip up. They boast a great chocolaty flavor and make a fun, quick dessert to bring to parties or serve to company.

—JENNIFER RAFFERTY MILFORD, OH

PREP: 20 MIN. • **BAKE:** 20 MIN. + COOLING
MAKES: 2 DOZEN

- 1 package German chocolate cake mix (regular size)
- ⅓ cup canola oil
- 1 egg

FILLING

- 1 package (8 ounces) reduced-fat cream cheese
- ⅓ cup sugar
- 1 egg
- 1 cup miniature semisweet chocolate chips

1. In a large bowl, combine the cake mix, oil and egg. Set aside 1 cup for topping. Press remaining crumb mixture into a 13x9-in. baking pan coated with cooking spray. Bake at 350° for 10-12 minutes or until set.

2. For filling, in a large bowl, beat cream cheese and sugar until smooth. Add egg; beat well. Spread over crust. Sprinkle with chocolate chips and reserved crumb mixture.

3. Bake for 18-20 minutes or until set. Cool on a wire rack. Cut into bars. Store in the refrigerator.

PER SERVING *187 cal., 9 g fat (3 g sat. fat), 24 mg chol., 207 mg sodium, 25 g carb., trace fiber, 3 g pro.* **Diabetic Exchanges:** *1½ starch, 1½ fat.*

Chocolate Angel Food Cake

This cake comes out tall and spongy with a mild cocoa flavor. A drizzling of chocolate icing gives this dessert just the right amount of sweetness.

—REBECCA BAIRD SALT LAKE CTY, UTAH

PREP: 35 MIN. • **BAKE:** 30 MIN. + COOLING
MAKES: 16 SERVINGS

- 12 egg whites
- 1 cup cake flour
- ⅓ cup baking cocoa
- ¾ teaspoon cream of tartar
- 1½ teaspoons vanilla extract
- ¼ teaspoon almond extract
- ⅛ teaspoon salt
- 1⅔ cups sugar

ICING
- 1¾ cups confectioners' sugar
- ⅓ cup baking cocoa
- ⅓ cup reduced-fat sour cream
- 1 tablespoon fat-free milk
- ¾ teaspoon vanilla extract

1. Place egg whites in a large bowl; let stand at room temperature for 30 minutes. Sift flour and cocoa together twice; set aside.

2. Add the cream of tartar, extracts and salt to egg whites; beat on medium speed until soft peaks form. Gradually add sugar, about 2 tablespoons at a time, beating on high until stiff glossy peaks form and sugar is dissolved. Gradually fold in flour mixture, about ½ cup at a time.

3. Gently spoon into an ungreased 10-in. tube pan. Cut through batter with a knife to remove air pockets. Bake on the lowest oven rack at 350° for 30-40 minutes or until lightly browned and entire top appears dry. Immediately invert the tube pan; cool completely, about 1 hour.

4. Run a knife around side and center tube of pan. Remove cake to a plate.

5. For icing, in a small bowl, beat the confectioners' sugar, cocoa, sour cream, milk and vanilla until smooth. Drizzle over the cake. Store in the refrigerator.

PER SERVING *195 cal., 1 g fat (trace sat. fat), 2 mg chol., 64 mg sodium, 43 g carb., 1 g fiber, 4 g pro.*

CHOCOLATE ANGEL FOOD CAKE

Rhubarb-Pineapple Crisp

We grow our own rhubarb, so I enjoy finding new ways to use it. Years ago when I first tried the rhubarb-pineapple combination, I thought it would be too strong, but I was pleasantly surprised.

—JUDY SCHUT GRAND RAPIDS, MI

PREP: 15 MIN. • **BAKE:** 30 MIN.
MAKES: 6 SERVINGS

- 2 cups sliced fresh or frozen rhubarb, thawed and drained
- 1 can (20 ounces) unsweetened pineapple tidbits, drained
- ½ cup sugar, divided
- 2 tablespoons plus ⅓ cup all-purpose flour, divided
- ⅓ cup quick-cooking oats

RHUBARB-PINEAPPLE CRISP

- ¾ teaspoon ground cinnamon
- ⅛ teaspoon salt
- ¼ cup cold butter
   Whipped cream, optional

1. In a large bowl, combine the rhubarb, pineapple, ¼ cup sugar and 2 tablespoons flour. Transfer to a 9-in. deep-dish pie plate coated with cooking spray.

2. In a small bowl, combine the oats, cinnamon, salt and remaining sugar and flour. Cut in butter until crumbly. Sprinkle over fruit. Bake, uncovered, at 350° for 30-35 minutes or until filling is bubbly and topping is golden brown. Cool for 5 minutes; serve with whipped cream if desired.

NOTE *If using frozen rhubarb, measure rhubarb while still frozen, then thaw completely. Drain in a colander, but do not press liquid out.*

PER SERVING *232 cal., 8 g fat (5 g sat. fat), 20 mg chol., 106 mg sodium, 39 g carb., 2 g fiber, 2 g pro.*

Pumpkin Spice Cake

A hint of cocoa and a sprinkling of chocolate chips makes this cake stand out from other pumpkin desserts. You could also make it with mashed sweet potatoes or butternut squash.

—**KATIE WOLLGAST** FLORISSANT, MO

PREP: 25 MIN. • **BAKE:** 50 MIN. + COOLING
MAKES: 16 SERVINGS

- 1 **can (15 ounces) solid-pack pumpkin**
- 1½ **cups sugar**
- ½ **cup buttermilk**
- ⅓ **cup canola oil**
- ⅓ **cup water**
- 2 **eggs**
- 2 **egg whites**
- 1 **teaspoon vanilla extract**
- 2 **cups all-purpose flour**
- 1 **tablespoon baking cocoa**
- 1½ **teaspoons ground cinnamon**
- 1 **teaspoon baking soda**
- 1 **teaspoon baking powder**
- ½ **teaspoon salt**
- ½ **teaspoon each ground nutmeg, allspice and cloves**
- ½ **cup raisins**
- ¼ **cup miniature semisweet chocolate chips**
  Confectioners' sugar
  Reduced-fat vanilla ice cream, optional

1. In a large bowl, beat the pumpkin, sugar, buttermilk, oil, water, eggs, egg whites and vanilla until well blended.
2. In a small bowl, combine the flour, cocoa, cinnamon, baking soda, baking power, salt, nutmeg, allspice and cloves; gradually beat into pumpkin mixture until blended. Stir in raisins and chocolate chips.
3. Transfer to a 10-in. fluted tube pan coated with cooking spray. Bake at 350° for 50-60 minutes or until a toothpick inserted near the center comes out clean.
4. Cool for 10 minutes before removing from pan to a wire rack to cool completely. Sprinkle with confectioners' sugar. Serve with ice cream if desired.
PER SERVING *223 cal., 7 g fat (1 g sat. fat), 27 mg chol., 204 mg sodium, 39 g carb., 2 g fiber, 4 g pro.*

Spiced Sweet Potato Pie

In my lightened-up version of Sweet Potato Pie, I cut down on sugar and added vanilla and bourbon to create cozy flavor without extra fat.

—**DIANA RIOS** LYTLE, TX

PREP: 15 MIN. • **BAKE:** 45 MIN. + COOLING
MAKES: 8 SERVINGS

- 2 **egg whites**
- 1 **egg**
- 1¾ **cups mashed sweet potatoes**
- ½ **cup 2% milk**
- ¼ **cup reduced-fat butter, melted**
- 1 **tablespoon bourbon**
- 1½ **teaspoons vanilla extract**
- ⅔ **cup packed brown sugar**
- 1 **tablespoon all-purpose flour**
- 1 **teaspoon ground cinnamon**
- ½ **teaspoon salt**
- ½ **teaspoon ground nutmeg**
- ¼ **teaspoon ground cloves**
- 1 **reduced-fat graham cracker crust (8 inches)**
- ½ **cup fat-free whipped topping**

1. In a large bowl, whisk the the first seven ingredients until blended. In another bowl, combine the brown sugar, flour, cinnamon, salt, nutmeg and cloves; gradually beat into the pumpkin mixture until blended. Pour into crust.
2. Bake at 350° for 45-55 minutes or until a knife inserted near the center comes out clean. Cool completely on a wire rack. Garnish with whipped topping. Store in the refrigerator.
NOTE *This recipe was tested with Land O'Lakes light stick butter.*
PER SERVING *285 cal., 7 g fat (3 g sat. fat), 35 mg chol., 350 mg sodium, 51 g carb., 2 g fiber, 4 g pro.*

PUMPKIN SPICE CAKE

Old-Fashioned Strawberry Pie

I've been cooking since I was a girl, and I especially enjoy making fresh, fruity desserts like this. It's a wonderful and light sweet to follow dinner—and a must when fresh berries are in season.

—ERICA COOPER ELK RIVER, MN

PREP: 30 MIN. • **COOK:** 10 MIN. + CHILLING
MAKES: 8 SERVINGS

- 1 sheet refrigerated pie pastry
- 1 package (3 ounces) cook-and-serve vanilla pudding mix
- 1½ cups water
- 1 teaspoon lemon juice
- 1 package (.3 ounce) sugar-free strawberry gelatin
- ½ cup boiling water
- 4 cups sliced fresh strawberries
- 3 ounces reduced-fat cream cheese
- 2 cups reduced-fat whipped topping, divided
- 1 teaspoon vanilla extract
- 8 fresh strawberries

OLD-FASHIONED STRAWBERRY PIE

1. On a lightly floured surface, unroll pastry. Transfer to a 9-in. pie plate. Trim pastry to ½ in. beyond edge of plate; flute edges. Line unpricked pastry with a double thickness of heavy-duty foil. Bake at 450° for 8 minutes. Remove foil; bake 5-7 minutes longer or until lightly browned. Cool on a wire rack.

2. In a small saucepan, combine pudding mix, water and lemon juice. Cook and stir over medium heat until mixture comes to a boil. Cook and stir 1-2 minutes longer or until thickened. Remove from the heat; set aside.

3. In a large bowl, dissolve gelatin in boiling water. Gradually stir in the pudding. Cover and refrigerate for 30 minutes or until thickened. Fold in sliced strawberries. Transfer to crust.

4. For topping, in another bowl, beat the cream cheese, ½ cup whipped topping and vanilla until smooth. Fold in remaining whipped topping. Cut a small hole in the corner of a pastry or plastic bag; insert a medium star tip. Fill with topping. Pipe topping around edges of pie; garnish with whole strawberries. Refrigerate for at least 1 hour before serving.

PER SERVING *259 cal., 12 g fat (7 g sat. fat), 13 mg chol., 220 mg sodium, 37 g carb., 2 g fiber, 3 g pro.*

Heavenly Chocolate Pie

I made this a little less sinful with fat-free, sugar-free and reduced-fat products. What a lovely way to give in to chocolate cravings!

—DONNA ROBERTS MANHATTAN, KS

PREP: 15 MIN. + CHILLING
MAKES: 8 SERVINGS

- 1 cup fat-free vanilla frozen yogurt, softened
- 2 cups fat-free milk
- 1 package (1.4 ounces) sugar-free instant chocolate pudding mix
- 1 package (1 ounce) sugar-free instant vanilla pudding mix
- 1 carton (8 ounces) frozen reduced-fat whipped topping, thawed, divided
- 1 reduced-fat graham cracker crust (8 inches)
  Chocolate curls, optional

1. In a large bowl, whisk yogurt until soft and smooth. Gradually whisk in milk until blended. Add pudding mixes; whisk 2 minutes longer. Let stand for 2 minutes or until soft-set.

2. Fold in 1 cup whipped topping. Transfer to crust. Top with remaining whipped topping and chocolate curls if desired. Refrigerate for at least 4 hours.

PER SERVING *235 calories, 6 g fat (4 g saturated fat), 2 mg cholesterol, 433 mg sodium, 40 g carbohydrate, trace fiber, 5 g protein.*

Creamy Lemon Cheesecake

My friend, Gwen, gave me this creamy, lip-smacking recipe, and it's been a crowd-pleaser at my house ever since. The homemade lemon curd on top adds a tart, special touch! The cheesecake can also be made in three store-bought graham cracker pie shells.

—ANNE HENRY TORONTO, ON

PREP: 35 MIN. • **BAKE:** 50 MIN. + CHILLING
MAKES: 16 SERVINGS

- 1 cup graham cracker crumbs
- 2 tablespoons butter, melted

FILLING
- 2 packages (8 ounces each) reduced-fat cream cheese
- 1 package (8 ounces) fat-free cream cheese
- 1⅓ cups sugar
- ⅓ cup lemon juice
- 1 tablespoon grated lemon peel
- 3 eggs, lightly beaten

TOPPINGS
- 1 cup (8 ounces) reduced-fat sour cream
- 4 teaspoons plus ½ cup sugar, divided
- 1 teaspoon vanilla extract
- 4½ teaspoons cornstarch
- ¼ teaspoon salt
- ¾ cup water
- 1 egg yolk, beaten
- ⅓ cup lemon juice
- 1 tablespoon butter
- 2 teaspoons grated lemon peel

CREAMY LEMON CHEESECAKE

1. Place a 9-in. springform pan coated with cooking spray on a double thickness of heavy-duty foil (about 18 in. square). Securely wrap the foil around pan.

2. In a small bowl, combine cracker crumbs and butter. Press onto the bottom of prepared pan. Place the pan on a baking sheet. Bake at 325° for 6-9 minutes or until set. Cool on a wire rack.

3. In a large bowl, beat cream cheeses and sugar until smooth. Beat in lemon juice and peel. Add eggs; beat on low speed just until combined. Pour over crust. Place springform pan in a large baking pan; add 1 in. of hot water to larger pan.

4. Bake at 325° for 40-45 minutes or until center is almost set. Let stand for 5 minutes. Combine the sour cream, 4 teaspoons sugar and vanilla; spread over top of the cheesecake. Bake 10 minutes longer. Remove springform pan from water bath. Cool on a wire rack for 10 minutes. Carefully run a knife around edge of pan to loosen; cool 1 hour longer.

5. In a small heavy saucepan, combine the cornstarch, salt and remaining sugar. Stir in water until smooth. Cook and stir over medium-high heat until thickened and bubbly. Reduce heat; cook and stir 2 minutes longer. Remove from the heat.

6. Stir a small amount of hot mixture into egg yolk; return all to the pan, stirring constantly. Bring to a gentle boil; cook and stir 2 minutes longer. Remove from the heat. Gently stir in the lemon juice, butter and lemon peel. Cool to room temperature without stirring.

7. Spread over the cheesecake. Refrigerate overnight. Remove sides of pan.

PER SERVING *260 cal., 11 g fat (7 g sat. fat), 84 mg chol., 305 mg sodium, 33 g carb., trace fiber, 8 g pro.*

Chocolate Orange Cake

I love the combination of chocolate and orange. To keep this popular treat lower in fat and calories, I use cocoa, light sour cream, neufchatel cheese and very little butter. The orange flavor comes through in every bite.

—LINDA DALTON STOUGHTON, MA

PREP: 25 MIN. • **BAKE:** 20 MIN. + COOLING
MAKES: 12 SERVINGS

- 2 teaspoons plus ⅓ cup baking cocoa, divided
- ⅓ cup quick-cooking oats
- ⅔ cup reduced-fat sour cream
- ⅓ cup sugar blend
- 2 eggs
- 3 tablespoons Triple Sec or orange juice
- 2 tablespoons butter, melted
- 5 teaspoons canola oil
- 1 teaspoon vanilla extract
- ⅔ cup all-purpose flour
- 1 teaspoon baking powder
- ½ teaspoon baking soda
- ¼ teaspoon salt
- ¼ cup miniature semisweet chocolate chips
- 2 teaspoons grated orange peel

FROSTING
- 4 ounces reduced-fat cream cheese

CHOCOLATE ORANGE CAKE

- ¼ cup confectioners' sugar
- 2 teaspoons grated orange peel
- 2 teaspoons orange juice

1. Coat an 8-in. square baking dish with cooking spray and sprinkle with 2 teaspoons cocoa; set aside. Place oats in a small food processor; cover and process until ground. Set aside.
2. In a large bowl, beat the sour cream, sugar blend, eggs, Triple Sec, butter, oil and vanilla until well blended. Combine the flour, ground oats, baking powder, baking soda, salt and remaining cocoa; gradually beat into the sour cream mixture until blended. Stir in chocolate chips and orange peel.
3. Transfer to reserved dish. Bake at 350° for 20-25 minutes or until a toothpick inserted near the center comes out clean. Cool completely on a wire rack.
4. For frosting, in a small bowl, beat cream cheese until fluffy. Add the confectioners' sugar, orange peel and juice; beat until smooth. Frost top of cake. Refrigerate leftovers.
NOTE *This recipe was tested with Splenda sugar blend.*
PER SERVING *192 cal., 9 g fat (4 g sat. fat), 51 mg chol., 210 mg sodium, 22 g carb., 1 g fiber, 5 g pro. Diabetic Exchanges: 2 fat, 1½ starch.*

S

Pineapple Apple Pie

This special pie is destined to become a family tradition! The apple and pineapple are divine together, and the crunchy topping is fun and fabulous! We like to serve it warm.

—KAREN BRINK ATWATER, OH

PREP: 20 MIN. • **BAKE:** 40 MIN. + COOLING
MAKES: 10 SERVINGS

PINEAPPLE APPLE PIE

- Pastry for single-crust pie (9 inches)
- 1 can (20 ounces) crushed pineapple in heavy syrup, undrained
- 3 medium tart apples, peeled and chopped
- ¼ cup all-purpose flour
- ½ teaspoon ground cinnamon
- ½ teaspoon ground nutmeg

TOPPING
- ½ cup quick-cooking oats
- ⅓ cup packed brown sugar
- ¼ cup all-purpose flour
- 2 tablespoons plus 2 teaspoons butter, melted

1. Line a 9-in. pie plate with pastry; trim and flute edges. In a large bowl, combine the apples and pineapple. Combine the flour, cinnamon and nutmeg; add to apple mixture and toss to coat. Transfer to pastry.
2. In a small bowl, combine the oats, brown sugar, flour and butter; sprinkle over filling.
3. Bake at 375° for 40-45 minutes or until topping is browned. Cover edges with foil during the last 15 minutes to prevent overbrowning if necessary. Cool on a wire rack.
PER SERVING *259 cal., 9 g fat (4 g sat. fat), 12 mg chol., 105 mg sodium, 43 g carb., 2 g fiber, 3 g pro.*

F

Chocolate Angel Cupcakes with Coconut Cream Frosting

They taste as heavenly as they sound. If you're looking for a new take on angel food cake, these coconut-topped chocolatey cakes are calling your name.

—**MANDY RIVERS** LEXINGTON, SC

PREP: 15 MIN. • **BAKE:** 15 MIN. + COOLING
MAKES: 2 DOZEN

- **1 package (16 ounces) angel food cake mix**
- **¾ cup baking cocoa**
- **1 cup (8 ounces) reduced-fat sour cream**
- **1 cup confectioners' sugar**
- **⅛ teaspoon coconut extract**
- **2½ cups reduced-fat whipped topping**
- **¾ cup flaked coconut, toasted**

1. Prepare cake mix according to package directions for cupcakes, adding cocoa when mixing.
2. Fill foil- or paper-lined muffin cups two-thirds full. Bake at 375° for 11-15 minutes or until cake springs back when lightly touched and cracks feel dry. Cool for 10 minutes before removing from pans to wire racks to cool completely.
3. For frosting, in a large bowl, combine sour cream, confectioners' sugar and extract until smooth. Fold in whipped topping. Frost cupcakes. Sprinkle with the coconut. Store in the refrigerator.

PER SERVING *142 cal., 3 g fat (2 g sat. fat), 3 mg chol., 154 mg sodium, 27 g carb., 1 g fiber, 3 g pro.* ***Diabetic Exchanges:*** *1½ starch, ½ fat.*

CHOCOLATE ANGEL CUPCAKES WITH COCONUT CREAM FROSTING

True Love Chocolate Cake

A college roommate gave me this amazing recipe and it's been my favorite ever since. To use it for other holidays, just replace the hearts with appropriately colored hard candies.

—**STEPHANIE BASKER** SALT LAKE CITY, UT

PREP: 35 MIN. • **BAKE:** 35 MIN. + COOLING
MAKES: 24 SERVINGS

- **¼ cup butter, softened**
- **1⅔ cups sugar**
- **2 eggs**
- **½ cup unsweetened applesauce**
- **2¼ cups all-purpose flour**
- **⅔ cup baking cocoa**
- **1¼ teaspoons baking powder**
- **1 teaspoon salt**
- **¼ teaspoon baking soda**
- **1¼ cups water**
- **1 cup (6 ounces) semisweet chocolate chips**

FROSTING

- **1 package (8 ounces) reduced-fat cream cheese**
- **⅓ cup confectioners' sugar**
- **1 teaspoon vanilla extract**
- **1 carton (8 ounces) frozen reduced-fat whipped topping, thawed**

TOPPING

- **¾ cup flaked coconut**
- **½ cup candy hearts**

1. In a large bowl, beat the butter and sugar until crumbly, about 2 minutes. Add the eggs, one at a time, beating well after each addition. Beat in the applesauce.
2. Combine the flour, cocoa, baking powder, salt and baking soda. Add to the butter mixture alternately with water, beating well after each addition. Fold in chips. Pour into a 13-in. x 9-in. baking pan coated with cooking spray.
3. Bake at 350° for 35-40 minutes or until a toothpick inserted near center comes out clean. Cool on a wire rack.
4. For frosting, in a bowl, beat cream cheese and confectioners' sugar until smooth. Beat in vanilla. Fold in the whipped topping. Frost the cake. Refrigerate until serving. Just before serving, sprinkle with coconut and candy. Refrigerate leftovers.

PER SERVING *238 cal., 9 g fat (6 g sat. fat), 29 mg chol., 201 mg sodium, 39 g carb., 1 g fiber, 4 g pro.*

PUMPKIN OATMEAL BARS
PAGE 283

**KAREN GRANT'S
STRAWBERRY MERINGUE TART**

PAGE 288

**BARBARA PRYOR'S
BANANA CHIP CAKE** *PAGE 286*

**JOAN HALLFORD'S
HOT COCOA SOUFFLE**
PAGE 292

Treat Yourself

Don't give up on your diet ... but certainly **don't give up dessert**. This is the chapter you've been waiting for—the one that offers you **dozens of way to indulge** in your favorite treats **without spoiling your healthy lifestyle.**

Pumpkin Oatmeal Bars

It took me a long time to develop this quick and easy recipe, but I'm so happy with how it turned out. These bars have it all—sugar and spice and a light, creamy pumpkin layer that's especially nice!

—ERIN ANDREWS EDGEWATER, FL

PREP: 30 MIN. • **BAKE:** 30 MIN. + COOLING
MAKES: 2 DOZEN

- 1 **package yellow cake mix (regular size)**
- 2½ **cups quick-cooking oats**
- 5 **tablespoons butter, melted**
- 3 **tablespoons honey**
- 1 **tablespoon water**

FILLING

- 1 **can (15 ounces) solid-pack pumpkin**
- ¼ **cup reduced-fat cream cheese**
- ¼ **cup fat-free milk**
- 3 **tablespoons brown sugar**
- 2 **tablespoons maple syrup**
- 1 **teaspoon ground cinnamon**
- 1 **teaspoon vanilla extract**
- ¼ **teaspoon ground allspice**
- ¼ **teaspoon ground cloves**
- 1 **egg**
- 1 **egg white**
- ¼ **cup chopped walnuts**
- 1 **tablespoon butter, melted**

1. In a large bowl, combine cake mix and oats; set aside ½ cup for topping. Add the butter, honey and water to the remaining cake mixture. Press onto the bottom of a 13-in. x 9-in. baking pan coated with cooking spray.
2. For filling, in a large bowl, beat the pumpkin, cream cheese, milk, brown sugar, maple syrup, cinnamon, vanilla, allspice and cloves until blended. Add egg and egg white; beat on low speed just until combined. Pour over crust. In a small bowl, combine the walnuts, butter and reserved cake mixture; sprinkle over filling.
3. Bake bars at 350° for 30-35 minutes or until set and edges are lightly browned. Cool on a wire rack. Cut into bars.
PER SERVING *186 cal., 7 g fat (3 g sat. fat), 18 mg chol., 180 mg sodium, 30 g carb., 2 g fiber, 3 g pro.* **Diabetic Exchanges:** *2 starch, 1 fat.*

S Honey Cheese Bars

If you like cheesecake, you'll love this light dessert. Walnuts lend a subtle nutty taste to the crust, and honey and lemon make the smooth topping delicious.

—EDNA HOFFMAN HEBRON, IN

PREP: 25 MIN. • **BAKE:** 30 MIN. + COOLING
MAKES: 16 BARS

- 1 **cup all-purpose flour**
- ⅓ **cup packed brown sugar**
- ¼ **cup cold butter, cubed**
- ½ **cup finely chopped walnuts**

FILLING

- 1 **package (8 ounces) reduced-fat cream cheese**
- ¼ **cup honey**
- 2 **tablespoons milk**
- 1 **tablespoon lemon juice**
- ½ **teaspoon vanilla extract**
- 1 **egg, lightly beaten**
  Additional honey, optional

1. In a small bowl, combine flour and brown sugar. Cut in butter until crumbly. Stir in walnuts. Press onto the bottom of an 8-in. square baking dish coated with cooking spray. Bake at 350° for 10-12 minutes or until lightly browned.
2. For filling, in a large bowl, beat the cream cheese, honey, milk, lemon juice and vanilla until blended. Add the egg; beat on low speed just until combined. Pour over crust. Bake 20-25 minutes longer or until set. Cool completely on a wire rack. Drizzle with additional honey if desired. Cut into bars. Store in the refrigerator.
PER SERVING *152 cal., 8 g fat (4 g sat. fat), 31 mg chol., 88 mg sodium, 16 g carb., trace fiber, 4 g pro.* **Diabetic Exchanges:** *2 fat, 1 starch.*

Family-Favorite Peanut Butter Cake

My grandmother and aunts made this for family gatherings to go along with fresh homemade ice cream. I now share it with my family and friends during our own special gatherings.

—**KEITH GABLE** GODDARD, KS

PREP: 20 MIN. • **BAKE:** 15 MIN. + COOLING
MAKES: 24 SERVINGS

- ½ cup creamy peanut butter
- 6 tablespoons butter, cubed
- 1 cup water
- 2 cups all-purpose flour
- 1½ cups sugar
- ½ cup buttermilk
- ¼ cup unsweetened applesauce
- 2 eggs, lightly beaten
- 1¼ teaspoons baking powder
- 1 teaspoon vanilla extract
- ½ teaspoon salt
- ¼ teaspoon baking soda

FAMILY-FAVORITE PEANUT BUTTER CAKE

FROSTING
- ¼ cup butter, cubed
- ¼ cup creamy peanut butter
- 2 tablespoons fat-free milk
- 1¾ cups confectioners' sugar
- 1 teaspoon vanilla extract

1. In a large saucepan, bring peanut butter, butter and water just to a boil. Immediately remove from heat; stir in flour, sugar, buttermilk, applesauce, eggs, baking powder, vanilla, salt and baking soda until smooth.

2. Pour into a 15-in. x 10-in. x 1-in. baking pan coated with cooking spray. Bake at 375° for 15-20 minutes or until golden brown and a toothpick inserted in the center comes out clean. Cool on a wire rack for 20 minutes.

3. In a small saucepan, melt butter and peanut butter over medium heat; add milk. Bring to a boil. Remove from the heat. Gradually whisk in the confectioners' sugar and vanilla until smooth. Spread over the warm cake. Cool completely on a wire rack. Store in the refrigerator.

PER SERVING *220 cal., 9 g fat (4 g sat. fat), 30 mg chol., 166 mg sodium, 31 g carb., 1 g fiber, 4 g pro.* **Diabetic Exchanges:** *2 starch, 1½ fat.*

S Blueberry Walnut Bars

With power-packing oats, walnuts and blueberries, kids aren't the only ones who are going to love this sweet treat. Health-minded parents can feel happy about these bars, too.

—**DAWN ONUFFER** CRESTVIEW, FL

PREP: 20 MIN. • **BAKE:** 10 MIN. + COOLING
MAKES: 12 SERVINGS

- ⅔ cup ground walnuts
- ½ cup graham cracker crumbs
- 2 tablespoons plus ⅓ cup sugar, divided
- ⅓ cup old-fashioned oats
- 3 tablespoons reduced-fat butter, melted
- 1 package (8 ounces) reduced-fat cream cheese
- 1 tablespoon orange juice
- ½ teaspoon vanilla extract
- ½ cup reduced-fat whipped topping
- 2 tablespoons blueberry preserves
- 1½ cups fresh blueberries

1. In a small bowl, combine walnuts, cracker crumbs, 2 tablespoons sugar, oats and butter. Press onto the bottom of an 8-in. square baking dish coated with cooking spray.

2. Bake at 350° for 9-11 minutes or until set and edges are lightly browned. Cool on a wire rack.

3. In a large bowl, beat cream cheese and remaining sugar until smooth. Beat in orange juice and vanilla. Fold in whipped topping. Spread over crust.

4. In a microwave-safe bowl, heat preserves on high for 15-20 seconds or until warmed; gently stir in the blueberries. Spoon over the filling. Refrigerate until serving.

NOTE *This recipe was tested with Land O'Lakes light stick butter.*

PER SERVING *167 cal., 9 g fat (4 g sat. fat), 17 mg chol., 125 mg sodium, 19 g carb., 1 g fiber, 3 g pro.* **Diabetic Exchanges:** *2 fat, 1 starch.*

Raspberry Swirl Frozen Dessert

My Raspberry Swirl is a family delight that can only be described as luscious. It can be made ahead and stored in the freezer until ready to serve.

—KAREN SUDERMAN SUGAR LAND, TX

PREP: 45 MIN. • **COOK:** 20 MIN. + FREEZING
MAKES: 12 SERVINGS

- ⅔ cup graham cracker crumbs
- 2 tablespoons butter, melted
- 5 teaspoons sugar

FILLING

- 3 eggs, separated
- ¼ cup plus 1 tablespoon water, divided
- 1 cup sugar, divided
- ⅛ teaspoon salt
- ⅛ teaspoon cream of tartar
- 1 package (8 ounces) reduced-fat cream cheese
- 1½ cups reduced-fat whipped topping
- 1 package (10 ounces) frozen sweetened raspberries, thawed

1. In a small bowl, combine the cracker crumbs, butter and sugar. Press into an 11-in. x 7-in. dish coated with cooking spray. Cover and refrigerate for at least 15 minutes.

2. Meanwhile, for filling, in a small heavy saucepan, combine the egg yolks, ¼ cup water, ½ cup sugar and salt. Cook and stir over low heat until mixture reaches 160° or is thick enough to coat the back of a metal spoon. Cool quickly by placing pan in a bowl of ice water; stir for 2 minutes. Set aside.

3. In a small heavy saucepan over low heat, combine the egg whites, cream of tartar and remaining water and sugar. With a portable mixer, beat on low speed until mixture reaches 160°. Transfer to a small bowl; beat on high until soft peaks form.

4. In a large bowl, beat the cream cheese until smooth. Gradually beat in the egg yolk mixture. Fold in the whipped topping, then egg white mixture. Drain raspberries, reserving 3 tablespoons juice. In a small bowl, crush half of berries with 1 tablespoon juice. Set the remaining berries and juice aside.

5. Spread a third of cream cheese mixture over crust; spoon half of crushed berry mixture over the top. Repeat layers. Cut through with a knife to swirl raspberries.

6. Top with remaining cream cheese mixture. Sprinkle with reserved berries and drizzle with remaining juice. Cover and freeze for 5 hours or until firm. Remove from the freezer 15 minutes before cutting.

PER SERVING *217 cal., 9 g fat (5 g sat. fat), 71 mg chol., 164 mg sodium, 32 g carb., 1 g fiber, 4 g pro.* **Diabetic Exchanges:** *2 starch, 1½ fat.*

RASPBERRY SWIRL FROZEN DESSERT

🅂 Cranberry Apple Crisp

I first tasted this apple crisp at a church potluck and thought it was delicious. I lightened the recipe by reducing the sugar and adding oats to replace some of the flour. You'll adore the results!

—CAROLYN DIPASQUALE MIDDLETOWN, RI

PREP: 15 MIN. • **BAKE:** 40 MIN.
MAKES: 8 SERVINGS

- 5 medium tart apples, sliced
- 1 tablespoon all-purpose flour
- 1 can (14 ounces) whole-berry cranberry sauce

TOPPING

- ¾ cup quick-cooking oats
- ⅓ cup packed brown sugar
- ¼ cup all-purpose flour
- 2 tablespoons plus 2 teaspoons wheat bran
- 2 tablespoons canola oil
- 2 tablespoons butter, melted
- ¾ teaspoon ground cinnamon
  Fat-free vanilla frozen yogurt, optional

1. In a large bowl, combine apples and flour; toss to coat. Stir in cranberry sauce. Transfer to a 13-in. x 9-in. baking dish coated with cooking spray.

2. In a small bowl, combine topping ingredients; sprinkle over apple mixture. Bake, uncovered, at 350° for 40-45 minutes or until topping is golden brown and fruit is tender. Serve with frozen yogurt if desired.

PER SERVING *259 cal., 7 g fat (2 g sat. fat), 8 mg chol., 36 mg sodium, 50 g carb., 4 g fiber, 2 g pro.*

good

Banana Chip Cake

This is my delectable version of Ben & Jerry's Chunky Monkey Ice Cream (my favorite!) in a cake. The hardest part is waiting for it to cool.

—**BARBARA PRYOR** MILFORD, MA

PREP: 25 MIN. • **BAKE:** 40 MIN. + COOLING
MAKES: 16 SERVINGS

- 1 package yellow cake mix (regular size)
- 1¼ cups water
- 3 eggs
- ½ cup unsweetened applesauce
- 2 medium bananas, mashed
- 1 cup miniature semisweet chocolate chips
- ½ cup chopped walnuts

1. In a large bowl, combine the cake mix, water, eggs and applesauce; beat on low speed for 30 seconds. Beat on medium for 2 minutes. Stir in the bananas, chips and walnuts.

2. Transfer to a 10-in. fluted tube pan coated with cooking spray and sprinkled with flour. Bake at 350° for 40-50 minutes or until a toothpick inserted near the center comes out clean. Cool for 10 minutes before removing from pan to a wire rack to cool completely.

PER SERVING *233 cal., 9 g fat (4 g sat. fat), 40 mg chol., 225 mg sodium, 38 g carb., 1 g fiber, 3 g pro.*

BANANA CHIP CAKE

S

Cranberry Pecan Bars

I've been making these bars for as long as I can remember. They look so pretty they're hard to resist. Try them with low-fat ice cream for a sweet-tart treat.

—**SANDRA BUNTE** COVINA, CA

PREP: 30 MIN. • **BAKE:** 30 MIN. + COOLING
MAKES: 1 DOZEN

- ¾ cup all-purpose flour
- ¾ cup quick-cooking oats
- ⅓ cup packed brown sugar
- ⅓ cup butter, melted

FILLING

- 1 package (12 ounces) fresh or frozen cranberries
- ½ cup cranberry juice, divided
- ½ cup golden raisins
- ⅓ cup honey
  Sugar substitute equivalent to 3 tablespoons sugar
- ½ teaspoon ground cinnamon
- ¼ teaspoon ground cloves
- ½ teaspoon cornstarch
- ¼ cup chopped pecans

1. In a small bowl, combine the flour, oats and brown sugar. Stir in butter until blended. Set aside ⅔ cup. Pat remaining mixture onto the bottom of a 9-in. square baking pan coated with cooking spray; set aside.

2. In a small saucepan, combine the cranberries, 7 tablespoons cranberry juice, raisins, honey, sugar substitute, cinnamon and cloves. Cook and stir over medium heat for 10-12 minutes or until berries pop.

3. Combine the cornstarch and remaining cranberry juice until smooth; stir into berry mixture. Bring to a boil; cook and stir for 1-2 minutes or until thickened.

4. Pour filling over crust. Sprinkle with pecans and reserved oat mixture. Bake at 350° for 30-35 minutes or until lightly browned. Cool on a wire rack. Cut into squares. Store in the refrigerator.

NOTE *This recipe was tested with Splenda no-calorie sweetener.*

PER SERVING *199 cal., 7 g fat (3 g sat. fat), 14 mg chol., 56 mg sodium, 33 g carb., 2 g fiber, 2 g pro.* **Diabetic Exchanges:** *1 starch, 1 fruit, 1 fat.*

CRANBERRY PECAN BARS

S C

Caramel Whiskey Cookies

A bit of yogurt replaces part of the butter in the traditional cookie, but you would never know. I get a lot of requests for these and can't make a cookie tray without them.

—PRISCILLA YEE CONCORD, CA

PREP: 30 MIN. • **BAKE:** 10 MIN./BATCH
MAKES: 4 DOZEN

- ½ cup butter, softened
- ½ cup sugar
- ½ cup packed brown sugar
- ¼ cup plain Greek yogurt
- 2 tablespoons canola oil
- 1 teaspoon vanilla extract
- 2½ cups all-purpose flour
- 2 teaspoons baking powder
- 1 teaspoon baking soda
- ¼ teaspoon salt

TOPPING

- 24 caramels or 1 cup Kraft caramel bits
- 1 tablespoon whiskey
- 3 ounces semisweet chocolate, melted
- ½ teaspoon kosher salt, optional

1. In a large bowl, beat butter and sugars until crumbly, about 2 minutes. Beat in the yogurt, oil and vanilla. Combine the flour, baking powder, baking soda and salt; gradually add to sugar mixture and mix well.
2. Shape into 1-in. balls. Place 2 in. apart on ungreased baking sheets. Flatten with the bottom of a glass dipped in flour. Bake at 350° for 7-9 minutes or until edges are lightly browned. Cool for 2 minutes before removing to wire racks.
3. In a microwave, melt caramels with whiskey; stir until smooth. Spread over cookies. Drizzle with chocolate; sprinkle with salt. Let stand until set. Store in an airtight container.

PER SERVING *93 cal., 4 g fat (2 g sat. fat), 6 mg chol., 83 mg sodium, 14 g carb., trace fiber, 1 g pro.*

Chocolate Raspberry Torte

The chocolate cake alone is wonderful, but the light raspberry filling elevates this torte to another level of deliciousness!

—SHARON KURTZ EMMAUS, PA

PREP: 30 MIN. • **BAKE:** 25 MIN. + COOLING
MAKES: 16 SERVINGS

- 2 cups sugar
- 1 cup water
- 1 cup buttermilk
- 2 eggs
- ½ cup unsweetened applesauce
- ¼ cup canola oil
- 2 teaspoons vanilla extract
- 2 cups all-purpose flour
- 1 cup baking cocoa
- 1 teaspoon baking powder
- ½ teaspoon salt
- ½ teaspoon baking soda
- 1 package (8 ounces) reduced-fat cream cheese
- ½ cup confectioners' sugar
- ¼ cup seedless raspberry jam
  Fresh raspberries, mint sprigs and additional confectioners' sugar, optional

1. In a large bowl, beat the sugar, water, buttermilk, eggs, applesauce, oil and vanilla until well blended. Combine the flour, cocoa, baking powder, salt and baking soda; gradually beat into sugar mixture until blended.
2. Transfer to two 9-in. round baking pans coated with cooking spray. Bake at 350° for 25-30 minutes or until a toothpick inserted near the center comes out clean. Cool for 10 minutes before removing from pans to wire racks to cool completely.

3. In a small bowl, beat the cream cheese, confectioners' sugar and jam until blended. Split each cake into two horizontal layers. Place a bottom layer on a serving plate; spread with a third of the filling. Repeat layers twice. Top with remaining cake layer. Garnish with raspberries, mint and additional confectioners' sugar if desired.
PER SERVING *281 cal., 8 g fat (3 g sat. fat), 37 mg chol., 223 mg sodium, 49 g carb., 2 g fiber, 5 g pro.*

CHOCOLATE RASPBERRY TORTE

FROZEN HOT CHOCOLATE

S Strawberry Meringue Tart

I got this recipe from a girlfriend and made a few minor changes to make it less fattening. It's a lovely, light and dreamy dessert that will charm guests!

—**KAREN GRANT** TULARE, CA

PREP: 25 MIN. • **BAKE:** 45 MIN. + STANDING
MAKES: 8 SERVINGS

- **3 egg whites**
- **⅛ teaspoon cream of tartar**
- **¾ cup sugar**

FILLING

- **1 package (8 ounces) reduced-fat cream cheese**
- **⅓ cup confectioners' sugar**
- **½ cup marshmallow creme**
- **1 cup reduced-fat whipped topping**
- **5 cups fresh strawberries, halved**
- **¼ cup strawberry glaze**

1. Line a large pizza pan with parchment paper; set aside. In a large bowl, beat egg whites and cream of tartar on medium speed until soft peaks form. Gradually add sugar, 1 tablespoon at a time, beating on high until stiff glossy peaks form and sugar is dissolved.

2. Spread into a 10-in. circle on prepared pan, forming a shallow well in the center. Bake at 225° for 45-55 minutes or until set and lightly browned. Turn oven off; leave meringue in oven for 1 to 1¼ hours.

3. For filling, in a large bowl, beat cream cheese and confectioners' sugar until smooth. Beat in marshmallow creme. Fold in whipped topping. Cover and refrigerate for at least 1 hour.

4. Just before serving, spread filling into meringue shell. Top with strawberries. Drizzle with glaze.

PER SERVING *196 cal., 6 g fat (4 g sat. fat), 16 mg chol., 123 mg sodium, 32 g carb., 2 g fiber, 4 g pro.* **Diabetic Exchanges:** *1½ starch, 1 fat, ½ fruit.*

S Frozen Hot Chocolate

Kids and all us wannabes in our family love this frozen treat for summer and winter. For a stiffer consistency, freeze mixture for 8 hours then scoop into goblets.

—**LILY JULOW** GAINESVILLE, FL

PREP: 15 MIN. + FREEZING
MAKES: 4 SERVINGS

- **¾ cup sugar**
- **½ cup baking cocoa**
- **2¾ cups 2% milk, divided**
- **¼ cup reduced-fat whipped topping**
- **4 teaspoons chocolate syrup**

1. In a large saucepan, combine sugar and cocoa. Gradually add the milk, reserving 2 tablespoons for blending; cook and stir until heated through and sugar is dissolved. Remove from the heat and let cool.

2. Transfer to an 8-in. square dish. Freeze for 2 hours or until edges begin to firm. Stir and return to freezer. Freeze 4 hours longer or until firm.

3. Just before serving, transfer to a food processor; cover and process with remaining milk until smooth. Garnish with whipped topping and chocolate syrup.

PER SERVING *285 cal., 5 g fat (3 g sat. fat), 13 mg chol., 88 mg sodium, 57 g carb., 2 g fiber, 8 g pro.*

STRAWBERRY MERINGUE TART

PHOTO ID

Candy Bar Cupcakes

Everyone in my family goes crazy for cupcakes, so I experimented to create these cream cheese-filled treats with a sweet Snickers surprise inside. I also lightened them up without anyone knowing. I guess the secret's out!

—**EDIE DESPAIN** LOGAN, UT

PREP: 40 MIN. • **BAKE:** 20 MIN. + COOLING
MAKES: 1½ DOZEN

- 1 **cup sugar**
- 1 **cup buttermilk**
- ¼ **cup canola oil**
- 1 **teaspoon vanilla extract**
- 1½ **cups all-purpose flour**
- ⅓ **cup baking cocoa**
- 1 **teaspoon baking soda**
- ½ **teaspoon salt**

FILLING
- 6 **ounces fat-free cream cheese**
- 2 **tablespoons confectioners' sugar**
- 1 **egg**
- 2 **Snickers candy bars (2.07 ounces each), finely chopped**

FROSTING
- ⅓ **cup butter, cubed**
- ⅓ **cup packed brown sugar**
- 3 **tablespoons fat-free milk**
- 1½ **cups confectioners' sugar**

CANDY BAR CUPCAKES

1. In a large bowl, beat the sugar, buttermilk, oil and vanilla until well blended. Combine the flour, cocoa, baking soda and salt; gradually beat into sugar mixture until blended.
2. For filling, in a small bowl, beat cream cheese and confectioners' sugar until light and fluffy. Add egg; mix well. Stir in the candy bars.
3. Fill paper-lined muffin cups one-third full with batter. Drop filling by tablespoonfuls into the center of each cupcake (cups will be about half full). Bake at 350° for 20-25 minutes or until a toothpick inserted in the filling comes out clean. Cool for 10 minutes before removing from pans to wire racks to cool completely.
4. For frosting, in a small saucepan, melt butter. Stir in brown sugar. Bring to a boil; cook for 2 minutes, stirring occasionally. Remove from the heat; stir in the milk, then confectioners' sugar. Cool until frosting reaches spreading consistency. Frost cupcakes.
PER SERVING *250 cal., 9 g fat (3 g sat. fat), 23 mg chol., 248 mg sodium, 40 g carb., 1 g fiber, 4 g pro.*

No-Stick Liners

When baking muffins or cupcakes in seasonal paper liners, I spray them first with nonstick cooking spray. The liner peels off very nicely, leaving zero crumbs behind!

—**PAMELA K.,**
MARTINSBURG, WEST VIRGINIA

Chocolate Anise Cannoli

A lavish treat that's unique enough to please guests who want to dabble in something different, these brandy-infused cannoli are the perfect size to dazzle on any dessert tray.

—MARIE RIZZIO INTERLOCHEN, MI

PREP: 35 MIN. • **BAKE:** 10 MIN. + COOLING
MAKES: 16 SERVINGS

- 16 wonton wrappers
  Butter-flavored cooking spray
- 1 tablespoon sugar
- ¼ cup dried cherries
- 1 tablespoon cherry brandy
- 2 packages (8 ounces each) reduced-fat cream cheese
- 1 cup confectioners' sugar
- ½ cup baking cocoa
- 3 tablespoons anise liqueur
- ¼ cup semisweet chocolate chips
- ¼ cup chopped shelled pistachios

1. Wrap a wonton wrapper around a metal cannoli tube. Moisten corner with water and seal. Transfer to an ungreased baking sheet. Repeat with remaining wrappers. Spritz with cooking spray; sprinkle with sugar.

2. Bake at 325° for 10-14 minutes or until golden brown. Cool 5 minutes. Remove shells from tubes; cool on a wire rack.

3. Meanwhile, place cherries in a small bowl. Add brandy; let stand for 10 minutes. Drain and coarsely chop cherries. In a large bowl, beat the cream cheese, confectioners' sugar, cocoa, liqueur and chopped cherries until blended.

4. In a microwave, melt chocolate chips; stir until smooth. Dip shell ends in chocolate; allow excess to drip off. Press into pistachios. Place on waxed paper; let stand until set.

5. Pipe filling into prepared shells. Serve immediately.

PER SERVING *175 cal., 9 g fat (5 g sat. fat), 21 mg chol., 174 mg sodium, 19 g carb., 1 g fiber, 5 g pro.*

CHOCOLATE ANISE CANNOLI

Dulce de Leche Rice Pudding

Take an old-fashioned treat and give it a modern, caramel-infused twist. I'm sure your whole family will love my sweet and salty version.

—CARLA CERVANTES-JAUREGUI
MODESTO, CA

PREP: 15 MIN. • **COOK:** 50 MIN.
MAKES: 6 SERVINGS

- 2 cups water
- ½ cup uncooked brown rice
- ½ cup uncooked long grain rice
- ¼ cup sugar
- 1½ cinnamon sticks (3 inches)
- 1 tablespoon butter
  Dash salt
- 1 can (12 ounces) evaporated milk
- 8 caramels
- 1 tablespoon coarse sugar
- ⅛ teaspoon kosher salt

DULCE DE LECHE RICE PUDDING

1. In a large saucepan, combine the first seven ingredients. Bring to a boil. Reduce heat; simmer, uncovered, for 30 minutes or until water is absorbed.

2. Stir in milk. Bring to a boil. Reduce heat; simmer, uncovered, for 12-16 minutes or until thick and creamy, stirring occasionally. Add caramels, stirring until melted. Discard the cinnamon sticks.

3. Spoon into dessert dishes. In a small bowl, combine coarse sugar and kosher salt; sprinkle over pudding. Serve warm or cold.

PER SERVING *294 cal., 7 g fat (4 g sat. fat), 24 mg chol., 166 mg sodium, 50 g carb., 1 g fiber, 7 g pro.*

Blueberry Cobbler

With a buttery biscuit topping and warm, thick blueberry filling, this home-style cobbler sure doesn't taste light.

—**MARY RELYEA** CANASTOTA, NY

PREP: 20 MIN. • **BAKE:** 30 MIN.
MAKES: 8 SERVINGS

- 4 **cups fresh or frozen blueberries, thawed**
- ¾ **cup sugar, divided**
- 3 **tablespoons cornstarch**
- 2 **tablespoons lemon juice**
- ¼ **teaspoon ground cinnamon**
- ⅛ **teaspoon ground nutmeg**
- 1 **cup all-purpose flour**
- 2 **teaspoons grated lemon peel**
- ¾ **teaspoon baking powder**
- ¼ **teaspoon salt**
- ¼ **teaspoon baking soda**
- 3 **tablespoons cold butter**
- ¾ **cup buttermilk**

1. In a large bowl, combine the blueberries, ½ cup sugar, cornstarch, lemon juice, cinnamon and nutmeg. Transfer to a 2-qt. baking dish coated with cooking spray.
2. In a small bowl, combine flour, lemon peel, baking powder, salt, baking soda and remaining sugar; cut in butter until the mixture resembles coarse crumbs. Stir in the buttermilk just until moistened. Drop by tablespoonfuls onto blueberry mixture.
3. Bake, uncovered, at 375° for 30-35 minutes or topping is until golden brown. Serve warm.
PER SERVING *231 cal., 5 g fat (3 g sat. fat), 12 mg chol., 220 mg sodium, 45 g carb., 2 g fiber, 3 g pro.* **Diabetic Exchanges:** *2 starch, 1 fruit, 1 fat.*

ⓢ Toffee Cheesecake Bars

I found this recipe many years ago by accident when searching for another recipe. Once I tried it, I decided it's a keeper for my Christmas collection. The bars just melt in your mouth.

—**EDIE DESPAIN** LOGAN, UT

PREP: 25 MIN. • **BAKE:** 20 MIN. + CHILLING
MAKES: 2½ DOZEN

- 1 **cup all-purpose flour**
- ¾ **cup confectioners' sugar**
- ⅓ **cup baking cocoa**
- ⅛ **teaspoon baking soda**
- ½ **cup cold butter**
- 1 **package (8 ounces) reduced-fat cream cheese**
- 1 **can (14 ounces) sweetened condensed milk**
- 2 **eggs, lightly beaten**
- 1 **teaspoon vanilla extract**
- 1¼ **cups milk chocolate English toffee bits, divided**

1. In a small bowl, combine the flour, confectioners' sugar, cocoa and baking soda. Cut in butter until mixture resembles coarse crumbs. Press onto the bottom of an ungreased 13-in. x 9-in. baking dish. Bake at 350° for 12-15 minutes or until set.
2. In a large bowl, beat cream cheese until fluffy. Add the milk, eggs and vanilla; beat until smooth. Stir in ¾ cup toffee bits. Pour over crust. Bake 18-22 minutes longer or until center is almost set.
3. Cool on a wire rack for 15 minutes. Sprinkle with remaining toffee bits; cool completely. Cover and refrigerate for 8 hours or overnight.
PER SERVING *169 cal., 9 g fat (5 g sat. fat), 39 mg chol., 120 mg sodium, 19 g carb., trace fiber, 3 g pro.* **Diabetic Exchanges:** *2 fat, 1 starch.*

TOFFEE CHEESECAKE BARS

Hot Cocoa Souffle

A friend invited me to go to a cooking demo at her church years ago, and one of the recipes prepared was this airy and absolutely fabulous souffle. It was so easy to prepare and tastes devilishly delicious.

—JOAN HALLFORD

NORTH RICHLAND HILLS, TX

PREP: 20 MIN. • **BAKE:** 40 MIN.
MAKES: 6 SERVINGS

- 5 **eggs**
- 4 **teaspoons plus ¾ cup sugar**
- ½ **cup baking cocoa**
- 6 **tablespoons all-purpose flour**
- ¼ **teaspoon salt**
- 1½ **cups fat-free milk**
- 2 **tablespoons butter**
- 1½ **teaspoons vanilla extract**

1. Separate eggs; let stand at room temperature for 30 minutes. Coat a 2-qt. souffle dish with cooking spray and lightly sprinkle with 4 teaspoons sugar; set aside.

2. In a small saucepan, combine the cocoa, flour, salt and remaining sugar. Gradually whisk in milk. Bring to a boil, stirring constantly. Cook and stir 1 2 minutes longer or until thickened. Stir in butter. Transfer to a large bowl.

3. Stir a small amount of hot mixture into egg yolks; return all to the bowl, stirring constantly. Add the vanilla; cool slightly.

4. In another large bowl with clean beaters, beat the egg whites until stiff peaks form. With a spatula, stir a fourth of the egg whites into the chocolate mixture until no white streaks remain. Fold in remaining egg whites until combined.

5. Transfer to prepared dish. Bake at 350° for 40-45 minutes or until the top is puffed and center appears set. Serve immediately.

PER SERVING *272 cal., 9 g fat (4 g sat. fat), 188 mg chol., 209 mg sodium, 41 g carb., 2 g fiber, 9 g pro.*

HOT COCOA SOUFFLE

F S C FAST FIX

Mocha Pecan Balls

Dusted in confectioners' sugar or cocoa, this six-ingredient dough rolls up into truffle-like treats—no baking needed.

—LORRAINE DAROCHA MOUNTAIN CITY, TN

START TO FINISH: 25 MIN.
MAKES: 4 DOZEN

- 2½ **cups crushed vanilla wafers (about 65 wafers)**
- 2 **cups plus ¼ cup confectioners' sugar, divided**
- ⅔ **cup finely chopped pecans, toasted**
- 2 **tablespoons baking cocoa**
- ¼ **cup reduced-fat evaporated milk**
- ¼ **cup cold strong brewed coffee**
  Additional baking cocoa, optional

MOCHA PECAN BALLS

1. In a large bowl, combine the wafer crumbs, 2 cups confectioners' sugar, pecans and cocoa. Stir in milk and coffee (mixture will be sticky).

2. With hands dusted in confectioners' sugar, shape dough into ¾-in. balls; roll in remaining confectioner's sugar or additional baking cocoa if desired. Store in an airtight container.

PER SERVING *61 cal., 2 g fat (trace sat. fat), 1 mg chol., 20 mg sodium, 10 g carb., trace fiber, trace pro. Diabetic Exchange: 1 starch.*

CHOCOLATE BLISS MARBLE CAKE

Chocolate Bliss Marble Cake

I serve this cake at all our family parties. I started making it when my husband had heart surgery and had to watch his diet.
—**JOSEPHINE PIRO** EASTON, PA

PREP: 40 MIN. • **BAKE:** 30 MIN. + COOLING
MAKES: 16 SERVINGS

- 5 **egg whites**
- ¼ **cup baking cocoa**
- ¼ **cup hot water**
- 1 **cup sugar, divided**
- 1 **cup fat-free milk**
- 3 **tablespoons canola oil**
- 1 **teaspoon vanilla extract**
- ¾ **teaspoon almond extract**
- 2½ **cups all-purpose flour**
- 3 **teaspoons baking powder**
- ½ **teaspoon salt**
- 1½ **cups reduced-fat whipped topping**
- 4 **ounces semisweet chocolate**
- 1½ **cups fresh raspberries**

1. Let egg whites stand at room temperature for 30 minutes. Dissolve cocoa in water; let stand until cool.
2. In a large bowl, beat ¾ cup sugar, milk, oil and extracts until well blended. Combine the flour, baking powder and salt; gradually beat into sugar mixture until blended.
3. In another bowl with clean beaters, beat egg whites on medium speed until soft peaks form. Beat in the remaining sugar, 1 tablespoon at a time, on high until stiff peaks form. Gradually fold into batter. Remove 2 cups batter; stir in the reserved cocoa mixture.
4. Coat a 10-in. fluted tube pan with cooking spray. Alternately spoon the plain and chocolate batters into pan. Cut through batter with a knife to swirl.
5. Bake at 350° for 30-35 minutes or until a toothpick inserted near the center comes out clean. Cool for 10 minutes before removing from pan to a wire rack to cool completely.
6. For topping, in a microwave, melt whipped topping and chocolate; stir until smooth.
7. Place cake on a serving plate. Drizzle with topping. Arrange raspberries in center of cake.
PER SERVING *215 cal., 6 g fat (2 g sat. fat), trace chol., 172 mg sodium, 37 g carb., 2 g fiber, 4 g pro.*

GLUTEN-FREE APPLE CIDER DOUGHNUTS
PAGE 296

**DESIREE GLANZERS
GLUTEN-FREE CHOCOLATE
CUPCAKES** PAGE 301

**SYLVIA GIRMUS
GLUTEN-FREE PIZZA CRUST**
PAGE 296

**CORLEEN HEIDGERKENS
GLUTEN-FREE SUGARPLUMS**
PAGE 298

Gluten-Free Goodies

There is hope for gluten-free baked goods after all! From **pie pastry to snack mix** to homemade sandwich bread, youll find **all the delicious treats you need** to satisfy your cravings.

Gluten-Free Flour Mix

My son and I have Celiac disease, so I use this flour mix to make our favorite dishes.
—**BERNICE FENSKIE** WEXFORD, PA

START TO FINISH: 5 MIN.
MAKES: 3 CUPS

- 2 **cups white rice flour**
- ⅔ **cup potato starch flour**
- ⅓ **cup tapioca flour**

In a small bowl, combine all ingredients. Store in an airtight container in a cool dry place for up to 1 year.
PER SERVING 1 tablespoon equals 29 cal., trace fat (0 sat. fat), 0 chol., trace sodium, 7 g carb., trace fiber, trace pro.

Alis Gluten-Free Pie Pastry

Everyone on a gluten-free diet should have a pie crust recipe like this. Its tender, nutty shell is the perfect base for all your pie favorites.
—**HARRIET STICHTER** MILFORD, IN

PREP: 15 MIN. + CHILLING
MAKES: PASTRY FOR ONE 9-INCH PIE.

INGREDIENTS FOR
 SINGLE-CRUST PIE

- 1 **cup gluten-free all-purpose baking flour**
- ⅓ **cup ground almonds**
- 3 **tablespoons sugar**
- ¼ **teaspoon salt**
- ¼ **teaspoon xanthan gum**
- 6 **tablespoons cold butter or margarine, cubed**
- 2 **tablespoons beaten egg**
- 1 **to 2 tablespoons ice water**

INGREDIENTS FOR
 DOUBLE-CRUST PIE

- 2 **cups gluten-free all-purpose baking flour**
- ⅔ **cup ground almonds**
- ⅓ **cup sugar**
- ½ **teaspoon salt**
- ½ **teaspoon xanthan gum**
- ¾ **cup cold butter or margarine, cubed**
- 1 **egg, beaten**
- 3 **to 4 tablespoons ice water**

In a large bowl, combine the flour, almonds, sugar, salt and xanthan gum. Cut in the butter until crumbly. Stir in egg. Gradually add water, tossing with a fork until dough holds together when pressed.

FOR SINGLE-CRUST PIE

1. Form into a disk and wrap in plastic wrap; refrigerate for 1 hour or until easy to handle.
2. Roll out pastry to fit a 9-in. pie plate. Transfer pastry to pie plate. Trim pastry to ½ in. beyond edge of plate; flute edges. Fill or bake shell according to recipe directions.

FOR DOUBLE-CRUST PIE

1. Divide dough in half so that one portion is slightly larger than the other; wrap each in plastic wrap. Refrigerate for 1 hour or until easy to handle.
2. Roll out larger portion of dough to fit a 9-in. pie plate. Transfer pastry to pie plate. Trim pastry even with edge of plate. Add filling. Roll out remaining pastry to fit top of pie; place over filling. Trim, seal and flute edges. Cut slits in top.
3. Cover edges with foil. Bake pie according to recipe directions, removing foil during the last 15-20 minutes of baking.
PER SERVING 172 cal., 11 g fat (6 g sat. fat), 39 mg chol., 141 mg sodium, 17 g carb., 2 g fiber, 3 g pro.

top tip
Label Smarts

Read all ingredient labels for possible gluten content prior to use. Ingredient formulas can change, and production facilities vary among brands. If you're concerned that your brand may contain gluten, contact the company.

Gluten-Free Apple Cider Doughnuts

I wanted to make a cider doughnut that tasted amazing; the fact that its gluten-free is just a bonus!

—**KATHRYN CONRAD** MILWAUKEE, WI

PREP: 20 MIN. + STANDING
BAKE: 15 MIN. + COOLING
MAKES: 10 DOUGHNUTS

- 2 cups gluten-free biscuit/baking mix
- ¾ cup sugar
- 1 package (¼ ounce) quick-rise yeast
- 1½ teaspoons baking powder
- ½ teaspoon salt
- ½ teaspoon apple pie spice
- ¼ teaspoon ground cinnamon
- ⅛ teaspoon baking soda
- ½ cup warm water (110° to 115°)
- 6 tablespoons butter, melted
- ¼ cup unsweetened applesauce, room temperature
- 1 tablespoon vanilla extract

GLUTEN-FREE APPLE CIDER DOUGHNUTS

GLAZE

- 1 cup apple cider or juice
- 1 tablespoon butter, softened
- ⅔ to ¾ cup confectioners sugar

1. In a large bowl, mix the first eight ingredients. In another bowl, whisk the water, butter, applesauce and vanilla until blended. Add to the dry ingredients; stir until blended. Cover and let rest for 10 minutes.
2. Cut a small hole in the corner of a food-safe plastic bag; fill with batter. Pipe into a six-cavity doughnut pan coated with cooking spray, filling cavities three-fourths full.
3. Bake at 325° for 11-14 minutes or until golden brown. Cool for 5 minutes before removing from pan to a wire rack. Repeat with remaining batter.
4. For glaze, in a small saucepan, bring apple cider to a boil; cook until liquid is reduced to 3 tablespoons. Transfer to a small bowl; stir in butter until melted. Stir in enough confectioners sugar to reach glaze consistency. Dip each doughnut halfway, allowing excess to drip off. Place on wire rack; let stand until set.

PER SERVING *273 cal., 8 g fat (4 g sat. fat), 18 mg chol., 565 mg sodium, 47 g carb., 4 g fiber, 4 g pro.*

⬚ Gluten-Free Pizza Crust

I live in a small town in Wyoming, and I can purchase the flours for this recipe in two local grocery stores. This is an ideal dough for children and adults alike who are gluten intolerant but who also crave pizza.

—**SYLVIA GIRMUS** TORRINGTON, WY

PREP: 20 MIN. + STANDING • **BAKE:** 20 MIN.
MAKES: 6 SERVINGS

- 1 tablespoon active dry yeast
- ⅔ cup warm water (110° to 115°)
- ½ cup tapioca flour
- 2 tablespoons nonfat dry milk powder
- 2 teaspoons xanthan gum
- 1 teaspoon unflavored gelatin
- 1 teaspoon Italian seasoning
- 1 teaspoon cider vinegar
- 1 teaspoon olive oil
- ½ teaspoon salt
- ½ teaspoon sugar
- 1 to 1⅓ cups brown rice flour
  Pizza toppings of your choice

1. In a small bowl, dissolve yeast in warm water. Add the tapioca flour, milk powder, xanthan gum, gelatin, Italian seasoning, vinegar, oil, salt, sugar and ⅔ cup brown rice flour. Beat until smooth. Stir in enough remaining brown rice flour to form a soft dough (dough will be sticky).
2. On a floured surface, roll dough into a 13-in. circle. Transfer to a 12-in. pizza pan coated with cooking spray; build up edges slightly. Cover and let rest for 10 minutes.
3. Bake at 425° for 10-12 minutes or until golden brown. Add toppings of your choice. Bake 10-15 minutes longer or until crust is golden brown and toppings are lightly browned and heated through.

PER SERVING *142 cal., 2 g fat (trace sat. fat), 1 mg chol., 223 mg sodium, 30 g carb., 3 g fiber, 4 g pro.* **Diabetic Exchange:** *2 starch.*

GLUTEN-FREE ANGEL FOOD CAKE

S Gluten-Free Sugar Cookies

These cake-like goodies are wonderful with a cold glass of milk. You can also use this recipe as a base and mix in dried cranberries or cherries, nuts or a variety of extracts.

—TASTE OF HOME TEST KITCHEN

PREP: 25 MIN. • **BAKE:** 10 MIN./BATCH
MAKES: 3 DOZEN

- ⅔ **cup butter, softened**
- 1 **cup sugar**
- 2 **eggs**
- ¼ **cup unsweetened applesauce**
- 4 **teaspoons grated lemon peel**
- 1 **teaspoon almond extract**
- 1⅓ **cups potato starch**
- 1⅓ **cups garbanzo and fava flour**
- 1 **cup tapioca flour**
- 1 **teaspoon salt**
- 1 **teaspoon xanthan gum**
- ½ **teaspoon baking soda**
- ⅓ **cup coarse sugar**

1. In a large bowl, cream butter and sugar until light and fluffy. Beat in the eggs, applesauce, lemon peel and extract. Combine the potato starch, garbanzo and fava flour, tapioca flour, salt, xanthan gum and baking soda; gradually add to creamed mixture and mix well.

2. Shape into 1½-in. balls and roll in coarse sugar. Place 2 in. apart on baking sheets coated with cooking spray. Bake at 350° for 7-9 minutes or until lightly browned. Remove from pans to wire racks.

NOTE *This recipe was tested with Bobs Red Mill garbanzo and fava flour.*
PER SERVING *110 cal., 4 g fat (2 g sat. fat), 21 mg chol., 116 mg sodium, 18 g carb., 1 g fiber, 1 g pro.* **Diabetic Exchanges:** *1 starch, ½ fat.*

F Gluten-Free Angel Food Cake

My daughter can't have gluten, and my husband is diabetic, so there are a lot of special-diet recipes in our house. This fruit-topped cake is a sweet treat that pleases all.

—ANNE WIEBE GLADSTONE, MB

PREP: 15 MIN. • **BAKE:** 45 MIN. + COOLING
MAKES: 16 SERVINGS

- 1½ **cups egg whites (about 10)**
- ¾ **cup plus ½ cup sugar, divided**
- ¼ **cup cornstarch**
- ¼ **cup white rice flour**
- ¼ **cup tapioca flour**
- ¼ **cup potato starch**
- 1½ **teaspoons cream of tartar**
- ¾ **teaspoon salt**
- ¾ **teaspoon vanilla extract**
   Assorted fresh fruit, optional

1. Place egg whites in a large bowl; let stand at room temperature for 30 minutes. Sift ¾ cup sugar, cornstarch, flours and potato starch together twice; set aside.

2. Add cream of tartar, salt and vanilla to egg whites; beat on medium speed until soft peaks form. Gradually add remaining sugar, about 2 tablespoons at a time, beating on high until stiff peaks form. Gradually fold in flour mixture, about ½ cup at a time.

3. Gently spoon into an ungreased 10-in. tube pan. Cut through the batter with a knife to remove air pockets. Bake on the lowest oven rack at 350° for 45-50 minutes or until lightly browned and entire top appears dry. Immediately invert pan; cool completely, about 1 hour.

4. Run a knife around side and center tube of pan. Remove cake to a serving plate. Top with fresh fruit if desired.
PER SERVING *101 cal., trace fat (0 sat. fat), 0 chol., 149 mg sodium, 23 g carb., trace fiber, 3 g pro.* **Diabetic Exchange:** *1½ starch.*

F S C FAST FIX
Gluten-Free Sugarplums

Grab one of these fruity-spicy bites early—they'll be gone before you can lick the sugar off your fingers!.

—CORLEEN HEIDGERKEN MILWAUKEE, WI

START TO FINISH: 25 MIN.
MAKES: 2½ DOZEN

- 1⅓ cups chopped walnuts
- 1 cup pitted dates
- 1 package (5 ounces) dried cherries
- ¼ cup honey
- 2 teaspoons grated orange peel
- 1 teaspoon ground cinnamon
- 1 teaspoon ground allspice
- ½ teaspoon ground nutmeg
- ¼ teaspoon ground ginger
- ½ cup coarse sugar

Place the walnuts, dates and cherries in a food processor; cover and process until finely chopped. Transfer to a small bowl; stir in the honey, orange peel and spices. Roll into 1-in. balls, then roll in sugar. Store in an airtight container in the refrigerator.

PER SERVING *84 cal., 3 g fat (trace sat. fat), 0 chol., 1 mg sodium, 13 g carb., 1 g fiber, 1 g pro.* **Diabetic Exchange: 1 starch.**

GLUTEN-FREE SUGARPLUMS

GLUTEN-FREE OATMEAL CHIP BARS

S
Gluten-Free Oatmeal Chip Bars

With two energetic boys who'd rather move around than sit and eat, I needed a gluten-free, hand-held treat that could double as a quick breakfast or snack. This is one of their favorites.

—SUSAN JAMES COKATO, MN

PREP: 20 MIN. • **BAKE:** 20 MIN. + COOLING
MAKES: 3 DOZEN

- ½ cup packed brown sugar
- 4 eggs
- 1½ cups mashed ripe bananas (3-4 medium)
- 1 cup peanut butter
- ½ teaspoon salt
- 6 cups gluten-free old-fashioned oats
- 1 cup gluten-free butterscotch chips
- 1 cup (6 ounces) semisweet chocolate chips

1. In a large bowl, beat brown sugar and eggs until well blended. Add bananas, peanut butter and salt until blended. Stir in the oats, butterscotch and chocolate chips.

2. Spread batter into a 15-in. x 10-in. x 1-in. baking pan coated with cooking spray. Bake at 350° for 20-25 minutes or until edges begin to brown. Cool completely on wire rack. Cut into bars.

PER SERVING *179 cal., 8 g fat (4 g sat. fat), 24 mg chol., 80 mg sodium, 23 g carb., 2 g fiber, 5 g pro.* **Diabetic Exchanges: 1½ starch, 1 fat.**

Gluten-Free Sandwich Bread

In my search for a satisfying gluten-free bread, this recipe emerged. Unlike some varieties, its soft and doesn't have a cardboard-like texture.

—DORIS KINNEY MERRIMACK, NH

PREP: 20 MIN. + RISING
BAKE: 30 MIN. + COOLING
MAKES: 1 LOAF (16 SLICES)

- 1 tablespoon active dry yeast
- 2 tablespoons sugar
- 1 cup warm fat-free milk (110° to 115°)
- 2 eggs
- 3 tablespoons canola oil
- 1 teaspoon cider vinegar
- 2½ cups gluten-free all-purpose baking flour
- 2½ teaspoons xanthan gum
- 1 teaspoon unflavored gelatin
- ½ teaspoon salt

1. Grease a 9-in. x 5-in. loaf pan and dust with gluten-free flour; set aside.

2. In a small bowl, dissolve yeast and sugar in warm milk. In a stand mixer with a paddle attachment, combine the eggs, oil, vinegar and yeast mixture. Gradually beat in the flour, xanthan gum, gelatin and salt. Beat on low speed for 1 minute. Beat on medium for 2 minutes. (Dough will be softer than yeast bread dough with gluten.)

3. Transfer to prepared pan. Smooth the top with a wet spatula. Cover and let rise in a warm place until dough reaches the top of pan, about 25 minutes.

4. Bake at 375° for 20 minutes; cover loosely with foil. Bake 10-15 minutes longer or until golden brown. Remove from pan to a wire rack to cool.

PER SERVING *110 cal., 4 g fat (trace sat. fat), 27 mg chol., 95 mg sodium, 17 g carb., 2 g fiber, 4 g pro. Diabetic Exchanges: 1 starch, ½ fat.*

GLUTEN-FREE SANDWICH BREAD

Gluten-Free Snack Mix

The buttery sweet cinnamon coating in this crunchy mix makes this snack almost addictive. Because it travels well, it makes an easy on-the-go snack.

—TASTE OF HOME TEST KITCHEN

PREP: 15 MIN. • **BAKE:** 10 MIN. + COOLING
MAKES: 10 CUPS

- 8 cups popped popcorn
- 2 cups Koala Crisp cereal
- 1 package (5 ounces) dried cherries
- ⅓ cup butter, cubed
- ⅓ cup honey
- ½ teaspoon ground cinnamon

1. In a large ungreased roasting pan, combine the popcorn, cereal and cherries. In a small saucepan, melt butter. Add honey and cinnamon;

GLUTEN-FREE SNACK MIX

cook and stir until heated through. Pour over popcorn mixture and toss to coat.

2. Bake at 325° for 15 minutes, stirring every 5 minutes. Cool completely. Store in airtight containers.

PER SERVING *½ cup equals 110 cal., 5 g fat (2 g sat. fat), 8 mg chol., 89 mg sodium, 16 g carb., 1 g fiber, 1 g pro. Diabetic Exchanges: 1 starch, 1 fat.*

Gluten-Free Carrot Cake

Pineapple is the secret ingredient in carrot cake that makes it extra luscious. This gluten-free version calls for xanthan gum, a corn-based thickener that can be found in your grocery store's baking aisle.

—TASTE OF HOME TEST KITCHEN

PREP: 35 MIN. • **BAKE:** 40 MIN. + COOLING
MAKES: 20 SERVINGS

- 1½ cups sugar
- 2 cans (8 ounces each) unsweetened crushed pineapple, drained
- 4 eggs
- ¾ cup reduced-fat mayonnaise
- 1½ cups white rice flour
- ½ cup potato starch
- ½ cup soy flour
- 2 teaspoons baking soda
- 2 teaspoons ground cinnamon
- 1 teaspoon xanthan gum
- ½ teaspoon ground ginger
- ¼ teaspoon salt
- 3¾ cups shredded carrots
- 1 cup flaked coconut

FROSTING

- 4 ounces reduced-fat cream cheese
- ¼ cup reduced-fat butter, softened
- 2½ cups confectioners sugar
- ¾ teaspoon grated orange peel
- ¼ teaspoon vanilla extract

1. In a large bowl, beat the sugar, pineapple, eggs and mayonnaise until well blended. Combine the rice flour, potato starch, soy flour, baking soda, cinnamon, xanthan gum, ginger and salt; gradually beat into sugar mixture until blended. Stir in carrots and coconut.

2. Pour into a 13-in. x 9-in. baking dish coated with cooking spray. Bake at 350° for 40-50 minutes or until a toothpick inserted near the center comes out clean. Cool on a wire rack.

3. For frosting, in a small bowl, beat cream cheese and butter until fluffy. Add the confectioners sugar, orange peel and vanilla; beat until smooth. Spread over top of cake. Refrigerate leftovers.

PER SERVING *287 cal., 9 g fat (4 g sat. fat), 52 mg chol., 311 mg sodium, 51 g carb., 2 g fiber, 4 g pro.*

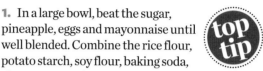

top tip

Xanthan Gum

In doughs and batters containing wheat, rye, barley or triticale flour, the protein gluten works as a binder and thickener, and also to trap tiny air bubbles that make your baked goods light and fluffy. In gluten-free baking, however, xanthan gum is needed to achieve similar results, so it's important not to skip this ingredient.

GLUTEN-FREE CARROT CAKE

PHOTO ID

Gluten-Free Chocolate Cupcakes

Both my boys have food allergies and really love these cupcakes! To make my own oat flour, I grind whole oats in my blender, just pulsing until they're flour.
—**DESIREE GLANZER** CARPENTER, SD

PREP: 15 MIN. • **BAKE:** 20 MIN. + COOLING
MAKES: 1 DOZEN

- 2 cups gluten-free oat flour
- 1 cup sugar
- ¼ cup baking cocoa
- 1 teaspoon baking soda
- ½ teaspoon salt
- 1 cup water
- ⅓ cup canola oil
- 1 teaspoon cider vinegar
- ½ teaspoon vanilla extract
- 2 teaspoons confectioners sugar

1. In a large bowl, combine the flour, sugar, cocoa, baking soda and salt. In another bowl, combine the water, oil, vinegar and vanilla. Stir into dry ingredients just until moistened.
2. Fill paper-lined muffin cups three-fourths full. Bake at 350° for 20-25 minutes or until a toothpick inserted near the center comes out clean. Cool for 10 minutes before removing from pan to a wire rack to cool completely. Dust with confectioners sugar.
PER SERVING *187 cal., 8 g fat (1 g sat. fat), 0 chol., 203 mg sodium, 29 g carb., 2 g fiber, 2 g pro.* **Diabetic Exchanges: 2 starch, 1 fat.**

GLUTEN-FREE
CHOCOLATE CUPCAKES

Gluten-Free Banana Pancakes

When one of my sons and I had to change to a gluten-free diet, I searched for recipes that tasted great. These pancakes are low-cal as well. I cook extras and freeze them. Then, when I'm short on time, I toss a couple in the toaster. You'll love the fluffy texture and chocolate chips.
—**SHAREN GUSTAFSON** SOUTH LYON, MI

PREP: 15 MIN. • **COOK:** 5 MIN./BATCH
MAKES: 12 PANCAKES

- 1 cup gluten-free all-purpose baking flour
- 3 teaspoons baking powder
- ½ teaspoon salt
- ⅔ cup gluten-free rice milk
- ¼ cup unsweetened applesauce
- 2 tablespoons olive oil
- 3 teaspoons vanilla extract
- 1⅓ cups mashed ripe bananas (3 medium)
- ½ cup semisweet chocolate chips, optional
   Maple syrup

1. In a large bowl, combine the flour, baking powder and salt. In another bowl, whisk the rice milk, applesauce, oil and vanilla; stir into dry ingredients just until moistened. Stir in bananas and chocolate chips if desired.
2. Pour batter by ¼ cupfuls onto a hot griddle coated with cooking spray; turn when bubbles form on top. Cook until the second side is golden brown. Serve with syrup.
PER SERVING *2 pancakes equals 173 cal., 6 g fat (1 g sat. fat), 0 chol., 407 mg sodium, 30 g carb., 3 g fiber, 3 g pro.* **Diabetic Exchanges: 2 starch, 1 fat.**

Gluten-Free Gingerbread Loaves

I only cook and bake gluten-free foods, and when I give these molasses-spiked loaves to friends, no one can taste the difference.

—ERIN MENDELSSOHN
BERMUDA DUNES, CA

PREP: 20 MIN. • **BAKE:** 35 MIN. + COOLING
MAKES: 3 MINI LOAVES (6 SLICES EACH)

- ¾ cup molasses
- ¾ cup boiling water
- ½ cup butter, softened
- ½ cup sugar
- 2 eggs
- 2½ cups gluten-free all-purpose baking flour
- 2½ teaspoons xanthan gum
- 2 teaspoons ground ginger
- 1 teaspoon baking powder
- ½ teaspoon baking soda
- ½ teaspoon salt

1. In a small bowl, combine molasses and boiling water; set aside.
2. In a large bowl, cream butter and sugar until light and fluffy. Add eggs. Gradually add molasses mixture. Combine the flour, xanthan gum, ginger, baking powder, baking soda and salt; gradually add to creamed mixture.
3. Transfer to three 5¾-in. x 3-in. x 2-in. loaf pans coated with cooking spray. Bake at 325° for 35-40 minutes or until a toothpick inserted near the center comes out clean. Cool for 10 minutes before removing from pans to wire racks.

PER SERVING *170 cal., 6 g fat (3 g sat. fat), 37 mg chol., 176 mg sodium, 28 g carb., 2 g fiber, 2 g pro.* **Diabetic Exchanges:** *2 starch, 1 fat.*

Gluten-Free Peanut Butter Blondies

This is a recipe I converted to be gluten-free so that my family could enjoy a comforting dessert. We were really craving brownies one night, and this cakelike treat hit the spot.

—BECKY KLOPE LOUDONVILLE, NY

PREP: 15 MIN. • **BAKE:** 20 MIN. + COOLING
MAKES: 16 SERVINGS

- ⅔ cup creamy peanut butter
- ½ cup packed brown sugar
- ¼ cup sugar
- ¼ cup unsweetened applesauce
- 2 eggs
- 1 teaspoon vanilla extract
- 1 cup gluten-free all-purpose baking flour
- 1¼ teaspoons baking powder
- 1 teaspoon xanthan gum
- ¼ teaspoon salt
- ½ cup semisweet chocolate chips
- ¼ cup salted peanuts, chopped

GLUTEN-FREE PEANUT BUTTER BLONDIES

1. In a large bowl, combine the peanut butter, sugars and applesauce. Beat in eggs and vanilla until blended. Combine the flour, baking powder, xanthan gum and salt; gradually add to peanut butter mixture and mix well. Stir in chocolate chips and peanuts.
2. Transfer to a 9-in. square baking pan coated with cooking spray. Bake at 350° for 20-25 minutes or until a toothpick inserted near the center comes out clean. Cool on a wire rack. Cut into squares.

PER SERVING *176 cal., 9 g fat (2 g sat. fat), 26 mg chol., 142 mg sodium, 22 g carb., 2 g fiber, 5 g pro.* **Diabetic Exchanges:** *1½ starch, 1½ fat.*

GLUTEN-FREE GINGERBREAD LOAVES

GLUTEN-FREE BANANA NUT MUFFINS

S
Gluten-Free Banana Nut Muffins

There's something therapeutic about making muffins. I baked these gluten-free muffins for our trip to see Grandma. Packed with nutritious whole grains, healthy proteins and fats, and just a touch of sweetness, these muffins are satisfying and delicious.

—GINGERLEMONGIRL

TASTE OF HOME ONLINE COMMUNITY

PREP: 20 MIN. • **BAKE:** 20 MIN.
MAKES: 1 DOZEN

- 1½ cups mashed ripe bananas (2 to 3 medium)
- ⅔ cup sugar
- 2 eggs
- ¼ cup fat-free plain yogurt
- 2 tablespoons plus 1½ teaspoons canola oil
- 1 teaspoon vanilla extract
- ½ cup millet flour
- ½ cup sorghum flour
- ½ cup tapioca flour
- 1 tablespoon ground flaxseed
- 2 teaspoons baking powder
- ½ teaspoon baking soda
- ¼ teaspoon xanthan gum
- ⅓ cup chopped walnuts

1. In a large bowl, beat the first six ingredients until well blended. In a large bowl, combine the flours, flax, baking powder, baking soda and xanthan gum; gradually beat into banana mixture until blended. Stir in walnuts.

2. Coat muffin cups with cooking spray or use paper liners; fill three-fourths full with batter. Bake at 350° for 18-22 minutes or until a toothpick inserted near the center comes out clean.

3. Cool for 5 minutes before removing from pan to a wire rack.
PER SERVING *191 cal., 6 g fat (1 g sat. fat), 35 mg chol., 135 mg sodium, 32 g carb., 2 g fiber, 4 g pro.* **Diabetic Exchanges:** *2 starch, 1 fat.*

Freezing Bananas

When bananas are overripe but you're not ready to bake, peel and mash the fruit with 1 teaspoon of lemon juice per 3 to 4 small bananas. Freeze in an airtight container for up to 6 months.

General Index

This handy index lists every recipe by food category and/or major ingredient,
so you can easily locate the recipes that best suit your tastes.

INDEXES

Alphabetical Index

This index lists all of the recipes in this book by title, making it easy to find your family's favorite dishes.